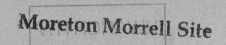

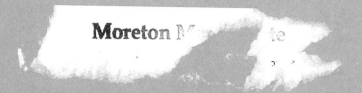

Research Methods for Leisure and Tourism

Research Methods for Leisure and Tourism

A Practical Guide

THIRD EDITION

A.J. VEAL

University of Technology, Sydney

 Prentice Hall
FINANCIAL TIMES

An imprint of **Pearson Education**

Harlow, England • London • New York • Boston • San Francisco • Toronto • Sydney • Singapore • Hong Kong
Tokyo • Seoul • Taipei • New Delhi • Cape Town • Madrid • Mexico City • Amsterdam • Munich • Paris • Milan

Pearson Education Limited
Edinburgh Gate
Harlow
Essex CM20 2JE
England

and Associated Companies throughout the world

Visit us on the World Wide Web at:
www.pearsoned.co.uk

First published 1992
Second edition published 1997
Third edition published 2006

ISBN-10 0-273-68200-8
ISBN-13 978-0-273-68200-4

British Library Cataloguing-in-Publication Data
A catalogue record for this book is available from the British Library

Library of Congress Cataloging-in-Publication Data
A catalog record for this book is available from the Library of Congress

10 9 8 7 6 5 4 3 2 1
10 09 08 07 06

Typeset in 9/12pt Stone Serif by 35
Printed in Great Britain by Henry Ling Ltd., at the Dorset Press, Dorchester, Dorset

The publisher's policy is to use paper manufactured from sustainable forests.

Summary Contents

Detailed Chapter Contents

9   Questionnaire surveys   231

10 Sampling   283

11 Survey analysis   297

12 Statistical analysis

List of Figures

List of Tables

List of Case Studies

Preface

The first edition of *Research Methods for Leisure and Tourism* was published in mid-1992 and the second in 1997. In this edition a number of changes have been made, including:

- updating of Statistical Package for the Social Sciences (SPSS) guidelines to Version 12;
- addition of more detail on qualitative data analysis, including a guide to the use of the *NVivo* computer package;
- summary case study exemplars of research in the leisure and tourism area drawn from the literature.

A number of other changes have been made in the light of my own and others' experience in using the book in teaching undergraduate and graduate students. I am particularly grateful to my UTS colleague Dr Simon Darcy for many helpful contributions to the development of this edition of the book.

The aims of the book remain: to provide a 'how to do it' text and also to offer an understanding of how research findings are generated in order to assist students and practising managers to become knowledgeable consumers of the research of others.

A.J. Veal
University of Technology, Sydney
May 2005

1 Introduction to research: what, why and who?

Introduction

Information, knowledge and understanding concerning the natural, social and economic environment have become the very basis of cultural and material development in contemporary societies and economies. An understanding of how information and knowledge are generated and utilised and an ability to contribute to that information and knowledge base through research can therefore be seen as key skills for managers in any industry sector and a key component of the education of the modern professional. Research is, however, not just a set of disembodied skills; it exists and is practised in a variety of social, political and economic contexts. The purpose of this book is to provide an introduction to the world of social research in the context of leisure and tourism, both as industries, public policy concerns and fields of academic inquiry and reflection. The aim is to provide a guide to the conduct of research, a critical understanding of existing theoretical and applied research and an appreciation of the role of research in the policy-making, planning and management processes of the leisure and tourism industries. This first chapter therefore addresses the preliminary questions of what research is, why it is done and who does it.

The focus of the book is leisure and tourism. While research methodology can be seen as universal, various fields of research – including leisure and tourism studies – have developed their own methodological emphases and bodies of experience. In some fields of enquiry scientific laboratory experiments are the norm, while in others social surveys are more common. While most of the principles of research are universal, a specialised text such as this reflects the traditions and practices in its field and draws attention to examples of relevant applications of methods and the particular problems and issues which arise in such applications.

The field of leisure and tourism is a large one, encompassing a wide range of individual and collective human activity. It is an area fraught with problems of definition – for example, in some contexts the word *recreation* is used synonymously with *leisure*, while in others recreation is seen as a distinct and limited part of leisure or even separate from leisure. In some countries the term *free time* is used in preference to the word leisure. In some definitions *tourism* includes *business travel*, while in others such travel is excluded. In some definitions *day-trips* are included in tourism, while in others they are excluded. The aim in this book is to be *inclusive* rather than *exclusive*. Leisure is taken to encompass such activities as: recreation; play; games; involvement in sport and the arts, as spectator, audience member or participant; the use of the electronic and printed media; live entertainment; hobbies; socialising; drinking; gambling; sight-seeing; visiting parks, coast and countryside; do-it-yourself; arts and craft activity; home-based and non-home-based activity; commercial and non-commercially based activity; and doing nothing in particular. Tourism is seen primarily as a leisure activity involving travel away from a person's normal place of residence, but also encompassing such activities as business travel, attending conventions and visiting friends and relatives, if for no other reason than that they invariably engage in leisure activities in addition to the activity which is the prime motivator for travel. Since the book covers leisure *and* tourism, day-tripping is included, regardless of whether or not it is viewed as part of tourism. Leisure and tourism are seen as activities engaged in by individuals and groups, but also as service industries which involve public sector, non-profit and commercial organisations.

Most of the book is concerned with *how* to do research, so the aim of this opening chapter is to introduce the 'what, why and who' of research. What is it? Why study it? Who does it?

What is research?

Research defined

What is research? The sociologist Norbert Elias defined research in terms of its aims, as follows:

> The aim, as far as I can see, is the same in all sciences. Put simply and cursorily, the aim is to make known something previously unknown to human beings. It is to advance human knowledge, to make it more certain or better fitting ... The aim is ... discovery.
>
> (Elias 1986: 20)

Discovery – making known something previously unknown – could cover a number of activities, for instance the work of journalists or detectives. Elias, however, also indicates that research is a tool of 'science' and that its purpose is to 'advance human knowledge' – features which distinguish research from other investigatory activities.

Scientific research

Scientific research is research which is conducted within the rules and conventions of science. This means that it is based on logic and reason and the systematic examination of evidence. Ideally, within the scientific model, it should be possible for research to be *replicated* by the same or different researchers and for similar conclusions to emerge (although this is not always possible or practicable). It should also contribute to a cumulative body of knowledge about a field or topic. This model of scientific research applies most aptly in the physical or natural sciences, such as physics or chemistry. In the area of *social science*, which deals with people as social beings and as members of communities, the scientific model must be adapted and modified, and in some cases largely abandoned.

Social science research

Social science research is carried out using the methods and traditions of social science. Social science differs from the physical or natural sciences in that it deals with *people* and their social behaviour, and people are less predictable than non-human phenomena. People can be aware of the research being conducted about them and are not therefore purely passive subjects; they can react to the results of research and change their behaviour accordingly. People in different parts of the world and at different times behave differently. The social world is constantly changing, so it is rarely possible to replicate research at different times or in different places and obtain similar results.

Three types of research

Elias' term *discovery* can be seen as, first, the process of *finding out* – at its simplest, therefore, research might just *describe* what exists. But to 'advance human knowledge, to make it more certain or better fitting' requires more than just the accumulation of information, or facts. The aim is also to provide *explanation* – to explain *why* things are as they are, and how they might be.

In this book, we are also concerned with a third function of research, namely *evaluating* – that is judging the success or value of policies or programmes. Three types of research can be identified corresponding to these three functions, as shown in Figure 1.1. In some cases particular research projects concentrate on only one of these, but often two or more of the approaches are included in the same research project.

1. Descriptive research

Descriptive research is very common in the leisure and tourism area, for three reasons: the newness of the field, the changing nature of the phenomena being studied, and the frequent separation between research and action.

Since leisure and tourism are relatively new fields of study there is a need to *map the territory*. Much of the descriptive research in the field might therefore be described as *exploratory*: it seeks to discover, describe or map patterns of behaviour in areas or activities which have not previously been studied. Explanation of what is discovered, described or mapped is often left until later or to other researchers.

Figure 1.1
Types of
research

1.	Descriptive research	finding out, describing what is
2.	Explanatory research	explaining *how* or *why* things are as they are (and using this to predict)
3.	Evaluative research	evaluation of policies and programmes

Leisure and tourism phenomena are subject to constant change. Over time, for example: the popularity of different leisure activities changes; the leisure preferences of different social groups (for example young people or women) change; and the relative popularity of different tourism destinations changes. A great deal of research effort in the field is therefore devoted to tracking – or monitoring – basic patterns of behaviour. Although a complete understanding and explanation of these changing patterns would be ideal, the providers of leisure and tourism services must be aware of, and respond to, changing market conditions whether or not they can be fully explained or understood; they therefore rely on a flow of descriptive research to provide up-to-date information.

There is often a separation between research projects and the policy, planning or management activity which gives rise to the commissioning of the research. So, for example, a company may commission a *market profile* study or a local council may commission a *recreation needs* study from a research team – but the actual use of the results of the research, in marketing or planning, is a separate exercise with which the research team is not involved: the research team may simply be required to produce a descriptive study.

2. Explanatory research

Explanatory research moves beyond description to seek to explain the patterns and trends observed. *Why* is a particular type of activity or destination falling in popularity? *How* do particular tourism developments gain approval against the wishes of the local community? *Why* are the arts patronised by some social groups and not others? Such questions raise the thorny issue of *causality*: the aim is to be able to say, for example, that there has been an increase in A because of a corresponding fall in B. It is one thing to discover that A has increased while B has decreased; but to establish that the rise in A has been *caused* by the fall in B is often a much more demanding task. To establish causality, or the likelihood of causality, requires the researcher to be rigorous in the collection, analysis and interpretation of data. It also generally requires some sort of theoretical framework to relate the phenomenon under study to wider social, economic and political processes. The issue of causality and the role of theory in research are discussed further in later chapters.

Once causes are understood, the knowledge can be used to *predict*. This is clear enough in the physical sciences: we know that heat causes metal to expand (explanation) – therefore we know that if we apply a certain amount of heat to a bar of metal it will expand by a certain amount (prediction). In the biological and medical sciences this process is also followed, but with less precision: it can be predicted that if a certain treatment is given to patients with a certain disease then it is *likely* that a *certain proportion* will be cured. In the social sciences this approach is also used, but with even less precision. For example, economists have found that demand for goods and services, including leisure and tourism goods and services, responds to price levels so that, if the price of a product or service is reduced then sales will generally increase. But this does not always happen because there are so many other factors involved – such as quality or the activities of competitors. Human beings make their own decisions and are far less *predictable* than non-human phenomena. Nevertheless *prediction* is a key aim of much of the research that takes place in the area of leisure and tourism.

3. Evaluative research

Evaluative research arises from the need to make judgements on the success or effectiveness of policies or programmes – for example whether a particular leisure facility or programme is meeting required performance standards or whether a particular tourism promotion campaign has been cost-effective. Evaluative research is highly developed in some areas of public policy, for example education, but is less well developed in the field of leisure and tourism (Shadish *et al.*, 1991). Again the issues facing the evaluative researcher are discussed in later chapters, particularly Chapters 3 and 14.

Why study research?

In general

Why study research? Research and research methods might be studied for a variety of reasons, as indicated in Figure 1.2. First, it is useful to be able to *understand* and *evaluate* research reports and articles which one might come across in an academic or professional context. It is therefore advantageous to understand the basis of such reports and articles. Second, many readers of this book may engage in research in an academic environment, where research is conducted for its own sake, in the interests of the pursuit of knowledge – for example for a thesis. Third, most readers will find themselves conducting or commissioning research for professional reasons, as managers. It is therefore particularly appropriate to consider the role of research in the policy-making, planning and management process.

Research in policy-making, planning and management processes

All organisations, including those in the leisure and tourism industries, engage in policy-making, planning and managing resources to achieve their goals. A variety of terms is used in this area and the meanings of terms vary according to the context and user. In this book:

- *policies* are considered to be the statements of principles, intentions and commitments of an organisation;
- *plans* are detailed strategies designed to implement policies in particular ways over a specified period of time;
- *management* is seen as the process of implementing policies and plans.

Figure 1.2
Why study
research?

- Understanding research reports, etc.
- Academic research projects
- Management tool in:
  - policy-making
  - planning
  - managing

Although planning is usually associated in the public mind with national, regional and local government bodies, it is also an activity undertaken by the private sector. Organisations such as cinema chains, holiday resort developers or sport promoters are all involved in planning, but their planning activities are less public than those of government bodies (Henry and Spink, 1990). Private organisations are usually only concerned with their own activities, but government bodies often have a wider responsibility to provide a planning framework for the activities of many public and private sector organisations. Examples of policies, plans and management activity in leisure and tourism contexts are given in Figure 1.3.

Both policies and plans can vary enormously in detail, complexity and formality. Here the process is considered only briefly, in order to examine the part played by research. Of the many models of policy-making, planning and management processes that exist, the *rational-comprehensive* model, a version of which is depicted in Figure 1.4, is the most traditional, 'ideal' model. It is beyond the scope of this book to discuss the many alternative models which seek to reflect more accurately real world decision-making, but guidance to further reading on this issue is given at the end of the chapter. Suffice it to say here, that these alternatives are often 'cut-down' versions of the rational-comprehensive model, emphasising some aspects of this model and de-emphasising, or omitting, others. Thus some reflect the view that it is virtually impossible to be completely *comprehensive* in assessing alternative policies; some reflect the fact that political interests often intervene before 'rational' or 'objective' decisions can be made; while others elevate community consultation to a central rather than supportive role. In nearly all cases the models are put forward as an *alternative* to the rational-comprehensive model, so the latter, even if rejected, remains the universal reference point.

In most of these models a research role remains – sometimes curtailed and sometimes enhanced. It is rare that all of the nine steps shown here are followed through in the real world. And its rare for research to inform the process in all the ways discussed below. The nine steps depicted in Figure 1.4 provide an agenda for discussing the

Level	Leisure Centre	Tourist Commission	Arts Centre	National Park
Policy	Maximise use by all age-groups	Extend peak season	Encourage contemporary composers	Increase non-government revenue
Plan	Two-year plan to increase visits by older people by 50 per cent	Three-year plan to increase shoulder season visits by promoting new festivals	Three-year plan to commission new work by contemporary composers	Three-year plan to implement user-pays programme
Management	Implement daily morning keep-fit sessions for older people	Choose festival themes, and implement	Select composers and commission and produce works	Implement user pays programme

Figure 1.3 Examples of policies, plans and management

Figure 1.4
The rational-
comprehensive
model of
planning/
management

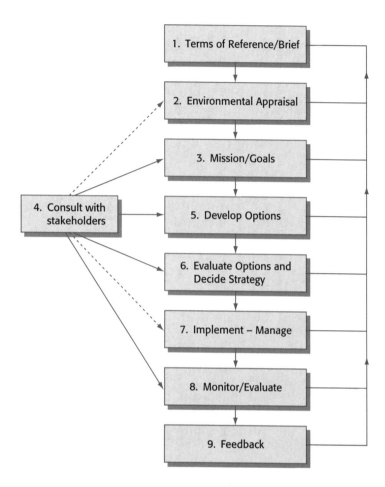

many roles of research in policy-making, planning and management processes. Two examples of how the process might unfold in leisure and tourism contexts are given in Figure 1.5.

1. Terms of reference/brief: The 'terms of reference' or 'brief' for a particular planning or management task sets out the scope and purpose of the exercise. Research can be involved right at the beginning of this process in assisting in establishing the terms of reference. For example, existing research on levels of sports participation in a community may result in a government policy initiative to do something about the level of sports participation; or research on environmental impacts of tourism growth may prompt a government to develop a sustainable tourism plan.

2. Environmental appraisal: An environmental appraisal involves the gathering of all information on the context of the task in hand. Information may relate to the organisation's internal workings or to the outside world, including actual and potential clients, and the activities of governments and competitors and physical resources.

Steps in the Planning/ Management Process (See Figure 1.4)	Young people and sport in a local community		Sustainable tourism in a tourism destination	
	Policy/Planning/management	Associated Research	Policy/Planning/management	Associated Research
1. Terms of reference	Increase young people's participation in sport	Existing research indicates 40 per cent participation rate	Develop local sustainable tourism strategy	Physical survey indicates road capacity reached
2. Environmental appraisal	Consider existing supply – demand	Existing programmes and infrastructure fully used	Examine current environmental impacts of tourism and future scenarios.	Extensive physical surveys (traffic + other environmental issues) + development of future tourism demand scenarios
3. Set Mission/ goals	Increase participation level to 60 per cent over 5 years	–	Develop policy to Increase tourism volume by 50 per cent over 10 years within acceptable environmental impact parameters	Study of likely increases in tourism demand over 10 years
4. Consult stakeholders	Consult sporting clubs, schools, young people	Survey indicates support among all groups and confirms feasibility	Consult community and tourism industry provider groups	Survey + meetings with community and tourism industry provider groups
5. Develop options	1. Publicity campaign 2. Free vouchers 3. Build more community facilities 4. Provide support to clubs/schools 5. Train leaders/coaches/teachers	Review of experience of each option in other regions, based on published accounts and a survey	1. Road-building/traffic management programme 2. Local public transport solution 3. Alternative accommodation development strategies	Survey of experience of similar destinations in similar stages of the tourism lifecycle
6. Evaluate options/ decide strategy	Evaluate options 1–5 Options 3 and 4 adopted	Each option costed; on basis of survey evidence, estimate made of cost-effectiveness of each option Options 3 and 4 recommended	Evaluate options 1 and 2 against range of options in 3 Options selected in light of evaluative research	Options 1 and 2 costed and evaluated against a range of accommodation development strategies (3) Options ranked in order of effectiveness and net environmental impact
7. Implement – manage	Implement options 3 and 4	–	Implement public transport and 3-star accommodation option	–
8. Monitor/ evaluate	Assess success in terms of increased participation	Survey indicates participation increase to 45 per cent after 1 year, but shortage of coaches/ leaders	Assess success in terms of tourism numbers and traffic congestion	Annual surveys of traffic conditions and tourism numbers undertaken. Persistent peak public holiday congestion problems noted
9. Feedback	Continue programme: increase resources for training coaches/leaders	–	Develop peak public holiday traffic management plan	–

Figure 1.5 Examples of planning/management tasks and associated research

Such information may be readily to hand and may just need collation, or it may require extensive research.

3. Mission/goals: Statements of the missions or goals of the organisation may already be in place if the task in hand is a relatively minor one, but if it is a major undertaking, such as the development of a strategic plan for the whole organisation, then the development of statements of mission and goals may be involved. It is very much a task for the decision-making body of an organisation (such as the board or the council) to determine its mission and/or goals, research may be directly involved when consultation with large numbers of stakeholders is involved, as discussed under step 4.

4. Consult with stakeholders: Consultation with 'stakeholders' is considered vital by most organisations and, indeed, is a statutory requirement in many forms of public sector planning. Stakeholders can include employees, clients, members of the general public, members of boards and councils and neighbouring or complementary organisations. Research can be a significant feature of such consultation, especially when large numbers of individuals or organisations are involved.

5. Develop options: In order to develop a plan or strategy, consideration must be given to what policies options are available to pursue the goals of the organisation, their feasibility, their likely contribution to the achievement of the goals and the best way to implement them. Research can be involved in the process of *identifying* alternative policy or planning options, for example, by providing data on the extent of problems or on stakeholder preferences.

6. Evaluate options and decide strategy: Deciding on a strategy involves selecting a course or courses of action from among all the options identified. This choice process may involve a complex process requiring a research to *evaluate* the alternatives. Typical formal evaluation techniques include cost–benefit analysis, economic impact analysis and environmental and social impact analysis (see Shadish *et al.*, 1991; Veal, 2002: 185–210), and the use of the *importance-performance* technique (Martilla and James, 1977; Harper and Balmer, 1989) or *conjoint analysis* (Claxton, 1994).

7. Implement – manage: Implementing a plan or strategy in the field of management. Research can be involved in day-to-day management in investigating improved ways of deploying resources and in providing continuous feedback on the management process – for example in the form of customer surveys. However, the line between such research and the monitoring and evaluation process is difficult to draw.

8. Monitor/evaluate: Monitoring progress and evaluating the implementation of strategies is clearly a process with which research is likely to be involved.

9. Feedback: The process comes full circle with the feedback step. The data from the monitoring and evaluation step can be fed back into the planning or management cycle and can lead to a revision of any or all of the decisions previously made. The monitoring and evaluation process may report complete success, it may suggest minor changes to some of the details of the policies and plans adopted, or it could result in a fundamental re-think, going 'back to the drawing board'.

Research formats in different contexts

Research for leisure and tourism planning/management is presented in many forms and contexts. A number of these are listed in Figure 1.6 and discussed briefly below. The formats are not all mutually exclusive: a number of them may arise in various aspects in a single research project.

Position statements are similar to the *environmental appraisals* discussed above. They are compilations of information on the current situation with regard to a topic or issue of concern, and are designed to assist decision-makers to become knowledgeable about the topic or issue and to take stock of such matters as current policies, provision levels and demand. For example if a local authority wishes to develop new policies for heritage conservation in its area, a position statement might be prepared listing what heritage currently exists, its ownership, quality, nature and state of preservation, existing policies, rules and regulations and types of use.

Market profiles are similar to position statements, but relate specifically to a *market*, particularly actual and potential consumers, but also suppliers. If an organisation wishes to start a project in a particular tourism or leisure market it will usually require a 'profile' of that market sector. How big is the market? What are its growth prospects? Who are the customers? What sub-sectors does it have? How profitable is it? Who are the current suppliers? Such a profile will usually require considerable research and can be seen as one element in the broader activity of market research.

Market research is a more encompassing activity. Research on the actual or potential market for a service can take place in advance of a service being established but also as part of the on-going monitoring of the performance of an operation. Market research seeks to establish the scale and nature of the market (the number of people who use or are likely to use the product or service and their characteristics) and consumer requirements and attitudes (the particular requirements or tastes of users or potential users of the product or service).

Market segmentation/lifestyle studies are also referred to as *psychographic* studies. Traditionally marketers attempted to classify consumers into sub-markets or segments on the basis of characteristics such as age, sex, occupation and income. Later they sought to classify people using not only these background social and economic characteristics

Figure 1.6
Research report
formats

- Position statements
- Market profiles
- Market research
- Market segmentation/lifestyle studies
- Feasibility studies
- Forecasting studies
- Leisure/recreation needs studies
- Tourism strategies/tourism marketing plans

but also on their attitudes, values and behaviour, including leisure activities and holiday behaviour. The best-known of such studies, the *VALS* typology (Values, Attitudes and Life Styles, – Mitchell, 1985), classified Americans into nine lifestyle groups: Survivor, Sustainer, Belonger, Emulator, Achiever, I-Am-Me, Experiential, Socially Conscious and Integrated. This system has been widely used in market research, including tourism research (e.g. Shih, 1986). Other lifestyle 'systems' include the *ACORN*, census-based system developed in Britain (Shaw, 1984) and the Australian *Age* lifestyle typology (*The Age*, 1982).

Feasibility studies investigate not only current consumer characteristics and demands, as in a market profile, but also future demand and such aspects as the financial viability and environmental impact of proposed development or investment projects. The decision whether or not to build a new leisure facility or launch a new tourism product is usually based on a feasibility study (Kelsey and Gray, 1986b).

Leisure/recreation needs studies are a common type of research in leisure planning. These are comprehensive studies, usually carried out for local councils, examining levels of provision and use of facilities and services, levels of participation in leisure activities, and views and aspirations of the population concerning leisure provision. In some cases a 'needs' study also includes a leisure or recreation 'plan', which makes recommendations on future provision; in other cases the plan is a separate document.

Tourism strategies/tourism marketing plans are the tourism equivalent of the recreation needs study. Recreation and leisure *needs* studies refer to the requirements of the local population, which are largely met within the local area, often with the emphasis on the public sector; tourism strategies or marketing plans refer to tourism *demands*, generated in a potentially wide range of regions and met within the destination region within which the host area is situated, by a mixture of public and private sector providers. Such tourism studies usually consider the capacity of the local area to meet the demands of growing numbers of tourists, in terms of accommodation, transport, existing and potential attractions and environmental impacts.

Forecasting studies form a key input to many plans. They might provide, for example, projections of demand for a particular leisure activity or for a particular type of tourist accommodation over a ten-year period. Forecasting is intrinsically research-based and can involve predicting the likely effects of future population growth and change, the effects of changing tastes, changing levels of income or developments in technology. Leisure and tourism forecasting have become substantial fields of study in their own right (Veal, 2002: 154–84; Archer, 1994).

Who does research?

This book is mainly concerned with how to conduct research, but it also aims to provide an understanding of the research process which will help the reader to become a knowledgeable, critical consumer of the research carried out by others. In reading research reports and articles, it is useful to bear in mind *why* the research has been done

Figure 1.7
Who does
research?

- Academics
- Students
- Government and commercial organisations
- Consultants
- Managers

and to a large extent this is influenced by *who* did the research and *who paid* for it to be done. Leisure and tourism research is undertaken by a wide variety of individuals and institutions, including academics and students, government and commercial research units, consultants and managers of leisure or tourism facilities and services, as listed in Figure 1.7. The respective roles of these research actors are discussed in turn below.

Academics

Academics, members of the paid academic staff of academic institutions, include professors, lecturers, tutors and research staff – in American parlance: 'the faculty'. In most academic institutions professors and lecturers are expected, as part of their contract of employment, to engage in both research and teaching. Typically a quarter or third of an academic's time might be devoted to research and writing. Promotion and job security depend partly (some would say mainly) on the achievement of a satisfactory track record in published research. Publication can be in various forms, including: refereed journals, un-refereed journals (such as professional magazines), books, reports/monographs (published by academic institutions or other agencies) and conference papers.

Publication of research in refereed journals is considered to be the most prestigious form in academic terms because of the element of 'peer review'. Articles submitted to such journals are assessed (refereed) on an anonymous basis by two or three experts in the field, as well as the editors. Editorial activity is overseen by a board of experts in the field. The main refereed journals in the leisure and tourism area are: *Journal of Leisure Research* (USA), *Annals of Tourism Research* (UK), *Leisure Sciences* (USA), *Tourism Management* (UK), *Leisure Studies* (UK), *Journal of Travel Research* (USA), *Society and Leisure* (Canada).

Some research conducted by academics requires little or no specific financial resources over and above the academic's basic salary – for example theoretical work and the many studies using students as subjects. But much research requires additional financial support, for instance, to pay full-time or part-time research assistants, to pay interviewers or a market research firm to conduct interviews, or to cover travel costs or the costs of equipment. The main sources of funding are university/college funds; government research councils; trusts/foundations; government departments or agencies; commercial companies; and non-profit organisations.

Universities tend to use their own funds to support research which is initiated by academic staff and where the main motive is the 'advancement of knowledge'. Most universities and colleges have research funds for which members of their staff can apply. Governments usually establish organisations to fund scientific research – for example the UK Social and Economic Research Council or the Australian Research Council. Many private trusts or foundations also fund research – for example the Ford Foundation and the Leverhulme Trust. Funds may come from the world of practice – for instance from a government department or agency, from a commercial company or from a non-profit organisation such as a governing body of a sport. In this case the research will tend to be more practically oriented. Government agencies and commercial and non-profit organisations fund research to solve particular problems or to inform them about particular issues relevant to their interests.

Generally academics become involved in funded research of a practically oriented nature when their own interests coincide with those of the agency concerned. For instance an academic may be interested in ways of measuring what motivates people to engage in certain outdoor recreation activities and this could coincide with an outdoor recreation agency's need for research to assist in developing a marketing strategy. Some academics specialise in applied areas – such as marketing or planning – so they are very often in a better position to attract funding from the 'practical world'. Academics may use funds to employ one or more research assistants who may also be registered for a higher degree – usually a PhD. This leads to the second academic source of research, namely students.

Students

PhD and Masters degree students are major contributors to research. Journals periodically publish lists of theses and dissertations completed in the area (Van Doren and Stubbles, 1976; Van Doren and Solan, 1979; Jafari and Aaser, 1988). Theses from most USA and UK universities are available on microfiche and, increasingly, on-line. In the science area research students often work as part of a team, under the direction of a supervisor who determines what topics will be researched by individual students within a particular research programme. In the social sciences this approach is less common, with students having more freedom of choice in their selection of research topic.

PhD theses are the most significant form of student research, but research done by Masters degree and graduate diploma students and even undergraduates can be a useful contribution to knowledge. Leisure and tourism are not generally well endowed with research funds, so even, for example, a small survey conducted by a group of undergraduates on a particular leisure activity or in a particular locality, or a thorough review of an area of literature, may be of considerable use or interest to others.

Government and commercial organisations

Government and commercial organisations often have their own in-house research organisations – for example, the Office of National Statistics in the UK, the former Bureau of Tourism Research in Australian and the US Forest Service Experiment Stations. Commercial organisations in leisure and tourism tend to rely on consultants for their social, economic and market research, although equipment manufacturers, for instance in sport, may conduct their own scientific research for product development.

Research conducted by commercial bodies is usually confidential but that conducted by government agencies is generally available to the public. Research reports from these organisations can therefore be important sources of knowledge, especially of a more practically oriented nature. For example, in nearly every developed country some government agency takes responsibility for conducting nation-wide surveys of tourism patterns and leisure participation rates (Cushman *et al.*, 2005a). This is descriptive research which no other organisation would have the resources to undertake.

Consultants

Consultants exist to offer their research and advisory services to the leisure and tourism industries. Some consultancy organisations are large, multi-national companies involved in accountancy, management and property development consultancy generally, and who establish specialised units covering the leisure and/or tourism field. Examples are Coopers and Lybrand and Price Waterhouse. But there are many other, smaller, specialised organisations in the consultancy field. Some academics operate consultancy companies as a 'side-line', either because of academic interest in a particular area or to supplement incomes or both. Self-employed consultancy activity is common among practitioners who have taken early retirement from leisure or tourism industry employment.

Managers

Managers in leisure and tourism who recognise the full extent of the management process should see research very much as part of their responsibilities. Managers may find themselves carrying out research on a range of types of topic, as indicated in Figure 1.8. Since most of the readers of this book will be actual or trainee managers, this is a most important point to recognise.

Successful management depends on good information. Much information – for example sales figures – is available to the manager as a matter of routine and does not require *research*. However, the creative utilisation of such data – for example to establish market trends – may amount to research. Other types of information can only be obtained by means of specific research projects. In some areas of leisure and tourism management even the most basic information must be obtained by research. For example, while managers of theatres or resorts routinely receive information on the level of use of their facilities from sales figures or bookings, this is not the case for the manager of an urban park or a beach. To gain information on the number of users of this type of facility it is necessary to conduct a specific data gathering exercise. Such data gathering may not be very sophisticated and some would say that it does not qualify as *research*, being just part of the management information system, but in the

Figure 1.8
Managers and
research

- ■ Research on customers
- ■ Research on potential customers
- ■ Research on staff
- ■ Research on performance
- ■ Research on competitors
- ■ Research on products

sense that it involves *finding out*, and sometimes *explaining*, it qualifies as research for the purposes of this book.

Most managers need to carry out – or commission – research if they want information on their users or customers, for example, where they come from (the 'catchment area' of the facility) or their socio-economic characteristics. Research is also a way of finding out customers' evaluations of the facility or service. It might be argued that managers do not themselves need research skills since they can always commission consultants to carry out research. However, managers will be better able to commission good research and evaluate the results if they are familiar with the research process themselves. It is also the case that few managers in leisure and tourism work in an ideal world where funds exist to commission all the research they would like; often the only way managers can get research done is to do it themselves.

Academics and the world of practice: the relevance of published research to planning and management

Who does research is important because it affects the nature of the research conducted and hence has a large impact on what constitutes the *body of knowledge* which students of leisure and tourism must absorb and on which leisure and tourism managers draw.

Academic research and publication is, to a large extent, a 'closed system'. Academics referee other academics' book proposals for commercial publishers; they are the editors of the refereed journals and serve on their editorial advisory boards and referee panels. They therefore determine what research is acceptable for publication. Practitioners therefore very often find published academic research irrelevant to their needs – this is hardly surprising since much of it is not designed for the practitioner but for the academic world. The student training to become a professional practitioner in the leisure or tourism field should not therefore be surprised to come across scholarly writing available on leisure and tourism which is not suitable for direct practical application to policy, planning and management. This does not mean that it is irrelevant, but simply that it does not necessarily focus explicitly on immediate practical problems.

Some research arises from academic interest and some arises from immediate problems being faced by the providers of leisure or tourism services. Much published academic research tends to be governed by the concerns of the various theoretical disciplines, such as sociology, economics or psychology, which may or may not coincide with the day-to-day concerns of the leisure or tourism industries. In fact part of the role of academic research is to 'stand apart' from the rest of the world and provide disinterested analysis, which may be critical and may not be seen as particularly supportive by those working in the industry. However, what some see as overly critical and unhelpful, or just plain irrelevant, others may see as insightful and constructive.

There are nevertheless applied disciplines which focus specifically on aspects of the policy, planning and management process, such as planning, management, marketing or financial management. While academic research in these areas can also be critical rather than immediately instrumental, it is more likely to be driven by the sorts of issues which concern the industry. In each of these theoretical and applied disciplines there is a distinctive body of leisure and tourism research. In addition there is research which draws on more than one discipline (multi-disciplinary) and research which occupies a niche somewhere between two or more disciplines (inter-disciplinary). Further, in the areas of *leisure studies* and *tourism studies* there is research which recognises no disciplinary allegiance. The disciplinary aspects of leisure and tourism research are examined in Chapter 2.

Summary

This chapter addresses the 'What?' of research in defining and introducing the concept of research and describes three types of research with which this book is concerned: descriptive research, explanatory research and evaluative research. The 'Why?' of research is discussed primarily in the context of policy-making, planning and management, since the majority of the users of the book will be studying for a vocational qualification. The links between research and the various stages of policy-making, planning and management are discussed using the rational-comprehensive model as a framework, and attention is drawn to the variety of forms that research reports can take in the management environment. *Who* conducts research is an important and often neglected aspect of research: in this chapter, the respective research roles of academics, students, governmental and commercial organisations, consultants and managers are discussed.

Test questions

1. What is the difference between research and journalism?

2. Outline the differences between *descriptive*, *explanatory* and *evaluative* research.

3. What are the broad differences between policy-making, planning and management, as presented in this chapter?

4. Summarise the potential role of research in three of the nine steps in the 'rational-comprehensive' model of the policy-making/planning/management process presented in this chapter.

5. Name three of the six formats which research reports might take, as put forward in this chapter, and outline their basic features.

6. Outline three of the six topics, as put forward in this chapter, on which managers might conduct or commission research.

7. Why does academic research often appear to be irrelevant to the needs of practitioners?

Exercises

1. Choose a leisure or tourism organisation with which you are familiar and outline ways in which it might use research to pursue its objectives.

2. Choose a leisure or tourism organisation and investigate its research activities. What proportion of its budget does it devote to research? What research has it carried out? How are the results of the research used, by the organisation or others?

3. Take an edition of a leisure or tourism journal, such as *Leisure Studies* or *Annals of Tourism Research*, and ascertain, for each article: why the research was conducted; how it was funded; and who or what organisations are likely to benefit from the research and how.

4. Repeat exercise 3, but using an edition of a journal outside the leisure/tourism field, for example a sociology journal or a physics journal.

5. Using the same journal edition as in exercise 4 above, examine each article and determine whether the research is descriptive, explanatory or evaluative.

Further reading

Models of planning and policy-making: introductory discussions: Parsons (1995:248ff); Veal (2002: 76–86); for a more advanced discussion, see Treuren and Lane (2003).

Tourism research methods: see Smith (1989) for a quantitative, geographical approach; Ryan (1994) for coverage of similar ground to this book; Dann, Nash and Pearce (1988) and Pearce and Butler (1993) for a number of methodological papers and, for a mine of information on all aspects of tourism research, see the comprehensive collection of papers edited by Ritchie and Goeldner (1994).

Leisure and tourism forecasting, see: Archer (1994); Veal (1987, 2002); Kelly (1987b); Martin and Mason (annual); Henley Centre for Forecasting (Quarterly).

Research in the planning process: Kelsey and Gray (1986a); Marriott (1987); Veal (1994).

Feasibility studies: Kelsey and Gray (1986b).

Psychographics/lifestyle: Wells (1974); Veal (1989a, 1993a, 2000); Chisnall (1991).

Evaluative research: Loomis (1987); Henderson and Bialeschki (1995); Pollard (1987); Shadish, Cook and Leviton (1991); Veal, 2002: 185–210.

2 Approaches to leisure and tourism research

Introduction

The aim of this chapter is to introduce a range of disciplines and paradigms within which leisure and tourism research is conducted. The chapter examines:

- *Disciplinary traditions*: reviews of a number of academic disciplines and their approaches to leisure and tourism research, including sociology, economics, geography, psychology, social psychology, history and philosophy.
- *Cross-disciplinary dimensions*: examination of a number of dichotomous research issues, including:
  - theoretical and applied research;
  - theoretical and empirical research;
  - induction and deduction;
  - descriptive and explanatory research;
  - experimental and non-experimental methods;
  - positivist and interpretive approaches;
  - quantitative and qualitative methods;
  - primary and secondary data and self-reported and observed data.

The disciplinary traditions of leisure and tourism research

Introduction

The bulk of published leisure and tourism research has arisen, not from the demands of the leisure and tourism industries, but from the interests of academics who owe allegiance to a particular discipline. Here we examine, very briefly, the contributions made to leisure and tourism research by academic disciplines that have been particularly significant in the field.

Disciplines are characterised by the particular aspect or dimension of the universe with which they are concerned, the theories which they develop for explanation and the techniques they use for research. Leisure and tourism studies is a multi-disciplinary, cross-disciplinary and inter-disciplinary field of study:

■ *Multi-disciplinary* means that research from a number of disciplines is used – for example the economics of leisure/tourism and the sociology of leisure/tourism.

■ *Cross-disciplinary* means that issues, theories, concepts and methods which are common to more than one discipline are involved – such as the *cross-disciplinary dimensions* listed above and discussed in the second half of this chapter.

■ *Inter-disciplinary* means that sub-fields of research which do not fit neatly into any particular discipline are involved – for example time–budget research.

An inter-disciplinary framework

Figure 2.1 provides a very simple, inter-disciplinary, conceptual representation of the world within which leisure and tourism exist, and which may assist in placing the various disciplinary approaches into perspective. It consists of five main elements:

■ people;

■ organisations;

■ services/facilities/attractions;

■ the linkages between these three; and

■ the physical environment within which everything takes place.

Figure 2.1
A leisure/
tourism studies
framework

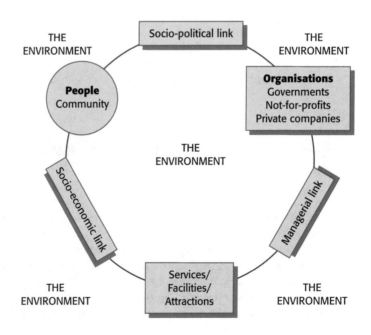

The linkages between people, organisations and services/facilities/attractions consist of processes such as:

■ Link A – market research and political activity;

■ Link B – marketing, buying, selling, employing, visiting/using services;

■ Link C – planning and investment.

The (physical) environment is all-pervasive and affects, and is affected by, all of the other elements in various ways. The boxes enclosing the elements are deliberately depicted with dotted lines to suggest that the elements should not be seen as hermetically sealed – indeed, the same people who make up organisations are also among the users of services/facilities/attractions, so most people play a role in, and move between, more than one of the elements of the system.

Disciplines in leisure and tourism studies

Disciplines vary in terms of their primary focus of attention within this system:

■ psychology and social psychology are focussed primarily on the *people* element, with some concerns with links A and B in Figure 2.1;

■ political science is concerned mainly with *organisations* and with link A to the people;

■ history can cover the whole system – but much of historical research in leisure studies has also had the same focus as political science;

■ economics at the macro-level is concerned with the whole system, while micro-economics is located around Link B, where the market process is at work;

■ sociology is concerned primarily with the people and with Link A and with organisations;

■ applied disciplines, such as planning, management and marketing, are based in organisations, then move along links A and C to the other elements of the system;

■ geography's basis is the interaction between the human parts of the system and the environment;

■ comprehensive social, economic and political systems of thought, such as Marxism or liberalism, encompass the whole system.

While much of this may seem fairly obvious, it is not always made explicit in the disciplinary literature, so that research is often criticised unfairly for ignoring phenomena which are outside its disciplinary scope. The above framework can be seen as an example of a *systems* model, a form of inter-disciplinary model which has been used particularly in tourism studies, and is discussed further below.

It is, of course, impossible to gain a complete appreciation of the research contribution and methods of any discipline without understanding the discipline as a whole. The student of leisure or tourism faces the daunting challenge of having to grasp the essence of a wide range of disciplinary contributions to the field. The discussions below, which relate to the academic disciplines of sociology, geography, economics, psychology and social psychology, history and anthropology and political science, are therefore inevitably somewhat superficial – some more than others – but references to more detailed reviews are given in the guide to further reading.

Sociology

Why do men tend to play sport more than women? How are the relationships between wealthy Western tourists and impoverished host populations in some tourist destinations to be interpreted? Why do middle-class, highly educated people make greater use of arts facilities and outdoor recreation areas than other groups? To what extent do people freely choose leisure activities and holiday destinations and to what extent is their choice limited by economic and social constraints or commercial manipulation? Who is involved and who is excluded when major decisions are made on leisure or tourism investment in local areas? Why do some groups in society engage in leisure activities which are viewed as 'deviant' or 'anti-social' by others and how do such activities come to be viewed as deviant or anti-social? These are the sorts of questions which sociological research in the field of leisure and tourism attempts to answer.

Sociologists have arguably been the most significant contributors to the field of leisure studies, but less significantly to the specific field of tourism studies. Although there is some overlap between the two fields, they are discussed separately below, and the sociology of leisure is discussed in three sections: first, the empirical tradition of surveys and quantitative models, second, the first wave on non-quantitative theorising, and third, the critical tradition.

Sociology of leisure I: social surveys and quantitative models

Much of the early research on leisure, and some current research, which appears to be 'sociological' has, in fact, not been carried out by sociologists trained in the discipline. This is true, for example, of many of the major leisure participation surveys which provide much of the basic factual information about patterns of participation (Cushman *et al.*, 1996; 2005a). Much *apparently* sociological research might therefore more aptly be called *social* research, since it is often somewhat pragmatic, and lacking in the theoretical framework which many formally trained sociologists would like to see.

Sociology is concerned with explaining or understanding social behaviour – particularly the behaviour of groups or classes of people. Early survey evidence on leisure participation from the 1960s was generally descriptive (e.g. BTA/Keele University, 1967; Sillitoe, 1969) – the aim was, in Elias' words quoted in Chapter 1: 'discovery'. Some of these early findings nevertheless fed directly into public policy debates: if participation in sport was low, should something not be done about it? If certain leisure activities were participated in primarily by the more well-off groups in society should efforts not be made to provide for the less well-off? In the context of rapidly rising populations, there was also concern about planning for the future.

The surveys were able to contribute to this policy process since, while they showed that some aspects of leisure behaviour exhibited uniform features across virtually all sections of society (for example, the importance of home-based leisure), others (for example engagement in the arts or sport) varied considerably between different groups in the community, depending on such social characteristics as family status, age, gender, educational level and ethnicity. Despite claims by some later commentators that these issues had been ignored in leisure studies, in fact they were very much at the heart of early leisure studies, as far back as the 1930s in the United States (Lundberg *et al.*, 1934: 92–3) and the 1960s in the UK (Sillitoe, 1969: 42–50). Researchers therefore pursued the idea that if only these relationships could be clearly identified, and provided that they were stable over time, it should be possible to develop *models* of leisure behaviour which could be used to 'predict' the patterns of participation of different social groups and therefore of society as a whole.

This research approach was *quantitative*, being highly statistical and concerned primarily with predicting numbers of participants and visits. It generally involved the construction of mathematical *models* of human behaviour (Christensen, 1988), with regression equations used to represent the relationships between leisure participation and *causal variables*, such as age, gender and income. The research can be seen as part of the *functionalist* tradition in sociology, which is based on the premise that elements in social systems can be studied in terms of the structure of the system and the functioning of its various interacting elements. It was also *normative*, in that it was largely embedded in the public policy process: the research undertaken was designed to assist in the process of planning for the sorts of leisure activities which the public sector provided for – such as sport, outdoor recreation and the arts. Most of the high-profile early American research was in this structural-functionalist-normative mode, much of it was of the quantitative/modelling type. But the highly quantitative approach held less sway in Britain where, for example, Stanley Parker's (1971) early influential work on the relationships between work and leisure, while being empirically based, was not markedly quantitative and did not involve quantitative modelling.

The modelling/prediction approach was eventually rejected by many sociologists, mainly because it did not work well in its own terms. In America, as John Kelly (1980) has pointed out, the models did not perform well, although in Britain more success was obtained (Settle, 1977; Veal, 1987: 152–4). But the main concern of later sociological commentators was that the approach lacked a framework of sociological theory: it was too pragmatic and in some cases it failed to answer the key questions.

Sociology of leisure II: explaining why

Methodologically the 'surveys and modelling' approach was challenged by sociologists who were not interested in quantitatively modelling and forecasting, but instead believed in the value of more sociological theory and in the use of qualitative as well as quantitative evidence. They wanted to know not just *what* people did with their leisure time but *why* and what leisure, and lack of leisure, meant to them. These more pragmatic and eclectic approaches had always been present in leisure studies, but had been somewhat overshadowed by the quantitative trend. While they came to the fore in the 1970s and 1980s and were later overshadowed by the critical trend discussed below, they continue as a significant element in leisure studies.

In Britain Rhona and Robert Rapoport epitomised this shift to a more qualitative, explanatory approach, while in the USA it was championed by John Kelly (1983). The Rapoports indicated the new trend with their book, *Leisure and the Family Life Cycle* (Rapoport and Rapoport, 1975), which was based on in-depth interviews with only about thirty people altogether; and in which detailed case studies of the motivations and feelings of individuals were reported. In fact their research was so individually oriented that it overlaps with the area of social psychology.

In the United States, a number of other areas were explored, including existential approaches to leisure, the benefits approach and leisure constraints. John Kelly's (1987a, 1994) *existential* and *symbolic interaction* approach explored leisure as a process of negotiation by the individual in the context of personal, social, community and professional relationships, commitments and ties. The development of the *benefits* and *constraints* approaches to leisure research in the 1980s continued the normative tradition discussed above. Benefits research sought to identify, evaluate and quantify the satisfactions individuals and communities gained from leisure as an input to planning and providing leisure services to maximise such benefits (see Driver *et al.*, 1991; Driver and Bruns, 1999). Constraints research focussed on the social, physical, psychic and economic factors which prevented individuals from gaining access to leisure benefits (Jackson and Scott, 1999). Empirically these approaches were supported by relatively small-scale social surveys, often with a psychological dimension.

The continuing value of the pragmatic tradition in leisure studies has been defended by Kenneth Roberts (1999: 221–6) against a number of the critical developments discussed below and also against some of the more experiential perspectives which have emerged from psychology, also discussed below (Roberts, 1999: 153–5).

Sociology of leisure III: critical approaches

In the 1980s the research traditions which had developed up to that point were attacked from a critical, neo-Marxist standpoint – typified by John Clarke and Chas Critcher's (1985) *The Devil Makes Work: Leisure in Capitalist Britain*. On one hand this work relied on a broader, often historically based, analysis of society and on the other hand it relied heavily on the findings of the *ethnographic* style of research which was emerging from the area of *cultural studies* and involved in-depth interaction with usually small groups of, often marginalised, individuals – such as members of youth gangs, ethnic minority groups and young working-class mothers. The intellectual sweep of the neo-Marxists was broader than that of earlier theorists, even though the contemporary empirical basis was, in some senses, a narrow one.

The neo-Marxist research introduced the *agency/structure* debate into leisure studies – that is the question of the extent to which individuals are *free agents*, exercising free choice in their lives, including their leisure choices, and the extent to which such choice is constrained and manipulated by the capitalist, economic and political *structure*, which is beyond the control of the individual (Rojek, 1989). Empirical research on relatively disadvantaged groups in society sought to demonstrate how such groups were exploited or marginalised by the system but often themselves sought to 'resist' such tendencies, thus demonstrating the neo-Marxist thesis of a deeply divided society.

The critical approach also raised questions about the role of the state (government and its associated agencies) in contemporary society. Traditionally leisure research had reflected the view that leisure services provided by the state provided for people's needs in response to democratic demands and this process should be supported and assisted, as in the case of the normative traditions mentioned above. The alternative view was that the state was merely a tool of the capitalist system, providing it with an acceptable 'human face' by providing those services which are not profitable but are necessary for a civilised society – research should therefore be critically focussed on revealing these 'contradictions' of the system. This debate led to a considerable growth in research on the state and public policy in leisure (Coalter, 1988, 1990; Moorhouse, 1989; Henry, 1993; Bramham *et al.*, 1993), involving interviews with policy-makers, analyses of government policy statements and legislation, and case studies of policy-making in individual cities. Explicit critiques of the neo-Marxist approach in leisure studies have been few (Moorhouse, 1989; Veal, 1989a), but it became less fashionable during the course of the 1990s, with the decline of Marxism as a political force in the world.

The 1980s also saw an attack on existing leisure research by *feminist* sociologists, who noted that much of the empirical work to date had been based on samples of men and, in focussing on factors such as occupation and work/leisure relationships, had ignored the day-to-day experience of women and their traditional responsibilities for child-care and unpaid domestic work. Further, it was argued that leisure research to-date had taken for granted the existence of freedom of choice in leisure and had therefore ignored the power relationships in society which limited or negated the range of choice for some groups, particularly women (Anderson, 1975; Deem, 1986; Wimbush and Talbot, 1988; Henderson *et al.*, 1989; Green *et al.*, 1990; Scraton, 1994). Much, but not all, of the empirical research underpinning the feminist contribution was qualitative in nature, concerned as it was to explore meanings and experiences of leisure among women.

The critical perspective in the sociology of leisure has, in recent years, been assumed by the idea of *postmodernism* (Rojek, 1995) and poststructuralism (Aitchison, 2000). The *modern* era of Western civilisation dates from the seventeenth century when science, rationality and the idea of *human progress* displaced traditional, largely religion dominated, values. Postmodernists argue that Western societies – and indeed most other parts of the world – are entering a new era, when values are becoming uncertain and the modern idea of progress no longer seems valid; the basis of modern economies and contemporary culture is becoming dominated by the ephemeral, fast-moving, world of the electronic communications media and the cultural 'products' which they purvey. One implication of this is a shift in the focus of the sociology of leisure to examine popular cultural forms, such as television (O'Connor and Boyle, 1993) and the world of Disney (Rojek, 1993), although there is also a tendency to add the term 'postmodern' to research on a wide variety of more mundane topics, such as the fun run (Wilson, 1995), rock climbing (Morgan, 1994) and social history (Seaton, 1994). The effect of these tendencies is to move parts of leisure sociology closer to a humanities approach, in which *the text*, or cultural artefact, rather than people, becomes the empirical focus and *cultural criticism* and *hermeneutics* (the interpretation of texts) are the research techniques deployed (e.g. Hultsman and Harper, 1992). Empirical research related to this approach therefore generally involves qualitative research, encompassing interviews, observation and the analysis of 'texts' as well as involvement with human subjects.

More recently, there have been calls for leisure sociology to embrace the ideas of *poststructuralism*, which rejects *structural* theories of society – be they functionalist, critical, neo-Marxist or feminist – but seeks to focus on the micro-level of human existence and the ways individuals and groups interact to create social environments and power relationships (Aitchison, 2000; Kelly, 1997; Wearing, 1998).

Space precludes examination of a number of other developments in the sociology of leisure, including Robert Stebbins' idea of *serious leisure* (Stebbins, 1992), the potential of *figurational sociology*, as propounded by Elias and Dunning (1986; see Maguire, 1988), the revisiting of *play* as a focus for research and theorising (Hamilton-Smith, 1994; Rojek, 1995, ch. 9) and the concept of *lifestyle* (Veal, 1993a).

The culmination of this brief history of the sociology of leisure is that the field is now characterised by a wide range of *social* or *sociological* research conducted within what Rojek (1985) refers to as *multi-paradigmatic rivalry* – that is alternative, competing traditions, with different ways of looking at the world. In addition an enormous range of research approaches is now deployed by sociologists studying leisure: quantitative methods are still used (see any edition of the American *Journal of Leisure Research*), major surveys continue to be conducted (mainly for government/policy purposes – see Cushman *et al.*, 2005b), and a variety of qualitative and experimental methods are also used. In short, anything goes.

Sociology of tourism

It is notable that, although leisure encompasses the major tourism activity of 'going on holiday', the general leisure literature rarely refers specifically to tourism or going on holiday. A further oddity in the leisure/tourism research tradition is that a great deal of North American research on leisure, which is concerned primarily with outdoor recreation, in fact involves studies of people who are staying away from home, often camping, while visiting major attractions such as national parks. So a great deal of what is recognised as *recreation research* in North America could in fact equally be seen as *tourism research* – but this is rarely, if ever, acknowledged. So research on the *sociology of tourism* is conventionally seen as separate from research on the *sociology of leisure*.

Dann and Cohen (1991: 157) point out that there is 'no single sociology of tourism', instead 'there have been several attempts to understand sociologically different aspects of tourism, departing from a number of theoretical perspectives'. They indicate that leisure is only one of the contexts in which tourism is studied; it is also viewed in the context of the sociology of migration and in the context of research on travel. Tourism research has been driven by private industry demands to a greater extent than leisure research; as a result tourism research is characterised by a predominance of economic and marketing and related psychological research, rather than sociological research. Indeed, John Urry has remarked that: 'There is relatively little substance to the sociology of tourism' (Urry, 1990: 7).

Erik Cohen (1984) divides sociological research on tourism into four 'issue areas': the tourist; relations between tourists and locals; the structure and functioning of the tourist system; and the social and environmental consequences of tourism. Reflecting the situation in leisure research, he concluded, in 1980:

> While a variety of often intriguing conceptual and theoretical approaches for studying the complex and manifold touristic phenomena have emerged, none has yet withstood rigorous empirical testing; while field-studies have proliferated, many lack an explicit, theoretical orientation and hence contribute little to theory building.   (Cohen, 1980: 388)

Dean MacCannell's (1976) seminal work on tourism as a 'quest for authenticity' linked tourism research to the area of *semiotics*, involving the study of symbols and signs, and this is reflected in John Urry's (1990) *The Tourist Gaze*. Such studies focus on tourism involving travel to strange places to 'see things', as opposed to the mass of tourism which is domestic and quasi-domestic (for example trips by northern Europeans to the Costa Del Sol) and involves going somewhere for 'sand, sea and sex'. The emergence of postmodern perspectives in sociology has affected tourism research as it has leisure research generally. The implications for research involve a similar shift towards areas previously the preserve of the humanities, as discussed in Chapter 9.

The paucity of theoretical sociological writing on tourism has been remedied in part in recent years by the collection of papers edited by Graham Dann (2002), entitled *The Tourist as a Metaphor of the Social World*, and Adrian Franklin's *Tourism; An Introduction* (2003). Parallelling developments in theory has been the development of empirical research on tourism to encompass a spread of methodologies, from the highly quantitative and deductive to the full range of qualitative and inductive approaches.

One of the main focuses of empirical research in the sociology of tourism has been on the social interaction between tourists and host communities and its effects (see Ryan, 1991 for summary). In recent years there has also been a tendency to move away from consideration of the phenomenon of mass tourism and to examine the behaviour patterns and motivations of smaller, more specialised groups, engaged in 'special interest' tourism, centring on such developments as 'eco-tourism' and activity-based holidays (see Weiler and Hall, 1992).

Geography

What is the relationship between where people live, their access to leisure facilities and their patterns of leisure participation? How do people's perceptions of and appreciation of different landscapes affect their leisure travel behaviour? How are the leisure and tourism trips of the population of a region accommodated and distributed within the region? How do people make use of outdoor recreation areas – how do they view crowding and congestion? What is the capacity of various environments to absorb visitors? These are the sorts of questions which geographical leisure and tourism research addresses.

Geographers have been very prominent in leisure research (Coppock, 1982) and have not generally restricted their interests to the formal confines of their discipline. For example, the Tourism and Recreation Research Unit of Edinburgh University was a creation of the Geography Department of the university and was at the forefront of the development of the modelling techniques discussed under sociology above (Coppock and Duffield, 1975). 'Social modelling' was extended to 'spatial modelling' with the aim of predicting not just levels of participation in activities in general, but levels of trips to particular recreation sites. This research was based on data gathered by interview surveys of the population in general and the users of particular recreation sites.

Of course geographers can be expected to be concerned primarily with spatial and environmental issues and also with large-scale natural and man-made phenomena such as the coastline, wilderness and human settlement patterns. Geography has indeed contributed a great deal of insight into these aspects of leisure research. Thus, for example, a considerable amount of research has been completed on the catchment areas of different kinds of leisure facilities – that is, surveys which ask people how far they travel to use facilities and which therefore establish the area which the facilities serve (Cowling *et al.*, 1983). Much of this research also included tourism sites. Traditionally geographers have focussed on recreation in 'green' areas, such as urban and national parks (e.g. Pigram, 1983), but a later text by Williams, entitled *Outdoor Recreation and the Urban Environment* (1995) indicates the contemporary range of the geographer's interest, covering environments as diverse as the domestic garden, urban thoroughfares, children's playgrounds, parks and sports facilities.

Tourism is of course quintessentially a geographical phenomenon and geography has made major contributions to research in that field (Mitchell, 1994; Smith, 1983; Pearce, 1987; Mitchell and Murphy, 1991), including studies of travel patterns and their modelling using the 'gravity model', tourism/recreation carrying capacity studies and regional development studies.

More recently geographers have embraced postmodern and poststructural perspectives, as exemplified by the volume *Leisure and Tourism Landscapes*, by Cara Aitchison *et al.* (2000) and *Leisure/Tourism Geographies* edited by David Crouch (1999). These studies overlap into sociology and also bridge the gap between leisure and tourism. As with sociology, they also mark the arrival of a full range of qualitative and quantitative research methods into the field.

Geographers have been at the forefront of various types of observational research (Burch, 1964; Tourism and Recreation Research Unit (TRRU), 1983). In particular they have demonstrated the use of aerial photography in examining the spatial distribution of recreational resources and utilisation and they have examined the way visitors make use of dispersed sites such as parks (Van der Zande, 1985; Glyptis, 1981a, 1981b). Geographers have also linked the concept of lifestyle with census information to create 'lifestyle maps' based on the common social characteristics of neighbourhoods; such characteristics being closely associated with leisure behaviour (Bickmore *et al.*, 1980; Shaw, 1984). A mixture of geography and psychological research has been responsible for a large amount of research on 'landscape perception' – that is, what it is that people find attractive about different kinds of landscape (Patmore, 1983: 212).

Economics

How do increases in incomes affect leisure expenditure and behaviour? How can an annual subsidy of £10 million to an opera company or a sports centre be justified?

What is the impact in terms of business turnover and jobs, of an event such as the Olympic Games? How significant is tourism, the arts or sport, in the economy? How will a change in the exchange rate affect international tourist arrivals? These are the sorts of question which economic research on leisure and tourism attempts to answer.

Economics is the discipline concerned with the 'allocation of scarce resources between competing ends' – that is, with what is produced by a society and with the distribution of what is produced – who gets what. Since leisure and tourism products and services now account for between 20 and 30 per cent of consumer spending in modern Western societies, the economics of leisure and tourism is of increasing importance. Most of the economics of leisure is, however, concerned with the public sector, where the free market forces with which economics is so concerned, are constrained or inoperative (Veal, 1989b). In the case of tourism, economists have drawn largely on macro-economics, that part of economics which is concerned with economies as a whole, including levels of economic output, multipliers, unemployment, international trade and so on.

The major focus of research in the economics of leisure has been on the public sector, particularly rural outdoor recreation and the arts. One of the major concerns of this area of research has been the economic valuation of the recreational, natural and aesthetic values of public recreation lands and wildernesses or of arts facilities, where entrance is often free or subsidised. Information on the users' willingness to pay is therefore not immediately available as a measure of their evaluation of the experience, as it is, say, with a commercial facility such as Disneyland. This therefore has spawned a great deal of research on 'cost–benefit analysis' – ways of measuring both the full costs and the full benefits to society of these publicly provided facilities.

As governments moved to the right in the 1980s and began to examine critically many areas of public enterprise with a view to expenditure cuts or privatisation, there was a burst of 'economic impact' studies – in which economists were engaged to establish the economic significance of the arts (Myerscough, 1988; Casey *et al.*, 1996) or sport (Henley Centre for Forecasting, 1986; DASETT, 1988a, 1988b). The general political/economic environment has also stimulated some research on the effects of pricing on demand (Coalter, 1993; Gratton and Taylor, 1995, 2000).

Another distinct area of the economic study of leisure has been the work on the economics of professional sport. Professional sport is a 'peculiar' – and fascinating – industry sector to economists because of the nature of competition, which is unlike that in other industries (Cairns *et al.*, 1986).

Of a more practical bent is the work of forecasters such as Martin and Mason, Sports Industries Research Centre, (annual) and the Henley Centre for Forecasting (quarterly), who produce regular forecasts of consumer expenditure on leisure products and services as a service to the leisure industries. Demand forecasting has been a major focus of tourism research (Eadington and Redman, 1991). In most countries, at least one organisation exists to produce forecasts of domestic and overseas tourist trips and such forecasts are often based on primarily economic models (Archer, 1987). In terms of research techniques, economists have tended to use similar methods to other social scientists, including household and site interviews, but they tend to have access to more government-collected data, for example on consumer expenditure, and tend to make use of quantitative methods, such as regression.

Psychology/social psychology

What satisfactions do people obtain from their leisure? How do people's perceptions of tourist destinations affect their decision to travel? What motivates people to engage in one form of leisure activity rather than another? How do people's relationships with family and friends affect their leisure behaviour? These are the sorts of question which psychological and social psychological research addresses.

In discussing sociological research, we have already referred to the work of the Rapoports and Kelly as social-psychological in nature, based as it is on attempts to understand the underlying motivations of individuals as well as their social interactions.

In a review of the contributions of psychology to leisure research, Roger Ingham (1986) classified the body of work into four main categories: motivation and needs ('why individuals do what they do'), satisfactions (the idea that 'particular types of leisure behaviour and experience lead to differential levels of satisfaction'), leisure as a state of mind (including Csikszentmihalyi's concept of 'flow'), and individual differences (including gender, age, personality and cultural differences). The field is divided into two general approaches, the 'experiential' approach of Neulinger and Csikszentmihayli and the broader approach dealing with reported motivations, satisfactions and attributions typified by the work of Iso-Ahola. Ingham pointed out that:

> By far the majority of psychological research has relied on the use of self-report questionnaire-derived data . . . Alternative methodological approaches are relatively rare: these could include detailed case studies, direct physiological recording, open-ended self-reporting, field experimentation, and careful observation and analysis of behaviour in different settings.
> (Ingham, 1986: 258)

In the second part of his review Ingham commends for the future the socio-psychological work of Kelly (1983), which involves viewing leisure as a medium in which individuals develop their identities, styles and social roles.

In the area of tourism Pearce and Stringer (1991) divide psychological research into five types: physiological and ergonomic (e.g. jet-lag and travellers' health problems); cognition (e.g. the use of maps and tourists' 'mindfulness' of areas visited); individual differences approaches (e.g. relationships between personality types and types of touristic experience sought, and links with motivation, psychographics and need); social psychology (including intra-individual, inter-individual and group processes); and environmental studies (e.g. perception of crowding). Pearce and Stringer argue that the psychology of tourism is not well developed but that: 'In the absence of a broad psychological thrust in tourism, geographers, sociologists, and leisure and recreation researchers are doing much work which at heart is psychological' (Pearce and Stringer (1991: 150).

Pearce's text, *The Ulysses Factor* (1988) includes a diverse collection of papers on visitor behaviour and attitudes in a variety of settings, including theme parks, museums, and natural environments. Ryan's (1995) *Researching Tourist Satisfaction* considers the psychology of the tourist from a market research point of view. In his theoretical review he reveals that research on tourist attitudes and satisfaction draws extensively on the same psychological basis as leisure research, including Maslow, Csikszentmihayli and Iso-Ahola.

There is clearly a link between psychology, consumer research and market research and this is reflected particularly in the growing body of research on tourism markets and marketing, exemplified by two volumes of papers on the *Consumer Pyschology of Tourism, Hospitality and Leisure* edited by Woodside *et al.* (1999) and Mazanec *et al.* (2001).

The methods of leisure and tourism psychology-related research are dominated by the small-scale self-completion questionnaire survey, sometimes of tourists in the field and sometimes of 'captive' groups, such as students, and typically involving Likert scales (see Chapter 10). The influence of psychology means that, more often than in other areas of research, the basic research model is traditionally positivistic and deductive.

History and anthropology

What are the historical roots of the practices, attitudes and institutions involved in contemporary leisure and tourism? To what extent has leisure time increased since pre-industrial times? How is change constrained by the effects of past actions and events? Historians, in addressing such questions, have been influential in the development of leisure research. For instance, Huizinga's classic work on play, *Homo Ludens* (1955), is largely historical and Young and Willmott's study of *The Symmetrical Family* (1973) has a firm base in historical analysis, as has Clarke and Critcher's *The Devil Makes Work* (1985). More recently, historians and theorists have produced histories of leisure, particularly in the nineteenth century (Cunningham, 1980; Bailey, 1978), which show how leisure has been an integral part of the development of the cultures and economies of Western capitalist societies. In fact one of the claims of the 1980s critics of earlier leisure research was that it was ahistorical, or at least that its view of history was naive.

A comprehensive history of leisure has, however, yet to be written. The available historical writing tends to jump from ancient Greece, with a brief dalliance in medieval Europe to observe the concept of 'carnival' as described by Bahktin (see Rojek, 1985: 85), to the industrial revolution in Europe. There is little material, in the English language literature, on history outside of Europe and North America. And there is virtually no reference to periods before the first millennium BC, even though it is clear that most leisure forms, such as music, dance, art, sport, gambling and drinking, have their origins in pre-history. By and large, anthropology has been ignored in leisure research, despite the wealth of leisure or play-related material in works such as Sahlins' *Stone Age Economics* (1972).

Most textbooks on tourism (e.g. Burkart and Medlik, 1981) provide an historical overview of the development of travel and tourism. Tourism is traced back to classical Greek and Roman times, to the emergence of the 'grand tour' in Europe in the seventeenth and eighteenth centuries and the development of spas and resorts. In Britain historical research has addressed some of the theoretical issues on social structure and change which have been addressed by sociologists (Urry, 1990), but in America studies have tended to be more descriptive case studies (Towner and Wall, 1991).

Some attention has been given to the anthropology of tourism in an historical sense (Nash and Smith, 1991), taking the history of tourism back beyond the classical period, but the 'anthropology of tourism' is also seen as a more contemporary phenomenon, drawing on the particular research approaches of anthropology in the study of (often clashing) relationships between cultures which arise as a result of tourism (Graburn and Moore, 1994).

While reviews of the contributions of history to leisure and tourism research tend not to discuss techniques, in fact one of the major contributions of historical analysis is to illustrate the use of secondary data sources, such as diaries, official records and reports and newspaper reports. Anthropological research methods, however, emerge through such areas as 'cultural studies' in the form of *ethnographical* methods, which are discussed in Chapter 8 on qualitative methods.

Political science

Despite the importance of public policy matters in leisure and tourism, the political dimension of the subject was neglected for many years. Important contributions began to be made in the 1980s and 1990s, including studies by Bramham and Henry (1985), Wilson (1988), Coalter (1990) and Henry (1993, 2001) in relation to leisure generally, and by Richter (1989, 1994) in relation to tourism. Case studies of the politics of local decision-making have emerged as an important contribution to this field in recent years (e.g. Henry and Paramio Salcines, 1998; Long, 2000; Jenkins and Stolk, 2003). While leisure studies research has focussed on the relationships between political ideology and leisure policy, in tourism the focus is less ideological and more to do with the role of tourism in political behaviour (Matthews and Richter, 1991). Typically, any empirical work in the area of the politics of leisure and tourism tends to draw on the historic record; however, being related to recent history, studies are often also supplemented with interviews with eyewitness political figures.

Approaches and dimensions

A number of alternative approaches to and dimensions of leisure and tourism research cut across the disciplines; some of them, as listed in Figure 2.2, are discussed here in the form of dichotomies. These are terms and ideas which recur in the literature and discourses on research; a basic understanding of them is therefore necessary if the literature and the discourses are to be understood. In general these themes arise in pairs – X and Y – so in many discussions they are presented as X *versus* Y. But X and Y are not always opposed to one another, they are often complementary, so here the form X *and* Y or the form X/Y is used.

Figure 2.2
Approaches/
dimensions/
issues

- Theoretical/applied
- Empirical/non-empirical
- Induction/deduction
- Descriptive/explanatory research
- Positivist/interpretive
- Experimental/non-experimental
- Primary/secondary data
- Self-reported/observed
- Qualitative/quantitative
- Validity and reliability

Theoretical and applied research

Theoretical research seeks to draw general conclusions about the phenomena being studied. *Applied* research, however, is less universal in its scope: it seeks not necessarily to create wholly *new* knowledge about the world but to apply existing theoretical knowledge to particular problems or issues. Such problems or issues may arise in particular policy, planning or management situations. Policy studies, planning and management are themselves fields of study which have developed a body of theory. Because they are related to areas of practice they can be seen as *applied disciplines*. In these fields, therefore, there can be such a thing as *applied theory*. The rational-comprehensive model of management portrayed in Figure 1.4 is an example of applied theory: research which sought to develop or elaborate the model in general would be theoretical whereas research which simply used the model as a framework for examining a problem in a particular organisation would be called applied.

Empirical and non-empirical research

The dichotomy here should probably be between *purely* empirical research, if such a thing exists, and *purely* theoretical research. Empirical research involves the collection and/or analysis of data – quantitative or qualitative, primary or secondary. The research is informed by observations or information from the 'real world'. It is, however, rare for any research project to be *purely* empirical – it is usually informed by some sort of theory or conceptual framework (see Chapter 3), however implicit.

It is possible to become 'carried away' with data and their analysis and to forget the theory which should make them *meaningful*. In such cases the disparaging term 'mindless empiricism' is sometimes used. Similarly, theoretical research with no reference to information about the 'real world' is likely to be of limited value. Typically – and ideally – theoretical and empirical research coexist and enhance each other; most research projects have complementary theoretical and empirical components.

A review of the contents of one or two editions of the main leisure or tourism journals will reveal the existence of both sorts of research – and the contributions which each can make. While the empirical studies provide some of the 'building blocks' of a great deal of research and knowledge, non-empirical contributions are needed to review and refine ideas and to place the empirical work in context. A book

Figure 2.3
Circular model
of the research
process

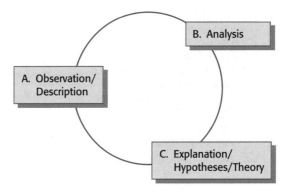

Based on: Williamson *et al.*, 1982, p 7.

like this inevitably devotes more space to empirical methods, because they involve more explicit, technical processes which can be described and 'taught'. It cannot, however, be too strongly stressed that a good review of the literature or a thoughtful piece of writing arising from deep, insightful, inspirational thinking about a subject can be worth a thousand, unthinking, surveys!

Induction and deduction

Induction and deduction refer to alternative approaches to explanation in research. It has been noted that research involves *finding out* and *explaining*. Finding out might be called the 'what?' of research – what is happening? What is the situation? Explaining might be called the 'how?' and the 'why?' of research – how do things happen? Why do they happen the way they do? What are the causes of different phenomena?

Finding out involves description and gathering of information. Explaining involves attempting to understand that information: it goes beyond the descriptive. Research methods can facilitate both these processes. Description and explanation can be seen as part of a circular model of research as illustrated in Figure 2.3.

The research process can work in two ways:

Inductive

■ begin at point A, *observation/description*
■ proceed to point B, *analysis*
■ arrive at point C, *explanation.*

Deductive

■ begin at point C, with a *hypothesis*
■ proceed to point A, *observation/description*, gathering data to test the hypothesis
■ proceed to point B, *analysis*, to test the hypothesis against the data.

A *hypothesis* is a proposition about how something might work or behave – an explanation which may or may not be supported by data, or possibly by more detailed or rigorous argument. A hypothesis may arise from informal observation and experience of the researcher or from examination of the existing literature. The term *theory* is also included at point C since, when more elaborate hypotheses or a number of inter-related hypotheses are involved, the term theory may be used. A theory can be similar to a hypothesis, in being propositional, or it may have been subjected to empirical validation – that is, testing against data.

A research project may involve a single circuit or a number of circuits of the process, possibly in both directions. If the research process begins with description, at point A, and moves from there to explanation, the process is described as *inductive*. The explanation is *induced* from the data – the data come first and the explanation later. If the process starts at point C then it is *deductive*; it involves *deduction*, where the process is based on prior logical reasoning. Case study 2.1 illustrates these ideas using an example on the relative popularity of two leisure activities.

Case Study 2.1   Tennis vs golf: inductive and deductive approaches

Inductive

An inductive approach to researching and explaining the relative popularity of tennis and golf could proceed as follows.

A descriptive survey shows that more people play tennis than play golf. This is just a piece of information; we cannot explain why this is so without additional information and analysis. If the research also reveals that it costs more to play golf than to play tennis then we could offer the explanation that relative popularity is related to price.

However, qualitative information from the survey might also indicate that more people consider tennis as being fun to play than consider golf to be fun. This suggests that tennis is intrinsically more attractive than golf for many people and its popularity is not related to price but to intrinsic enjoyment.

On the other hand, the research might indicate that there are more tennis courts available than golf courses in the particular community being studied, suggesting that, if there were more golf courses available, then golf would be more popular – implying that popularity is related to availability of facilities.

In this example, a series of possible explanations is being *induced* from the data. In its most fully developed form the explanation amounts to a theory. In this case a theory of sports participation might be developed relating levels of participation to costs of participation, intrinsic satisfactions and supply of facilities, perceived attractiveness of the activity and facilities, and so on.

Deductive

A deductive approach to the topic would proceed as follows. On the basis of reading and existing theory on leisure activities generally, the following two hypotheses are put forward:

Hypothesis 1: if sport A is more expensive to play than sport B, then sport B will be more popular than sport A.

Hypothesis 2: if more facilities are available for sport B than for sport A then sport B will be more popular than sport A.

To test these hypotheses a research project is designed to collect information on:

a. the levels of participation in the two sports – tennis and golf
b. the costs of participating in the two sports
c. the availability of facilities for the two sports in the study area

The two hypotheses would then be tested using the data collected. The data collection and outcomes are limited by the hypotheses put forward. In this example the idea of 'intrinsic motivation', which featured in the inductive approach, was not identified. In this case the research is guided from the beginning by the initial hypotheses. The process is deductive.

In practice data are rarely collected without some explanatory model in mind – otherwise how would we know what data to collect? So there is always an element of deduction in any research. And it is not possible to develop hypotheses and theories without at least some initial information on the subject in hand, however informally obtained; so there is always an element of induction. Thus most research is partly inductive and partly deductive.

Whether hypotheses or theories containing the explanation are put forward at the start of a research project or arise as a result of data analysis, they represent the key creative part of the research process. Data collection and analysis can be fairly mechanical but interpretation of data and the development of explanations requires at least creativity and, at best, inspiration!

Descriptive and explanatory research

In Chapter 1 the difference between descriptive and explanatory research was discussed and it is appropriate to raise the issue again here. *Descriptive* research aims to describe, as far as possible, what is. The focus is not on explanation. *Explaining* the patterns in observed or reported data usually involves establishing that one phenomenon is caused by another. For example, descriptive research might show that a tourism destination is losing market share. Explanatory research would seek to establish whether this was caused by, for example, price movements or ineffective marketing. This raises the question of *causality*: whether A is caused by B. Labovitz and Hagendorn (1971: 4) state that there are 'at least four widely accepted scientific criteria for establishing causality. These criteria are association, time priority, nonspurious relation and rationale.'

Association is a 'necessary condition for a causal relation' – that is, A and B must be associated in some way – for example, A increases when B decreases.

> There are two characteristics of an association that generally strengthen the conclusion that one variable is at least a partial cause of another. The first is magnitude, which refers to the size or strength of the association . . . The second . . . is consistency. If the relation persists from one study to the next under a variety of conditions, confidence in the causal nature of the relation is increased. (Labovitz and Hagendorn, 1971: 5)

Time priority means that for A to be the cause of B then A must take place before B.

Nonspurious relationships are defined as associations between two variables that 'cannot be explained by a third variable' (Labovitz and Hagendorn, 1971: 9). This means that it must be established that there is no third factor, C, which is affecting both A and B.

Rationale means that statistical or other evidence is not enough; the conclusion that A causes B is not justified simply on the basis of an observed relation; it should be supported by some plausible, theoretical or logical explanation to suggest how it happens.

These matters are taken up again in Chapters 3 and 13.

Positivist and interpretive research

The positivist/interpretive dichotomy refer to schools of thought or traditions – or *paradigms* – in the social sciences. *Positivism* is a framework of research, similar to that adopted by the natural scientist, in which the researcher sees people as phenomena to be studied from the outside, with behaviour to be explained on the basis of facts and observations gathered by the researcher, using theories and models developed by researchers. Some sociologists are highly suspicious of such attempts to translate natural science approaches into the social sciences (e.g. Rojek, 1989: 70). They believe that it is inappropriate to draw conclusions about the causes and motivations of human behaviour on the basis of the type of evidence used in the natural sciences. In the social sciences the term 'positivist' has almost become a term of abuse (Giddens, 1974: 2).

The *interpretive* model places more reliance on the people being studied to provide their own explanations of their situation or behaviour. The interpretive researcher therefore tries to 'get inside' the minds of subjects and see the world from their point of view. This of course suggests a more flexible approach to data collection, usually involving qualitative methods and generally an inductive approach.

In the 1990s numerous commentators, in calling for more interpretive and qualitative research, frequently referred to the positivist approach as dominant in leisure and tourism studies (e.g. Godbey and Scott, 1990; Howe, 1991; Hultsman and Harper, 1992; Glancy, 1993; Hemingway, 1995; Wearing, 1998). Since the 1990s, with the wide range of research approaches evident in published research, particularly outside North America, this has become more difficult to substantiate (Veal, 1994).

Experimental and non-experimental methods

The popular image of the scientist is someone in a white coat in a laboratory, conducting experiments. The experimental method of research involves the scientist attempting to control the environment of the subject of the research and measuring the effects of controlled change. Knowledge based on the experimental method progresses on the basis that, in a controlled experimental situation, any change in A must have been brought about by a change in B because everything except A and B has been held constant. The researcher therefore aims to produce conditions such that the research will fulfill the requirements for causality discussed above.

In the world of human beings, with which the social scientist deals, there is much less scope for experiment than in the world of inanimate objects or animals with which natural scientists deal. Some situations do exist where experimentation with human beings in the field of leisure or tourism can take place. For instance it is possible to experiment with variations in children's play equipment; it is possible to conduct experiments with willing subjects; and it is possible to experiment in management situations, for instance by varying prices or advertising strategies in relation to leisure or tourism services. But many areas of interest to the leisure or tourism researcher are not susceptible to controlled experiment.

For example, the researcher interested in the effect of people's level of income on their behaviour cannot take a group of people and vary their incomes in order to study the effects of income on leisure participation or tourism behaviour – it would be difficult to find people on executive salaries willing voluntarily to spend a year living on a student grant in the interests of research! Further, unlike the scientist experimenting with rats, it is not possible to find two groups of humans identical in every respect except for their level of income. Even more fundamentally, it is of course not possible to vary people's social class or race. In order to study these phenomena it is necessary to use *non-experimental* methods, that is, it is necessary to study differences between people as they exist.

So, for example, in order to study the effects of income on leisure participation patterns or touristic behaviour it is necessary to gather information on the leisure and travel behaviour patterns of a range of people with different levels of income. But people differ in all sorts of ways, some of which may be related to their level of income and some not. For example, two people with identical income levels can differ markedly in terms of their personalities, their family situation, their physical health, and so on. So, in comparing the behaviour of two groups of people, it is difficult to be sure which differences arise as a result of income differences and which as a result of other differences. The results of the research are therefore likely to be less clear-cut than in the case of the controlled experiment.

Some areas within the broad field of leisure and tourism do lend themselves to experimental research: these are the areas which are closest to the natural sciences, namely psychology and the human movement aspect of sports research. Thus in the case of psychological research, it is possible to set up experiments in which people are subject to 'stimuli' – for example the viewing of photographs or videos – and to study their reactions. In the case of human movement, subjects can be asked to engage in particular forms of physical exercise and their physical and psychological reactions can be measured. Although some of the techniques and approaches described in this book are applicable to experimental as much as non-experimental research, the experimental method is not dealt with specifically here.

Primary and secondary data

In planning a research project it is advisable to consider whether it is necessary to go to the expense of collecting new information (*primary* data, where the researcher is the first user) or whether existing data (*secondary* data, where the researcher is the secondary user) will do the job. Sometimes existing information is in the form of research already completed on the topic or a related topic; sometimes it arises from non-research sources, such as administration. A fundamental part of any research project is therefore to scour the existing published – and unpublished – sources of information for related research. Existing research might not obviate the need for the originally proposed research, but it may provide interesting ideas and points of comparison with the proposed research.

Even if the research project is to be based mainly on new information it will usually be necessary also to make use of other, existing, information – such as official government statistics or financial records from a leisure or tourism facility or service. Such information is generally referred to as *secondary data*, as opposed to the *primary data*, which is the new data to be collected in the proposed research. The topic of secondary data is dealt with in Chapter 6.

Self-reported and observed data

The best, and often the only, sources of information about individuals' leisure or tourism behaviour or attitudes are the individuals' own reports about themselves. Much leisure and tourism research therefore involves asking people about their past behaviour, attitudes and aspirations, generally using interviews or respondent-completed questionnaires. There are some disadvantages to this approach, mainly that the researcher is never sure just how honest or accurate people are in responding to questions. In some instances people may deliberately or unwittingly distort or 'bend' the truth – for instance in understating the amount of alcohol they drink or overstating the amount of exercise they take. In other instances they may have problems of recall – for instance in remembering just how much money they spent on a recreational or holiday trip some months ago – or even yesterday!

The alternative to relying on people to tell the researcher what they do, is for the researcher to use an alternative source of evidence. For instance, to find out how children use a playground or how adults make use of a resort area or a park it would probably be better to watch them than to try to ask them about it. Patterns of movement and crowding can be *observed*. Sometimes people leave behind evidence of their behaviour – for instance the most popular exhibits at a museum will be the ones where the carpet is most worn, and the most used beaches are likely to be those where the most litter is dumped. Generally these techniques are referred to as *observational* or *unobtrusive* techniques and are dealt with in Chapter 7.

Qualitative and quantitative research

Much leisure and tourism research involves the collection, analysis and presentation of statistical information. Sometimes the information is innately quantitative – for instance the numbers of people engaging in a list of leisure activities in a year, the number of tourists visiting a particular holiday area or the average income of a group of people. Sometimes the information is qualitative in nature but is presented in quantitative form – for instance numerical 'scores' calculated from asking people to indicate levels of satisfaction with different services, where the scores range from 1, meaning 'very satisfied', to 5, meaning 'very dissatisfied'.

The *quantitative* approach to research involves statistical analysis. It relies on numerical evidence to draw conclusions or to test hypotheses. To be sure of the reliability of the results it is often necessary to study relatively large numbers of people and to use computers to analyse the data. The data may be derived from questionnaire surveys, from observation involving counts, or from secondary sources.

In fact there can be said to be two approaches to quantitative research, which we will refer to as type A and type B research. Type A research makes use of statistical methods and tests, as outlined in Chapter 13. Type B research is also based on numerical data, but makes little or no use of statistical tests: its most sophisticated statistical measure is usually the percentage. Type B research is very common in the British tradition of leisure and tourism research. For example, in reading the British journal *Leisure Studies*, it is notable that, whereas there are many articles which present numerical information, very few utilise statistical tests and techniques, such as the chi-square tests, t-tests, analysis of variance, correlation or regression discussed in Chapter 13. This is in marked contrast to the leading American *Journal of Leisure Research*, where a substantial proportion of the articles include numerical data which make use of such tests. Type B research is more informal than type A and is closer in approach to qualitative methods.

The *qualitative* approach to research is generally not concerned with numbers. It involves gathering a great deal of information about a small number of people rather than a limited amount of information about a large number of people. The information collected is generally not presentable in numerical form. It is used when a full and rounded understanding of the leisure or tourist behaviour and situation of a few individuals, however 'unrepresentative' they may be, is required, rather than a limited understanding of a large, 'representative' group.

The methods used to gather qualitative information include observation, informal and in-depth interviewing and participant observation. Research studying groups of people using non-quantitative, anthropological approaches, is referred to as ethnographic research or ethnographic fieldwork. Such methods were initially developed by anthropologists, but have been adapted by sociologists for use in their work. Qualitative methods are considered in Chapter 8.

While the debate between protagonists of qualitative and quantitative research can become somewhat partisan, it is now widely accepted that the two approaches complement one another (Bryman and Bell, 2003). Thus quantitative research is often based on initial qualitative work. It is even possible that the two approaches are moving closer together, as computers are now being used to analyse qualitative data (Miles and Weitzman, 1994; Richards and Richards, 1994), as shown in Chapter 8.

Validity and reliability

Validity is the extent to which the information collected by the researcher truly reflects the phenomenon being studied. Leisure and tourism research are fraught with difficulties in this area, mainly because empirical research is largely concerned with people's behaviour and with their attitudes, and for information on these the researcher is, in the main, reliant on people's own reports in the form of responses to questionnaire-based interviews and other forms of interview. These instruments are subject to a number of imperfections, which means that the validity of leisure and tourism data can rarely be as certain as in the natural sciences. For example, data on the number of people who have participated in an activity at least once over the last month (a common type of measure used in leisure research) covers a wide range of different types of involvement, from the person who participates for two hours every day to the person who accidentally engaged in the activity just once for a few minutes. So the question of what is a *participant* can be complex. More detailed questioning to capture such complexity can be costly to undertake on a large scale.

Reliability is the extent to which research findings would be the same if the research were to be repeated at a later date or with a different sample of subjects. Again it can be seen that the model is taken from the natural sciences where, if experimental conditions are properly controlled, a repetition of an experiment should produce identical results wherever and whenever it is conducted. This is rarely the case in the social sciences, because they deal with human beings in differing and ever-changing social situations. While an individual person's report of his or her behaviour may be accurate, when it is aggregated with information from other people, it presents a snap-shot picture of a group of people, which is subject to change over time, as the composition of the group changes, or as *some* members of the group change their patterns of behaviour. Further, identical questions asked of people in different locations, even within the same country or region, are likely to produce different results, because of the varying social and physical environment. This means that the social scientist, including the leisure and tourism researcher, must be very cautious when making general, theoretical, statements on the basis of empirical research. While measures can be taken to ensure a degree of generalisability, strictly speaking, any research findings relate only to the subjects involved, at the time and place the research was carried out.

Summary

The aim of this chapter is to provide an introduction to the disciplinary context and traditions of leisure and tourism research and to introduce some general dimensions of social science research. It begins with a conceptual framework for studying leisure and tourism as a whole, within which the partial perspectives of individual disciplines can be located. This is followed by a brief overview of the contributions of individual disciplines to leisure and tourism research, covering: sociology, geography, economics, psychology/social psychology, history and anthropology and political science. The review indicates that most of the disciplines contributing to leisure and tourism research now make use of a wide variety of research methods. The final part of the chapter covers a range of generic, dichotomous social science issues which arise in the literature and with which the leisure and tourism researcher should be familiar. They are: theoretical and applied research; empirical and non-empirical research; induction and deduction; descriptive and explanatory research; positivist and interpretive research; experimental and non-experimental research; primary and secondary data; self-reported and observed data; qualitative and quantitative research; and validity and reliability.

Test questions

1. What are the basic differences between theoretical and applied research?

2. What are the basic differences between empirical and non-empirical research?

3. What are the basic differences between the inductive and deductive approaches to research?

4. What are the basic differences between descriptive and explanatory research?

5. What are the basic differences between the positivist and interpretive approaches to research?

6. What are the basic differences between experimental and non-experimental research?

7. What is the basic difference between primary and secondary data?

8. What is the basic difference between self-reported and observed data?

9. What are the basic differences between qualitative and quantitative research?

10. What are validity and reliability?

Exercises

1. Examine any issue of either *Leisure Studies* or *Annals of Tourism Research* and classify the articles into disciplinary areas. Contrast the key questions which each article is addressing.

2. Using the same journal issue as in exercise 1, determine whether the articles are: a. empirical or non-empirical; b. deductive or inductive; c. positivist or interpretive.

3. Using either *Leisure Studies* or *Annals of Tourism Research*, take an issue of the journal at two-yearly intervals over 10 or 12 years and summarise the apparent change over time in the topics addressed and methods used in the articles.

4. Select one of the following topics and examine it from the point of view of three different disciplines:
   a. the impact of tourism on the host community;
   b. inequalities in sports participation;
   c. inequalities in participation in the arts;
   d. the rise of 'special interest' tourism;
   e. the effects of recreation/tourism on the environment;
   f. the role of leisure/tourism in the urban environment.

Further reading

The journal *Leisure Studies,* has published a number of articles which review the contributions of various disciplines to leisure research; these are by: Coppock (1982) on geography; Parry (1983) on sociology; Vickerman (1983) on economics; and Ingham (1986, 1987) on psychology. And in 1989 it published an analysis and review of the contribution of historians to leisure studies in Britain by Bailey (1989). These reviews are now somewhat dated but provide useful historical introductions to the field.

Books edited by Barnett (1988) and Jackson and Burton (1989, 1999) provide disciplinary reviews of leisure research in more detail than those presented above.

For contributions and overviews on the sociology of leisure, see Jarvie and Maguire's (1994) *Sport and Leisure in Social Thought*; Wearing's (1998) *Leisure and Feminist Theory*; Aitchison's (2003) *Gender and Leisure*; and Roberts' (1999) *Leisure in Contemporary Society*. On cultural studies, see During (1993) and McRobbie (1994). On the geography of leisure, see: Williams (1995) *Outdoor Recreation and the Urban Environment*; Crouch (1999) *Leisure/Tourism Geographies*; and Aitchison *et al.* (2000) *Leisure and Tourism Landscapes*. On economics, see: Gratton and Taylor (2000). On psychology, see: Kleiber (1999).

The journal *Annals of Tourism Research* devoted a special issue to 'Tourism Social Sciences' in 1991 (Graburn and Jafari, 1991), covering such disciplines as: sociology (Dann and Cohen, 1991); geography (Mitchell and Murphy, 1991); history (Towner and Wall, 1991); psychology (Pearce and Stringer, 1991); political science (Matthews and Richter, 1991); and economics (Eadington and Redman, 1991). As with the reviews of leisure studies mentioned above, these are now dated, but provide useful historical introductions.

Tourism research is discussed from an interdisciplinary perspective and from the point of view of sociology and psychology in Pearce and Butler (1993) and Dann (2002), while Ryan (1995) and Pearce (1982, 1988) address the psychology of tourism particularly as it affects motivation and satisfaction. Edwards (1991) provides a discussion of the reliability of tourism statistics.

For discussion of qualitative versus quantitative research see: Kelly (1980); Kamphorst *et al.* (1984); Borman *et al.* (1986); Krenz and Sax (1986); Godbey and Scott (1990); Henderson (1990); Veal (1994); and Bryman and Bell (2003), chs. 21 and 22.

For a discussion of the experimental method in leisure research see Havitz and Sell (1991).

3 Starting out: research plans and proposals

Introduction: the research process

This chapter examines:

- stages in the planning of research projects;
- the formulation and presentation of research proposals and tenders.

Planning a research project

A research plan or proposal must summarise how a research project is to be conducted in its entirety; consequently preparation of a plan or proposal involves examination of the whole research process from beginning to end. In this chapter, therefore, a certain amount of cross-referencing is required to later chapters, where elements of the process are dealt with in detail.

The research process can be envisaged in a number of ways, but for the purposes of discussion in this chapter it is divided into nine main elements, as shown in Figure 3.1. The enormous variety of approaches to research suggests that all research projects do not follow precisely the same sequence of procedures. In particular, the first four elements depicted – selecting the topic, reviewing the literature, devising a conceptual framework and deciding the key research questions – rarely happen in the direct, linear way that the numbered sequence implies. There is generally a great deal of 'to-ing and fro-ing' between the elements. Hence, in Figure 3.1, these elements are located on a circle, implying that a number of circuits may be necessary before proceeding to element 5. Each of the nine elements in Figure 3.1 is discussed in turn below.

To illustrate the process in operation, three case studies are appended to this chapter. Using the terms introduced in Chapter 1, case study 3.1 is clearly *explanatory* research with evaluative features and arises from a hypothetical management problem; it seeks to find an explanation for a decline in the number of visitors to a leisure or tourism facility. Case study 3.2 deals with the role of the holiday as a leisure activity and lies somewhere between descriptive and explanatory research. Case study 3.3 is

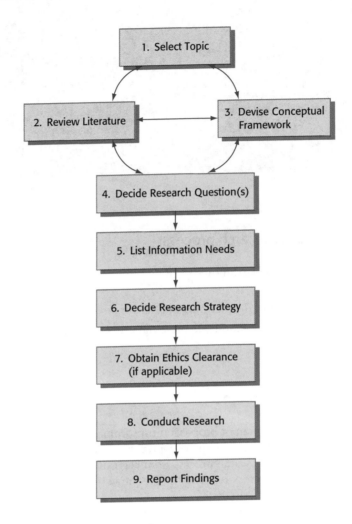

Figure 3.1
Elements in the research process

evaluative in nature, considering the relationship between a local authority's object-ives for leisure services and how its performance should be assessed. The case studies cover the first six elements of the process shown in Figure 3.1. Because of space limita-tions they are presented in somewhat abbreviated form, but the essential process is illustrated.

1. Select a topic

How do research topics arise? They may arise from a range of sources, including: the researcher's personal interests; issues identified as a result of reading in the research literature; a policy or management problem; an issue of social concern; a popular or media issue; published research agendas; and/or brainstorming, which may draw on a number of the above sources. Examples of topics arising from these sources are shown in Figure 3.2.

Source of topic	Examples of topics
a. Personal interest (usually combined with one or more of b–f)	■ A particular sport – trends, motivations, satisfactions ■ Leisure access and needs of a particular ethnic or age group ■ Tourism conflicts in a particular (home) locality ■ A particular professional group – its ethos, history and future
b. The literature	■ Does Csikzentmihayli's (1990) idea of 'flow' apply to participation in sport X, or to tourist trips to destination Y? ■ How do MacCannell's (1976) ideas on 'signs' relate to 'sun, sea, sand, sex' holidays, as opposed to sight-seeing holidays? ■ What is known about the leisure activity of 'taking a holiday', as opposed to the activity of choosing a tourism destination?
c. Policy/management	■ Why are visits to leisure facility X declining? ■ What market segments should be used to develop a strategy for promoting sport X, arts venue Y, or tourism destination Z? ■ What are the leisure needs of community X?
d. Social	■ The impact of growing tourism on a local environment ■ Leisure needs of single parents ■ The role of sport in a third world community
e. Popular/media	■ Are recreational drugs harmful? ■ Are city streets less safe than they used to be? ■ Who goes to 'rave' parties and what do they get out of them?
f. Published research agendas	Both of the following examples include a wide range of potential research topics: ■ *An Australian Leisure Research Agenda* (Lynch and Brown, 1995) ■ 'Tourism research: policy and managerial priorities for the 1990s and beyond' (Ritchie, 1994)
g. Brainstorming	■ Conduct a 'brainstorm' session on any of the above topics/sources – a means of exploring the potential of a–f

Figure 3.2 Examples of research topics from different sources

Personal interest

Personal interest can give rise to a research project in a number of ways. For example, the researcher may be personally involved in a sport or other leisure activity, may be a member of a particular social group, based on gender, ethnicity or occupation, or may live in or have visited a particular tourism location and so be personally aware of certain local issues or problems. Using personal interest as a focus for research has advantages and disadvantages. The advantage lies in the knowledge of the phenomenon which researchers already have, the possibility of access to key individuals and information sources, and the high level of motivation which is likely to be brought to the research. The disadvantage is that the researcher may be unduly biassed and may not be able to view the situation 'objectively'; familiarity with the subject of the research may result in too much being taken for granted so that the researcher cannot 'see the wood for the trees'.

Personal interest is generally just a starting point in selecting a topic. If the selected topic area is initially fairly broad, deciding on a *specific focus* for the research will usually depend on consideration of one or more of the other four sources discussed below.

While a particular personal interest in the research topic may be referred to in writing up a research project – generally in a Foreword or Preface rather than in the main body of the report – it is often not mentioned in formal reports of research, such as journal articles. Personal interest may therefore be a component in the process of selecting a research topic, but does not alone generally provide a sufficient rationale or focus for a research project; it is necessary to develop additional criteria for selection of a specific topic from among the other sources discussed below.

The research literature

The research literature is the most common source of topics for academic research. A researchable topic derived from reading of the literature can take a variety of forms. It may arise from an informal scanning of the literature which stimulates a spark of interest in a topic, or it may arise from a more critical and focussed reading. Much reported research is very specific to time and place, so that even a widely accepted theory might be subject to further testing and exploration. Thus it may be that a certain theory or theoretical proposition has never been tested empirically, or it merits further empirical testing for a variety of reasons, as set out in Figure 3.3.

Reason	The theories/propositions/observations history	Example
Geographical	May have been tested only in one country/region	– Theory established using US data could be tested in another country. – Behaviour patterns of urban residents – are they replicated in rural areas?
Social	May have been established on the basis of the experience of one social group only	– Theory based on men's experience – does it apply to women? – Theory tested on middle-class subjects – does it apply to working-class people?
Temporal	May be out of date	Theory on youth culture established in the 1960s – is it still valid?
Contextual	May have been established in fields other than leisure/tourism	Foucault's (1979) theories on power are based on studies in a hospital – are they relevant in the tourism industry?
Methodological	May have been tested using only one methodology	Conclusions from a qualitative study could be tested quantitatively

Figure 3.3 Reasons for re-visiting theories/propositions/observations from the literature

A topic may, however, be inspired not by theory, but by other material from the literature. For example, a particular research technique might be of interest, and the aim is then to find a suitable setting to explore the use of the technique. An historical account could inspire a researcher to explore the history of an area or an activity or a group of people.

Clearly, therefore, identifying a topic from the literature requires a special, *questioning, exploratory* approach to reading research literature: the aim is not just to identify what the literature *says*, but also what it does *not* say or the *basis* for assertions made. The process of critically reviewing the literature is discussed further below under Review the literature, and in Chapter 5. If the research literature is to be the main source of ideas for a research topic then the first two elements of the research process – 1. Select a topic; and 2. Review the literature – are effectively combined.

A policy or management issue/problem

Policy or management topics are often specified by a leisure or tourism organisation, but students or academics interested in policy or management issues can also identify such topics. For example: tourism forecasting is done not only by, and at the behest of, government and commercial tourism bodies but also by academics; and surveys of users of leisure or tourist facilities or cost–benefit analyses of programmes and projects can be conducted by interested academics as well as leisure service organisations. The difference is that the results of academic research will often be made public, will generally be presented so as to highlight their more general implications rather than the particular application to the facility or programme being studied, and will be concerned as much with the *methodology* of the study as with its substantive findings. Research carried out by or for an industry organisation, on the other hand, may often not be made public, the wider implications of the research might not be examined and the methodology, while it must be sound, will often not be of particular interest to the sponsoring organisation. Research sponsored by government bodies lies somewhere in between these two situations: the results of the research may be very specific, but will often not be confidential.

It is common for policy or management topics to be outlined by an organisation in a *brief* or set of *terms of reference* for a funded research or consultancy project. Research organisations – usually consultants – are invited to respond in the form of a competitive *tender* to conduct the project. This type of procedure has its own set of practices and conventions, as discussed later in this chapter under Responsive proposals – briefs and tenders (see pp. 77–9).

Social concern

Social concern can give rise to a wide range of research topics. For example, concern for certain deprived or neglected groups in society can lead to research on the leisure needs or behaviour of members of such groups. Concern for the environment can lead to research on the environmental impact of tourism in sensitive areas. Often such research is closely related to policy or management issues, but the research may have a more limited role, seeking to highlight problems rather than necessarily seeking to devise solutions.

Popular/media

A *popular issue* can inspire research that seeks to explore popular beliefs or conceptions, especially where it is suspected that these may be inaccurate or contestable. 'Popular' usually means 'as portrayed in the media'. For example, this might be seen as the motivation for much research on media portrayals of such phenomena as sporting crowd violence and 'alienated youth' (Rowe, 1995: 4) or a major controversial leisure or tourism development.

Published research agendas

From time to time public agencies, professional bodies or individual academics publish 'research agendas', based on an assessment, often made by a committee, of the research needs of a field of study. Lynch and Brown (1999) provide a review and summary of such agendas for leisure/recreation in Britain, Australia and North America and Ritchie (1993) and Faulkner *et al.* (2003) have presented agendas for the field of tourism. Often the aim of the initiating body is to implement the published research agenda itself, but in other cases the idea is for researchers in the field generally – including students – to respond by adopting topics in the agenda for their own research. Students looking for 'relevant' research topics know that if their topic is selected from such a published list, then there will be at least a few people 'out there' who will be interested in the results!

Brainstorming

Brainstorming involves a group of two or more people bouncing ideas off one-another in discussion in pursuit of inspiration or solutions to a problem. Typically this might be done with the aid of a board or 'butcher's paper' to write down ideas as they emerge. It can be seen as a separate source of ideas for a research topic or a way of refining ideas from any or all of the sources discussed above.

Selecting the topic

What makes an acceptable research topic? There is no single, or simple, answer to this question. In general it is not the topic itself which is 'good' or 'bad' but the way the research is conceptualised – see element 3, Devise conceptual framework – and how the research question(s) is or are framed – see element 4, Decide research question(s). A key question is whether the topic has already been researched by someone else – hence the need for a review of the literature, as discussed in element 2, Review the literature. But even when a topic has already been researched there is invariably scope for further research – sometimes this is pointed out by the original researcher! Thus the first four elements of the research process – select topic, review literature, conceptualise, define research questions – form an iterative, often 'messy', process, which is invariably difficult, challenging and frustrating. But it is essential to get this stage right or the rest of the research effort may be wasted.

Type of purpose/motivation	Features
Pursue knowledge for its own sake	Academic/scientific criteria – but may combine with others below

Ideologically driven:
– Conservative
– Reformist
  – e.g. social-democratic
  – e.g. environmental
– Radical/critical
  – e.g. neo-liberal
  – e.g. neo-Marxist
  – e.g. radical-feminist
  – e.g. anti-globalist
	
	– defence/acceptance of the status quo
	
	– a more egalitarian society
	– sustainability
	
	– defence/extension of the market
	– demonstration of class conflict/exploitation
	– demonstration of patriarchy/women's oppression
	– demonstrate undesirable features of global market trends

Policy/management: – Critical – Instrumental	 – critiques current policy/management – may reflect one or more radical/critical stances above – accepts broad philosophy of organisational milieu being studied

Figure 3.4 Purposes of research

The purpose of research

The *purposes* of a research project can shape the choice of topic and the subsequent research design. Three types of purpose are discussed here, namely: knowledge for its own sake; ideological/political purposes; and policy/management purposes; and their key features are summarised in Figure 3.4. These purposes or motivations for research are often not explicitly stated, but are generally implicit. They affect the choice of topic and the overall shaping of the research process.

Knowledge for its own sake

The classic purpose of research is to 'add to knowledge' for its own sake, or for the general good as judged by the researcher. Some researchers continue to be driven by this goal in all or some of their research, and work in an institutional environment where it can be pursued. Much 'unfunded' research undertaken by academics in their own time is of this nature. But even in such a 'pure' situation, other, less noble, although not necessarily illegitimate, purposes may be involved – for example personal career advancement.

Ideological/political

Many academic researchers are motivated wholly or in part by an ideological or political agenda. It could be said that *all* are so motivated, and in certain areas of the social sciences this is a valid point. Many social scientists might be described as *reformist*, in that they are motivated by a general desire for 'a more equitable society' and their research will tend to at least be consistent with such a goal, if not centrally concerned with it. Thus, for example, much leisure research is concerned with equality and inequality of access to leisure opportunities and much tourism research is concerned about unjust exploitation of host communities. Similarly, in both fields, environmental protection and sustainability is often an implicit or explicit concern. If none of these concerns is apparent, but the research is dealing with social issues, the implicit stance may be taken as *conservative* – implying contentment with the political, social and/or economic status quo. In contrast some researchers are guided by one or more of a number of ideological positions which seek fundamental change in society and might be described as *radical* or *critical*. On the right of the political spectrum is radical 'New Right' thinking which endorses market processes and seeks their extension and might be termed *neo-liberal*. There is relatively little research in leisure studies with this outlook, although it is implicit in some tourism research which is concerned with the development of tourism. By contrast, those on the left with, for example, neo-Marxist beliefs, are opposed to the market system and those with radical feminist beliefs seek to demonstrate the effects of patriarchal power. Thus neo-Marxists John Clarke and Chas Critcher state that 'the study of leisure for its own sake . . . is an irrelevancy. The purpose of studying any particular element of the social order is to . . . understand the ways in which one particular element is shaped by other structures . . .' (Clarke and Critcher, 1985: xiii) and the epilogue to their book discusses how 'socialism as a movement might benefit from an active appreciation of leisure' (232). Feminist Betsy Wearing seeks to develop the concept of leisure as 'a potential site for resistance to and subversion of hegemonic masculinity' (Wearing, 1998: xvi).

Policy/management

The purpose of research which is policy-related or management-related seems obvious enough – to address policy or management problems. But the stance adopted can vary and can be affected by the ideological positions outlined above. Some research might be seen as *critical*, in that it steps outside the policy or management milieu of the public or private sector organisations being studied and adopts reformist or leftist perspectives when it critiques processes such as privatisation or 'managerialism' or seeks to demonstrate the inequitable outcomes of certain policies or management practices. Research which seeks to make private sector operations more efficient or profitable and generally accepts the broad philosophical stance of the field being studied can be seen as *instrumental*.

2. Review the literature

Introduction

The process of reviewing the existing research literature is sufficiently important for a complete chapter to be devoted to it in this book (Chapter 5). 'Reviewing the literature' is a somewhat academic term referring to the process of identifying and engaging with previously published research relevant to the topic of interest. The process can play a number of roles, as listed in Figure 3.5 and discussed further in Chapter 5.

Figure 3.5
Roles of the
literature in
research

- Entire basis of the research
- Source of ideas on topics for research
- Source of information on research already done by others
- Source of methodological or theoretical ideas
- Basis of comparison
- Source of information that is an integral/supportive part of the research

In many cases the review undertaken in the early stages of the research has to be seen as a 'preliminary' or 'interim' literature review only, since time does not always permit a thorough literature review to be completed at the start of a project. Part of the research programme itself may be to explore the literature further. Having invest-igated the literature as thoroughly as possible, it is usually necessary to proceed with the research proposal in the hope that all relevant material has been identified. Exploration of the literature will generally continue for the duration of the project. Researchers always run the risk of coming across some previous – or contemporaneous – publication which will completely negate or upstage their work just as they are about to complete it. But that is part of the excitement of research! In fact, unlike the situ-ation in the natural sciences, the risk of this happening in the leisure and tourism field is minimal, since research in this area can rarely be replicated exactly. In the natural sciences research carried out in, say, California can reproduce exactly the findings of research carried out in, say, London. In leisure and tourism research, however, this is not the case – a set of research procedures carried out in relation to residents of California could be expected to produce very different results from identical proced-ures carried out in London – or even New York – simply because leisure and tourism research is involved with unique people in varying social settings.

Conducting the review

Where possible, attempts should be made to explore not just published research – the *literature* – but also unpublished and on-going research. This process is very much 'hit and miss'. Knowing what research is on-going or knowing of completed but unpub-lished research usually depends on having access to informal networks, although some organisations produce registers of on-going research. Once a topic of interest has been identified it is often clear, from the literature, where the major centres for such research are located and to discover, from direct approaches or from websites, annual reports or newsletters, what research is currently being conducted at those centres. This process can be particularly important if the topic is a 'fashionable' one. However, if this is the case, the communication networks are usually very active, which eases the process. In this respect papers from conferences and seminars are usually better sources of information on current research than books and journals, since the latter have long gestation periods, so that the research reported in them is generally based on work carried out two or more years prior to publication.

As will be discussed in Chapter 5, a review of the literature should be con-cluded with a *summary* which provides an overview of the field, its substantive and methodological merits and deficiencies or gaps, and an indication of how such conclusions are related to the research task in hand.

What discipline?

In an academic context, especially for undergraduate or graduate projects, it is helpful to consider what *discipline(s)* the project is related to. In some cases this is obvious because the project is linked to a particular disciplinary unit – for example, marketing. In other cases the project is a 'capstone' exercise which may draw on one or more of any of the subjects studied in the course. Often, the fact that a topic does not have an obvious disciplinary 'label' results in student researchers failing to draw on available disciplinary theories and frameworks and failing to take the opportunity to demonstrate the knowledge they have gained during the course of their studies! For example, if the research topic is to do with the subject of *golf*, searching library catalogues and databases using the keyword 'golf' will undoubtedly produce a certain amount of useful material. But consideration of whether the focus of the study is to be on golf management, golf marketing; the social context of golf or the motivations of golf players opens up the possibility of applying generic theories and relating the research to comparable studies on other phenomena in the area of management, planning, sociology and psychology respectively. An important question to ask is, therefore: what disciplinary field(s) is this research related to? What theories and ideas can be drawn from the literature in this discipline or these disciplines?

3. Devise a conceptual framework

The idea of a conceptual framework

The development of a conceptual framework is arguably the most important part of any research project and also the most difficult. And it is the element which is the weakest in many research projects. A *conceptual framework* involves *concepts* involved in a study and the *hypothesised relationships between them*. In this discussion the term conceptual framework has been used to cover a wide range of research situations. Thus such a term can be used in applied research when the framework adopted might relate to such activities as planning or marketing. In such cases, ideas for conceptual frameworks may readily be found in the planning or marketing literature. When the research is more academically oriented, the term *theoretical framework* might equally well be used. Miles and Huberman describe conceptual frameworks as follows:

> A conceptual framework explains, either graphically or in narrative form, the main things to be studied – the key factors, constructs or variables – and the presumed relationships among them. Frameworks can be rudimentary or elaborate, theory-driven or commonsensical, descriptive or causal.
> (Miles and Huberman, 1994: 18)

The concepts identified and the framework within which they are set determines the whole course of the study. In exploring the conceptual framework for the study the researcher is asking: What's going on here? What processes are at work or likely to be at work? Sometimes the framework is developed from individual reflection or 'brain-storming' and sometimes it arises from the literature – indeed, an existing framework from the literature might well be used and merely adapted for application in a new situation. Where a number of areas of literature have been reviewed and provide the basis for the research, the skill is to draw the theoretical ideas together into a common framework – even if the aim is to show the incompatibility between two or more perspectives. Obviously, such links should be clearly and fully explained in the exposition of the framework.

Different types of research – descriptive, explanatory or evaluative – tend to call for different styles of conceptual framework. *Descriptive research* rarely requires an elaborate conceptual framework, but clear definitions of the concepts involved are required. In some cases this can nevertheless be a considerable undertaking, for example when the descriptive task is to decide people's time use, and a taxonomy and associated coding system must be devised for every conceivable form of leisure and non-leisure activity (see United Nations Statistics Division, n.d.), or when the task is to gather data on the many types of tourist expenditure and activity. Both *explanatory* and *evaluative* research call for well-developed conceptual frameworks which form the basis for the explanation or evaluation work required from the research.

The development of a conceptual framework can be thought of as involving four elements, as depicted in Figure 3.6. The element 'Identification of concepts' should, perhaps, be the starting point, but this is rarely the case: the tendency is to think about relationships first, and then identify and define the concepts involved, as this becomes necessary. In fact the exercise is generally *iterative* – that is, it involves going backwards and forwards, or round and round, between the various elements until a satisfactory solution is reached. The four elements are discussed in turn below.

1. Explore/explain the relationships

Relationships may represent power relationships, influencing factors, money or information flows or simply a sequence of elements in a process. The postulated

Figure 3.6
Development of a conceptual framework

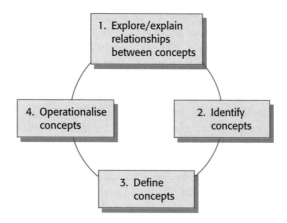

Stage	Statements/hypotheses (concepts are in italics)
A.	*Participation* in a leisure or tourism activity arises as a result of an individual (or household/family) decision-making process.
B.	Whether or not a person participates could depend on a variety of *events and circumstances*. For example: – the *availability of and access to facilities* may by good or bad; – *advertising and promotion* may vary in quantity and influence; – the *cost* of participation may be high or low; – a *chance event*, such as meeting up with a group of friends, may trigger *participation*
C.	Whether or not individuals participate will also depend on their *characteristics*, such as: – *age* – *income* – *personality* and – *past experience* in participating in that or similar experiences

relationships correspond to the theory which underpins the conceptual framework. Explaining a conceptual framework may be a lengthy and complex process, especially when links with the literature are involved. The example in Figure 3.7 is very simple. It shows how the ideas develop from a simple statement (Stage A) to a more complex statement or series of statements (Stage C) as the ideas develop. In the example, the statements are expressed in the form of hypotheses; they could alternatively be expressed as questions, for example: 'To what extent is the decision influenced by income?'

One aid to the development of a conceptual framework is to use the device of a *concept map*, sometimes referred to as a *mind map*. While some concept maps are more 'self-evident' than others, a concept map *is* only an optional aid – a full narrative discussion and explanation always forms the core of the conceptual framework. A concept map merely illustrates or summarises the discussion.

Concept mapping can be seen as a form of visual 'brainstorming' and can be done alone or as part of a group exercise. The idea is to write down, on a piece of paper or a board or flip-chart, all the concepts which appear to be relevant to a topic, in any order which they come to mind. Then begin to group the concepts and indicate linkages between them. This is likely to involve a process of trial and error. Figure 3.8 illustrates the framework described in Figure 3.7. Three versions of the concept map correspond to the three stages in Figure 3.7.

The concept map then, depicts *concepts* – usually depicted in boxes or circles – and the *relationships* between concepts – usually represented by lines between the concepts, with or without directional arrows. Different types of concept might be represented by different shaped boxes. The concepts and their relationships are explained in the accompanying text (Figure 3.7). The key relationships identified at stages A, B and C in the process are labelled accordingly.

Figure 3.8
Concept map
example

(Related to stages in Figure 3.7)

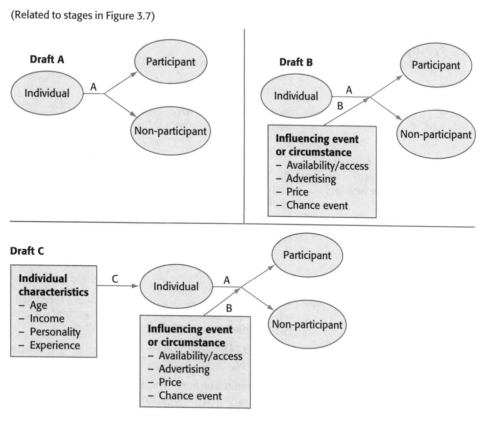

2. Identify concepts

Concepts are general representations of the phenomena to be studied – the 'building blocks' of a study. They might involve types of individuals (e.g. 'manager'), groups of individuals (e.g. 'gang') or organisations (e.g. 'firm') of their characteristics or actions. The first column of Figure 3.9 lists the concepts encountered in Figures 3.7 and 3.8.

3. Define concepts

Concepts must be clearly defined for research purposes. Dictionary definitions or definitions from the research literature may be used, but it is often necessary to be selective or adaptive. Figure 3.9 includes suggested definitions for the concepts listed there. Definitions might be very rudimentary in the early stages of the exercise and become more detailed and complex with time: as we talk about 'X' we have to clarify 'exactly what we mean' by 'X'.

4. Operationalise concepts

If a concept lends itself to quantification then *operationalisation* involves deciding how it might be *measured*. If the concept is qualitative in nature, the process involves deciding how the concept might be identified or assessed in a non-quantified manner when

Concept*	Definition	Operationalisation
1. Participant:		
a. In leisure	Person who engages in relatively freely chosen activity during leisure time.	Participation in activity identified as 'leisure' at least once in preceding year.
b. In tourism	Person who travels away from home for leisure purposes**	Travel for leisure purposes at least 40km from home with at least one overnight stay in preceding 3 months.
2. Circumstances/events		
a. Availability of/access to:		
– Leisure facilities	Preferred leisure facilities at affordable price available in home community.	Range of facilities within day-trip range at or below a various 'benchmark' costs – e.g. $10, $20, $30 a head.
– Tourism opportunities	Holiday services at preferred destinations available at affordable price.	Range of two-week holidays of different sorts available at a range of 'benchmark' costs, related to household income.
b. Advertising/promotion	Leisure/tourism advertising/promotion to which individual is exposed.	Individual's recall of a specified list of advertisements/promotions in last 3 months.
c. Cost (of participation)	Total cost of leisure/tourism experience.	Costs of ranges of activities as indicated in 2a and 2b above.
d. Chance event	Unplanned occurrence which affects decision to participate.	Events which individual claims affected recent decisions to participate: experience, advice from friend/relative, item read or seen in the media.

3. Individual characteristics	Individual attributes (which influence leisure/tourism decisions), for example:
	  a. Age
	  b. Income
	
	  c. Personality
	  d. Past leisure/tourism experience
		
		a. Age last birthday
		b. Annual household income before tax
		c. Results of Myers-Briggs test
		d. Leisure: activities undertaken in last six months (from checklist); Tourism: trips taken in last 5 years.

* Concepts appearing in Figure 3.8, Draft C. ** NB some definitions of tourism include other purposes, such as business

Figure 3.9 Examples of concepts – definition and operationalisation

conducting qualitative research, such as in-depth interviews. Examples of operationalisation of concepts are shown in Figure 3.9. Most of the concepts lend themselves to quantification and measurement, at least in part, but concepts 2a, 2b and 2d have qualitative characteristics and could be treated either way.

To some extent operationalisation involves thinking ahead as to how information might, in practice, be gathered about a concept: it is an indication of the practical

Concept	Definition	Operationalisation
City park	Park within the city	All parks within Detroit city boundaries
Regional park	Park outside the city	All parks located in three counties surrounding Detroit city
Race	Ethnic/racial identity	Subjects' response to self-identification question with the following categories: 'black, Hispanic, white, other'
Marginality	Limitations on participation due to a. limited income or b. access to transportation	*Objective indicators*: a. annual income and b. automobile ownership *Subjective indicators*: subjects' reported perception of: a. 'expense' as a barrier to park use, and b. transportation barriers to park use
Subcultural preferences	Unconstrained preference for use or non-use of parks	Coded responses to open-ended question on non-use of parks or reasons for not using parks more often, such as 'no interest' or 'prefer to do other things'
Inter-racial constraints	Actual or subjective feelings of racial discrimination resulting in feelings of being 'uncomfortable' or 'unwelcome' in parks	Coded responses to open-ended questions on reasons for use/non-use of parks and specific questions on experience of 'negative reactions of other people' in parks

Source: West, 1989

Figure 3.10   Case study: operationalisation of concepts

implications of the definition. Often arbitrary or pragmatic choices have to be made in order to 'operationalise' the project. For example, should 'leisure participation' involve 'regular' participation to be counted as 'participation' or is 'once a year' adequate? Or, what distance should someone have to be travelling away from home to be classified as a 'tourist' – 40km or 50km or 25km? These may be arbitrary decisions, or decisions based on the need to gather data which is comparable to other, existing, data.

Figure 3.10 summarises the discussion of the operationalisation of concepts used by Patrick West (1989) in a study of the use of parks by ethnic minorities in Detroit. The study sought to discover whether black and white Detroit residents had different patterns of use of city parks and regional parks and whether black residents' use of parks was constrained by ethnic sub-cultural tastes, marginality (limitations of income or transport) or racial discrimination. Figure 3.10 presents the operationalisation aspects of the study in tabular form, but in the article they are presented in narrative form over two pages.

Models

A theoretical framework might also be called a *model*, particularly when the research is quantitative in nature. For example the relationship between holiday-taking and a person's social and economic circumstances could be expressed in quantitative modelling terms as shown in Figure 3.11. A survey of holiday-taking would identify various groups with different levels of income and holiday frequency, and statistical analysis

The theory	The frequency of holiday-taking of a particular group is positively related to the group's average level of income
Variables	H = number of holiday trips per year N = income pa in $'000s
Equation	H = a + bN
Example of calibrated equation	H = 0.1 + 0.05 N
Use of the equation used for prediction (assume N = $30k)	H = 0.1 + 0.05 x 30 = 0.1 + 1.5 = 1.6 trips pa

Figure 3.11   Conceptual framework as quantifiable model

could be used to 'calibrate' the equation, that is, find values for the 'parameters' a and b, so that the level of holiday-taking of a particular group could be predicted once the average income of that group was known. In Figure 3.11 hypothetical parameters of 0.1 and 0.05 are presented to illustrate the approach and an example is given of how such an equation might be used to estimate or predict holiday expenditure of groups with given income levels, now or in the future. The technicalities of the statistical process are not pursued further here, but are touched on again in Chapter 12, when the technique of regression is discussed. More complex models could be developed, including, perhaps, people's age and occupation, the price of travel, exchange rates, and so on. Indeed, such models are used to predict future tourism demand to and from different countries and regions.

Examples of conceptual frameworks in leisure and tourism studies

The example given in Figure 3.8 relates to leisure participation decision-making, including the decision to take a holiday. More elaborate versions of this type of framework are presented in Brandenburg *et al.* (1982) and Veal (1995), which relate to leisure in general, although this can include the leisure activity of taking a holiday trip.

An example of a framework specifically geared to decision-making or choice in regard to holiday-taking is that presented by Witt and Wright (1992: 50) and is reproduced in modified form in Figure 3.12. In Witt and Wright's original formulation the diagram referred only to choice of a holiday and holiday destination, but the same process could apply equally to decision-making in relation to deciding to participate in any leisure activity at a leisure facility, so in Figure 3.12 the term 'HD/LF' is used, meaning 'holiday destination or leisure facility'.

Some of the discussions and diagrams presented in this book are examples of conceptual frameworks. For example, Figure 1.4 presents a conceptualisation of the 'rational-comprehensive model of the management process. Some of the boxes as presented in Figure 1.4 are expressed as verbs, but they can quite easily be expressed as nouns, as shown in Figure 3.13. There is not an extensive discussion of the rationale behind the model in Chapter 1, but such a rationale could be presented, as in, for example, Veal (2002: 91–113).

Further examples of conceptual frameworks are presented in the case studies at the end of the chapter.

Figure 3.12
Holiday/leisure
facility choice:
conceptual
framework

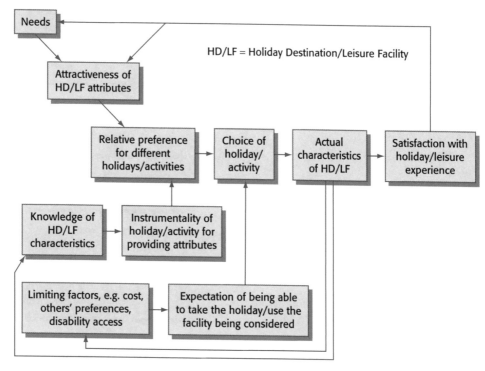

Source: based on Witt and Wright, 1992: 50

Conceptual frameworks for policy/planning/management/marketing tasks

In many cases research is part of a specific management task, of the sort discussed at the end of Chapter 1 and listed in Figure 1.5 – for example, marketing study or a customer service quality study. In these cases the conceptual framework for the research may be part of a wider task. Often the 'research question' is clear from the beginning, because it is to resolve the management problem or task. Planning, marketing or management frameworks from the applied literature may be used as the basis for the research framework. Two examples are given in Figure 3.14. One concerns a market research study for a proposed new facility or attraction and the other concerns a customer service quality study using the SERVQUAL approach. The latter is similar to what is sometimes referred to as the *importance/performance* approach to assessment and decision-making (see Veal, 2002: 110–11; 220–1).

Conceptual frameworks and inductive research

One reaction to this discussion of conceptual frameworks is to observe that the approach seems inconsistent with the *inductive* approach, as discussed in Chapter 2, in which theory is derived from the data rather than data being used to test pre-existing theory. In particular, it seems inconsistent with the more apparently open-ended approaches such as *grounded theory* and informal, flexible approaches used in *qualitative*

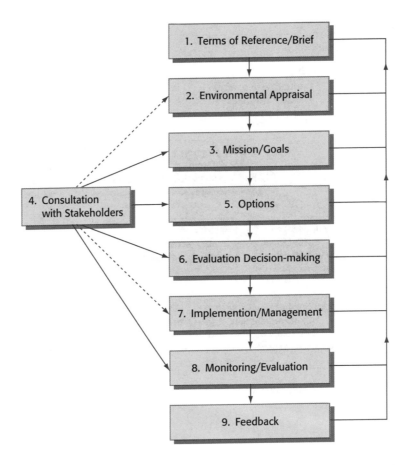

Figure 3.13
The rational-
comprehensive
management
model as
conceptual
framework

research. However, as Miles and Huberman (1994: 17) indicate, in their book on *Qualitative Data Analysis*, conceptual frameworks are just as vital for qualitative research as for quantitative – arguably more so.

In fact, a conceptual framework need not be a straitjacket: it can be a flexible, evolving device. As will be discussed in Chapter 8, in qualitative research, theory development and data collection and analysis are often intertwined, rather than being sequential. But the researcher rarely starts with an absolutely blank conceptual framework – there is usually some sort of rudimentary framework drawn from the literature or other sources. As a minimum there will be an initial list of relevant concepts with which the researcher is concerned and without which it is difficult to know what questions to ask or what issues to explore. In some cases the researcher may start with a framework from the literature which is seen as unsatisfactory in some way: the aim of the research then is not to validate the framework but to do the opposite and replace it with an improved – and possible very different – model. The conceptual framework drawn up at the beginning of the research project can be seen as the 'first draft'; as data gathering and analysis proceeds, further drafts will emerge, to incorporate new insights arising from the research. The developing conceptual framework becomes the focus of the research process.

A. Market research study

Aim: to assess the size and nature of the market for a potential new tourist/leisure attraction.

Strategy (concepts are indicated in italic): 1. to obtain information on the general level of *demand for this type of attraction* in the community at large, and the *market profile* of visitors to existing similar attractions, using national or regional data; 2. to estimate the *current level of demand* and *future level of demand* for this type of attraction in the specified *market area*, based on *local demand, day-trip demand* and *tourist demand*; 3. to assess *existing provision* of this type of attraction in the locality and the likely *market share* which the new attraction might attract; 4. to conduct a consumer study of *quality* of existing provision to guide developers on the design of the proposed new attraction.

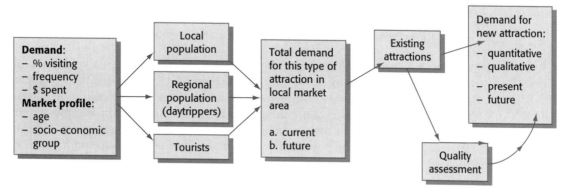

B. Customer service quality study

Aim: To assess customers' satisfaction with a leisure/tourism facility/service.

Strategy (concepts in italic): Use the SERVQUAL approach to customer service quality measurement (see Parasuraman *et al.*, 1985; Howat *et al.*, 2003), which compares customers' *expectations* concerning various *attributes of service quality* with customers' assessment of actual *performance* of the service in regard to those attributes. The *difference* or *disconfirmation* between the two assessments provides information for managers on areas of service quality which require *management action*.

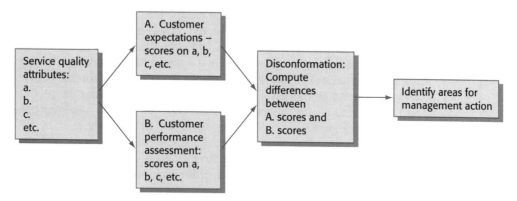

Figure 3.14 Examples of conceptual frameworks for management/planning projects

4. Decide research question(s)

Research question, problem or hypothesis?

The focus of a research project might be expressed as a *question*, a *problem* or a *hypothesis*.

■ A question requires an answer.

■ A problem requires a solution.

■ A hypothesis is expressed as a statement, which must be proved 'true' (consistent with the evidence), or 'false' (not consistent with the evidence).

The difference between and relationships between the question-based approach and the hypothesis-based approach are illustrated in Figure 3.15, which uses the *problem* of declining visitor numbers at a leisure/ tourism site as an illustrative example. In part A, the simple version, the issue of declining visits at a leisure/tourism site is expressed on the left as a *question*, with the research process seeking to produce an answer to the question. On the right the possible explanation is expressed as a *statement/hypothesis*, which is tested by the research process to come up with a conclusion. In the example given here, the hypothesis is consistent with the evidence. In practice, the two approaches are often quite similar. Thus a more detailed sequence of events is shown in part B of Figure 3.15. This shows a *range* of hypotheses being tested, rather than a single one. This is similar to the range of possible answers which might be explored to answer the research question.

The hypothesis format is more common in the natural sciences while the research question format is more common in the social sciences. The latter lends itself to descriptive and inductive research, while the former is more appropriate for explanatory and deductive research, as discussed in Chapter 2. For most of the book the research question format is assumed, but the hypothesis format is integral to certain forms of statistical analysis and so is used in Chapter 13.

In some cases the research *topic* selected by the researcher is quite specific from the beginning and is initially expressed in the form of a question: the subsequent literature review and the conceptual framework are then the process by which this specific issue is analysed and placed in the context of existing knowledge. This is demonstrated in the example used in Figure 3.15 on declining visitor numbers at a site.

The conceptual framework can involve *decision-making models* as presented in Figure 3.12 – that is, the research is designed to explore the causal factors and processes involved in people's decisions to visit a site or destination in order to discover how others might be persuaded to visit, or how they might be persuaded to visit again. The literature review would involve a review of similar existing models and a review of existing research on the various factors which influence people to choose a destination or visit a leisure site.

In other cases the topic is initially quite vague: it is an area of interest without a very specific focus. In such cases the literature review and the process of developing a conceptual framework help to focus the topic and determine what exactly should be researched. The aim is to focus the research on one or more very specific questions which can be answered by the research. This is inevitably an iterative process; a

Research question	Hypothesis
A. Simple version	
1. *Pose research question*: Why have visitor levels declined in the last two years at site X?	1. *State hypothesis*: Visitor levels declined in the last two years at site X because of the attraction of newer, better value sites.
2. Conduct research.	2. Conduct research.
3. *Answer*: Because of the attraction of newer, better value sites.	3. *Result*: Consistent with the evidence.
B. More detailed version	
1. *Pose research question*: Why have visitor levels declined in the last two years at site X?	1. *Develop hypotheses*: Brainstorm/review literature/make enquiries as to range of possible reasons for decline in attendances.
2. *Develop research strategy:* Brainstorm/review literature/make enquiries as to range of possible reasons for decline in visits. Compile list of possible reasons: a. attraction of newer, better value facilities b. declining income in local catchment c. downturn in tourist numbers d. decline in quality of the facility e. increase in prices.	2. *Formulate/state hypotheses:* Visit levels have declined because of: a. attraction of newer, better value facilities b. declining disposable income in local catchment c. downturn in tourist numbers d. decline in quality of the facility, or e. increase in prices, . . . or a combination of the above.
3. *Conduct research* Collect evidence/data to discover which reasons are plausible.	3. *Conduct research* Collect evidence/data and test all five hypotheses.
4. *Answer*: Because of the attraction of newer, better value sites.	4. *Results*: a. Consistent with evidence; b. Not consistent; c. Not consistent; d. Not consistent; e. Not consistent.

Figure 3.15 The research question *vs* the hypothesis

question that looks simple and answerable, once subject to thought, reading and analysis, often develops into many questions which become conceptually too demanding to deal with in one project or which cannot be managed in the time and with the resources available. In such a situation a smaller part of the problem must be isolated for research. This does not mean that the complex, 'big picture' must always be ignored – there is always a case, when writing up a research project, for setting it in its wider context and explaining how and why the particular focus was adopted.

Research questions or objectives?

Often research projects have a set of practical *objectives* but these should not be confused with research *questions*. Nor should objectives be confused with the list of *tasks* necessary to conduct the research – as discussed under *research strategy* below. Thus, for example, to say: The purpose of this research is to conduct a survey of a group of clients ...' is to confuse ends with means. The survey, in this case, is being conducted for a purpose, to answer the research question(s), not as an end in itself. Of course, a research question can be embedded in an objective; thus it is possible to say:

> The objective of this research is to answer the following question: Why are attendances falling?

The one possible exception to this rule is the sort of research project which is aimed at establishing a database for a range of possible future uses. For example, the national statistics office of most countries conducts the population census every five or ten years as a service to a multitude of users who use the data for a wide range of purposes – so 'conducting a census of the population' could be said to be the objective of the research project. But even in this case, most of the possible future uses are known: the project assumes at least a prior range of policy-oriented research questions, related to trends in ageing, educational needs, health matters, and so on. Few leisure or tourism researchers find themselves in this sort of 'open-ended' data collection situation: data should generally not be collected for their own sake or in the hope that they 'might come in useful'.

Primary and secondary questions

In most situations the idea of *primary* and *subsidiary* questions is helpful. The subsidiary questions are necessary steps towards answering the primary question. For example, in Figure 3.14, a number of unknowns are indicated in the diagrams, which could be turned into subsidiary research questions. Thus, in study A, the 'market profile' could be translated into the question: 'What is the profile of existing visitors to this type of attraction?' Compiling an inventory of competing local attractions pre-supposes the subsidiary question: 'What are the competing local attractions for the proposed development?' This idea is further illustrated in the case studies at the end of the chapter.

5. List information needs

The research question(s) and the conceptual framework should give rise to a list of *information needs* or *requirements*. In some cases the information requirements are quite clear and the likely sources of information are straightforward. For example, in the case of example A in Figure 3.14, each of the concepts suggests the need for data to determine its nature or to measure it. This is illustrated in Figure 3.16. It also suggests some likely sources for this information, but some types of information can be obtained from a variety of sources, so the decision on the source of the information is a separate issue and is discussed further below. The information needs are only indicated in abbreviated form here in Figure 3.16: for example, a 'market profile' for a particular type of attraction could involve more than just age and socio-economic group. This is clearly linked to the idea of 'operationalising' concepts, as discussed above. Again the case studies at the end of this chapter provide further illustrations of such lists.

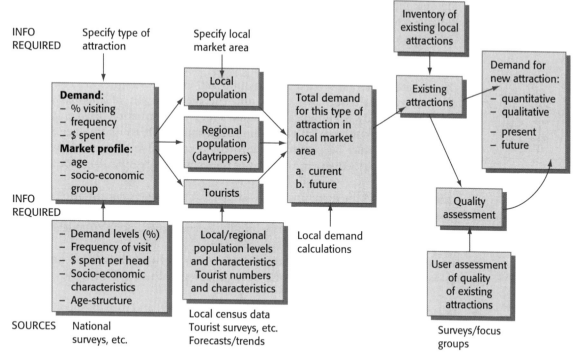

Figure 3.16 Information needs

6. Decide research strategy

Development of a *research strategy* involves making decisions on a number of aspects of the research process, as listed in Figure 3.17.

a. Project elements/stages

Often a research project will involve a number of different elements, or 'sub-projects' – for example gathering of primary and secondary data or data gathering in different locations or in different time-periods. This is clearly illustrated in the project shown in Figure 3.14, where there is an initial 'sub-project' to establish the nature of the market, a second sub-project to assess nature and scale of the local market base, then a third sub-project to estimate demand for the proposed attraction. A project may be devised in stages, particularly when one part is dependent on the findings from another. For example, stage 1 might involve some fieldwork in a particular location and, depending

Figure 3.17
Research
strategy

a. Identify project elements/stages
b. Decide information gathering techniques to be used
c. Decide data analysis techniques to be used
d. Decide budget
e. Draw up timetable

on the outcomes of stage 1, stage 2 might involve more in-depth work in the same location or conducting work in a second location.

b. Information gathering techniques to be used

It is at this stage that alternative information gathering techniques are considered. While the *operationalisation of concepts* and the identification of *information needs* processes may already have indicated certain types of information source, it is here that the detail is determined. For each item of information listed under stage 5 above, a range of sources may be possible. Judgement is required to determine just what techniques to use, particularly in the light of time and resources available, or likely to be made available.

A further review of the literature can be valuable at this stage, concentrating particularly on techniques used by previous researchers, and asking such questions as: have their chosen methods been shown to be limiting or even misguided? What lessons can be learned from past errors?

The range of information gathering methods which are most likely to be considered at this stage, are those covered in the following chapters of this book, namely:

- utilisation of existing information, including published and unpublished research and secondary data (Chapters 5 and 6);
- observation (Chapter 7);
- qualitative methods: including ethnographic methods, participant observation, informal and in-depth interviews, group interviews or focus groups (Chapter 8);
- questionnaire based surveys: including household face-to-face surveys, street surveys, telephone surveys, user/site surveys, postal surveys (Chapter 9).

These individual techniques are not discussed further here since they are covered in general terms in Chapter 4 and in detail in subsequent chapters, as indicated.

Where the process of information gathering involves going out into the 'field' – for instance to conduct interviews or to undertake observation – the planning of *fieldwork* needs to be considered. In the case of experimental research the proposed programme of experiments would be considered here. If the proposed research does not involve primary data collection then this will not be a consideration. Where extensive data collection is involved then the organisation of fieldwork may be complex, involving recruitment and training of field staff (e.g. interviewers), obtaining of permissions, including ethics committee clearance in universities (as discussed below), and organisation of data processing and analysis.

c. Approach to data analysis

Data analysis may be simple and straightforward and may follow fairly logically from the type of information collection technique to be used. This is particularly the case when the research is descriptive in nature. In some cases, however, the analysis of data may be complex and thought needs to be given to the time and the skills which will be required to undertake the analysis. Consideration must be given to the format of the data which will be collected and just how its analysis will answer the research questions posed. The planned analysis procedures have implications for data collection. For example, Case study D involves comparison of holiday-takers and non-holiday-takers, implying that an adequate sample of the two groups would need to be collected and ways would need to be found to compare their characteristics, patterns of holiday-taking, local leisure participation and perceptions. Where qualitative data are to be collected, for example using in-depth interviews, thought must be given to how the results of the interviews will be analysed. Details of analysis methods which are appropriate and possible for different data collection techniques are discussed in subsequent chapters, but it must be borne in mind that, when planning a project, full consideration should be given not only to the *collection* of data but also to its *analysis*.

d. Budget and e. Timetable

In some situations key aspects of the budget and timetable are fixed. For example a student may have available only her or his own labour and no other resources and may be required to submit a report by a specified date. Similarly, research consultancies usually have an upper budgetary limit and a fixed completion date. In other situations, for example when seeking a grant for research from a grant-giving body, or permission to conduct an 'in-house' project, the proposer of the research is called upon to recommend both budget and timetable. Whatever the situation, the task is never easy, since there is rarely enough time or money available to conduct the ideal research project, so compromises invariably have to be made.

The research strategy and timetable can be represented in various graphical formats; examples are shown in Figures 3.18 and 3.19.

Figure 3.18
Example of research programme diagrammatic representation

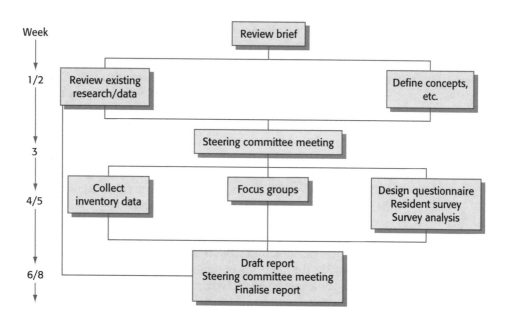

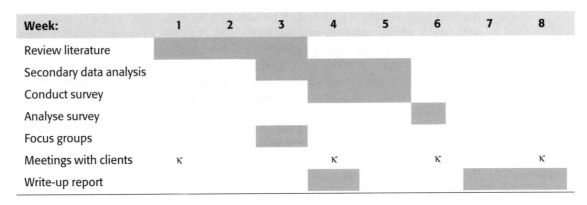

Figure 3.19   Example of research project timetable

7. Obtain ethics clearance

Introduction: research ethics

Ethical behaviour is important in research, as in any other field of human activity. Certain ethical considerations, concerned with such matters as plagiarism and honesty in reporting of results, arise in all research, but additional issues arise when the research involves human subjects, in both the biological and social sciences. The principles underlying 'research ethics' are universal – they concern things like honesty and respect for the rights of individuals.

Professional groups, such as market researchers, have established explicit 'codes of ethics' to which members are obliged to adhere (e.g. BMRA, n.d.). Most universities now have codes of ethics enforced by ethics committees. Typically, undergraduate and graduate projects are covered by a generic code of behaviour, but research proposals for theses and funded research by academics which involve humans or animals must be individually submitted for approval by the University Ethics Committee.

Codes of research ethics have intrinsic value in protecting the rights of humans and animals who may become involved in research, but they also serve a professional and organisational function. Researchers may be subject to litigation and can lose professional indemnity if they are not seen to have adhered to the appropriate code of ethics. A related consideration is the question of public relations and the standing of organisations responsible for the research within the community. Some practices may be ethical, but still give offence, so the value of the data collected using such practices must be weighed against the ill-will which may be generated.

Ethical issues arise in the design and conduct of research and in the reporting of results. With regard to the design and conduct of research many codes of ethics deal with practices in laboratories, but this discussion is concerned with ethical issues in the 'field'. As far as the reporting of results is concerned, the same ethical principles apply, regardless of the methods involved.

The general principles usually invoked in codes of research ethics are:

a. that no *harm* should befall the research subjects;

b. that subjects should take part *freely*; and

c. that subjects should take part on the basis of *informed consent*.

These ideas are discussed further below.

a. Harm

The question of harm arises particularly in medical/biological research, where an individual's health may be put at risk by an experimental procedure. But such risks can also arise in psychological research, where stress and distress can arise, and in socio-psychological research where inter-personal relationships can be damaged. In social research, where most leisure and tourism research falls, the question of 'harm' is more likely to arise in the use of data rather than in the collection process, in particular over the issue of confidentiality and privacy.

Privacy is a valued right in Western society. Even if no serious harm is *apparently* done, people can still be offended and suffer stress if their affairs are made public or divulged to certain third parties. There is therefore an obligation on the researcher to ensure confidentiality of any data collected. In many questionnaire survey situations, the issue of confidentiality of data does not arise since the data are collected anonymously. But even in such an anonymous situation, informants may be reluctant to give certain types of information to 'a complete stranger'. Where such sensitivity is encountered, the usual approach is to stress the voluntary nature of the information-giving process.

In some research projects named individuals are inevitably involved – for example where the number of subjects is small and they are key figures associated with particular organisations or communities. In this case the issue of confidentiality does arise. Where data are collected directly from the individual, care must be taken to adopt the journalist's practice of checking whether information is being given 'on the record' or 'off the record'. Thus, in interviews where sensitive matters arise, it is wise to ask informants whether they are prepared to be quoted. However, some information is obtained from third parties, and the researcher, like the journalist, must give careful consideration to just how such information is to be used. Unlike newspapers, few research organisations can afford to take the risk of publishing defamatory material, even if it does make a good story!

When data are confidential, measures must be taken to protect that confidentiality through ensuring the security of the raw data, such as interview tapes/transcripts/questionnaires. And care must be taken in the way the results are written up. Data can be stored with code-numbers or false names, with a key to the code-numbers or names being kept securely in a place apart from the data. Postal surveys are an 'in between' case. If returns cannot be identified, then there is no way of identifying non-respondents in order to send reminders. Sending reminders to *everyone* is costly, and an irritation to those who have already responded. One solution is to place an identifying number on the return envelope rather than on the questionnaire, with an assurance that the number will not be transferred to the questionnaire.

In reporting results, the use of false names or numbers to identify individuals, organisations, events, places and communities is the obvious solution, although it is often not sufficient. For those 'in the know', the places and the people involved in the research project may be all too easily identifiable. Occasionally this is exacerbated by the author's own list of 'acknowledgements', which clearly identifies people and places! The situation is akin to the phenomenon of novelists using friends or acquaintances in their books: some are flattered and others are very offended!

Confidentiality issues often arise with regard to the relationship between the researcher and the sponsoring organisation. In particular, if the sponsoring organisation 'owns' the data, the researcher may wish to protect the confidentiality of informants by *not* passing on to the sponsoring organisation any information which could identify informants by name.

b. Free choice

It seems obvious that subjects should not be coerced to become involved in research projects, but there are some 'grey' areas. Some of these are institutional and some are intrinsic to the design and nature of the research.

In universities, students are often used as subjects in research. In some places students are *required* to be available for a certain amount of experimental or survey work conducted by academic staff, and in some cases they receive credit for this involvement. Although, no doubt, students can 'opt out' of such activities, there is moral pressure on them to conform and possibly fear of sanctions if they do not. Clearly it is unethical for the university to allow such undue moral pressure to be brought to bear.

Other 'captive group' cases involve classes of school children or members of organisations, whose participation is agreed to by the person in charge. Again, while opting out may be possible, in practice it may be difficult and the subject is, to all intents and purposes, coerced. Research in prisons and mental and other hospitals raises similar questions about genuine freedom of choice on the part of the subject.

The principle of freedom of choice is constantly infringed by governments: it is an offence, for example, not to complete the population census forms or to refuse cooperation with a number of other official surveys. In these cases, the social need for accurate data is considered to outweigh the citizen's right to refuse to give information.

In some types of research choice on the part of the subject is virtually impossible – such as observational research where large numbers of subjects are involved – for example, studies of traffic flows, pedestrian movements or crowd behaviour. In many observational research situations, if the subjects knew that they were being observed they might well modify their behaviour, and so invalidate the research. This would apply particularly in situations where anti-social, and even illegal, behaviour may be involved. These considerations might apply in research ranging from people's interpersonal behaviour in a gym through to research on the milieu of prostitution, gambling or drinking.

The problem of freedom to participate arises particularly in research using participant observation (Bulmer, 1982). The whole basis of such research may rely on the researcher being accepted and trusted by the group being investigated: this may not be forthcoming if it is known that the participant is a researcher. If the researcher does 'come clean', there is the risk – even the likelihood – of the subjects modifying their behaviour, thus invalidating the research. To what extent is it ethical for researchers to disguise their identity to the people they are interacting with and studying – in effect to lie about their identity? When researchers are involved with groups engaging in illegal and/or anti-social activities, for example drug-taking or some youth gangs, where do their loyalties lie?

In a celebrated case in recreation research, Moeller and his colleagues (1980a) used *incognito* interviewers, posing as campers, to investigate campers' attitudes to pricing and discovered different results from those collected by formal, identified interviewers. The ethics of this practice raised considerable controversy in the *Journal of Leisure Research* (Christensen, 1980; LaPage, 1981; Moeller *et al.*, 1980b).

If it is accepted that the research of this type is permissible, despite the lack of freedom of consent, then the issue of confidentiality in reporting, as discussed above, comes even more to the fore.

c. Informed consent

In experimental research, where there is a risk, however remote, of physical harm to the subject (for example where allergies might be involved, or a risk of muscle strains, or even of heart attack), it is clearly necessary for the subject to be fully aware of the risks involved in order to be able to give their 'informed consent' to participate. The level of risk of harm is a matter of judgement, and often only the researcher is fully aware of the extent of risk involved in any given research procedure. This raises the question of the extent to which the subject can be fully 'informed'. Subjects can never be as fully informed as the researcher. A judgement has to be made about what is reasonable. In the traditional science laboratory setting, verbal and written explanations of the nature of the research are given to the potential subjects and they are asked to sign a document indicating their agreement to being involved in the research. A researcher could of course 'go through the motions' of following this procedure, but abuse it by providing misleading information about the level of risk – hence the need for clear guidelines and monitoring of these matters.

Such physical or mental risks do not generally arise in leisure and tourism research, but they are only one aspect of being 'informed'. There may be a moral dimension also. For example, some people may object to being involved in research which is being conducted for certain public, political or commercial organisations. So being informed also involves being informed about the purpose of the research and the nature of the sponsor or beneficiary.

In some cases the status of the researcher is ambivalent, for example when students conduct a project on behalf of a client organisation, or when part-time students conduct research for a university assignment using their fellow employees as subjects or conduct research on competitors. It is clearly unethical for students to identify themselves only as students and not to identify to their informants the organisation which will be the beneficiary of the research.

But again there are some grey areas. In some cases the research would be invalidated if subjects knew fully what its purpose was: for example, quasi-experimental research on people's attitudes based on reactions to pictures, or to interviewers of differing race or gender. In some attitudinal research, for example on potentially sensitive topics such as race or sex, it may be thought that responses will be affected if respondents are told too much about the research and therefore placed 'on their guard'. Clearly such deception raises ethical issues and judgements have to be made about whether the value of the research justifies the use of mild deception.

In some cases the provision of detailed information to informants, and obtaining their written consent is neither practicable nor necessary. Thus the typical leisure or tourism survey:

■ is anonymous,
■ involves only a short interview (e.g. 3 or 4 minutes),
■ involves fairly innocuous, non-personal questions,
■ takes place at a facility/site with the agreement of the management or authorities.

In this type of situation most respondents are not interested in detailed explanations of the research. Most people are familiar with surveys and their main concern is that the interview should not take up too much of their time! Potential respondents can become impatient with attempts to provide detailed explanations of the research and would prefer to 'get on with it'. Often questions about the purpose of the survey, if they arise at all, do so later during the interview process, when the respondent's interest has been stimulated.

A suggested set of guidelines for such surveys is as follows:

1. Interviewers should be identified with a badge including their name and the name of the organisation involved (the host organisation or university).
2. Interviewers should be fully briefed about the project so that they can answer questions if asked.
3. If a respondent-completion questionnaire is used, a brief description of the purpose of the project should be provided on the questionnaire (but not too long so that it takes a long time to read), with phone numbers for those requiring more information.
4. Interviewers approaching potential respondents should introduce themselves and seek cooperation using the following words, or similar: 'We are conducting a survey of users of ——, would you mind answering a few questions?'
5. Telephone numbers of supervisors should be available and can be given to respondents if required.
6. A short printed handout should be available with more information for those respondents who are interested.

General research ethics

The discussion so far has been concerned with the relationship between the researchers and subjects or informants and, to some extent, with client organisations. We should not leave this topic without considering a number of other issues, some of which might be considered 'obvious' to the moral person, but which are nevertheless included for completeness.

■ *Competence*: A researcher should not embark on research involving the use of skills in which they have not been adequately trained; to do so may risk causing harm to subjects, may be an abuse of subjects' goodwill, may risk damaging the reputation of the research organisation, and may involve waste of time and other resources.
■ *Literature review*: Any research should be preceded by a thorough review of the literature to ensure, as far as possible, that the proposed research has not already been done elsewhere.
■ *Plagiarism*: The use of others' data or ideas without due acknowledgement and, where appropriate, permission, is unethical.
■ *Falsification of results*: The falsification of research results or the misleading reporting of results is clearly unethical.

8. Conduct research

Actually conducting the research is what the rest of this book is about. However, it cannot be stressed enough that good research will rarely result if care is not taken over the preparatory processes discussed in this chapter. In a more positive vein, good preparation can ease the rest of the research process considerably. Often inexperienced researchers move too rapidly from stage 1, selecting the topic, to stage 8, conducting the research. This can result in the collection of data which is of doubtful use, and the researcher being presented with a problem of making sense of information which has been laboriously collected, but does not fit into any framework. If the above process is followed then every item of information collected should have a purpose, since it will have been collected to answer specific questions. This does not of course mean that the unexpected will not happen and 'serendipitous' findings may not arise, but at least the core structure of the research should be 'under control'.

It might be thought that inductive research, 'grounded theory' and various forms of qualitative research require less preparation, but in practice this is rarely the case. As will be discussed in Chapter 8, in qualitative research it is certainly true that there is often a more fluid, evolutionary structure to the research design, but a sound preparatory base is still vital.

9. Report findings

The question of writing up research results is not discussed in detail here because the whole of the final chapter of the book is devoted to this topic. Unlike the actual conduct of the research, which inexperienced researchers invariably rush into too quickly, beginning the writing up of results is often delayed too long, so that insufficient time is left to complete it satisfactorily. An outline of the research process, as presented here, can itself be part of the problem, in that it implies that the writing up process comes right at the end. In fact, the writing of a research report can begin almost as soon as the project begins, since all the early stages, such as the review of the literature and the development of the conceptual framework, can be written up as the project progresses.

Research proposals

Introduction

Research proposals of two broad kinds are discussed here. The first is the *self-generated* research proposal of the sort prepared by students seeking approval for research for a project or thesis on a topic of their own choosing or by academics seeking funds for a research project of their own devising. The second is the *responsive* proposal prepared by consultants responding to research briefs prepared by potential clients. Students can also be required to prepare responsive proposals when they conduct projects for real or hypothetical clients. Planners and managers seeking 'in-house' resources to conduct research fall somewhere between the two situations described.

In each case the proposal is a written document, which may or may not be supported by a 'live' presentation, and which must be convincing to the person or persons who will decide whether the research should go ahead. The writers of a research proposal are faced with the difficult task of convincing the decision-makers of: the value of the research; the soundness of the proposed approach; the valuable and original insights which they will bring to the project; and their personal capability to conduct the research. In some cases the decision-making person or persons will be experts in the field, while in other cases they may be non-experts, so care must be taken to ensure that the proposal is understandable to all concerned. Clarity of expression and succinctness are often the key qualities looked for in these situations.

Self-generated research proposals

Academic research proposals, for student theses/projects or for academics seeking funding, not only have to describe what research is to be done and how, but must also provide a rationale for the choice of topic. The topic and its treatment must be seen to be appropriate, in terms of scale and complexity, to the particular level of project involved, be it an undergraduate project, a PhD thesis or a funded project involving a team of researchers over a number of years.

In general the academic research proposal must cover the material dealt with in this chapter. In some cases considerable work will already have been completed before the proposal is submitted. This could apply in the case of a PhD proposal, which might be based on as much as a year of preparatory work, or a proposal from an experienced academic who has been working in a particular field for a number of years. In such cases, the proposal may present considerable completed work on elements 1 to 6 of the research process as discussed above; funding being sought only to actually conduct the fieldwork part of the research and write up the results – elements 7 to 9. In other cases little more than the selection of the topic may have been completed and the proposal outlines a programme to undertake elements 2 to 9. Some proposals contain a preliminary review of the literature with a proposal to undertake more as part of the project. Some proposals are very clear about the conceptual framework to be used, while in other cases only speculative ideas are presented. While bearing in mind, therefore, that there can be substantial differences between proposals of various types, the checklist in Figure 3.20 is offered as a guide to the contents of a proposal.

Figure 3.20
Research
proposal
checklist:
self-generated
research

1. Background and justification for selection of topic (see Element 1 above).
2. (Preliminary) review of the literature (Element 2).
3. Conceptual/theoretical framework/theoretical discussion (Element 3).
4. Statement of research questions or hypotheses (Element 4).
5. Outline of data/information requirements and research strategy (Elements 5 and 6).
6. Details of information collection methods (chapters 4–9):
   ■ structured by the research strategy, but including:
     – outline of any additional literature to be reviewed (chapter 5);
     – summary of any secondary data sources to be used;
     – outline of fieldwork to be conducted – qualitative and/or quantitative, including, as appropriate:
       – sample/subject selection methods (chapter 10);
       – measures to ensure quality;
       – justification of sample sizes.
7. Consideration of ethical implications (Element 7).
8. Details of data analysis methods (chapters 6–9, 11–12).
9. Timetable or work/tasks.
10. Budget – where applicable – costing of each element/stage/task (Section 6d above).
11. Report/thesis chapter outline or indication of number and type of publications.
12. Resources/skills/experience/'track record' (necessary when seeking funds).

Responsive proposals – briefs and tenders

A *brief* is an outline of the research which an organisation wishes to be undertaken. Consultants wishing to be considered to undertake the project must submit a written, costed proposal or 'tender'. Usually briefs are prepared by an organisation with a view to a number of consultants competing to obtain the contract to do the research. In some cases potential consultants are first asked, possibly through an advertisement, to indicate their 'expression of interest' in the project; this will involve a short statement of the consultants' capabilities, their 'track record' of previous consultancies and staff available. In some cases public bodies maintain a register of accredited consultants with particular interests and capabilities, who may be invited to tender for particular projects. In the light of such statements of interest or information in the register, a *short-list* of consultants is sent the full brief and invited to submit a detailed proposal. Successful tenders are not usually selected on the basis of price alone (the budget is in any case often a fixed sum) but on the quality of the submitted proposal and the track record of the consultants.

Briefs vary in the amount of detail they give. Sometimes they are very detailed, leaving little scope for consultants to express any individuality in their proposals. In other cases they are very limited and leave a great deal of scope to consultants to indicate proposed methods and approaches. Client organisations experienced in commissioning research can produce briefs which are clear and 'ready to roll'. In other situations it is necessary to clarify the client's meanings and intentions. For example a client might ask for a study of the 'leisure needs' of a community – in which case it would be necessary to clarify what the client means by 'leisure' – for example whether home-based leisure, holidays, entertainment, restaurants or nightclubs are to be included. If a client asks for the 'effectiveness' of a programme to be assessed it may be necessary to clarify whether a statement of objectives or a list of performance criteria for the programme already exists, or whether that must be developed as part of the research.

Paradoxically, problems can arise when client organisations are over-specific about their requirements. For example an organisation may ask for a 'user survey' or 'visitor survey' to be conducted. It is not easy to decide what should be included in such a survey without information on the management or policy questions which the resultant data are intended to answer. Is the organisation concerned about declining attendances? Is it wanting to change its 'marketing mix'? Is it concerned about the particular mix of clientele being attracted? Is it concerned about future trends in demand? It would be preferable in such a situation for the client to indicate the nature of the management problem and leave the researcher to determine the most suitable research approach to take, which might or might not include a survey.

Sometimes there is a hidden agenda which the researcher would do well to become familiar with before embarking on the research. For example, research can sometimes be used as a means to defuse or delay difficult management decisions in an organisation. An example would be where a leisure or tourism service is suffering declining attendances because of poor maintenance of facilities and poor staff attitudes to customers; this is very clear to anyone who walks in the door, but the management decides to commission a 'market study', in the hope that the answer to their problem can be found 'out there' in the market – when in fact the problem is very much 'in there', and their money might be better spent on improving maintenance and staff training than on research!

A situation where the client's requirements may seem vague is when the research is not related to immediate policy needs but to possible future needs or simply to satisfy curiosity. For example, a manager of a leisure or tourism facility might commission a visitor survey (perhaps because there is spare money in the current year's budget) without having any specific policy or management problems in mind. In that case the research will need to specify hypothetical or potential policy or management issues and match the data specifications to them.

What should a proposal contain? The first and golden principle is that it should *address the brief*. It is likely that the brief will have been discussed at great length in the commissioning organisation; every aspect of the brief is likely to be of importance to some individual or section in the organisation, so *all* aspects of the brief should be considered in the proposal. So, for example, if the brief lists, say, four objectives, it would be advisable for the proposal to indicate very clearly how each of the four objectives will be met. A proposal must therefore indicate:

■ what is to be done?
■ how is it to be done?
■ when will it be done?
■ what will it cost?
■ who will do it?

A typical responsive proposal might include elements as shown in Figure 3.21.

Figure 3.21
Research
proposal
checklist –
responsive
research

1. Brief summary of key aspects of the proposal, including any unique approach and particular skills/experience of the consultants.
2. Re-statement of the key aspects of the brief and interpretation/definition of key concepts.
3. Conceptual framework/theoretical discussion (Element 3).
5. Research strategy – methods/tasks (Element 6).
6. Details of information collection methods (chapters 4–9):
   - structured by the research strategy, but including:
     - outline of any additional literature to be reviewed (chapter 5);
     - summary of any secondary data sources to be used;
     - outline of fieldwork to be conducted – qualitative and/or quantitative, including, as appropriate;
     - sample/subject selection methods (chapter 10);
       - measures to ensure quality;
       - justification of sample sizes.
7. Timetable of tasks, including interim reporting/meetings with clients/draft and final report submission (Section 6e above).
8. Budget: costing of each element/stage/task (Section 6d above).
9. Chapter outline of report and, if appropriate, details of other proposed reporting formats – e.g. interim reports, working papers, articles.
10. Resources available, staff, track record.

Case studies of research project planning

Because of the importance of the planning process in the conduct of research three case studies are included in the chapter to illustrate the process.

Case study 3.1 is concerned with a specific problem identified in a management situation: the declining level of visits at a facility – in this case a museum.

Case study 3.2 arises from an academic interest: the neglect of the idea of 'the holiday' in leisure and tourism research.

Case study 3.3 also arises from a management situation – evaluation of a local authority's recreation services.

Summary

This chapter covers the process of planning a research project and preparing a research proposal. It is structured around nine 'elements': 1. selecting the topic; 2. reviewing the literature; 3. devising a conceptual framework; 4. deciding the research questions; 5. listing information needs; 6. deciding a research strategy; 7. obtaining ethics clearance; 8. conducting the research; and 9. reporting the findings. The term 'elements' is used rather than 'stages' or 'steps', since the eight elements do not always appears in the precise order indicated. In particular, the first elements listed take place in a variety of orders, often in an iterative process. The overview of the research process is followed by a discussion of research proposals – self-generated proposals, where the researcher initiates the research, and responsive proposals, which respond to a research brief from a commissioning organisation.

Test questions

1. In this chapter, it is suggested that a research topic might arise from five different sources – what are the five sources?

2. What is a concept?

3. What is meant by 'operationalisation' of a concept?

4. What is a conceptual framework?

5. What is the difference between a research question and a hypothesis?

6. What are the differences between a self-generated research proposal and a responsive research proposal and what implications do they have for the content of the two types of proposal?

Exercises

1. Select three articles from an issue of a leisure or tourism journal and identify the basis of their choice of research topic.

2. Select any article from a copy of a leisure or tourism journal and: a. identify the key concepts used in the article; and b. draw a simple concept map to show how the concepts are related.

3. Draw a concept map for a possible research project on either: a. the effects of American culture on British leisure; or b. the effects of the ageing of the population on trends in tourism in Western countries.

4. Write a case study, similar in structure and length to Case studies 3.1 or 3.2, on a topic of your own choice.

Further reading

The best reading material for this chapter would be examples of successful research grant applications and proposals written in response to tenders. Completed research reports, whether academic or non-academic, vary in the amount of detail they provide about the development of the process.

Approaches to tourism research: Pizam (1994) and Ryan (1995).
Concepts in tourism: Chadwick (1994).
Selection of a research topic: Howard and Sharp (1983: ch. 2).
Stages in the research process: Most general and specific research methods texts deal with the stages in the research process, for example, Kidder (1981); Burgess (1982); Williamson, *et al.* (1982); Kelsey and Gray (1986a); Kraus and Allen (1987) and Hudson (1988).
Conceptual frameworks: Miles and Huberman (1994): 18–22. Examples of conceptual frameworks, in leisure studies, see Veal (1995); Brandenburg *et al.* (1982); Marans and Mohai (1991) and, in tourism, see Echtner and Ritchie (1993); Witt and Wright (1992).
Concept maps: Buzan (1995); Howell and Badmin (1996: 243–50).
Research ethics: Bulmer (1982); Kimmel (1988); Sieber (1992) and Punch (1994).

Case study 3.1   Facility Use

This case study outlines the sequence of six elements in the research process which leads up to the preparation of a responsive research proposal. The outline is presented in a summary form to illustrate the process.

1. Select Topic[1]

The topic has been presented by the management of a museum. While attendances from tourists have been rising, attendances by members of the local community have been declining over a number of years and the management would like to know why.

2. Review literature relevant to museum visitation[2]

The literature to be reviewed covers museums and leisure/tourism facility management generally. There is an extensive research literature on museum visitors and part of the proposed research will therefore involve a detailed examination of this literature. At this planning stage three sources have been drawn on to provide a starting point for the study. The first two suggest that the decline could be related to trends in the general community, while the third suggests that the problem may lie with the management of the museum itself.

■ Bennett and Frow (1991) show that gallery and museum users are overwhelmingly drawn from the more highly educated, higher-income social groups, suggesting that attendance and non-attendance at such facilities may be something to do with changing class/education/income trends in the community.

■ Rojek (2000: 22–4),[3] suggests that the phenomenon of 'fast leisure' might be a characteristic of the postmodern age – the equivalent of 'fast food'. This idea reflects the on-going debate in the literature concerning the idea of 'time squeeze' (Bittman 1998). Arguably the idea of visiting a museum is not consistent with the 'fast leisure' idea, so the decline in museum visiting could be due to this broad socio-cultural trend.

---

[1] This type of topic could also apply to other sorts of leisure facility or a tourist destination.

[2] This is a very short literature review for illustrative purposes. A more extensive review would be expected in an academic study. A brief review such as this might well be presented in a consultancy report, but would generally have been based on a much more extensive investigation of relevant literature. It is quite instrumental in nature (see chapter 5 for discussion of 'instrumental'). It would have been helpful to have found a study on 'declining attendances at museums and their cure', but this was not the case. The review is presented here as a *fait accompli*, but will have involved considerable searching/reading/assessing before coming up with the selected items.

[3] Note that page numbers are given for the Rojek reference because 'fast leisure' is just one of many topics discussed in one part of a wide-ranging book.

■ The problem may lie with the management of the museum. The literature on customer service and service quality[4] may therefore offer ideas on how to research the problem of declining attendances. The SERVQUAL model has been applied in leisure and tourism contexts (Howat *et al.*, 1996; Langer, 1997; Williams, 1998; Veal, 2002: 219–20) and relates customers' *expectations* concerning aspects of their experience with the *actual experience*.

3. Conceptual framework/theoretical discussion: models of museum visitation[5]

All three of the perspectives presented in the literature review will be explored in this study. Since this is a study with limited resources and scope, and the museum is a small one, the issues of general social change identified by Bennett and Frow (1991) and Rojek (2000) will be explored in the context of the local community which the museum serves, that is the population living within its *catchment area*.[6] The three literature resources examined above can be said to reflect different 'models' of museum visiting/demand. In practice, however, they appear to complement one another, as the following discussion suggests.

Model 1 Social class etc. and demand
The socio-economic characteristics of the local population may have changed over recent years, resulting in a decline in numbers in the groups from which museum visitors are traditionally drawn. This suggests a simple model in which the changing level of *visitor demand* is determined by the changing size of *target demographic demand segments* between the current time-period and some earlier time, as shown in Figure 3.22.

Model 2 'Fast leisure'
Whether or not there have been changes in the size of the target demographic segments, as Model 1 posits, Rojek's 'fast leisure' phenomenon could also be at work. This is difficult to research empirically in a local community because, while it might be possible to measure the current 'pace' of leisure, such information would not be available, say, five or ten years ago. However, if people *feel* that they are rushed, perhaps because of longer paid working hours and more demanding domestic commitments, they may be able to articulate this change in a survey response. There are, for example, data available at national level on people's perceptions of whether

---

[4] See the discussion of 'what discipline?' in chapter 3, and the need to look beyond the specific topic for useful ideas.
[5] Either or both of these headings could be used, or perhaps, something like 'Analysis of the problem' or 'Modelling visitor demand'. . .
[6] Note that all the *concepts* mentioned in the discussion appear in the diagram/concept map.

Figure 3.22
Museum study:
Model 1 – social
class etc. and
changing visitor
demand

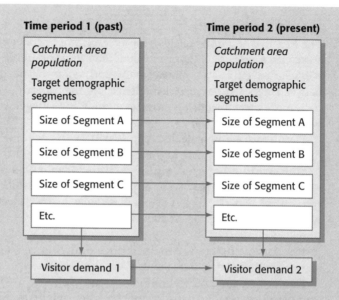

Figure 3.23
Museum study:
Models 1+2 –
social class,
'perceived time
squeeze' and
changing visitor
demand

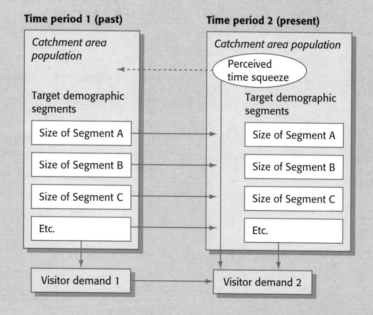

they feel 'pressed for time' (ABS, 1998: 12; Zuzanek and Mannell, 1998). Model 1 as presented in Figure 3.23 reflects an 'objective' measure of change, but it could be modified to include a 'subjective' dimension, which might be called *perceived time squeeze*, as shown in Figure 3.23.

Model 3 Service quality

The SERVQUAL model relates visitors' *expectations* concerning aspects of a visit to the *actual experience*. It involves initial identification of *key service dimensions* which are seen as critical to management and visitors. The pattern of discrepancies between expectations and experience on the various service dimensions – the pattern of *disconfirmation* – provides a guide to management on where action may be necessary.

Because we are here dealing with a pattern of declining visitation, current users may not be the best guide to the quality of experience at the museum: they may be first-time visitors or regular visitors who are tolerant of poor quality aspects of their visit. *Lapsed* visitors may be of more interest. It is possible to conceive of information on the expectations vs actual experience being collected from lapsed users as well as current users. These SERVQUAL ideas have been added to Figure 3.23 to provide Figure 3.24.

It is possible that one, two or all three of the above models might contribute to an explanation of declining demand at the museum.

Figure 3.25 presents definitions of the concepts involved in the conceptual framework and indications as to how they might be operationalised S that is delimited in a way that they can be measured or assessed in an operational research project.

Figure 3.24
Museum study:
Models 1+2+3
– social class,
'perceived time
squeeze' and
service quality
elements and
changing visitor
demand

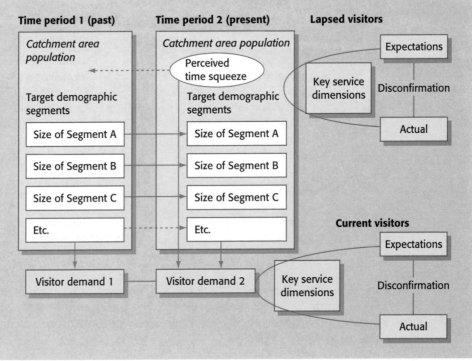

Concept*	Definition	Operationalisation**	RQ No.
Catchment area	Geographical area from which most visitors are drawn	Area where **70 per cent of visitors live**	a
Target demographic segments (TDS)	Demographic/socio-economic groups living in the catchment area and most likely to visit museums	– Segment A: **Managerial/ professional group** – Segment B: **35–44 age-group** – *etc.* (e.g., as indicated by ABS report 4114.0)	b, c
Visitor demand	Current number of visits to the museum	Number of **visits in a calendar year** (see Fig. 9.15 for alternative measures of leisure)	c
Perceived time squeeze	Individual's subjective feeling of being pressed for time	ABS method: Individual response to question as to whether person **feels 'pressed for time'** – Always/often, Sometimes, Rarely/never (e.g., as in ABS report 4153.0)	d, e
Key service dimensions (KSD)	Those aspects of a service or visit considered important by visitors and/or management	List of key service dimensions **determined by focus groups** with visitors and management	f
Lapsed visitors	Persons who have visited the museum but no longer do so	Lapsed visitors = persons who last visited the museum **more than 12 months ago**, but live within the catchment area	h
Visitor expectations re KSD	The level of service/quality of experience visitors expect to find in regard to KSD	Response, using **Likert-scales**, in regard to statements on the importance/expectations of each KSD	g, h
Visitor actual experience	Level of satisfaction with the KSD	Response, using **Likert-scales**, in regard to satisfaction with each KSD	g, h
Disconfirmation	Discrepancy between expectations and actual experience re KSD	Difference between **expectation and satisfaction scores** for each KSD	g, h

* See Fig. 3.24. ** Items in bold are key operationalisation decisions.
ABS = Australian Bureau of Statistics (www.abs.gov.au)

Figure 3.25 Museum project: list of concepts, definitions and operationalisation

4. Decide research questions[7]

Primary question[8]

Why are attendances at the museum falling?

---

[7] This section distils the theoretical discussion into a series of questions around which the research can be focussed.

[8] The questions track the discussion of the conceptual framework and concept maps.

Subsidiary questions

General

a. What is the catchment area of the museum, from which most visitors are drawn?

Model 1 social class etc. and demand

b. What are the target demographic segments (TDS) which are attracted to museums/ this museum?

c. What was the relationship between visitor demand and population in the TDSs living in the catchment area, between time period 1 and time period 2?

Model 2 'fast leisure'

d. Are people in the TDSs living in the catchment area feeling 'time squeezed'?

e. If the answer to (d) is 'yes,' is this likely to be affecting museum visiting?

Model 3 service quality

f. What are the 'key service dimensions' (KSD) for the museum?

g. What are *current* visitors' expectations, actual experience and disconfirmation with regard to the KSDs?

h. What are *lapsed* visitors' expectations, actual experience and disconfirmation with regard to the KSDs?

5. List information needs: what do we need to know?

Information needed to answer each of the subsidiary questions is listed in Figure 3.26 together with possible sources for the information.

6. Decide research strategy: studying the museum market

From the above process a number of elements of a possible research strategy emerge, as indicated below. The feasibility of such a strategy will need to be evaluated in relation to available time and resources. The strategy assumes that the museum does not have data available from an existing recent visitor survey.[9]

1. *Focus groups* of managers and users to establish KSDs.

2. A *survey of current visitors* to:
   ■ establish catchment area of the museum;
   ■ for Model 3: collect SERVQUAL data.

---

[9] Typically, the reason for choice of these particular methods might need to be given, although in most cases the data collection method flows readily from the discussion of information requirements. In some cases there are alternatives – e.g. household survey or postal or quota survey?

	Item	Information required	Likely sources
a.	Catchment area	Data on where visitors to the museum travel from 70 per cent cut-off	User survey (new survey or museum's past survey if available)
b.	Target demographic segments (TDS)	Data on demographic/socio-economic groups with high museum visit rates – for this museum (if available) or museums in general	ABS report No. 4114.0 or museum's past survey if available
c.	Change in period 1–2 in: – TDS population numbers in catchment area – visitor demand at museum	For period 1 and period 2: – catchment area TDS numbers – annual visitor numbers in periods 1 and 2 – population census – museum's own data	
d.	Catchment area TDS and time squeeze	Information on subjective feelings of catchment area TDS members	Survey of catchment area TDS
e.	Effects of time squeeze on museum-visiting	Information on museum visiting patterns of catchment area TDS members	Survey of catchment area TDS
f.	List of key service dimensions (KSD)	Information on customers' and managers' views on important aspects of a museum visit	Focus groups of customers and managers
g.	Current visitors' evaluation of expectations and actual experience re KSDs	Current visitors' scores on KSD expectation and actual experience scales	User survey
h.	Lapsed visitors' evaluation of expectations and actual experience re KSDs	Lapsed visitors' scores on KSD expectation and actual experience scales	Catchment area social survey

Figure 3.26 Museum project: information needs and likely sources

3. Confirm Target Demographic Groups from *secondary data* and/or *visitor survey*.

4. For Model 1: conduct *secondary data analysis*, using *population census data* for the catchment area for the last two censuses, particularly in relation to TDSs, and museum's own *attendance data* for the last 4–5 years.

5. Conduct *household survey* within catchment area:
   ■ for Model 2: to establish extent of time squeeze of museum visitors/non-visitors;
   ■ for Model 3: collect SERVQUAL data from lapsed users.

Case study 3.2   The holiday as leisure

1/2. Select topic and review the literature

The topic is: the role of the holiday in the leisure repertoire of the individual, and arises from an examination of the literature on the sociology of both leisure and tourism.

The sociology of leisure literature is represented in this review by the work of a number of authors, including Parker (1976), Roberts (1978), Rapoport and Rapoport (1975), Clarke and Critcher (1985), Rojek (1995) and Driver *et al.* (1991). In general, an examination of these works reveals that the sociology of leisure has been largely focused on the leisure needs/demands of individuals living in particular communities or social groups. Thus, for example, well-known writers have analysed the needs of individuals in their work, family and educational setting (Parker, 1976: 65–102), their life-cycle situation (Rapoport and Rapoport, 1975) and in relation to their personal satisfactions (Kelly and Godbey, 1992: 195–326). A broader type of leisure sociology seeks to situate leisure in the social, economic and cultural fabric of the nation state (Roberts, 1978: 41–92; Clarke and Critcher, 1985; Rojek, 1995). Research on the benefits of leisure to the individual (Driver *et al.*, 1991) is concerned particularly with the question of equity: who has access to leisure time and resources and who does not? Which socio-economic groups participate and which do not? While leisure includes holiday-taking, the sociology of leisure literature rarely refers to holiday-taking explicitly – it might be said, therefore, that the sociology of leisure is concerned with leisure in the local community: what might be referred to as *local leisure*.

The approach in the sociology of tourism, represented here by Cohen (1972), MacCannell (1976), Urry (1990) and Krippendorf (1987), is very different. Here people are referred to as *tourists* and are seen as *consumers*, comparatively disembodied from their community of origin or other social roles. The focus of most research in the sociology of tourism is on the tourist *destination*, with tourists' geographical origins merely serving to furnish them with certain attributes, such as a certain level of income and a set of 'cultural baggage', and information on these and on demographic characteristics is required only as inputs to effective marketing. The 'five star' tourist is the main focus of attention – those who are unable to go on holiday, or can only afford to take their holidays locally, are rarely the focus of interest. For example, Cohen's (1972) seminal paper on the sociology of tourism classifies tourists as types of consumer; MacCannell (1976) is concerned with how tourists interpret tourist sites; and Urry (1990) focuses largely on the cultural impact of tourists and the tourism industry on host communities. The exception is Krippendorf (1987) who sets tourism in the context of leisure and everyday life. However, Krippendorf's empirical sources are limited and, being a Swiss author, much of the research evidence on which he draws is in German and is therefore somewhat inaccessible to an English-speaking audience. Of those who do *not* go on holiday, Krippendorf considers only the privileged, who do not need to go on holiday because of their non-stressful lifestyles (1987, p. 16). He therefore ignores those who are unable to go on holiday because of financial or other constraints. With the exception of this partial treatment, therefore, it appears that the tourism literature has been unconcerned with the question of equity. It has generally ignored those who are prevented from going on holiday as a result of socio-economic circumstances.

A concept which might be used to link the two areas of research is the notion of *quality of life* (Marans and Mohai, 1991). Both local leisure and tourism can be seen as contributing to a person's quality of life – and lack of opportunities for either could be seen as resulting in a poor quality of life. The question therefore arises as to what are the respective contributions of local leisure and holiday-taking to a person's quality of life – and, conversely, what effect does a lack of local leisure and holiday-taking opportunities have on a person's quality of life? This issue *could* be studied at a 'macro' level, exploring the political and economic reasons for its neglect by researchers, government and industry, but, at this stage, it seems appropriate to study the phenomenon at the level of the individual.

3. Establish conceptual framework

It is suggested from the above brief review of the literature that an individual's quality of life is related to social and economic circumstances, such as income, housing and personal relationships, but also to access to local leisure and to holidays. It is posited that high-quality local leisure and holiday experiences can enhance quality of life through contributing to such things as relief of stress, social interaction, exercise, relaxation, enhanced status and education. While it is likely to be difficult to identify the separate effects of social and economic circumstances, local leisure experience and holiday experience on quality of life, this exploratory study will seek to establish whether there is evidence of holiday experience playing a role in this process. The model to be explored is presented in the concept map, Figure 3.27. The list of concepts which will be empirically explored, together with their definitions and indicative operationalisation, are listed in Figure 3.28.

Figure 3.27
Holiday as
leisure:
concept map

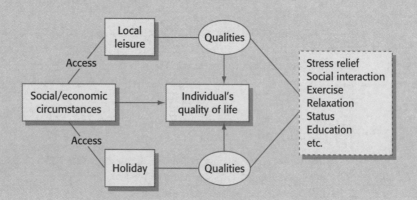

Concept	Definition	Operationalisation
Holiday	Staying overnight away from normal place of residence, for leisure purposes	Period of at least 5 days spent at least 40 km from normal place of residence, for leisure purposes
Local leisure	Leisure activity in normal place of residence	Leisure activity within 40 km of home
Qualities (of leisure/ holidays)	Perceived and actual characteristics of the activity which contribute positively to a person's quality of life	Benefits such as: relaxation, relief of stress, exercise, social bonding, education, 'flow' experiences . . .
Social/ economic circumstance	Social characteristics and circumstances likely to influence/constrain leisure – e.g. age, gender, occupation, family responsibilities	Age; occupation; gender; whether partnered; whether children, if so, what age(s); income; level of education
Quality of life	To be explored in the literature as part of project	To be explored in the literature

Figure 3.28   Holiday as leisure: concepts, definitions and operationalisation

4. Decide research questions

Major question

4.0   What contribution does a holiday make to a person's quality of life, compared with local leisure activity?

Subsidiary questions

4.1   How is 'quality of life' defined and how can it be measured?

4.2   What characteristics/qualities of local leisure contribute to a person's 'quality of life'*?

4.3   What characteristics/qualities of a holiday contribute to a person's 'quality of life'*?

4.4   What effect does lack of a holiday have on a person's 'quality of life'*?

4.5   Can local leisure compensate for lack of a holiday?

4.6   How are items 4.2–4.5 perceived by the individual?

4.7   How do items 4.2–4.6 vary with social/economic situation of the individual? (*As defined in 4.1.)

5. List information needs

5.1   Information on 'quality of life' and its measurement.[†]

5.2   Individual perceptions of value of leisure activities.

5.3   Individual perceptions of quality of life.

5.4 Individual perceptions of value of a holiday.

5.5 Individual perceptions of effects of lack of holiday.

5.6 Characteristics of holiday takers and non-holiday takers – e.g. age, gender, family situation, occupation, education, health, income.

† As a result of information gained under 5.1, it is likely that 'quality of life' can be measured by subjective assessment by the individual and possibly by 'objective' measures, such as health or levels of stress. The proposed project concentrates on subjective assessment only.

6. Decide research strategy

6.1 Review literature on quality of life.

6.2 Conduct in-depth interviews to explore items 5.2–5.5.

6.3 Taking account of the results of 6.2, conduct questionnaire survey in a local community, seeking a 50/50 quota of:
- people who have been on holiday (5 days or more, 40 km+) in the last year;
- people who have not been on holiday (5 days or more, 40 km+) in the last year.

6.4 Undertake questionnaire survey to collect information from the two groups addressing items 5.2–5.6 by asking questions on:
- local leisure activities undertaken;
- perceived characteristics of leisure and their contribution to quality of life;
- perceived characteristics of holiday and its contribution to quality of life;
- perceived consequences for quality of life of not going on holiday;
- social/economic characteristics: age, gender, family situation, occupation, income.

6.5 Compare perceptions of people who have and people who have not been on holiday and groups in varying social/economic situations.

Case Study 3.3   Evaluating public recreation services

1. Select topic

The topic is the evaluation of the performance of a public leisure or recreation service, such as that which might be provided by a local authority.

2. Review literature

Hatry and Dunn (1971) give an example of how concepts can be isolated from a set of objectives for a public recreation service. Their suggested objectives for a public recreation service are:

> Recreation services should provide for all citizens, to the extent practicable, a variety of adequate, year-round leisure opportunities which are accessible, safe, physically attractive, and provide enjoyable experiences. They should, to the maximum extent, contribute to the mental and physical health of the community, to its economic and social well-being and permit outlets that will help decrease incidents of antisocial behaviour such as crime and delinquency.
>
> (Hatry & Dunn, 1971: 13)

Other literature will be examined in the course of the proposed study, but meanwhile, from this statement a number of concepts, which constitute criteria for effectiveness, can be isolated:

a. adequacy
b. enjoyableness
c. accessibility
d. (un)crowdedness
e. variety

f. safety
g. physical attractiveness
h. crime avoidance
i. health
j. economic well-being.

The first criterion, adequacy, suggests the provision of a range of services which, as a result of criteria b–g, lead to outcomes h–j.

3. Devise conceptual framework

The Hatry and Dunn framework suggests that services with a high score on a range of qualities (enjoyable, accessible, uncrowded, varied, safe, physically attractive) will attract high levels of usage (effect 1); this in turn should lead to certain outcomes (effect 2 – low/reduced level of crime; high/enhanced level of health; and a high level of/enhanced economic well-being) which are the ultimate criteria for judging the success of public recreation services. These relationships are illustrated in the concept map, Figure 3.29. A list of concepts and their definitions and operationalisation are presented in Figure 3.30.

Figure 3.29
Recreation
services project:
concept map

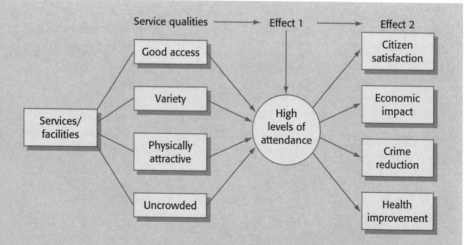

4. Decide research questions

Main question

4.0   To what extent is the authority achieving its goals in recreation provision?

Subsidiary questions

4.1   To what extent is the authority achieving its goals with regard to: (a) adequacy; (b) enjoyableness; (c) accessibility; (d) (un)crowdedness; (e) variety; (f) safety; (g) physical attractiveness; (h) crime avoidance; (i) health; (j) economic well-being?

5. List information requirements

In this case the information requirements are clearly listed in the 'operationalisation' column 3 of Figure 3.30.

6. Decide research strategy

6.1   Gather all available data on attendance levels – relate to census of population to estimate numbers of users and non-users (a).

6.2   Plot all facilities on map and use census data to indicate populations living within y kilometres and x minutes travel (b).

6.3   Undertake study of waiting times/crowding in all facilities (d).

6.4   Gather information on range of programmes/activities offered (e).

6.5   Conduct community/household survey and/or user surveys on citizen satisfaction with services and perceptions of facility attractiveness (a, b).

6.6   Collect data on crime rates (h).

Concept	Definition	Operationalisation
a. Adequacy of service	Services which meet community demand; provision of access to all	Level of attendance; number of participants and non-participants; persons living within x minutes and y kilometres of facilities; crowdedness indices (waiting times, ratios of use to capacity, user perceptions)
b. Enjoyableness	Providing pleasure for users/participants	Level of attendance; number of participants and non-participants; citizen satisfaction
c. Accessibility	Facilities within x minutes and y kilometres travelling for all of the community	Persons living within x minutes and y kilometres of facilities
d. (Un)crowdedness	Facilities not perceived as crowded by users	Crowdedness indices (waiting times, ratios of use to capacity, user perceptions)
e. Variety	Range of different activities on offer	Number of different activities catered for
f. Safety	Accident-free environment	Number of accidents
g. Physical attractiveness	Facilities which appear attractive to users and interested non-users (e.g. neighbours)	Index of facility attractiveness (user and non-user perceptions) – especially re parks and open space
h. Crime avoidance	Services which help reduce crime by providing creative outlets for energies	Reported crime rates in community
i. Health	Facilities/services which promote health (e.g. through exercise)	Illness measures
j. Economic wellbeing	Facilities/services which contribute to jobs, income, etc.	Business income; jobs; property values

Figure 3.30 Recreation services project: concepts, definitions and operationalisation

6.7 Collect data on community health and use of services (possible survey/study on fitness) (i).

6.8 Economic study: collect data on new business investment, job, property values. Possible survey of businesses (j).

On an annual basis, or some other suitable cycle, compare the above with past values and/or set targets.

4 The range of research methods

Introduction – horses for courses

In this chapter the range of alternative research methods and criteria for their use are examined in broad terms, as an introduction to the techniques to be covered in more detail in subsequent chapters. Initially, a range of 'major' methods is considered, including the roles of scholarship and research, together with the idea of 'just thinking', and the use of existing literature, secondary data, observation, qualitative methods and questionnaire-based surveys. The qualitative–quantitative debate is also considered. The middle section of the chapter considers a number of approaches and techniques which are subsidiary to one or more of the major methods, in that they are a variation on or an application of the major method or cut across a number of the major methods. Consideration is given to 'multiple methods', with a discussion of the concept of *triangulation* and of the *case study method*. Finally, the process of choosing a method is examined.

Choosing appropriate research methods or techniques is clearly vital. In this book we espouse the principle that every technique has its place; the important thing is for researchers to be aware of the limitations of any particular method and not to make claims which cannot be justified by the research methods used, by themselves or others. There has been much debate in recent years, especially in the sociological literature, about appropriate methods for leisure and tourism research, particularly concerning the relative merits of qualitative as opposed to quantitative methods (e.g. Kelly, 1980; Rojek, 1989; Henderson, 1990). The commentaries have often been very partisan in tone, as if there were a contest going on between the two approaches and as if there were some sort of conspiracy at work to maintain quantitative methods as the dominant research mode in leisure studies. While this domination may be apparent in leisure studies in the United States, it is less apparent in the literature emanating from other countries (Veal, 1994). In tourism research quantitative and qualitative research approaches seem to co-exist without the apparent rivalry seen in leisure studies.

There is a tendency, in the literature, for commentators to defend the methods in which they themselves are skilled. It is rare to find a researcher who is experienced in the full range of techniques as, for example, discussed in this book. It is hoped that the new generation of researchers in leisure and tourism will be competent in a wide range of skills and will therefore adopt a balanced and non-partisan approach to their use. As Henderson (1990: 179) points out in discussing qualitative versus quantitative methods: 'Ideally, a researcher who understands the array of methods available through both quantitative and qualitative approaches will be able to address the ways to best study the issues related to leisure.'

It is possible for research to be conducted entirely quantitatively, entirely qualitatively, or using a mixture of both approaches (Kamphorst *et al.*, 1984; Bryman and Bell, 2003: 479–94). It is quite common for large-scale quantitative research to be planned on the basis of prior, exploratory, qualitative studies, as Peterson (1994) discusses in relation to tourism research.

In this book a *horses for courses* approach is adopted; techniques are not intrinsically *good* or *bad*, but are considered to be *appropriate* or *inappropriate* for the task in hand. Further, it is maintained that it is not a question of good or bad techniques which should be considered, but good or bad *use* of techniques.

The range of major research methods

The range of major methods to be examined is listed in Figure 4.1. These are discussed below and a number of additional subsidiary or cross-cutting techniques are discussed later in the chapter.

Scholarship

Although the dividing line between *scholarship* and *research* can be difficult to draw, it is useful to consider the differences between the two. Scholarship involves being well informed about a subject and also thinking critically and creatively about a subject and the accumulated knowledge on it. Scholarship therefore involves *knowing the literature*, but also being able to synthesise it, analyse it and critically appraise it. Scholarship is traditionally practised in the role of teacher, but when the results of scholarship are published they effectively become a contribution to research.

Research involves the generation of new knowledge. Traditionally this has been thought of as involving the gathering and presentation of new data – empirical research – but clearly this is not a necessary condition for something to be considered 'research'. New insights, critical or innovative ways of looking at old issues, or the identification of new issues or questions – the fruits of scholarship – are also contributions to knowledge. Indeed, the development of a new framework or *paradigm* for

Figure 4.1
The range of
major research
methods

- Scholarship
- 'Just thinking'
- Existing sources – using the literature
- Existing sources – secondary data
- Observation
- Qualitative methods
- Questionnaire-based surveys

looking at a field can be far more significant than a minor piece of empirical work using an outmoded paradigm.

Recognising therefore that research does not have to be empirical, the first method discussed below is *just thinking*.

Just thinking

There is no substitute for thinking! Creative, informed thinking about a topic can be the only process involved in the development and presentation of a piece of research, although it will usually also involve consideration of the literature, as discussed below.

But even when data collection is involved, the difference between an *acceptable* piece of research and an *exceptional* or *significant* piece of research is usually the quality of the creative thought that has gone into it. The researcher needs to be creative in identifying and posing the initial questions or issues for investigation, creative in conceptualising the research and developing a research strategy, creative in analysing data and creative in interpreting and presenting findings. Texts on research methods, such as this, can provide a guide to mechanical processes, but creative thought must come from within the individual researcher – in the same way that the basics of drawing can be taught but *art* comes from within the individual artist.

Existing sources – using the literature

There is virtually no research that can be done which would not benefit from some reference to the existing literature and for most research such reference is essential. It is possible for a research project to consist only of a review of the literature: in comparatively new areas of study, such as leisure and tourism, especially when they are multidisciplinary as leisure and tourism are, there is a great need for the consolidation of existing knowledge which can come from good literature reviews.

The review of the literature often plays a key role in the formulation of research projects; it indicates the state of knowledge on a topic and is a source of, or stimulant for, ideas, both substantive and methodological.

A review of the literature can be important even when it uncovers no literature on the topic of interest. To establish that *no* research has been conducted on a particular topic, especially when the topic is considered to be of some importance to the field, can be a research finding of some significance in its own right. The literature review process is discussed in detail in Chapter 5.

Existing sources – secondary data

Clearly, if information is already available which will answer the research questions posed, then it would be wasteful of resources to collect new information for the purpose. As discussed in Chapter 6, large quantities of information are collected and stored by government and other organisations as routine functions of management, including sales figures and visitor numbers, income and expenditure, staffing, accident reports, crime reports and health data. Such data are referred to as *secondary* data, because their primary use is administrative and research is only a secondary use. Even when such data are not ideal for the research at hand, they can often provide answers to some questions more quickly and at less cost than new data.

Secondary data need not be quantitative. Historians for example, use diaries, official documents or newspaper reports as sources – such sources may be seen as secondary, since they were not initially produced for research purposes, but for historians themselves some of them are seen as primary sources. In policy research such documents as the annual reports or minutes of meetings of organisations might be utilised.

In some cases data have been collected for research as opposed to administrative purposes but may not have been fully analysed, or they may have been analysed only in one particular way for a particular purpose, or even not analysed at all. Secondary analysis of research data is a potentially fruitful, but widely neglected, activity.

Observation

The technique of observation is discussed in Chapter 7. Observation has the advantage of being unobtrusive – indeed, the techniques involved are sometimes referred to as *unobtrusive* techniques (Kellehear, 1993). Unobtrusive techniques involve gathering information about people's behaviour without their knowledge. While in some instances this may raise ethical questions (see Chapter 3), it clearly has advantages over techniques where the subjects are aware of the researcher's presence and may therefore modify their behaviour, or where reliance must be placed on subjects' own recall and description of their behaviour, which can be inaccurate or distorted.

Observation may be the only possible technique to use in certain situations, for example, when researching illicit activity, which people may be reluctant to talk about, or when researching the behaviour of young children (for example their play patterns) who may be too young to interview.

Observation is capable of presenting a perspective on a situation which is not apparent to the individuals involved. For example, the users of a crowded part of a recreation or tourist area may not be aware of the uncrowded areas available to them – the pattern of use of the site can only be assessed by observation. Observation is therefore an appropriate technique to use when knowledge of the presence of the researcher is likely to lead to unacceptable modification of subjects' behaviour, and when mass patterns of behaviour not apparent to individual subjects are of interest.

Qualitative methods

The nature of qualitative methods

Qualitative techniques stand in contrast to *quantitative* techniques. The main difference between the two groups of techniques is that quantitative techniques involve numbers – quantities – whereas qualitative techniques do not. In the case of qualitative techniques the information collected does not generally lend itself to statistical analysis and conclusions are not based on such analysis. By contrast, with quantitative techniques, the data collected are susceptible to statistical analysis and the conclusions are based on such analysis.

In consequence there is a tendency for qualitative techniques to involve the gathering of large amounts of relatively detailed information about relatively few cases (people, organisations, facilities, programmes, locations) and for quantitative techniques to involve the gathering of relatively small amounts of data on relatively large numbers of cases. It should be emphasised, however, that this is just a *tendency*. It is possible, for example, for a quantitative research project to involve the collection of, say, 500 items of data on only 20 people and for a qualitative research project to involve the collection of relatively little information on, say, 200 people. The difference lies in the nature of information collected and the way it is analysed.

Situations for the use of qualitative methods

In what situations are qualitative techniques used? They tend to be used:

- when the focus of the research is on meanings and attitudes (although these can also be studied quantitatively);
- when exploratory theory building rather than theory testing work is called for;
- when the researcher accepts that the concepts, terms and issues must be defined by the subjects and not by the researcher in advance;
- when interaction between members of a group is of interest.

Qualitative techniques are not appropriate when the aim of the research is to make general statements about large populations, especially if such statements involve quantification.

Types of qualitative method

- *Informal and in-depth interviews* usually involve relatively small numbers of individuals being interviewed at length, possibly on more than one occasion. Relatively large amounts of information are generally collected from relatively small numbers of people. This is in contrast to questionnaire-based surveys which usually involve gathering relatively small amounts of structured information from relatively large numbers of people.

- *Group interviews or focus groups* apply the informal/in-depth interview approach to groups of people rather than separate individuals.

- *Participant observation* involves the researcher becoming a participant in the phenomenon being studied.

- *Analysis of texts* are the main focus of research in some fields of inquiry – for example research on politicians' speeches or on media coverage of an event. The analysis and interpretation of the content of published or unpublished texts is referred to as *content analysis* or *hermeneutics*. The technique has not traditionally been widely used in leisure and tourism studies, but with the developing linkages with cultural studies, and the widening of the scope of *text* to include a wide variety of *cultural products*, such as film and television, advertising and postcards, the technique is attracting increasing attention. Approaches to the analysis of texts may be qualitative or quantitative, but for convenience are discussed along with qualitative methods in Chapter 8.

Questionnaire-based surveys

The nature of questionnaire-based surveys

Questionnaire-based surveys come in a variety of forms and these are discussed in detail in Chapter 9. The term questionnaire-*based* survey is used because such surveys can take two formats: a face-to-face or telephone *interview format*, where the interviewer reads out the questions from the questionnaire and records the answers, and the *respondent-completion format*, where the respondent reads the questions and writes answers on the questionnaire or on-screen, and no interviewer is involved.

Questionnaire-based surveys are probably the most commonly used technique in leisure and tourism research. This is partly because the basic mechanics are relatively easily understood and mastered, but also because so much leisure and tourism research calls for the sorts of general, quantified statement referred to above. Thus for example, governments want to know how many people engage in sport; managers want to know how many people are dissatisfied with a service and marketers want to know how many people are in a particular market segment. All these examples come from practical policy/management situations, which emphasises that most of the resources for survey research come from the public or private sector of the leisure/tourism industries. Academic papers are very often a secondary spin-off from research which has been sponsored for such specific, practical purposes.

Unlike qualitative techniques, where the researcher can begin data collection in a tentative way, can return to the subjects for additional information and can gradually build the data and concepts and explanation, questionnaire-based surveys require researchers to be very specific about their data requirements from the beginning, since they must be committed irrevocably to a questionnaire.

A further key feature of questionnaire-based surveys is that they depend on respondents' own accounts of their behaviour, attitudes or intentions. In some situations – for example in the study of 'deviant' behaviour or in the study of activities which are socially approved (e.g. playing sport) or disapproved of (e.g. smoking or drinking) – this can raise some questions about the validity of the technique, since accuracy and honesty of responses may be called into question.

Questionnaire-based surveys are used when quantified information is required concerning a specific population and when individuals' own accounts of their behaviour and/or attitudes is acceptable as a source of information.

Types of questionnaire survey

Questionnaire surveys in the leisure and tourism field can be divided into six types:

■ Household survey   people are selected on the basis of where they live and are interviewed in their home – sometimes referred to as 'community survey' or 'social survey'.

- Street survey   people are selected by stopping them in street, in shopping malls, etc. – sometimes referred to as 'quota' survey.

- Telephone survey   interviews are conducted by telephone.

- Mail survey   questionnaires are sent and returned by mail – sometimes 'postal survey'.

- Site or user survey users of a leisure or tourism facility or site are surveyed on-site – sometimes referred to as 'visitor survey' and sometimes as 'intercept survey'.

- Captive group survey members of groups such as classes of school children, members of a club or employees of an organisation are surveyed.

Questionnaire-based surveys are considered in more detail in Chapters 9 and 10.

Subsidiary and cross-cutting techniques

The somewhat inelegant term 'subsidiary and cross-cutting' is used to describe a number of techniques which are subsidiary to one or more of the major methods discussed above, in that they are a variation on or an application of the major method (e.g. Delphi technique, which uses questionnaires) or cut across a number of major methods (e.g. action research, which can use any or all of the major methods). The techniques discussed here are listed in Figure 4.2 and discussed in turn below, and an indication is given of how they relate to the pattern of the book.

Coupon surveys/conversion studies

In marketing research use can be made of information from the responses of the public to advertising coupons – that is where the public is invited in an advertisement to write

Figure 4.2
Subsidiary and cross-cutting techniques

- Coupon surveys/conversion studies
- En route/intercept surveys
- Time–budget surveys
- Experience sampling method
- Panel studies
- Longitudinal studies
- Media-sponsored surveys
- Action research
- Historical research
- Textual analysis
- Delphi technique
- Projective techniques
- The use of scales
- Meta-analysis

or telephone for information on a product. The data can be used to indicate the level of interest in the product on offer (compared with other products or with the same product in previous periods) and also to indicate the geographical spread of the interested public. The question then arises as to the extent to which people who respond to such advertising actually become customers. Thus conversion studies are designed to examine the extent to which enquirers *convert* to become customers (Woodside and Ronkanen, 1994).

En route/intercept surveys

In tourism research surveys of tourists while travelling are sometimes referred to as *en route* surveys (Hurst, 1994). Such surveys may be conducted in aeroplanes, at airports or while travelling by car (when travellers are waved into lay-bys for survey purposes with the assistance of police). In this book this type of survey, which invariably involves a questionnaire, is considered to be a special case of site or user surveys, as discussed in Chapter 9. Since respondents are 'intercepted' at or near a destination, site or attraction the term *intercept survey* is sometimes used, and if all approaches to the destination, site or attraction are covered, the term *cordon* survey may be used.

Time-budget surveys

There is a long tradition in leisure studies of investigating people's allocation of time between such categories as paid work, domestic work, sleep and leisure (Szalai, 1972; Pentland *et al.* 1999). The approach is not used in tourism research because it involves respondents keeping a diary of a day's activities; holiday-makers are, by definition, not at home to undertake such an exercise. The method could of course be adapted to study holiday-makers' activities at their destinations, but no known example of such a study exists. Time-budget – or time-use – research is basically a special case of the household survey and some reference is made to it in that context in Chapter 9.

Experience sampling method (ESM)

The experience sampling method, or ESM, is a development of the time-budget survey/diary method which has been pioneered by Mihaly Csikszentmihalyi (Csikszentmihalyi and Larson, 1987). For the period of the study – typically a few days – study participants wear watches which are programmed to 'beep' at a set number of times each day, typically six or eight. When the watch beeps, or as soon as practically possible thereafter, the study participant completes a short questionnaire in a booklet carried with the participant at all times. Information on activities being undertaken, where and who with, and attitudes and feelings can be recorded in the questionnaire. In a recent variation on the method, the watch and questionnaire are replaced by a mobile telephone text message and text responses to questions sent automatically under the control of suitable software. The method has the advantage of recording activities and feelings accurately in 'real time', rather than relying on recall. While the amount of information which can be gathered in any one episode is limited, the cumulative amount of information gathered, together with any information included in a preliminary conventional questionnaire, can be substantial. The details of the method are not pursued further in this book, but references to examples of its use are provided in the further reading section.

Panel studies

Market research companies often maintain *panels* of individuals for some of their surveys. Panels are made up of a representative cross-section of the public who agree to be on call for a series of surveys over a period of time. Often some financial reward is paid to panel members, but this cost is off-set by the savings in not having to continually select and contact new samples of respondents. While managing such panels presents particular problems, the range of survey methods which can be used with panels – by telephone, by mail or by face-to-face interview – is the same as for normal one-off samples (LaPage, 1994). Panel studies can therefore be seen as a particular form of household questionnaire survey.

Longitudinal studies

Longitudinal studies involve surveying the same sample of individuals periodically over a number of years (Young *et al.* 1991). Such studies are of course expensive because of the need to keep track of the sample members over the years, and the need to have a large enough sample at the beginning to allow for the inevitable attrition to the sample over time. They are, however, ideal for studying social change and the combined effects of social change and ageing. While longitudinal studies are a recognised technique in the social sciences, and leisure and tourism activity may feature in some studies, there are no known examples specifically focussed on leisure or tourism.

Media-sponsored surveys

Newspapers, magazines and radio and television stations often run opinion poll-type surveys among their readers, listeners and viewers. At the local level the public's views on an issue may be canvassed by the inclusion of some sort of form in a newspaper, which readers may fill in and return, and radio and television stations often run 'phone in' polls on topical issues. The results of these exercises have entertainment value, but should not generally be taken seriously. This is mainly because there is no way of knowing whether either the original population (the readers/listeners/viewers who happen to read, hear or view the item) or the sample of respondents are representative of the population as a whole. In most cases they are decidedly unrepresentative, in that the audiences and readership of particular media outlets tend to have particular socio-economic characteristics and only those with pronounced views, one way or the other, are likely to become involved in the process.

Action research

The common image of research is as a detached, 'clinical' process reporting objectively on what is discovered. When a researcher is personally committed to the topic under investigation, whether that be self-interest-related, such as the fortunes of a company, or a social cause, like saving the environment, efforts are still generally made to abide by the rules of science, for ethical reasons or because of the general belief that 'good research' is more effective research. Some types of research can, however, be deliberately designed to involve the researcher in the topic and for the research to be overtly part of the process of bringing about change – such research is termed 'action research'. This type of research is less usual in the leisure and tourism context than in some areas of social policy, such as housing or ethnic affairs. There are, however, examples of research in the leisure and tourism areas which are politically committed. For example, in the leisure sector a considerable amount of feminist research can be seen as overtly committed to the feminist cause, while in the tourism sector there has been research which has exposed the exploitative practices of sex tourism (Oppermann, 1998; Ryan and Hall, 2001).

Historical research

History is of course a major discipline with its own approaches to research. Historical research arises in the leisure and tourism research environment in at least two contexts; biographical research, discussed as a qualitative approach in Chapter 8, and in case study research, discussed below. It can also be seen as a form of secondary data analysis, since historians are invariably dependent on documents contemporary to a period, which were compiled for purposes other than historical research. As a discipline, history is part of the humanities, although in the context of leisure and tourism research it clearly extends into the social sciences when history is presented as a partial explanation for contemporary phenomena. Compared with the social science literature, in historical literature there is a tendency for the question of method to be played down or taken for granted. While historical accounts are generally conducted in a scholarly manner, with detailed reference to sources, just how the source material has been used and analysed is not always clear: thus there is rarely a 'methods' section in historically based articles (see, for example, two recent examples in *Leisure Studies*: Philips, 2004; and Snape, 2004). Historical methods are not pursued in this book, but some sources are indicated in the further reading section.

Textual analysis

In some fields of inquiry the focus of research is textual – for example, the content of organisations' annual reports, politicians' speeches or advertising messages. The analysis and interpretation of the content of published or unpublished texts is referred to as *content analysis* (generally when the analysis is quantitative) or *hermeneutics* (generally when the analysis is of a more qualitative nature). The technique has not traditionally been widely used in leisure and tourism studies, but with the development of postmodernism and the widening of the scope of *text* to include a wide variety of cultural products such as company documents, advertising material, websites and letters, the approach is attracting increasing attention. Further reference to this approach is made in Chapter 8.

Delphi technique

The Delphi technique (named after the classical Greek 'Delphic oracle'), is a procedure involving the gathering and analysing of information from a panel of experts on future trends in a particular field of interest. The experts in the field (e.g. leisure or tourism) complete a questionnaire indicating their views on the likelihood of certain developments taking place in future; these views are then collated and circulated to panel members for further comment, a process which might be repeated a number of times before the final results are collated. The technique is used in some areas of business and technological forecasting, and has been used to a limited extent in leisure and tourism. In this book the technique is not examined explicitly, but to some extent it involves questionnaire design and analysis, as covered in Chapter 9.

Projective techniques

Projective techniques might be termed 'what if?' techniques, in that they involve subjects responding to hypothetical – projected – situations. For example subjects might be asked to indicate how they might spend a particular sum of money if given a free choice, or how they might spend additional leisure time if it were made available, or they might be invited to respond to photographs of particular locations (Ryan, 1995: 124). While the technique can become elaborate and specialised, in this book it is considered to be an extension of questionnaire-based surveys and possibly of focus-group interviews.

The use of scales

Scales are numerical indexes used to measure constructs or variables which are generally not intrinsically quantitative. Typically subjects are asked to respond to questions using rating scales and the scores are combined to produce a scale or index of the phenomenon of interest. In Chapter 9 the development and use of customised scales in questionnaires is discussed, but it is quite common for researchers to make use of standardised scales which have been developed by others. The advantage of the use of existing scales is that researchers are not continually 'reinventing the wheel' by devising their own measure of a particular phenomenon. Widely used scales have generally been subject to considerable testing to ensure validity – that is that they measure what they are intended to measure. Further, the use of common measures facilitates comparability between studies. The disadvantage is, of course, that any fault in the scale validity may be replicated across many studies and a fixed scale may not fully reflect different socio-economic environments or change over time.

The use of such scales is widespread, particularly in psychology and related disciplines – the best-known being personality indicators, such as the Myers-Briggs scale (see McGuiggan, 2000). Bruner and Hensel (1992) list no less than 588 scales used in marketing research: most are related to generic topics, such as consumer motivation and attitudes, but others are designed for use in specific settings, including leisure and tourism. For example, among the scales listed are:

72.	Cooking enjoyment	262.	Sports enthusiasm
74.	Co-viewing TV (parent/child)	268.	Time management
147.	Involvement (television)	269 & 270.	Time pressure
186.	Pleasure	274.	Venturesomeness
193.	Pricing issues (air travel)	277.	Volunteerism (benefits)
219.	Restriction of TV viewing	278.	Volunteerism (family/job constraints)
226.	Safety (air travel)	279.	Volunteerism (willingness)
227.	Satisfaction (air travel)		
261.	Sports activeness		

Scales have not been widely utilised in the mainstream of leisure and tourism research. However, two examples developed in the United States are: the *Paragraphs About Leisure* (PAL) scale, developed by Howard Tinsley and his associates, and the Recreation Experience Preference (REP) scale developed by Bev Driver and associates (see Driver, Tinsley and Manfredo, 1991). They both seek to relate participation in different leisure activities to a range of psychological benefits to be derived from leisure. Researchers in the area of sport and exercise often make use of scales related to physical and mental health, such as that developed by Ware *et al.* (1994). Despite the considerable amount of psychologically influenced research using scales in such areas as destination choice and tourist satisfaction (see Woodside *et al.*, 2000 and Mazanec *et al.*, 2001), the use of specialised standardised scales has not emerged in tourism research. Examples of the use of scales in leisure and tourism research are listed in the further reading section.

Meta-analysis

One approach to research combines the feature of a literature review and secondary data analysis and involves a quantitative appraisal of the findings of a number of projects on the same topic. The technique, known as *meta-analysis* (Glass *et al.* 1981), is suitable for the sort of research where findings are directly comparable from one study to another – for example, when the key findings are expressed in terms of correlation and regression coefficients between particular variables (see Chapter 13). In a meta-analysis, the reported findings of a large number of individual research projects in the same area provide the basis for further exploration and analysis of the area. Typically, because many studies are involved and must be compared on a common basis, only relatively simple relationships can be examined. Examples of studies using meta-analysis in the leisure and tourism area are given in the further reading section.

Multiple methods

Many research methods involve the use of more than one method or technique. Two multi-method situations are discussed here: first the idea of *triangulation* and second, the *case study method*.

Triangulation

Triangulation gets its name from the land surveying method of fixing the position of an object by measuring it from two different positions, with the object being the third point of the triangle. In research, the triangulation method involves the use of more than one research approach in a single study to gain a broader or more complete understanding of the issues being investigated. The methods used are often complementary in that the weaknesses of one approach are complemented by the strengths of another. Triangulation often utilises both qualitative and quantitative approaches in the same study. Duffy (1987: 131) has identified four different ways that triangulation can be used in research, namely: analysing data in more than one way; using more than one sampling strategy; using different interviewers, observers and analysts in the one study; and using more than one methodology to gather data.

If triangulation methods are to be used in a study the approaches taken will depend on the imagination and the experience of the researcher. However, it is important that the research question is clearly focussed and not confused by the methodology adopted, and that the methods are chosen in accordance with their relevance to the topic. In particular the *rationale* for using triangulation should be outlined, and the possible weaknesses of one method and the ways in which the additional method might overcome such a weakness should be explained. This is clearly relevant to the issue of validity and reliability discussed in later chapters.

Often 'triangulation' is claimed in a study because more than one data source and/or analytical method are used, to address different aspects of the research question, or even different research questions. However, it is when the different data/methods address the *same* question that true triangulation can be said to have occurred. Figure 4.3

Figure 4.3
Triangulation

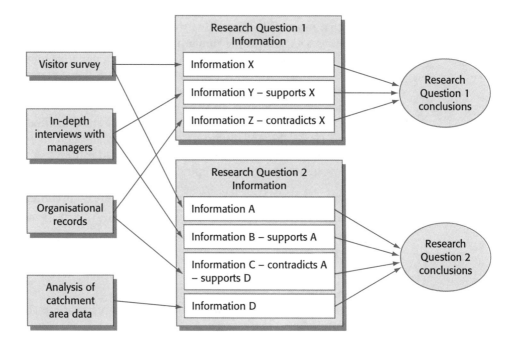

presents an example where four data collection methods are used to address two research questions. A research report on a project where triangulation is claimed should therefore compare and contrast the findings from the multiple methods. Whether the multiple methods produce similar or different findings should then be an issue for discussion.

Case studies

Introduction

A case study involves the study of an example – a case – of the phenomenon being researched. The aim is to seek to understand the phenomenon by studying single examples. Cases can consist of individuals (e.g. Rapoport and Rapoport, 1975; Saunders and Turner, 1987), communities, whole countries (e.g. Williams and Shaw, 1988; Bramham *et al.*, 1993), organisations and companies (e.g. Harris and Leiper, 1995) or places and projects (e.g. Murphy, 1991). Often a research project using the case study method will involve a number of *contrasting* cases, but studied in a similar manner. Case studies can range from small-scale vignettes to major projects in their own right. The case study as research method can encompass any or all of the techniques discussed in this book.

The case study *research method* should be distinguished from other uses of cases. The best-known use is in the law, where legal cases are important in setting precedents. Cases are also used in medicine and can become the basis of teaching, particularly in the area of psychology. Business cases or case studies are widely used for teaching purposes, the best-known being the Harvard Business School cases (Harvard Business School, n.d.).

The fact that research projects using the case study method typically involve only one or a few cases suggests some similarity with qualitative research methods and in some texts the case study method is subsumed under 'qualitative methods' (e.g. Finn, *et al.*, 2000: 81) but, as Yin (2003: 14) states: '. . . the case study strategy should not be confused with "qualitative research" . . . case studies can be based on any mix of quantitative and qualitative evidence'. In fact, the use of a variety of types of data and types of data analysis can be said to be a key feature of the case study method.

Robert Yin (2003: 13–14) discusses the case study method in relation to other research approaches, including experiments, surveys and histories, and concludes that the case study can be defined as an empirical inquiry that:

■ investigates a contemporary phenomenon within its real-life context; when

■ the boundaries between phenomenon and context are not clearly evident;

■ copes with the situation in which there are many more variables of interest than data points;

■ relies on multiple sources of evidence, with data needing to converge in a triangulating fashion;

■ benefits from the prior development of theoretical propositions to guide data collection and analysis.

To some extent all social research is a case study at some level, since all research is geographically and temporally unique. Thus, for example, a survey of 500 visitors to a particular leisure or tourism site can be seen as a case study of the site and even a nationwide opinion survey of, say, 20,000 people in a Western country carried out in 2004, could be seen, in one sense, as a case study of the opinion of the population of one affluent country in the early twenty-first century. To be seen as case studies in the full sense, however, these studies would need to involve more than just a survey – they would require additional information, in the first example, on the site and its environment and history, and in the second example, on the social and demographic characteristics of the country and perhaps on factors which were likely to influence opinion now and in the past. Thus the sheer variety of types of data and types of data analysis would offer a 'rich' description of the *case* – the site or the country and its people.

This section considers in turn: the purposes of case studies; the merits of the case study method; types of case study; data collection and data analysis. A number of examples of case study research in the leisure/tourism environment are then presented.

Purposes

Some commentators (for example, Zikmund, 1997: 108) have implied that the case study method is used only for 'exploratory' purposes but, while it can certainly be used for such a purpose, as Robert Yin (2003: 3) asserts: 'case studies are far from being only an exploratory strategy'. They can be the basis of substantive research projects in their own right.

Because, in case study research, only one or a few cases are examined, the method does not seek to produce findings that are generally or universally representative. Thus a case study of an organisation does not conclude: 'this explains the behaviour of organisation X, therefore it will explain or predict the behaviour of the 50,000 similar organisations in similar situations or a significant proportion of them'. However, if research has *no* implications beyond the particular case at a particular time and place, there would be little point in conducting it. Case study conclusions can, however, present general propositions relating to theory and policy issues and to possibilities, so they might be in the form: 'this explains the behaviour of organisation X, which is contrary to theoretical expectations, suggesting the possible need for some modification to the theory', or 'this explains the behaviour of organisation X, suggesting that other types of organisation might be examined to see whether the explanation applies more widely'. Thus, while case study research may not result in generalisations about a population, it can have valid things to say in relation to theory in the case of explanatory research and in relation to policy in the case of evaluative research. A number of scenarios can be envisaged in regard to theory and policy, as shown in Figure 4.4.

In the case of *explanatory* research a case study can be used to *test the applicability of an existing theory*. This might occur in situations where a theoretical proposition has never been tested empirically or where it has not been tested in a particular environment. Thus many propositions about leisure have in fact been developed using empirical evidence from sport – a case study of a non-sporting leisure activity could therefore

Type of	Research purpose	Case study outcomes
Explanatory research	Testing a single existing theory	Case study *confirms* applicability of theory in at least one setting or, alternatively, *raises doubts* as to applicability of theory and suggests modification or alternatives.
	Testing alternative/ competing theories	Case study demonstrates that one theory works better than the other in a particular situation, or that neither works.
	Develop theory where none exists	The task of the case study is to suggest *possible* theory.
Evaluative research	Testing effectiveness of a single policy	Case study *confirms* effectiveness of the policy in at least one setting or, alternatively, *raises doubts* as to effectiveness of the policy and possibly suggests modification or alternatives.
	Testing alternative/ competing policies	Case study demonstrates that one policy is more effective than the other in a particular situation, or that neither works.
	Establish need for policy measures	The case study outlines the current problems and their likely causes and suggests the need for policy action.

Figure 4.4   Scenarios for case study research

be used to test the universality of such propositions. If the theory is found to be non-applicable in a case study situation, this does not necessarily 'disprove' it, but can raise doubts as to its universality. In the case of policy-related *evaluative* research the corresponding research task would be to test the effectiveness of a policy or type of management practice. For example, while the impact of promotional policy could be examined by use of aggregate national statistics on customer/participant numbers, it could also be examined by means of a case study of the experience in one or two communities or neighbourhoods, particularly if the results of the national statistical analysis were unclear or indicated an apparent lack of impact.

Where there are *competing theories or theoretical perspectives*, especially if there is empirical evidence supporting both, a case study might be used to explore the reasons for the apparent impasse. This might be done by bringing to bear a much wider range of data than has hitherto been done, or it might be achieved by means of contrasting cases. Again, case studies are unlikely to be definitive, but may point in certain theoretical or empirical directions. Clearly a similar approach could be followed in evaluative research – for example, the effect of differing promotional campaigns in two facilities or in the same facility over two time-periods, could be examined by case studies.

Where *no known relevant theoretical framework* exists to address a topic, or those that purport to do so are seen as inadequate, one possible task of the case study can be to develop new theoretical propositions or insights, which are consistent with the case study data and which might be further tested by additional empirical study. The corresponding situation in evaluative research is where no policies exist and research is undertaken to establish whether there is a need for a policy.

Merits of the case study approach

The particular merits of the case study method can be summarised as follows.

- The ability to place people, organisations, events and experiences in their social and historical context.
- Ability to treat the subject of study as a whole, rather than abstracting a limited set of pre-selected features.
- Multiple methods – triangulation – are implicit and seen as a strength.
- The single, or limited number of, cases offers a manageable data collection task when resources are limited.
- Flexibility in data collection strategy allows researchers to adapt their research strategy as the research proceeds.
- There is no need to generalise to a defined wider population.

Design of case studies

While the case study method offers flexibility, it does not absolve the researcher from undertaking the usual initial preparatory steps – specifying research questions, reviewing the literature, establishing a theoretical framework and determining data needs and sources – as discussed in Chapter 3. As in any research, it is important to plan to avoid the problem of having collected a lot of data and not knowing what to do with it. While the method offers flexibility in the research strategy, this is rarely unlimited – for example, in some circumstances it may be possible to interview people, or ask them for data, a number of times as new issues emerge in the course of the research, but in other circumstances this may not be possible.

In addition to the general guidance on the planning of research projects set out in Chapter 3, three specific issues are discussed here: defining the unit of analysis; selection of cases and data gathering.

Defining the unit of analysis. While it might be a somewhat obvious point to make: it is necessary to be clear about the *unit of analysis* in case study research. For example, if the unit of analysis – the case – is a department within a large organisation, it is important to keep the analysis at the departmental level. Thus, for example, the policies and practices of the parent organisation are inevitably relevant, but they are 'given' influences on the department, the research is not *about* the parent organisation. Conversely, data on the staff of the department will form part of the research, but only in so far as they contribute to an understanding of the operation of the department as a unit.

Selecting the case(s). Of key importance in the case study method is the selection of the case or cases. This is, of course, comparable to sampling in a quantitative study. Four types of case-selection can be considered.

- *Purposive*. Where multiple cases are involved, the selection of cases is likely to be purposive – for example in selecting a range of facilities of similar or different sizes, in the same or different sectors, in comparable or contrasting geographical locations or of similar or contrasting levels of popularity.

■ *Illustrative*. Often the case(s) will be deliberately chosen to increase the likelihood of illustrating a particular proposition – for example, if the research is concerned with leadership success, then *successful* organisations with high-profile leaders may be deliberately chosen.

■ *Typical/atypical*. The case may be chosen because it is believed to be typical of the phenomenon being studied, or it may be deliberately chosen as an extreme or atypical case. Thus, a study examining the secrets of success in a particular leisure/tourism sector might well select the *most* successful facility for study.

■ *Pragmatic*. In some cases the selection of cases may be pragmatic – for example, when the researcher has ready access to a company, possibly because he or she is an employee of it.

Whatever the rationale for the selection of a case or cases, it should be clearly articulated in the research report, and the implications of the selection discussed.

Data gathering. A case study project generally uses a number of data sources and data gathering techniques, including: the use of documentary evidence; secondary data analysis; in-depth interviews; questionnaire surveys; observation; and participant observation. The process of selecting data sources and collection techniques is the same as in any other research process, as discussed in Chapter 3. In that chapter, the idea that different data sources might be used in the same project to address different research questions or aspects of research questions is illustrated; in particular, it is noted that all data collection should be linked to the research questions – even in cases where the research questions are being modified as the research progresses.

When a number of disparate data types and sources are involved, two other issues should be born in mind:

■ *consistency of the unit of analysis* – if, for example, staffing and financial data are involved, it is important that the data relate to the same organisational unit;

■ *temporal consistency* – ideally all data should relate to the same time-period – this is related to the issue of the unit of analysis, since reorganisation can result in changes in the size, composition and functions of organisational units over time.

Analysis

To the extent that the design of the case study, or parts of it, resembles that of more formalised research projects, with fixed research questions and corresponding data collection and analysis procedures, the analysis process will tend to be deductive in nature; the data analysis will be designed to address the questions posed in advance. But a case study can involve qualitative methods with a recursive, more inductive format, as discussed in Chapter 7. Indeed, the flexibility of the whole case study approach suggests a more inductive approach. Thus the discovery, in the course of the research, of a previously unknown source of information might lead the researcher to ask the question: can this data add something to the research? While the new data source might help in addressing the existing research questions in unanticipated ways, it could also suggest whole new research questions.

Three main methods of analysis are outlined by both Burns (1994: 324–5) and Yin (1994: 106–18):

■ *pattern matching* – relating the features of the case to what might be expected from some existing theory;

■ *explanation building* – often an iterative process whereby a logical/causal explanation of what is discovered is developed by to-and-fro referencing between theory/explanation and data;

■ *time series analysis* – explanations are developed on the basis of observing change over time.

In fact, all forms of analysis are possible within the context of a case study. It is the pulling together of the results of analyses of different sorts to form coherent conclusions which presents the challenge.

Case studies in practice

Two examples of case studies conclude the chapter. The case studies provide brief details on each study, but the reader can, of course, follow up the original references for the full report on the research. The first case study uses a combination of secondary data, textual and qualitative analysis and the second presents a historical narrative.

Secondary data/textual/qualitative

Case study 4.1 summarises research by Victoria Carty on a single aspect of the behaviour of a single organisation, the sports apparel multi-national Nike. As Case study 4.1 suggests, Nike has been the focus of considerable research and commentary as perhaps the most high profile of a number of such companies which outsource their manufacturing to Third World, cheap labour countries and have therefore been the particular focus of criticisms from anti-globalisation activists, such as Naomi Klein (1999). This study, however, focusses on a different ethical issue, namely whether Nike's rhetoric about treating women as respected customers is followed through in their advertising. The study uses a number of data sources but in particular illustrates the use of content analysis of print, poster and television advertising as a research method.

Case study 4.1   Nike, advertising and women

Source: Victoria Carty (1997) Ideologies and forms of domination in the organization of the global production and consumption of goods in the emerging postmodern era: a case study of Nike Corporation and the implications for gender. *Gender, Work and Organization*, 4(4), 189–201.

Methods/approaches:

Case study; secondary sources and textual analysis (TV and print advertising)

Topic:

Nike Corporation's advertising and marketing in relation to women.

This study draws on a number of information sources and theoretical perspectives to explore and critique the *modus operandi* of sportswear manufacturer Nike, particularly in regard to their treatment of women. The main information sources are: existing accounts of the development of Nike from the academic and popular literature and examples of Nike advertising on television and in print. Theoretical perspectives include: theories of globalisation and postmodernism; and the concept of 'global commodity chains', which geographically trace manufactured products from the point of consumption to the point of manufacturer. The thesis of the study is that Nike's advertising aimed at Western women consumers projects an image of the independent woman while their manufacturing practices exploit Third World women who make up the majority of its manufacturing labour, employed at low wages and in poor conditions in its own factories and those of its sub-contractors. The research sets out to demonstrate the validity of well-established theoretical frameworks which are critical of the role of multi-national global corporations, particularly in the production of fashion products where the costs of manufacturing are heavily outweighed by the costs of marketing and the retail mark-up. Thus, using a case study of a single firm, the study seeks to 'illustrate the interdependencies between production and consumption, or economics and culture, as organized in the global economy'.

Above, we have discussed the proposition that, while conclusions from case studies can, strictly speaking, apply only to the 'case' involved in the study, they would be of limited use if they did not at least raise the possibility of wider implications. Here the implication is that Nike may not be unique among multi-national companies in its exploitative approach to women.

The historical narrative

Case study 4.2 presents a history of events over a ten-year period, in which the Euro Disney theme park and resort, north of Paris, was conceived, planned, developed and opened, up to its third year of operation, when it made its first profit, following a series of losses. Based on participant observation, interviews and secondary sources, it covers a wide range of development, design, marketing and financial issues.

Case study 4.2 Euro Disney

Andrew Lainsbury 2000, *Once upon an American Dream: The Story of Euro Disneyland*. Lawrence, KS: University of Kansas Press.

Methods/approaches:	*Topic*:
Participant observation, In-depth interviews, Secondary sources, Historical	Theme park investment/ development/management

This book-length case study is based on the experiences of the author, a graduate in American Studies, in a year spent working as a general hand (and a period playing Prince Charming) in the Euro Disney theme park and resort, north of Paris. Opened in 1992 amid much publicity and controversy over its appropriateness and viability in a European context, the development had a chequered history in its early years. The book has five main chapters, dealing with: 1. The development of the idea of a European Disneyland and the political activity of selecting and securing a site; 2. The design, or 'imagineering', of the project; 3. Marketing of the project; 4. The financial struggles of the early years; and 5. The global Disney operation.

The book is written in a popular, narrative style, but is underpinned by extensive endnotes and references. The historical accounts draw mostly on press coverage which, given the high profile of the Walt Disney Company, was extensive. Use is also made of the considerable body of research literature on Disney, which comprises a mixture of popular and academic books, and papers in journals in such fields as cultural, media and American studies (Univ. of California, Berkeley, Library, n.d.).

Numerous themes emerge in each of the chapters. Thus chapter 1 provides an insight into the common phenomenon of countries and communities competing to attract industry and jobs, the financial and other 'deals' that are struck to attract enterprises, and the 'Not in My Back Yard' (NIMBY) politics of communities living in the immediate neighbourhood of proposed projects – in France the Disney project led to the establishment of the 'Association for the Protection of People Concerned by the Euro Disney Development'. Chapter 1 also discussed the clash of cultures between 'old Europe' and 'new America', an increasingly salient issue in an era of globalisation.

Much of chapter 2 is design-oriented rather than business-oriented, but the 'vertical integration' practice of Walt Disney Company in developing not only the theme park but also the ancillary hotels and golf courses – which it failed to do in the original Disneyland in California – is outlined. Chapter 3 outlines the complex strategy for marketing the project, both before and after its opening.

The development made substantial losses in its early years and chapter 4 documents the various measures taken to 'rescue' the project by improving income and attendance, cutting costs and reorganising its finances. This resulted in the achievement of the first profits in 1995. The final chapter examines briefly the international development of Disney theme parks and the growth of competitors.

While the book does not present 'hard' research data, it uses a variety of perspectives, issues and data sources to explore the saga of Euro Disney and therefore presents a valid case study of a major trans-national investment project.

Summary

This chapter complements Chapter 3 in setting out in brief the range of research methods available to the leisure and tourism researcher. It reinforces the message of Chapter 3, that research methods should ideally be selected on the basis of their suitability to answer the research questions posed, not on the basis of some prior preference for a particular method. Initially the 'major' research methods are reviewed, namely: scholarship; 'just thinking'; the use of existing information – the literature and secondary data; observation; qualitative methods; and questionnaire-based surveys. The first two are included to emphasise that research is not just about deploying techniques, but also involves being well-informed about the field and *thinking* about the problems and issues being researched. The other major methods foreshadow subsequent chapters which deal with them in detail. The middle section of the chapter briefly introduces a number of approaches and techniques which are subsidiary to one or more of the major methods, in that they are a variation on or an application of the major method, or cut across a number of the major methods. The approaches and techniques covered are: coupon surveys/conversion studies; en route/intercept surveys; time-budget surveys; panels; longitudinal studies; media-sponsored surveys; action research; historical research; textual analysis; the Delphi technique; projective techniques; the use of scales; and meta-analysis. In the penultimate section of the chapter consideration is given to 'multiple methods', with a discussion of the concept of triangulation and of the case study method. More attention is given to the latter because it can involve a range of methods and is not considered separately in later chapters. The final section considers the process of choosing a method.

Choosing a method

The process of choosing appropriate research methods for a research task is part of the whole process of planning and designing a research project, as discussed in Chapter 3. Here a number of considerations which should be borne in mind are discussed, as listed in Figure 4.5.

The research question or hypothesis

Much of the decision on how to research a topic is bound up in the basic research question or hypothesis. As discussed in Chapter 3, the 'research question' can take a variety

Figure 4.5
Considerations in selecting a research method

- The research question or hypothesis
- Previous research
- Data availability/access
- Resources
- Time
- Validity, reliability and generalisability
- Ethics
- Uses/users of the findings

of forms, but generally it will point the researcher in the direction of certain data sources – for example, in relation to visitors, facilities or organisations. Certain types of data also suggest certain types of analysis.

Previous research

If the proposed research is closely keyed into the literature and previous research, then the methods used in that research are likely to influence the choice of methods. The aim may be to replicate the methodology used in previous studies to achieve comparability, to improve on the methods used, or to deliberately adopt a contrasting methodology.

Data availability/access

In some cases an obvious existing data source presents itself, and may even have prompted the research in the first place. For example, a set of archives of an organisation can provide the basis for historical research. Official data which has been published but only superficially analysed could be analysed in more depth. Access to a sample of people, such as the workforce or customer-base of an organisation, can be seen as an opportunity too good to miss. In other cases *lack* of access shapes the research – for example, ethical or practical issues may preclude some research on children, so data may have to be gathered from parents.

Resources

Clearly the resources of staff and money will have a major effect on the type and scale of the research to be conducted.

Time

Time is also often a limitation. Research using the current year's attendance data must be completed quickly if it is to be used to influence next year's strategic planning.

Validity, reliability and generalisability

Validity is the extent to which the data collected truly reflect the phenomenon being studied. Leisure/tourism research faces difficulties in this area, especially in the measurement of attitudes and behaviour, as there are always doubts about the true meanings of responses made in surveys, interviews, and self-reported accounts of behaviour. The concept of validity is discussed in Chapter 2.

Reliability is the extent to which research findings would be the same if the research were to be repeated at a later date, or with a different sample of subjects. Caution should be exercised when making general statements on the basis of just one study.

Generalisability refers to the probability that the results of the research findings apply to other subjects, other groups, and other conditions. While measures can be taken to ensure a degree of generalisability, strictly speaking, any research findings relate only to the subjects involved, at the time and place the research was carried out.

Ethics

Ethical issues also limit choices of research method. Reference has already been made to ethical issues surrounding research on children: further examples of ethical issues in leisure/tourism research are discussed in Chapter 3.

Uses/users of the findings

The uses and users of the research are often taken for granted, but they are an important factor in shaping research. If substantial investment will depend on the results of the research then a more extensive and thorough-going project will be required than if the research is to be used only to generate ideas. When life and death issues are at stake – for example, in medical research on the effects of a treatment for a disease – much more precision is needed in the results than if, for example, an organisation merely wishes to know the socio-economic characteristics of its customers.

Test questions

1. What is 'scholarship'?
2. Define each of the following:
   a. Coupon surveys/conversion studies
   b. En route/intercept surveys
   c. Time-budget surveys
   d. Panel studies
   e. Longitudinal studies
   f. Media-sponsored surveys
   g. Action research
   h. Historical research
   i. Textual analysis
   j. The Delphi technique
   k. Projective techniques
   l. The use of scales
   m. Meta-analysis
3. What is triangulation and why is it used in research?
4. What are the characteristics which distinguish case study research?
5. If case study research cannot generalise to a wider population, what can it do?

Exercises

Exercises involving the major methods and subsidiary and cross-cutting methods arise in the subsequent chapters. Here, the focus is on the case study method.

1. Read and critically evaluate, from a methodological perspective, the original report of one of the case studies presented in this chapter.

2. A number of leisure/tourism-related multi-national companies have attracted media and research attention over the years – often of a critical nature. Examples are Nike (as discussed in Case study 4.1) because of its employment practices, McDonald's because of the nutritional levels of its food, and media companies because of their tendency to gain monopoly status in some markets. Select one such company and, using the Internet and library sources, produce a case study of its recent research and media coverage, noting both the comments of the critics and the responses of the company.

3. Interview one person concerning their consumption habits with regard to one class of leisure or tourism products or services – for example, entertainment, alcoholic drink, air travel. Explore the subject's motivations and rationale for choice of brands. As this is a case study, we might expect to draw on more than one source of information for the study: so examine the advertising of a selection of the subject's preferred and rejected brands to see whether this throws light on the type of consumer the subject is.

Further reading

The methodological debate: see Kelly (1980); Borman *et al.* (1986); Krenz and Sax (1986); Rojek (1989); Henderson (1990); Bryman and Bell (2003), Chapter 21, 'Breaking down the quantitative/qualitative divide'.

Coupon surveys/conversion studies: Woodside and Ronkainen (1994).

En route surveys: Hurst (1994).

Time-budget studies: Zuzanek and Veal (1998); Pentland *et al.* (1999).

Experience sampling method (ESM): Csikszentmihalyi and Larson (1987); Schneider *et al.* (2004).

Panel surveys: Kasprzyk *et al.* (1989); LaPage (1994); Rose (2000).

Longitudinal studies: in the social sciences see Young *et al.* (1991); an Australian longitudinal study on women's health includes questions on leisure, but at the time of writing, leisure-related results have been published only from the first, 1996, survey – an up-to-date list of papers emerging from the project can be found on the project web-site at: www.newcastle.edu.au/centre/wha.

Action research: Reason and Bradbury (2001); McNiff, and Whitehead (2002); see White (2004) for statement of 'action' dimension of feminist leisure research.

Historical research: Williams (2003); Ladkin (2004); Storey (2004); see the further reading section in Chapter 1 for examples.

Textual analysis: Prior (2003); television coverage of sport: Billings and Tyler Eastman (2002); sport: Rowe (2004); corporate advertising: Carty (1997) – see Case study 4.1.

Delphi technique: Green, Hunter and Moore (1990); Moeller and Shafer (1994); Veal (2002: 169–70).

Projective techniques: Semeonoff (1976).

Use of scales: Ware *et al.* (1994); Leisure and tourism and the Myers-Briggs personality indicator: McGuiggan (2000); physical and mental health scales used in leisure research: Brown *et al.* (2001).

Meta-analysis: outdoor recreation economic values: Shrestha and Loomis (2003); contingent valuation and cultural resources: Noonan (2003).

Case studies: The most commonly referred-to text on case study research is Robert Yin's (1994, 2003) *Case Study Research*. See also Bromley (1986) and Stake (1994) for a general treatment of the topic and Craig Smith (1991), Rose (1991) and Burns (1994: 312–31) for brief overviews. Robert Stake's (1995) book, *The Art of Case Study Research*, is more discursive and is oriented particularly towards the education sector. In leisure studies, see: Henderson (1991: 88–90). In tourism studies, see: Ryan (1995:115–17). Examples: a sporting/social club in a residential community: Wynne (1986, 1998); city governance and sport: Henry and Paramio Salcines (1998); city governance and tourism: Long (2000); tourism planning: Murphy (1991).

5 Reviewing the literature

Introduction: an essential task

The aim of this chapter is to explain the importance, for any research project, of reviewing previous research and being aware of existing writing – the literature – on a topic. In addition the chapter indicates general sources of information on leisure and tourism studies literature, sets out the mechanics of compiling bibliographies and recording bibliographical references and considers the *process* of reviewing the literature for research purposes.

Reviewing previous research or writing on a topic is a vital step in the research process. The field of leisure and tourism studies comprises relatively new areas of academic enquiry which are wide-ranging and multi-disciplinary in nature. Research is not so plentiful in the field that we can afford to ignore research which has already been completed by others. As discussed briefly in Chapters 3 and 4, the literature can serve a number of functions, as indicated in Figure 5.1.

The aim of research of an academic nature is to add to the body of human knowledge. In most societies that body of knowledge is generally in written form – the literature. To presume to add to that body of knowledge it is therefore necessary to be familiar with it and to indicate precisely how the proposed or completed research relates to it. In research which is of a consultancy nature, where the *primary* aim is not to add to knowledge but to use research to assist directly in the solution of policy, planning or management problems, a familiarity with existing knowledge in the area is still vital. Much time and valuable resources can be wasted in 're-inventing the wheel' to devise suitable methodologies to conduct a project, or in conducting projects with

Figure 5.1
The roles of
the literature
in research

- The entire basis of the research
- Source of ideas on topics for research
- Source of information on research already done by others
- Source of methodological or theoretical ideas
- Source of comparison between your research and that of others
- Source of information that is an integral or supportive part of the research – for example statistical data on the study area population

inadequate methodologies, when reference to existing work can provide information on tried and tested approaches.

Identifying relevant literature is often a demanding task. It involves: a careful search for information on relevant published and, if necessary, unpublished work; obtaining copies of relevant items and reading them; making a list of useful items to form a *bibliography*; and assessing and summarising aspects which are salient for the research proposal or the research report.

The value of bibliographies

This chapter focusses on reviewing the literature in relation to planned research projects, but the development of a bibliography can be a useful end in itself. It might be thought that modern electronic search methods have made the compilation and publication of bibliographies on specific topics obsolete, but this is not the case. While they are continually developing, electronic databases are still incomplete, especially with regard to older published material and 'ephemeral' material, such as conference papers and reports and working papers not published by mainstream publishers. In addition, electronic databases do not provide an *evaluation* of material: they rarely distinguish between a substantial research paper and a lightweight commentary with no original content. Further, full-text databases are not universally available, so electronic systems will only be able to identify items on the basis of their titles or, in some cases, key words and abstracts. Most existing databases do not indicate, for example, whether a report on 'recreation activities' includes data on a specific activity, such as golf, or whether a report on 'holiday patterns' mentions a specific form of holiday, such as backpacking. A great deal of useful work can therefore still be done in compiling bibliographies on specific topics, thus helping to consolidate the 'state of the art' and saving other researchers a great deal of time and trouble in searching for material.

Examples of published bibliographies in the leisure and tourism area are listed in the further reading section at the end of the chapter and considerable scope exists for the development of similar bibliographies on other topics. A number of websites list on-line bibliographies, as indicated in Appendix 5.1.

Searching

Where can the researcher look for information on existing published research on a topic? In this section a number of sources are examined, as listed in Figure 5.2.

Library catalogues

Modern libraries have computerised catalogues which are accessed via terminals within the library and can also be accessed from remote locations via the Internet. In many university and college libraries it is now possible to access the catalogues of a

Figure 5.2
Sources of
information

- Library catalogues
- Published bibliographies
- Published indexes and electronic databases
- The Internet
- General leisure/tourism books
- Reference lists
- Beyond leisure and tourism

number of libraries, often worldwide. Searches can be made on the basis of the titles of publications or using key words assigned to publications by the library. This can be very helpful as a starting point in establishing a bibliography. But it is *only* a starting point, particularly for the researcher with a specialist interest.

If search words such as *leisure, tourism, sport* or *the arts* are used, the typical computerised catalogue will produce an enormous number of references – possibly running to thousands, and far too many to be manageable. But if, for example, more specialised terms, such as *female golfers* or *Asian backpackers* are entered, the catalogue will produce few references, sometimes none at all. Whether a large or small number of references is produced, a proportion will be of a 'popular' nature, concerned with, for example, how to play golf, biographies of golfers, or backpacker guides to budget accommodation in Europe. Such material may be of interest to some researchers, but will be of little use if the researcher is interested in such aspects as levels of participation in golf, the socio-economic characteristics of golfers or trends in the numbers of backpackers. But the fact that this latter type of research material is not listed by the computerised catalogue does not mean that it does not exist in the library. The catalogue search is based only on the *titles* of catalogued items and on the *keywords* which the librarian or publisher has decided to include. Library catalogues generally do not contain references to individual articles in journals, individual chapters in books which are collections of readings, or individual papers in collections of conference papers. To identify these more detailed items, other sources must be used, as discussed below.

Neither can a library catalogue indicate, for instance, whether a general report on *sport* or *recreation* or *tourism* includes any reference to a specific leisure activity or a particular type of tourism. And of course the catalogue will not identify publications which, while they deal with one topic, provide a suitable methodology for studying other topics. Such material can only be identified by actually reading – or at least perusing – original texts.

Published bibliographies

Reference has already been made to the value of bibliographies on particular topics. Libraries usually have a separate section for bibliographies and it may be worth 'browsing' in that section, especially when the topic of interest is interdisciplinary. While many bibliographies have been published in 'hard copy' form over the years (see further reading for examples), the trend recently has been to publish these resources on the Internet, as indicated in Appendix 5.1.

Published indexes and electronic databases

Published indexes are specialist listings of bibliographical material published on a regular basis by specialist libraries or research centres. Such indexes readily lend themselves to production in CD-ROM format or to being made available on the Internet. Often they are available in more than one format. An example is the most extensive and well-established index and electronic database of leisure and tourism publications: *Leisure, Recreation and Tourism Abstracts (LRTA)*.

LRTA has been published quarterly since 1975 by the UK organisation CAB International and is available as a hard-copy quarterly publication and on-line in libraries which subscribe. Each quarterly issue includes about 600 references and very detailed author and subject indexes which make searching relatively easy. *LRTA* has the advantage of drawing on a much wider database than most individual libraries and it includes listings of individual journal articles, book chapters and conference papers.

The *Social Sciences Citation Index*, available in most university libraries and on-line, is a comprehensive listing of papers from thousands of social science journals, cross-referenced by author and subject. In addition, items of literature referred to by authors in papers are themselves listed and cross-referenced, so that further writings of any cited author can be followed up. Unfortunately many leisure and tourism journals are not included in the database, but the index nevertheless includes references to a considerable amount of leisure and tourism material.

The Internet

The Internet has rapidly become a significant source of information for researchers. The world of the Internet develops at such a rate that it is impossible for printed textbooks to be up-to-date in conveying the range of sources available. While general 'Google' type searches are possible, they are a rather blunt tool compared with specialist sources. In university libraries, general academic journal databases, such as EBSCO and Ingenta, are automatically available. Some key specialist sources are listed in Figure 5.3.

Figure 5.3
Internet sites

The following list is indicative only. Each site provides a wealth of information, including: bibliographies, information on conferences, journals and on-going research, and cross-references to other sites.

Site	Address
CABI leisure-tourism site	www.leisuretourism.com
Laboratory for Leisure, Tourism and Sport	www.playlab.uconn.edu/mylab.html
Sport Management Information Centre	www.unb.ca/web/sportmanagement
World Tourism Organisation	www.world-tourism.org/publications/
UTS On-line Leisure Bibliographies	www.business/uts.edu.au/lst/research/bibs.html

General leisure and tourism publications

The researcher should be aware of publications which contain information on specific activities or aspects of leisure or tourism. For example, Chapter 6 discusses national leisure participation and tourism surveys which contain information on as many as 100 leisure activities, on tourism flows of different types and a number of background items such as age and income. They are therefore a source of basic statistical information on many topics of interest.

General introductory books on leisure or tourism may have something to say on the topic of interest or may provide leads to other sources of information via the index and bibliography. Examples are, in the area of leisure:

- Cushman *et al.* (2005) *Free Time and Leisure Participation: International Perspectives*
- Torkildsen (2005) *Leisure and Recreation Management*
- Kelly and Godbey (1992) *Sociology of Leisure*
- Jackson and Burton (1999) *Leisure Studies: Prospects for the Twenty-first Century*
- Jarvie and Maguire (1994) *Sport and Leisure in Social Thought*
- Driver *et al.* (1991) *Benefits of Leisure*
- Veal and Lynch (2001) *Australian Leisure*

In the area of tourism:

- Ritchie and Goeldner (1994) *Travel, Tourism and Hospitality Research*
- Burkart and Medlik (1981) *Tourism: Past, Present and Future*
- Ryan (1995) *Researching Tourist Satisfaction*
- Leiper (1995) *Tourism Management*

In addition, there are a number of specialist encyclopaedias, with most entries including bibliographic references. Examples of specialist encyclopaedias include:

- Jenkins and Pigram (2003) *Encyclopedia of Leisure and Outdoor Recreation*
- Weaver (2000) *Encyclopedia of Tourism*
- Jafari (2000) *Encyclopedia of Tourism*
- Brukner *et al.* (2003) *Encyclopedia of Exercise, Sport and Health*
- Sherrow (1996) *Encyclopedia of Women and Sports*
- Levinson and Christensen (1996) *Encyclopedia of World Sport: From Ancient Times to the Present.*
- Pendergast and Pendergast (1999) *St. James Encyclopedia of Popular Culture.*

Searching through such texts, using the contents pages or the index, can be a somewhat 'hit and miss' process, but can often be rewarded with leads which could not be gained in any other way. Even scanning through the contents pages of key journals, such as *Leisure Studies* or *Annals of Tourism Research*, may produce relevant material which would not be identified by conventional searches.

Reference lists

Most importantly, the lists of references in the books and articles identified in initial searches will often lead to useful material. Researchers interested in a particular topic should be constantly on the alert for sources of material on that topic in anything they are reading. Sometimes key items are encountered when they are least expected. The researcher should become a 'sniffer dog' obsessed with 'sniffing out' anything of relevance to the topic of interest. In a real-world research situation this process of identifying as much literature as possible can take months or even years. While a major effort should be made to identify material at the beginning of any research project, it will also be an on-going exercise, throughout the course of the project.

Beyond leisure and tourism

Lateral thinking is also an aid to the literature search task. The most useful information is not always found in the most obvious places. Some commentators have remarked on how many researchers fail to look beyond immediate *leisure* or *tourism* material. Leisure and tourism are inter-disciplinary areas of study, not disciplines in their own right – they do not have a set of research methods and theories uniquely their own. Much is to be gained from looking outside the immediate area of leisure or tourism studies. For example, if the research involves measurement of *attitudes* then certain *psychological* literature will be of interest; if the research involves the study of leisure or tourism *markets* then general *marketing* journals may be useful sources and if the research involves the leisure activities of the *elderly* then *gerontology* journals should be consulted.

Obtaining copies of material

If material is not available in a particular library it can often be obtained through the *inter-library loan* service. This is a system through which loans of books and reports can be made between one library and another. In the case of journal articles the service usually involves the provision of a photocopy. In theory any item published in a particular country should be available through this system since it is connected with national copyright libraries – such as the British Lending Library in Boston Spa or the National Library in Australia – where copies of all published items must be lodged by law. Practices vary from library to library, but in academic libraries the service is often available to postgraduate students but undergraduate students may only access it through a member of academic staff.

For researchers working in metropolitan areas the other obvious source of material is specialist libraries, particularly of government agencies. For example, in London, Sports England and English Tourist Board (now 'VisitBritain') libraries are major resources for leisure and tourism researchers. In metropolitan areas and some other regions there is also often a cooperative arrangement between municipal reference libraries such that particular libraries adopt particular specialist areas – so it can be useful to discover which municipal library service specialises in leisure and/or tourism.

The full texts of journals are increasingly available via the Internet sources discussed above, in libraries which subscribe to the appropriate services. This means that copies of complete articles can be downloaded and printed out, not just the reference.

Compiling and maintaining a bibliography

What should be done with the material once it has been identified? First, a record should be made of everything which appears to be of relevance. The researcher is strongly advised to start a file of every item of literature used. This can be of use not only for the current research project but also for future reference – a personal bibliography can be built up over the years. Such record keeping can be done using cards, but is best done on a computer, using a wordprocessor or a database program, which can also store key-words. This has the attraction that when there is a need to compile a bibliography on another topic in future, a start can be made from your personal bibliography by getting the computer to copy designated items into a new file. In this way the researcher only ever needs to type out a reference once! Specialist packages, such as *Endnote* and *Pro-Cite*, now becoming available, which store reference material in a standard format, but will automatically compile bibliographies in appropriate formats to meet the requirements of different report styles and the specifications of different academic journals.

It takes only seconds to copy out the *full details* of a reference when it is first identified. It is advisable to have a stock of blank cards or a notebook always at hand for such purposes. If this practice is adopted, hours of time and effort can be saved in not having to chase up details of references at a later date. Not only should the details be recorded accurately, as set out below, but a note should be made on the card or in the database about the availability of the material – for example, the library catalogue reference, or the fact that the item is *not* in the library, or that a photocopy or electronic copy has been taken.

Reviewing the literature

Reviewing the literature on a topic can be one of the most rewarding – and one of the most frustrating – of research tasks. It is a task where a range of skills and qualities needs to be employed – including patience, persistence, insight and lateral thinking.

Types of literature review

The review of the literature can play a number of roles in a research project, as outlined above, and this leads to a number of approaches to conducting a review, as listed in Figure 5.4.

Figure 5.4
Types of
literature
review

- Inclusive bibliography
- Inclusive/evaluative
- Exploratory
- Instrumental
- Content analysis/hermeneutics

Inclusive bibliography

The *inclusive* approach to reviewing the literature seeks to identify everything that has been published on a particular topic. The compilation of such a bibliography may be a significant achievement in itself, independent of any research project with which it may be connected. It becomes a resource to be drawn on in the future by others. Such a bibliography does not amount to a 'review' of the literature if there is no accompanying commentary, although classification of entries into categories (e.g. books, articles, government reports) or time-periods can be seen as the beginning of such a process. In some cases bibliographies merely list the reference details; in other cases they include abstracts of the contents – in which case they are referred to as *annotated* bibliographies. A number of examples of comprehensive bibliographies are listed in the further reading section.

Inclusive/evaluative review

The *inclusive/evaluative* approach takes the inclusive approach a stage further by providing a commentary on the literature in terms of its coverage and its contribution to knowledge and understanding of the topic. Examples of such reviews are the review of the tourism forecasting literature by Calantone *et al.* (1987) and a review of the literature on the concept of *lifestyle* (Veal, 1993a, 2000). The latter is summarised in Case study 5.1.

Case study 5.1   Lifestyle and leisure literature review

Source: A.J. Veal (1993a) The concept of lifestyle: a review. *Leisure Studies*, 12 (4), 233–52; and A.J. Veal (2000) *Lifestyle and Leisure: A Bibliography and Review*. School of Leisure and Tourism Studies, University of Technology, Sydney. On-line Bibliography 8, available at: www.business.uts.edu.au/lst/research/bibs.html

Methods: Literature review   *Topic*: Lifestyle

This review arose because, in the mid-1980s, the author was required to teach a course on 'leisure and lifestyle'. A preliminary scan of the literature revealed that the term 'lifestyle' was widely used in leisure and tourism research but it was generally ill-defined, defined differently by different authors, or was not defined at all. Further detailed investigation identified some 400 references making substantial use of the term and indicated that the concept of lifestyle had a number of histories and associated meanings in different disciplines and study areas. These included:

- *Weberian* – early sociological formulation by Max Weber.
- *Sub-cultural* – ways of life associated with different sub-cultural groups (for example, youth sub-cultures).
- *Psychological* – outlook on life established in the first few years of life.
- *Market research/psychographics* – quantitative analysis of values, attitudes and socio-economic characteristics.
- *Spatial research* – ways of life associated with a type of residential location (for example, suburban, rural).
- *Leisure styles* – groupings of types of leisure.
- *Socialist lifestyles* – ways of life approved of and planned for by East European communist regimes of the 1960s and 1970s.

As a result of examining this body of literature, it was suggested that, in seeking a generic definition for the concept of lifestyle, a number of dimensions should be considered, namely:

- *Activities/behaviour* – including leisure, tourism, consumption, work and home activity patterns.
- *Values and attitudes* – political, moral, aesthetic.
- *Individuals versus groups* – whether a 'lifestyle' is only a group phenomenon.
- *Group interaction* – whether interaction among individuals adopting particular lifestyles is required to develop and reinforce a lifestyle.
- *Coherence* – whether a lifestyle requires some sort of internal aesthetic or moral coherence.
- *Recognisability* – whether a lifestyle must be recognised by others to exist.
- *Choice* – whether adoption of a *lifestyle* involves choice on the part of an individual, compared with a 'way of life' which might be imposed.

The contribution of this review was to identify the variety of independent uses and definitions of the concept arising from its multi-disciplinary antecedents and to analyse the concept in terms of its constituent elements.

A common variation on the inclusive/evaluative type of review might be termed *literature analysis* and involves a quantitative analysis of temporal trends in the content and/or authorship of the literature in a particular field or in a particular journal. For example, Riley and Love (2000) present an analysis of the contents of four tourism journals since their inception to show the changing proportion of articles using qualitative methodology through the 1970s and 1990s. Burdge (1989) analysed the contents of two leisure studies journals over the 1970s and 1980s to show the changing disciplinary mix of the contributing authors.

An even more formalised quantitative approach to analysing the literature is known as *meta-analysis*, as discussed in Chapter 4. This involves a systematic, quantitative appraisal of the findings of a number of projects focussed on the same topic. The technique is suitable for the sort of research where findings are directly comparable from one study to another – for example when the key research findings are expressed in terms of correlation or regression coefficients (see Chapter 12). In this approach the reported findings of the research themselves become the subject of research and the number of reported projects can become so large that it is necessary to *sample* from them in the same way that individuals are sampled for empirical research. Examples are listed in the further reading section.

Exploratory review

The *exploratory* approach is more focussed and seeks to discover existing research which might throw light on a specific research question or issue. This is very much the classic literature review which is the norm for academic research and best fits the model of the research process outlined in Chapter 3. Comprehensiveness is not as important as the focus on the particular question or issue. The skill in conducting such a review lies in keeping the question or issue in sight, while 'interrogating' the literature for ideas and insights which may help shape the research. The reviewer needs to be open to useful new ideas, but must not be side-tracked into areas which stray too far from the question or issue of interest.

Instrumental review

An example of the *instrumental* approach is the brief review in Case study 3.1 in Chapter 3. Here the focus of the research is a management issue and the literature is used as a source of suitable ideas on how the research might be tackled. The criterion for selection of literature is not to present a picture of the state of knowledge on the topic, but merely to identify a useful methodology for the project in hand.

Content analysis and hermeneutics

Content analysis and *hermeneutics* are techniques which involve detailed analysis of the contents of a certain body of literature or other documentary source as *texts*. The text becomes a focus of research in its own right rather than being merely a report of research. The texts might be, for example, novels, politicians' speeches or the contents of advertising. Content analysis tends to be quantitative, involving, for example, counting the number of occurrences of certain phrases. Hermeneutics tends to be qualitative in nature, the term being borrowed from the traditional approach to analysis and interpretation of religious texts. The essence of this approach is discussed in Chapter 8, in relation to the analysis of in-depth interview transcripts.

Reading critically and creatively

Reviewing the literature for *research* purposes involves reading the literature in a certain way. It involves being concerned as much with the methodological aspects of the research (which are not always well reported) as the substantive content. That is, it involves being concerned with *how* the conclusions are arrived at as well as with the conclusions themselves. It involves being critical – questioning rather than accepting what is being read. The task is as much to ascertain what is *not* known, as it is to determine what *is* known. This is different from reading for other purposes, such as some essay-writing. In the latter instance a particular substantive critical issue may be being explored, but the research basis or overall scope of the literature being discussed may not be an issue.

As material is being read, a number of questions might be asked, as set out in Figure 5.5. The questions relate to both individual items and to the body of literature as a whole.

Figure 5.5
Questions to ask
when reviewing
the literature

a. Individual items
■ What is the (empirical) basis of this research?
■ How does the research relate to other research writings on the topic?
■ What theoretical framework is being used?
■ What geographical area does the research refer to?
■ What social group(s) does the research refer to?
■ When was the research carried out and is it likely still to be empirically valid?

b. In relation to the literature as a whole
■ What is the *range* of research that has been conducted?
■ What *methods* have generally been used and what methods have been neglected?
■ What, in summary, does the existing research tell us?
■ What, in summary, does the existing research *not* tell us?
■ What contradictions are there in the literature – either recognised or unrecognised by the authors concerned?
■ What are the *deficiencies* in the existing research, in substantive or methodological terms?

It can be helpful to be conscious of the appropriate way in which the contents of an item of literature should be reported. A number of styles of reporting are used, including:

■ Smith believes . . . thinks . . . is of the opinion . . .

■ Smith argues . . .

■ Smith establishes . . .

■ Smith observes . . .

■ Smith speculates . . .

■ Smith puts forward the possibility that . . .

■ Smith concludes . . .

An author's opinion or beliefs may be important if the author is someone who deals in opinions and beliefs, such as a politician or cleric, but we generally expect more than just statements of belief from academic literature. An academic may be influenced by particular ideological or religious beliefs – for example a well-known theorist in the field of leisure, Josef Pieper, author of *Leisure, the Basis of Culture*, was a Catholic priest and this is not irrelevant to his work, but if his work had been merely a statement of faith it would not have been as influential as it has been in the development of leisure theory. A review of the literature should convey accurately the basis of the material presented, whether it be opinion, the result of argument or presentation of empirical evidence, informal observation or speculation. The type of literature being summarised is therefore important: newspaper and popular and professional magazine articles are not subject to the same checks and balances as academic journal articles; and reports emanating from leisure or tourism organisations or from politically motivated organisations cannot always be relied on to tell 'the truth, the whole truth and nothing but the truth'. Of course such material may appear in a literature review, but its status and the way it is reported and interpreted should be treated with caution and subtlety.

Care should be taken when referring to textbooks. Textbooks, such as this one, may contain some original contributions from the author, but will mostly contain summaries of the state of knowledge in a field, with some material attributed to specific sources and some not. Generally, in a research report, particularly a thesis, original scholarly sources rather than textbooks should be referred to where possible.

As regards the substantive content of the literature, a major challenge for a reviewer is to find some framework to classify and analyse it. In the case of an inclusive literature review, literature might be classified chronologically, by geographical origin or by discipline. For other types of review, themes or issues are likely to be more important. Reviewing the literature in this way can be similar to the development of a conceptual framework for a research project, as discussed in Chapter 3. Some sort of diagrammatic, concept map, approach, as indicated in Figure 5.6, may be helpful. Such a diagram

Figure 5.6
Making sense of
the literature

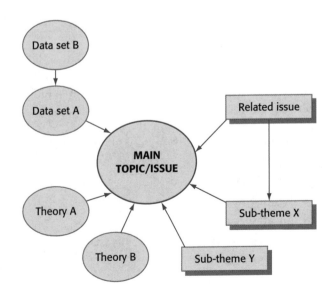

might be devised before starting a review, or may be developed, inductively, as the review progresses.

Summarising

A review of the literature should draw *conclusions* and *implications for the proposed research programme*. It is advisable to complete a review by presenting a *summary* which addresses the second set of questions in Figure 5.5. This summary should lead logically to the research project in hand. It should make clear to the reader just how the proposed research relates to the existing body of literature – whether it is seeking to: add to the body of knowledge in a unique way; fill a gap in knowledge; up-date existing knowledge; correct or contradict some aspect of existing knowledge; or simply use ideas from the literature as a source of ideas or comparison. When a large amount of literature with similar format is being reviewed it may be helpful to summarise it in a tabular quasi-meta-analytical form, using headings such as: geographical area covered, sample size, independent variables used, year of survey.

Referencing the literature

The purpose of referencing

What is the purpose of referencing? First, referencing is evidence of the writer's scholarship: it indicates that the particular research report is related to the existing body of knowledge. This is not only of importance to teachers marking student assignments or theses – it is part and parcel of the development of knowledge. Second, references enable the reader of the research report to check sources – either to verify the writer's interpretation of previous research or to follow up areas of interest.

Recording references

A number of standard or conventional formats exist for recording references to the literature. The conventions have been established by leading academic organisations and publishers. Guides are produced by organisations such as the American Psychological Association (2001) and the Australian Government Publishing Service (see Snooks and Co., 2002), to which the reader is referred for more detail. The formats presented here do not conform to any one standard approach but offer a style which, if followed consistently, would be acceptable in most academic contexts. In what follows, the word *text* refers to the main body of the research report or article.

The general format recommended for recording references is as shown in Figure 5.7.

In some systems the date is put at the end, but when using the *author/date* or *Harvard* system, as discussed below, the date should follow the author name as indicated.

Note that the part of the reference which is in *italic* is the title which would be found in a library catalogue. Thus what is found in a library catalogue is the name of the periodical, not the title of the article, so it is the *title of the periodical* that is in italic. In the case of a chapter from a book, the title of the book is found in the catalogue, not the title of the chapter, so the *title of the book* is in italic.

Figure 5.7
Standard/
generic
reference
formats

■ *A book or report:*
   Author(s), Initials (Year) *Title of Book or Report in Italic*. Place of publication: Publisher.

■ *An article from a periodical (journal/magazine/newspaper):*
   Author(s), Initials (Year) Title of article. *Title of Periodical in Italic*, Volume number (Issue number), Page numbers.

Note that the *publisher* of a book is not the same as the *printer* of the book (in the case of this book, the *publisher* is Pearson Education, but the *printer* is Henry Ling Ltd. References do not need to refer to the printer. And note that it is *not* necessary to refer to the publisher in the case of periodicals.

Some examples of reference formats are set out in Figure 5.8 to illustrate the principles.

Particular note should be made that, in the book chapter example, the main reference is to the author(s) of the chapter, not to the editor(s) of the book.

Internet references are becoming increasingly common. One of the problems with this medium is that some sources disappear or their website address (URL) changes over time, so that it is difficult for the reader to follow them up. For individual publications it is often advisable to give the index or 'list of publications' address rather than the often long and complex address of the individual publication. The general principle to be followed is that an Internet reference should include all the details which would normally apply to hard copy items, *plus* the website URL *and* the date accessed. The place of publication is not always clear from the website, but can generally be found with a little effort. If accessing a journal article via the Internet, it is not necessary to give the website address unless the journal is known to be only published electronically. Published style guides are now available for referencing in relation to this evolving medium, for example, *The Columbia Guide to Online Style* (Walker and Taylor, 1998).

Some guidelines suggest that newspaper articles should be referenced with the title of the article rather than, as here, with the author or the name of the newspaper. The important point to note is that, once a style is adopted, it should be consistent throughout the report.

Referencing and referencing systems

There are two commonly used referencing systems: the 'author/date' system, sometimes referred to as the 'Harvard' system, and the 'footnote' or 'endnote' system. These two systems are discussed in turn below.

The author/date or Harvard system

Basic features

In the author/date, or 'Harvard', system, references to an item of literature are made in the text by using the author's name and the year of the publication; at the end of

1.	**A book**	Ryan, C. (1991*) Recreational Tourism: A Social Science Perspective.* London: Routledge.
2.	**An edited book**	Ritchie, J.R.B. and Goeldner, C.R. (eds) (1994) *Travel, Tourism, and Hospitality Research: A Handbook for Managers and Researchers.* 2nd edn, New York: John Wiley and Sons.
3.	**A chapter from an edited book**	Gunn, C.A. (1994) A perspective on the purpose and nature of tourism research methods. In J.R.B. Ritchie and C.R. Goeldner (eds) *Travel, Tourism, and Hospitality Research: A Handbook for Managers and Researchers.* 2nd edn, New York: John Wiley and Sons, 3–12.
4.	**A published conference report** (NB in the example, the printed proceedings were published two years after the conference was held)	Ruskin, H. and Sivan, A. (eds) (1995) *Leisure Education: Towards the 21st Century, Proceedings of the International Seminar of the World Leisure and Recreation Commission on Education, Jerusalem, August, 1993.* Provo, Utah: Brigham Young University Press.
5.	**A published conference paper**	Veal, A.J. (1995) Leisure studies: frameworks for analysis. In H. Ruskin and A. Sivan (eds) *Leisure Education: Towards the 21st Century, Proceedings of the International Seminar of the World Leisure and Recreation Commission on Education, Jerusalem, August, 1993.* Provo, Utah: Brigham Young University Press, 124–36.
6.	**A government agency report, authored and published by the same agency**	Sport England (1999) *Best Value Through Sport: Case Studies.* London: Sport England.
7.	**A journal article**	Ravenscroft, N. (1993) Public leisure provision and the good citizen. *Leisure Studies*, 12 (1), 33–44.
8.	**A newspaper article with named author**	Hornery, A. (1996) Market researchers facing major hurdles. *Sydney Morning Herald*, 11 April, p. 26.
9.	**A newspaper item without a named author**	*Sydney Morning Herald* (1996) Our green future, 7 June, p. 12.
10.	**An Internet source**	Veal, A.J. (2003) *Education, Training and Professional Development in Leisure: A Bibliography.* On-line Bibliography 10, Sydney: School of Leisure and Tourism Studies, University of Technology, Sydney, available at: www.business.uts.edu.au/lst/research/bibs.html (accessed Jan 2005).

Figure 5.8   Examples of references

the paper or report, references are listed in alphabetical order. Thus, a sentence in a report might look something like this:

Research on women and leisure in the 1970s and 1980s included work in Britain by Deem (1986), in Canada by Bella (1989), in the United States by Bialeschki and Henderson (1986) and in Australia by Anderson (1975).

Note that authors' initials are not used in these references (unless there are two authors with the same surname). If one author has two or more references in the same year, they are listed as, for example, 2002a, 2002b. At the end of the report a list of references is provided, arranged in alphabetical order, as follows.

References
Anderson, R. (1975) *Leisure: An Inappropriate Concept for Women?* Canberra: AGPS.
Bella, L. (1989) Women and leisure: beyond androcentrism. In E.L. Jackson and T.L. Burton (eds) *Understanding Leisure and Recreation.* State College, PA: Venture, 151–80.
Bialeschki, M.D. and Henderson, K. (1986) Leisure in the common world of women. *Leisure Studies,* 5(3), 299–308.
Deem, R. (1986) *All Work and No Play? The Sociology of Women's Leisure.* Milton Keynes: Open University Press.

Style variation

The style of presentation can be varied; for instance, the above statement could be made drawing less explicit attention to specific authors.

Interest in research on women and leisure was widespread in the 1970s and 1980s in the English speaking world, as work from authors in the Britain, Canada, the United States and Australia indicates (Anderson, 1975; Bialeschki and Henderson, 1986; Deem, 1986; Bella, 1989).

Specifics and quotations

When referring to *specific points* from an item of literature, rather than making a general reference to the whole item, as above, page references should be given to the specific point of interest. This is particularly important when referring to a specific point from a substantial publication like a book, for example:

Aitchison (2003: 135–58) makes the link between gender issues and leisure management practices.

When *quoting* directly from a source, page references should also be given:

Iso-Ahola makes the point that: 'To survive as an academic field, scholars must supply evidence that their methods of investigation are valid and reliable rather than "soft"' (1980: 49).

A longer quotation would be indented in the page, without quotation marks, and handled like this:

Iso-Ahola argues the case for scientific research in the leisure area and states:

> To survive as an academic field, scholars must supply evidence to the effect that their methods of investigation are valid and reliable rather than 'soft'. This becomes increasingly important in obtaining grants from sources inside and outside academic institutions.
>
> (Iso-Ahola, 1980: 49)

Advantages and disadvantages

The author/date system is an 'academic' style. Its disadvantage is therefore that referencing is very 'up-front', even obtrusive, in the text. It is not an appropriate style for some practically oriented reports, particularly where the readership is not academic. Large numbers of references using this style tend to 'clutter up' the text and make it difficult to read. The system also has the disadvantage that it does not incorporate footnotes (at the foot of the page) or endnotes (at the end of the chapter or of the book). However, one view is that footnotes and endnotes are undesirable anyway – that if something is worth saying it is worth saying in the text. If notes and asides are nevertheless considered necessary it is possible to establish a footnote system for this purpose in addition to using the author/date system for references to the literature only. This of course becomes somewhat complex. If footnotes or endnotes are considered necessary then it is probably best to use the footnote style for everything, as discussed below.

The advantages of the author/date system are that it saves the effort of keeping track of footnote or endnote numbers; it indicates the date of publication to the reader; the details of any one item of literature only have to be written out once; and it results in a tidy, alphabetical list of references at the end of the document.

Footnote or endnote system

Basic features

The *footnote* style involves the use of numbered references in the text and a list of corresponding numbered references at the foot of the page, at the end of each chapter or at the end of the report or book. The term footnote originates from the time when the notes were invariably printed at the foot of each page – and this can be seen in older books. However, printing footnotes at the bottom of the page came to be viewed as too complex to organise and too expensive to set up for printing, so it was generally abandoned in favour of providing a list of notes at the end of each chapter or at the end of the book. Consequently *endnotes* are now more common. Ironically, the advent of word-processing has meant that the placing of footnotes at the bottom of the page can now be done automatically by computer. Most word-processing packages offer this feature, automatically making space for the appropriate number of footnotes on each page and keeping track of their numbering and so on. Publishers have, however, generally adhered to the practice of placing the notes all together at the end of the chapter or book.

The actual number reference in the text can be given in brackets (1) or as a superscript: [1]. Using the footnote system, the paragraph given above appears as follows:

Research on women and leisure in the 1970s and 1980s included Deem's[1] work in Britain, Bella's[2] work in Canada, Bialeschki and Henderson's[3] work in the United States and Anderson's[4] work in Australia.

The list of notes at the end of the report appear in the numerical order in which they appear in the text:

Notes
1. Deem, R. (1986) *All Work and No Play? The Sociology of Women's Leisure.* Milton Keynes: Open University Press.
2. Bella, L. (1989) Women and leisure: beyond androcentrism. In E.L. Jackson and T.L. Burton (eds) *Understanding Leisure and Recreation.* State College, PA: Venture, 151–80.
3. Bialeschki, M.D. and Henderson, K. (1986) Leisure in the common world of women. *Leisure Studies*, 5(3), 299–308.
4. Anderson, R. (1975) *Leisure: An Inappropriate Concept for Women?* Canberra: AGPS.

It can be seen that this format is less obtrusive in the text than the author/date system. In fact it can be made even less obtrusive by using only one footnote, as follows:

Research on women and leisure in the 1970s and 1980s included work by researchers in Britain, Canada, the United States and Australia.[1]

At the end of the report the reference list then appears as follows:

Notes
1. In Britain: Deem, R. (1986) *All Work and No Play? The Sociology of Women's Leisure.* Milton Keynes: Open University Press.

   In Canada: Bella, L. (1989) Women and leisure: beyond androcentrism. In E.L. Jackson and T.L. Burton (eds) *Understanding Leisure and Recreation.* State College, PA.: Venture, 151–80.

   In the USA: Bialeschki, M.D. and Henderson, K. (1986) Leisure in the common world of women. *Leisure Studies*, 5(3), 299–308.

   In Australia: Anderson, R. (1975) *Leisure: An Inappropriate Concept for Women?* Canberra: AGPS.

Multiple references

It should never be necessary to write a reference out in full more than once in a document. Additional references to a work already cited can be made using *op. cit.* or references back to previous footnotes. For example, the above paragraph of text might be followed by:

Deem pioneered the study of women and leisure in Britain.[2]

The footnote would then say:

2. Deem, *op. cit.*   OR   2. See footnote 1.

Specifics, quotations

Page references for specific references or quotations are given in the footnote rather than the text. So the Iso-Ahola quotation given above would look like this:

> Iso-Ahola makes the point that: 'To survive as an academic field, scholars must supply evidence to the effect that their methods of investigation are valid and reliable rather than 'soft'.[4]

The footnote would then say:

> 4. Iso-Ahola, S.E. (1980) Tools of social psychological inquiry. Chapter 3 of *The Social Psychology of Leisure and Recreation*, Dubuque, IA: Wm. C. Brown, p. 49.

Further quotations from the same work might have footnotes as follows:

> 5. Iso-Ahola, *op. cit.* p. 167.

Advantages and disadvantages of the footnote/endnote system

One of the advantages of the footnote system is that it is less obtrusive than the author/date system and it can accommodate authors' notes in addition to references to the literature, as discussed above. A disadvantage of the system is that it does not result in a tidy, alphabetical list of references. This diminishes the convenience of the report as a source of literature references for the reader. Some writers therefore resort to producing a bibliography in addition to the list of references. This results in extra work, since it means that references have to be written out a second time (but see 'Comparing two systems' below). Keeping track of footnotes or endnotes and their numbering is much less of a disadvantage than it used to be, since this can now be taken care of by the computer.

Comparing two systems

The features, advantages and disadvantages of the two systems, author/date and footnote/endnote, are summarised in Figure 5.9.

One way of combining the advantages of both systems is for the list of notes in a footnote/endnote system to consist of author/date references and then to provide an alphabetical list of references at the end of the report. So the list of footnotes for the above paragraph would then appear as follows:

Notes
1. Deem, 1986.
2. Bella, 1989.
3. Bialeschki and Henderson, 1986.
4. Anderson, 1975.

Feature	Harvard/Author-date	Footnote/Endnote
Reference in text	Author (date)	Number, e.g.:[1]
Reference format	Author (date) *Title*. Publishing details.	1. Author *Title*. Publishing details, date
Reference list format	Alphabetical list at end of report	Numbered list at: – foot of pages, or – end of chapters, or – end of report
Advantages	– alphabetical bibliography – easy to use – date of publication conveyed in text	– unobtrusive in text – can add other notes/comments
Disadvantages	– obtrusive in text – can't add notes	– can be difficult to use without computer – no alphabetical bibliography

Figure 5.9 Reference systems: features, advantages and disadvantages

An alphabetical bibliography would then follow which would be the same as for the author/date system. This approach is particularly useful when making several references to the same document.

Referencing issues

Secondhand references

Occasionally you make a reference to an item which you yourself have not read directly, but which is referred to in another document which you have read. This can be called a *secondhand* reference. It is misleading, somewhat unethical, and dangerous, to give a full reference to the original if you have not read it directly yourself. The reference should be given to the secondhand source, *not* to the original. For example:

> Kerlinger characterises research as 'systematic, controlled, empirical, and critical investigation of hypothetical propositions about the presumed relations among natural phenomena'.
> (quoted in Iso-Ahola, 1980, p. 48)

In this instance the writer has not read Kerlinger in the original but is relying on Iso-Ahola's quotation from Kerlinger. The Kerlinger item is not listed in the references; only the Iso-Ahola reference is listed. It is ethical to treat the secondhand reference this way and it is also safe, since any inaccuracy in the quotation then rests with the secondhand source.

In academic research reports – journal articles and theses – secondhand references should be avoided and every effort made to access and refer to the original source.

Excessive referencing

A certain amount of judgement must be used when a large number of references is being made to a single source. It becomes very tiresome when repeated reference is made to the same source on every other line of a report! One way to avoid this is to be very 'up-front' about the fact that a large section of your literature review is based on a single source. For example, if you are summarising MacCannell's work on tourism, rather than have large numbers of formal references to MacCannell cluttering up the text, it may be preferable to create a separate section of the report and announce it as follows:

> *The Work of MacCannell*
> This section of the review summarises MacCannell's (1976) seminal work, *The Tourist: A New Theory of the Leisure Class* . . .

Subsequently, formal references need only be given when using specific quotations.

Latin abbreviations

A number of Latin abbreviations are used in referencing.

et al.   If there are more than two authors of a work, the first author's name and *et al.* may be used in text references, but all authors should be listed in the bibliography: *et al.* stands for the Latin *et alia*, meaning 'and the others', and is generally presented in italic.

op. cit.   stands for the Latin *opere citato*, meaning 'in the work cited'.

ibid.   In the footnote system, if reference is made to the same work in consecutive footnotes, the abbreviation *ibid.* is sometimes used, short for *ibidem*, meaning 'the same'.

Summary

This chapter provides an overview of the process of reviewing the literature, as a research tool in its own right and as an essential element of any research project. It is noted that a literature review can have a number of purposes and can take a number of forms, ranging from being the entire basis of a research project to being the source of ideas and methods for conducting a research project. The mechanics of searching for relevant literature is examined, including library catalogues, published bibliographies and indexes and electronic sources. The process of reviewing the literature is examined, addressing the sorts of questions which should be asked when conducting such a review for research purposes. Finally, the chapter reviews the process of referencing the literature, examining the characteristics and advantages and disadvantages of the author/date or 'Harvard' system and the footnote or endnote system.

Test questions

1. What are the potential uses of the literature review in research?

2. Name three different sources of bibliographical information and their advantages and limitations.

3. What is the difference between conducting a literature review for the purpose of writing an essay compared with providing the context for a research project?

4. What are the advantages and disadvantages of the author/date referencing system compared with the footnote/endnote system?

5. What is a 'secondhand' reference?

Exercises

1. Compile an *inclusive* bibliography on a topic of your choice, using the sources outlined in this chapter.

2. Choose a research topic and:
   a. investigate the literature using a library computerised catalogue and any other electronic database available to you;
   b. explore the literature via literary sources, such as reference lists and indexes in general textbooks, journal contents and lists of references in articles;
   c. compare the nature and extent of the bibliography arising from the two sources.

Further reading

Examples of bibliographies:
An early example on the sociology of leisure: Meyersohn (1958)
On tourism generally: Baretje (1964); Goeldner (1994)
On tourism and travel research: Goeldner and Dicke (1980)
On recreational use of beaches: Veal (1997)
On the Olympic Games: Mallon (1984); Veal and Toohey (2003)
On leisure, sport and ethnicity: Geary et al. (1996)
On disability and tourism: Darcy (1998)
On urban parks: Veal (2004)
On education, training and professional development in leisure: Veal (2003a)

Evaluative literature reviews:
On the concept of lifestyle: Veal (1993a, 2000)
On tourism forecasting: Calantone et al. (1987)

Meta-analysis:
Generally: Glass et al. (1981)
On international tourism demand: Crouch and Shaw (1991)
On contingent valuation (willingness-to-pay) and the arts: Noonan (2003)
On contingent valuation (willingness-to-pay) and outdoor recreation economic values: Shrestha and Loomis (2003)

Style manuals:

- American Psychological Association (APA) (1983) and www.apastyle.org; AGPS style manual: Snooks & Co. (2002)
- Electronic style manual: Walker & Taylor (1998); APA guidelines at: www.apastyle.org/elecref.html

Appendix 5.1 On-line Leisure and Tourism Bibliographies

University of Technology, Sydney, School of Leisure, Sport and Tourism

Website: www.business.uts.edu.au/lst/research/bibliographies.html

Bibliographies
1. Recreational Use of Beaches
2. The Olympic Games
3. History of Leisure in Australia
4. Gambling in Australia
5. Arts Policy, Participation, Management & Economics
6. Leisure, Sport and Ethnicity
7. People with a Disability and Tourism
8. Lifestyle and Leisure
9. Urban Parks and Open Space Planning and Management
10. Education, Training and Professional Development in Leisure

University of Connecticut – Playlab

Website: http://playlab.uconn.edu/frl.htm

Bibliographies
1. Leisure/Tourism Motivation
2. Video Games
3. Tourist Roles
4. Sport & Education
5. Youth and Sport
6. Martial Arts
7. Tourism Marketing/Market Research
8. Economics of Sport
9. Sport Law
10. Leadership in Sport
11. Sport and Gender
12. Sport and Ideology
13. Sport Counseling
14. Sport Subcultures

15. Economic Impacts of Tourism and Sport
16. Life Satisfaction
17. Anthropology of Play/Sport
18. Ecotourism
19. Sport Violence/Aggression
20. Sociocultural Impacts of Tourism
21. Learned Helplessness in Leis/Sport
22. Deviance in Sport
23. Sport and the Media
24. Sport Marketing
25. Sport Tourism I
26. Sport and Religion/Ritual
27. Judo
28. Psychosocial Benefits of Sport/Exercise
29. Sport Tourism II
30. Concepts of Leisure
31. Leisure Education/Counselling
32. Corporate Fitness
33. Motivation and Sport Participation
34. Sport Promotion
35. Gender Issues in Sport
36. Tourism in Greece
37. Sport and Ethnic Minorities in Britain
38. Information Technology in Tourism & Hospitality
39. Sport Sponsorship
40. Tourism in the Middle East
41. Tourism/Hospitality Sources (comprehensive)
42. Tourism Forecasting/Time Series Analysis
43. Sport/Exercise and Mood I
44. Labor Relations in Sport
45. Sport and Politics
46. Sport and Title IX
47. Leisure Satisfaction
48. Leisure Attitudes
49. Sport and Drugs
50. Sport and Gender Preference
51. Sport and the Olympics (a)
52. Forecasting in Sport and Leisure
53. The Fan in Sport
54. Repeat Visitors To Tourist Destinations
55. Comprehensive Tourism Page from Greece
56. Sport and the Olympics (b)
57. Sport and Commercialization
58. Anxiety and Performance in Sport

59. Sport Management Strategy
60. Sport & Finance
61. Sport and Drugs II
62. Sport and Gender II
63. Sport & Finance II
64. Therapeutic Recreational Service
65. Physical Activity and Health
66. Tourism/Casino Development Impacts
67. Influence of Attitude/Behavior and Participation in Sports, Leisure and Exercise
68. Sport, Exercise and Mood II

International Centre for Research and Study on Tourism (CIRET), Aix-en-Provence, France

Website: www.ciret-tourism.com

Bibliographies
Access to the large general tourism bibliography and the specialist bibliographies listed here is subject to a fee.

1. Ecotourism, March 1997, 143pp., €30
2. Alternative-sustainable Tourism. March 1997, 144pp., €30
3. Urban Tourism, 153pp., €32
4. Tourism and History, 167pp., €35
5. Tourism in Australia, 188pp., €40
6. Tourism in Japan, 50pp., €12
7. Tourism and Life Cycle, 70pp., €16
8. Tourism, Ethnic Groups, Aborigines, 81pp., €18
9. Tourism and Ethics, 54pp., €12
10. Senior Tourism, 137pp., €30
11. Tourism, Leisure and Family, 39pp., €11,000
12. Tourism in the Himalayas, the Hindu-kush and the Karakorum, 145pp., €30
13. Woman, Leisure, Sport and Tourism, 58pp., €12
14. Tourism and Museums, 75pp., €17

6 Secondary data: sources and analysis

Introduction

In this chapter consideration is given to the use of existing sources of data, as opposed to the collection of new data which is the subject of most of the rest of the book. The chapter examines mainly published statistical sources, such as the census and national leisure and tourism participation surveys, but other sources, such as archives and management data are also included.

In undertaking research it is clearly wise to use existing information where possible, rather than embarking on expensive and time-consuming new information collection exercises. One aspect of this has already been touched on in Chapter 5 in relation to the use of the literature. In searching the literature the researcher may come across references to statistical or other data which may not have been fully analysed or exploited by the original collectors of the data, because of their particular interests or limitations on time or money. Or data may be available which are open to alternative analyses and interpretations. In other cases information may exist which was not originally collected for research purposes – for example the administrative records of a leisure or tourism organisation – but which can provide the basis for research.

Primary data are new data specifically collected in a research project – the researcher is the *primary user* of such data. *Secondary* data already exist and were collected for some other (primary) purpose but which can be used a second time in the current project – the researcher is the *secondary user*. Further analysis of such data is referred to as *secondary analysis*.

As with the literature, secondary data can play a variety of roles in a research project, from being the whole basis of the research to being a vital or incidental point of comparison. Some advantages and disadvantages of using secondary data are listed in Figure 6.1.

A considerable amount of leisure and tourism data is collected on a regular basis at considerable cost, particularly by government agencies. Often the immediate policy requirements of the data are quite limited – for example to announce a global figure on tourism numbers or numbers of participants in sport. In a sector where research funds are limited, it would seem unwise for the research community to waste such resources by failing to extract all possible research potential from them. This requires careful consideration of ways in which available data might be used, and often calls

Figure 6.1
Advantages and
disadvantages of
using secondary
data sources

Advantages

■ *Timing* – data may be instantly available.
■ *Cost* – cost of collecting new data avoided.
■ *Experience* – the 'trial and error' experience of those who collected the original data can be exploited.
■ *Scale* – secondary data may be based on larger samples than would otherwise be possible.
■ *Serendipity* – inductive process of data analysis may yield serendipitous findings, which may not have arisen with primary, purpose-designed data collection.

Disadvantages

■ *Design* – secondary data has been designed for another purpose, so may not be ideal for current project.
■ *Analysis limitations* – if access to the raw data for re-analysis is not possible, opportunities for analysis/manipulation of the data for the current project may be limited.

for a quasi-inductive approach to research, posing the question: what can these data tell us?

Six main sources of secondary data are listed in Figure 6.2 and examined in turn in this chapter. Where appropriate, reference is made to examples in Britain and Australia. At the end of the chapter a number of case studies are presented to demonstrate the use of such data in planning and management in the field of leisure and tourism.

National leisure participation surveys

The national leisure survey phenomenon

In most developed countries surveys of leisure participation are conducted by government departments or agencies on a regular basis. In the USA such surveys have been conducted since the early 1960s, particularly on outdoor recreation (Cordell *et al.*, 2005). Other countries began collecting leisure participation data in the 1970s and 1980s – the volume edited by Cushman *et al.* (2005a) includes data from fifteen countries.

■ In Britain the *General Household Survey* (GHS), commissioned by government agencies and conducted by the Office for National Statistics and its predecessors, has provided leisure participation information every 3–5 years since 1973 (Gratton and Veal, 2005). In later runs of the survey the scope of the leisure questions was

Figure 6.2
Types of
secondary data

■ National leisure participation surveys
■ Tourism surveys
■ Economic surveys
■ The census of population
■ Management data
■ Documentary sources

reduced to cover sport and physical recreation only, so that information on arts participation has been gathered by a separate survey conducted for the Arts Council. Examples of the results from these surveys are shown in Table 6.1.

■ In Australia the Commonwealth government commissioned the first of a series of national *Recreation Participation Surveys* in 1985/86, which was replaced in the 1990s by the *Population Survey Monitor* omnibus surveys conducted by the Australian Bureau of Statistics (ABS) and covering sport and physical recreation only. This was superseded in 2001 by the annual Exercise Recreation and Sport Survey (ERASS) conducted by the Australian Sports Commission and the Standing Council on Recreation and Sport (SCORS) (Veal, 2003b, 2005). More recently the ABS has used its *General Social Survey* omnibus survey to collect data on sport and physical recreation and some arts activities – results from this survey are shown in Table 6.2.

While such surveys have been carried out in a number of countries over the last two decades, each country has adopted different design principles, so that the findings are generally not comparable – for example, differences in the designs of the surveys used in Tables 6.1 and 6.2 mean that the participation levels in Great Britain and Australia cannot be compared. A number of attempts at international comparisons have indicated this problem but little effort has been made to harmonise data collection methods in different countries (Kamphorst and Roberts, 1989; Hantrais and Kamphorst, 1987; Cushman *et al.*, 2005a).

National leisure surveys, and their regional equivalents, are the main source of information available to researchers on overall participation levels in a range of leisure activities. A number of issues arise in the use of these important databases, including

Table 6.1   Leisure participation, Great Britain, 1996/2002

	% of population aged 16+ participating in:		
	A. 4 weeks before interview	B. Year before interview	Ratio of B to A
Home-based leisure, 1996*			
Watching television	99	na	na
Visiting/entertaining friends or relations	96	na	na
Listening to radio	88	na	na
Listening to records/tapes	78	na	na
Reading books	65	na	na
Gardening	48	na	na
Do-it-yourself	42	na	na
Dressmaking/needlework/knitting	22	na	na
Sports and physical activities, 1996*			
Walking (at least 2 miles)	44.5	68.2	1.5
Any swimming	14.8	39.6	2.7
Swimming: indoor	12.8	35.1	2.7
Swimming: outdoor	2.9	14.9	5.1

Table 6.1 (*continued*)

	% of population aged 16+ participating in:		
	A. 4 weeks before interview	B. Year before interview	Ratio of B to A
Keep fit/yoga	12.3	20.7	1.7
Snooker/pool/billiards	11.3	19.2	1.7
Cycling	11.0	21.4	1.9
Weight training	5.6	9.8	1.8
Any soccer	4.8	8.5	1.8
Soccer: outdoor	3.8	6.9	1.8
Soccer: indoor	2.1	4.8	2.3
Golf	4.7	11	2.3
Running/jogging	4.5	8.0	1.8
Darts	–	8.6	na
Ten-pin bowling/skittles	3.4	15.5	4.6
Badminton	2.4	7.0	2.9
Tennis	2.0	7.1	3.6
Any bowls	1.9	4.6	2.4
Carpet bowls	1.1	3.0	2.7
Lawn bowls	0.9	2.8	3.1
Fishing	1.7	5.3	3.1
Table tennis	1.5	5.3	3.5
Squash	1.3	4.1	3.2
Weight lifting	1.3	2.6	2.0
Horse riding	1.0	3.0	3.0
Cricket	0.9	3.3	3.7
Shooting	0.8	2.8	3.5
Self-defence	0.7	1.7	2.4
Climbing	0.7	2.5	3.6
Basketball	0.7	2.0	2.9
Rugby	0.6	1.3	2.2
Ice skating	0.6	3.2	5.3
Netball	0.5	1.4	2.8
Sailing	0.4	2.3	5.7
Motor sports	0.4	1.6	4.0
Canoeing	0.4	1.6	4.0
Hockey	0.3	1.1	3.7
Skiing	0.3	2.6	8.7
Athletics – track & field	0.2	1.2	6.0
Gymnastics	0.2	0.7	3.5
Windsurfing/boardsailing	0.2	1.1	5.5
At least 1 activity (excl. walking)	45.6	65.9	1.4
At least 1 activity	63.6	81.4	1.3
Attendance at cultural events, England, 2001**			
Film at a cinema or other venue	19	55	2.9
Play or drama	5	27	5.4
Carnival, street arts or circus	4	23	5.8
Art, photography or sculpture exhibition	6	19	3.2
Craft exhibition	4	17	4.3

Table 6.1 (*continued*)

	% of population aged 16+ participating in:		
	A. 4 weeks before interview	B. Year before interview	Ratio of B to A
Pantomime	–	13	na
Cultural festival	2	10	5.0
Event connected with books or writing	2	8	4.0
Event including video or electronic art	2	7	3.5
A musical	4	24	6.0
Pop or rock concert	4	18	4.5
Classical music concert	3	10	3.3
Opera or operetta	1	6	6.0
Jazz concert	2	5	2.5
Folk or country & western concert	–	3	na
Other music	–	9	na
All types of live dance performance	–	12	na
Contemporary dance	–	3	na
Ballet	–	2	na
Participation in arts activities, England, 2001**			
Read for pleasure	na	73	na
Buy a novel, fiction, play or poetry for yourself	na	49	na
Write any stories or plays	na	3	na
Write any poetry	na	3	na
Clubbing	na	25	na
Other dance (but not fitness class)	na	8	na
Ballet	na	1	na
Play a musical instrument for own pleasure	na	9	na
Sing to an audience (or rehearse)	na	4	na
Play a musical instrument to an audience (or rehearse)	na	3	na
Write or compose a piece of music	na	2	na
Perform in opera or operetta	na	0	na
Perform or rehearse in a play or drama	na	2	na
Painting, drawing, print making or sculpture	na	14	na
Photography as an artistic activity	na	6	na
Buy any original works of art	na	6	na
Make any films or videos as an artistic activity	na	2	na
Textile crafts such as embroidery, sewing, etc.	na	14	na
Buy any original handmade crafts	na	12	na
Wood crafts	na	6	na
Other crafts (e.g., calligraphy, pottery, jewellery making)	na	4	na
Create original artworks or animation using computer	na	4	na
Help run an arts/cultural event or arts organisation	na	4	na

Sources:
* *General Household Survey* – Office for National Statistics (1997) (Sample size: 15,700)
** Arts in England survey – Skelton *et al.* (2002) (Sample size: 6,042)
na = not available – = number less than 0.05%

Table 6.2 Leisure participation, Australia, 2002

	% of population aged 18+ participating in year prior to interview		% of population aged 18+ participating in year prior to interview
Sport/physical activities*			
Aerobics	10.9	Scuba diving	0.4
Aquarobics	0.3	Shooting sports	0.6
Athletics/track and field	0.2	Soccer (outdoor)	2.6
Australian Rules football	2.1	Soccer (indoor)	0.9
Badminton	0.6	Softball	0.3
Baseball	0.3	Squash/racquetball	1.7
Basketball	2.4	Surf sports	2.0
Billiards/snooker/pool	0.4	Swimming	10.9
Boxing	0.3	Table tennis	0.6
Bush walking	3.2	Tennis	6.8
Canoeing/kayaking	0.5	Tenpin bowling	0.9
Carpet bowls	0.5	Touch football	1.7
Cricket (indoor)	0.9	Triathlon	0.3
Cricket (outdoor)	2.5	Volleyball	1.1
Cross country running	0.5	Walking for exercise	25.3
Cycling	5.7	Waterskiing/powerboating	0.9
Dancing	1.8	Weight training	0.9
Darts	0.3	Yoga	2.1
Fishing	3.5	Sport spectating**	48.2
Golf	7.5		
Hockey (outdoor)	0.5	**Visiting cultural venues/events***	
Horse riding/equestrian		Art galleries	24.9
activities/polo	0.9	Museums	25.0
Ice/snow sports	0.9	Zoological parks and aquariums	40.0
Lawn bowls	1.9	Botanic gardens	41.6
Martial arts	1.5	Libraries	42.1
Motor sports	0.9	Classical music concerts	9.0
Netball	3.1	Popular music concerts	26.4
Rock climbing	0.5	Theatre performances	18.0
Roller sports	0.6	Dance performances	10.9
Rugby union	0.6	Musicals and operas	18.7
Rugby league	0.7	Other performing arts	20.4
Running	4.6	Cinemas	69.9
Sailing	0.7	At least one cultural venue/event	88.2

Source: Australian Bureau of Statistics (ABS) *General Social Survey* (2002a, 2002b, 2002c) (Sample size: 15,500)

* ABS 2003a; ** ABS 2003b; *** ABS 2003c

questions of validity and reliability, sample size, the participation reference period used, the age range of the population covered, the range of activities included, and availability of information on the social characteristics of respondents. These topics are discussed in turn below.

Validity and reliability

National leisure surveys suffer from the limitation of all interview surveys in that they are dependent on respondents' own reports of their patterns of leisure participation. How sure can we be, therefore, that the resultant data are accurate? We cannot be absolutely sure, as discussed in Chapter 9, however, a number of features of national surveys such as those discussed here lend credence to their reliability and value as sources of data:

1. national government statistical organisations have an enviable reputation for quality and professionalism in their work;
2. the surveys are often based on large sample sizes;
3. the fact that there has been little dramatic variation in the findings of the various surveys over the years is reassuring (Gratton and Tice, 1994; Gratton and Veal, 2005) – erratic and unexplainable fluctuations in reported levels of participation would have led to suspicions that the surveys were unreliable, but this has not happened.

Some commentators have questioned the validity of participation surveys, conducting experiments which show that there is a tendency for respondents to exaggerate levels of participation substantially, at least in relation to some activities (Chase and Godbey, 1983; Chase and Harada, 1984). However, as Boothby (1987) suggests, some of the defects of surveys can be overcome by attention to certain aspects of design.

Sample size

It is generally the case that the larger the sample size the more reliable and precise are the survey findings. The surveys discussed here are based on samples of around 15,000 interviews. These surveys are therefore large and subject to only minimal 'statistical error' – a term explained in Chapter 10.

Main question – participation reference period

The main question respondents have traditionally been asked in the British GHS is what leisure activities they have engaged in during their leisure time *in the previous four weeks*. Four weeks is the participation 'reference period'. As shown in Table 6.1, in 1996, for most activities, the survey also included a question on participation in the previous year, as did the 2001 'Arts in England' survey. Table 6.1 includes the ratio of the one year to the 4-week figures. It can be seen that for most sports, the ratio is between 1.5 and 3, that is, between one and a half and three times as many people take part in these activities in the course of a year as take part in an average month. For sporting activities which are likely to be holiday-based for most people (e.g. skiing, windsurfing, sailing, swimming outdoors), the ratios are higher. The ratios are also generally higher for cultural events. Thus the choice of reference period affects the level of participation recorded, but it affects different activities differently.

Early Australian surveys used a reference period of just two weeks (Darcy, 1994; Veal, 2003b, 2005), but recent surveys have used only the one year reference period, as shown in Table 6.2. This is becoming the international norm (Cushman *et al.*, 2005b: 284). This practice has the advantage of covering participation in all seasons of the year in one survey and including a larger proportion of the infrequent participants. However, it has the disadvantage of introducing possible errors in respondents' recall of their activities over such a long time-period. Use of the four-week reference period has the advantage of likely increased accuracy, but the disadvantage that seasonal variation must be covered by interviewing at different times of the year.

As a result of this methodological issue, it is important to note that leisure participation surveys do not indicate the total number of people who take part in an activity, but rather the number that take part in a *specified time-period*. This illustrates an important point about survey data in general: the meaning of information and the uses to which it can be put depend vitally on the way the data are collected. Abuse of this feature has resulted in the popularity of the cynical phrase, 'lies, damned lies and statistics', but the essence of a professional and ethical approach to research is to work at understanding the basis of data as fully as possible and present the results as clearly and truthfully as possible.

Age range

Participation surveys are restricted in terms of age range covered. Some include respondents as young as 12 years old, while some cover only those aged 18 and over. And some have upper age limits. The British surveys presented here cover people aged 16 and over, while the Australian survey covers people aged 18 and over. The reasons for not interviewing young children are three-fold. First, it may be difficult to obtain accurate information from very young children; second, it may be considered ethically unacceptable to subject children to the sort of questioning which adults can freely choose to face or not. Third, there is a question as to when children are considered to engage in their own independent leisure activities as opposed to being under the control of parents. Some surveys present data on children from 'proxy' interviews, in which questions about children's activities are answered by parents: an example is the Australian Bureau of Statistics (2000a) survey of children's participation in culture and leisure activities.

The lower age limit has effects on the results, in that for some activities – for example swimming or cycling – young teenagers may be a significant proportion of total participants. For other activities – for example gardening or going to the opera – the age limit may be inconsequential because young people are not among the most frequent participants. When using data from leisure participation surveys, particularly when seeking to compare results from different surveys, it is therefore important to bear in mind the age range covered.

Individual activities and sample size limitations

The leisure surveys reported in Tables 6.1 and 6.2 cover a wide range of home-based, indoor, outdoor, sporting and cultural activities. As can be seen, for many activities, the proportion of the population participating is small – often 1 per cent or less. However, even 1 per cent of the adult population of Britain is almost half a million people, so small percentages can represent large numbers of people. Although the sample size of the surveys is large, the small percentages produce correspondingly small sub-samples of participants – often only 20 or 30 respondents – so the scope for detailed analysis of participants in individual activities is limited. A further limitation of the sample size is that there are limits on the extent to which the surveys can be sub-divided to give detailed results for regions of the country.

Social characteristics

In addition to the basic information on participation, national leisure surveys generally include a wide range of background information on the people interviewed, including such variables as gender, occupation, age, education level reached, size of family or household unit and country of birth. This information can be used to examine levels of participation by different social groups from either an equity or a marketing point of view, and can also be used to predict demand, as future changes in the underlying social structure of the community affect patterns of demand; this is explored in Case study 6.1.

The importance of participation surveys

Leisure participation surveys, despite their limitations, are the main source of information, not only on overall levels of participation but also on differences in participation between different groups in the community, such as the young and the old, men and women, and different occupational groups. Any leisure researcher or professional should therefore be fully familiar with such key data sources.

Tourism surveys

Detailed data on domestic and international tourists are also obtained by means of interview surveys. In the case of *international* tourism, however, certain data are also available from government international arrivals and departures statistics, which are collected by immigration authorities at ports of entry. The advantage of this latter source of information is that it lends itself to a certain degree of international comparison, a task which is undertaken by the Organisation for Economic Cooperation and Development (OECD) and the World Tourism Organisation (OECD, annual; World Tourism Organisation, annual). However, the information on each traveller is limited, so recourse must also be had to surveys for much of the data on international tourists.

In Britain the main source of information on domestic tourism is the *UK Tourism Survey*, commissioned each year since 1971 by Tourism England. This is a home-based survey with a substantial monthly sample size, which records origins and destinations of trips with at least one overnight stay in the previous two months. A similar survey, the *National Visitor Survey*, is conducted in Australia, under the auspices of the government agency, Tourism Research Australia. Tables 6.3 and 6.4 indicate the sort of data available from these surveys. As with leisure surveys, a considerable amount of additional information is available from each survey, including regions visited, type of accommodation used, levels of expenditure and socio-demographic characteristics.

Information on overseas visitors to Britain and British trips overseas is collected via the *International Passenger Survey*, conducted each year by the Office for National Statistics. It records such information as destinations, length of trip, levels of

Table 6.3 Domestic tourism, UK, 2003

Trips by UK residents within UK	
No. of trips	151.0 millions
No. of nights	490.5 millions
Spending	£26,482 millions
Purpose of trip	%
Holiday, pleasure/leisure	46.7
Visiting friends and relatives, mainly as holiday	13.6
Business	14.8
Other VFR	22.7
Other	2.2
Length of holiday trips	%
1–3 nights	63.0
4–7 nights	28.7
8+ nights	8.2

Source: StarUK, 2003 (Sample size: 50,000)

Table 6.4 Domestic tourism, Australia, 2001

Trips by Australian residents within Australia	
No. of trips	74.6 millions
No. of nights	289.6 millions
Spending	A$38,262 millions
Purpose of trip	%
Holiday/leisure	43.1
Visiting friends and relatives	32.2
Business	20.1
Other	4.6

Source: Bureau of Tourism Research, 2002 (Sample size: 70,000)

Table 6.5 International tourism, UK, 2003

Country of residence	Arrivals, by purpose of journey					Nights spent in UK per visitor
	Holiday	VFR*	Business	Misc.	Total** '000s	Average
N. America						
Canada	199	307	78	68	652	11.3
USA	1,365	864	725	391	3,346	8.4
EU Europe						
France	1,048	774	1,007	245	3,073	4.5
Germany	810	625	934	241	2,611	5.9
Irish Republic	537	1,019	534	398	2,488	3.9
Netherlands	520	362	556	110	1,549	4.5
Spain	307	449	338	112	1,206	9.1
Italy	379	219	399	172	1,168	6.9
Belgium	317	192	337	90	936	2.8
Sweden	173	143	174	43	533	5.8
Other EU Europe	363	319	407	134	1,223	6.2
Non-EU Europe						
Switzerland	163	151	195	55	564	6.2
Other non-EU Europe	508	408	619	321	1,856	12.3
Rest of the world						
Australia	304	285	57	76	723	18.1
Other	980	862	607	340	2,788	18.0
Total	7,973	6,978	6,967	2,797	24,715	8.2

Source: Office for National Statistics (2004a). (Sample size: 251,000) Individual countries with total visits > 500,000 listed here
* VFR = Visiting friends and relatives; ** individual countries

expenditure and places and attractions visited. The equivalent Australian survey is the *International Visitor Survey*. Information from these surveys is shown in Tables 6.5 and 6.6.

As with leisure surveys, the data on tourist trips is influenced by the definition of 'tourist' and the reference time-periods used. Most definitions of tourism require a person to stay away from their normal place of residence for at least one night and travel a certain minimum distance to qualify as a tourist. This means that people who take a trip from London to Southend or Brighton, but do not stay overnight, are not classified as tourists, but as day-trippers. Even people travelling across international borders – such as those taking day-trips across the English Channel – are not tourists by this definition. Comprehensive data on border crossings are no longer collected in Europe because of the sheer volume of such crossings and the increasing liberalisation of travel regulations. Thus, while they are collected by governments and their agencies for official purposes, the 'hard' data on tourism flows are, in reality, every bit as 'soft' as the data on leisure participation (Edwards, 1991).

Table 6.6 International tourism, Australia, 2003–04

Country of residence	Arrivals, by Purpose of journey					Nights spent in Australia per visitor
	Holiday	VFR*	Business	Education	Total** '000s	Average
New Zealand	375.1	234.2	180.5	5.3	838	13
Japan	518.8	33.1	42.9	30.4	646	17
Hong Kong	56.0	31.7	17.9	12.0	120	30
Singapore	118.9	30.8	40.7	17.3	219	20
Malaysia	87.3	29.6	16.1	16.4	154	28
Indonesia	34.8	14.0	10.4	16.7	81	45
Taiwan	70.8	10.2	6.6	6.8	96	21
Thailand	33.3	10.8	14.4	12.0	72	34
Korea	133.9	19.2	21.0	18.9	197	29
China	89.6	24.0	60.5	28.1	208	41
Other Asia	33.5	28.3	24.4	14.3	118	37
USA	162.4	75.2	93.2	37.4	403	25
Canada	42.1	26.9	13.1	2.5	89	35
UK	332.2	220.9	47.9	5.8	645	41
Germany	89.0	18.0	13.6	11.0	137	46
Other Europe	210.1	80.6	49.0	36.1	401	42
Other	100.4	63.8	40.1	14.8	252	31
Total	2,488.1	951.1	692.5	285.8	4,675	28

Source: Tourism Australia (2004). (Sample size 19,800) data relate to year ended June 2004
* VFR = Visiting friends and relatives. Individual purpose numbers do not add to total because for some visitors, purpose was not recorded; ** individual countries

Economic surveys

In most developed countries surveys of *household expenditure* are conducted on a regular basis. In Britain this survey is an annual one and is called the *Expenditure and Food Survey*, while the Australian equivalent, the *Household Expenditure Survey*, is conducted every five years. These surveys collect information from a cross-section of families throughout their respective countries on their weekly expenditure on scores of items, many of which relate to leisure and tourism. Table 6.7 presents data related to leisure and tourism which have been abstracted from the latest surveys (2003 for the UK and 2003/04 for Australia) and converted into annual expenditure figures. Such data exclude a significant, but not separately identified, component of leisure-related expenditure, such as leisure clothing and some aspects of expenditure on housing and food. Although the data categories between the two countries are not strictly comparable, they both indicate that leisure accounts for about a quarter of all household expenditure.

The other form of available economic data relates to employment in the leisure and tourism industries. Data are available from national statistical agencies on employment in a number of leisure and tourism industry sectors – for example, in the UK in the Office National Statistics (Annual (a)), and in Australia in ABS (2004).

Table 6.7   Household leisure expenditure

Expenditure item	UK 2002–03 £ per annum	Aust. 2003–04 $A per annum
Alcoholic drink	307	1,213
Tobacco	281	601
Audio-visual, photographic, computer equipment	426	1,150
Games, toys, hobbies	114	122
Computer software and games	57	70
Sporting, camping, outdoor recreation equipment	42	553
Gardening equipment, plants	156	273
Pets, pet food	151	477
Sports admissions, subscriptions, fees	291	341
Cinema, theatre, museums etc.	83	230
TV, video, Internet rental, subs	250	49
Miscellaneous entertainment	52	519
Photographic	26	142
Gambling (net)	192	285
Newspapers, magazines, books, stationery	343	438
Package holidays – domestic	47	1,074
Holiday accommodation – domestic	130	
Package holidays – abroad	608	731
Holiday accommodation – abroad	125	
Holiday spending	333	*
Restaurant & café meals	588	987
Leisure transport**	924	2,173
Total	5,526	11,428
Total household expenditure	21,122	39,614
% Leisure	26.1	23.6

Source: Derived from: UK: 2002–2003 Expenditure and Food Survey (ONS, 2004b: 42–47); Australia: Household Expenditure Survey, 2003-04 (ABS,2005).

* Not separately listed.

These economic data sources provide the basis for the regular leisure expenditure forecasting and market trend analysis reports produced by such organisations as the *Henley Centre for Forecasting* (Henley Centre for Forecasting, quarterly).

The population census

And it came to pass in those days, that there went out a decree from Caesar Augustus, that all the world should be taxed . . . And all went to be taxed, every one into his own city.

(Luke, 2: 1–3)

This quotation from the Bible indicates that the taking of a census of the whole population, for taxation and other purposes, is a long-standing practice of governments. Another well-known historical example is the *Domesday Book*, compiled by William the Conqueror for the whole of England in the eleventh century.

The *population census* is an important source of information and any aspiring recreation or tourism manager should be fully aware of its content and its potential. A complete census of the population is taken in Britain by the Office for National Statistics every ten years; the latest was 2001, and before that 1991, 1981 and so on. In Australia, because the population is growing relatively rapidly, the Australian Bureau of Statistics undertakes a census every five years. As in most countries, it is a statutory requirement for householders (and hoteliers, hospital managers, boarding school principals and prison governors) to fill out a census form on 'census night', indicating the number of people, including visitors, in the building, and their age, gender, occupation and so on. Some people escape the net, for instance people sleeping rough or illegal immigrants, but generally the information is believed to be reliable and comprehensive.

Data from the census are available at a number of levels, from national down to the level of Census Collection Districts (CCDs) or Enumeration Districts (EDs), as indicated in Figure 6.3. CCDs are small areas, with populations of around 250 to 500, which a single census collection officer deals with on census night. By adding together data from a few CCDs, a leisure facility manager can obtain data on the demographic characteristics of the population of the catchment area of the facility. An enormous amount of information is available on each of these areas, as listed in Figure 6.4.

It can be seen that none of the census information, with the possible exception of working hours, is concerned directly with leisure or tourism. So why should the census be of interest to the leisure or tourism researcher? Four typical uses can be envisaged.

1. Planning facilities and conducting feasibility studies

As is demonstrated in Case study 6.1, census data can be invaluable when planning new facilities or conducting feasibility studies since, along with other types of data, they provide the basis for estimating likely demand.

2. Area management/marketing

Many managers in the leisure and tourism industries have responsibility for a particular geographical area, whether that be a whole country, a region, a local government area or the catchment area of a particular facility or service. One of the cardinal rules

Figure 6.3
Census data: levels of availability

Britain	Australia
National	National
Regions	State
Counties	Postal codes
Local government areas	Local government areas
Parliamentary constituencies	State and federal Parliament electorates
Enumeration districts (EDs)	Census Collection districts (CCDs)

Figure 6.4
Census data
available

Resident population

■ Number of males/females
■ Number/proportion in 5-year age-groups (and single years for under 20s)
■ Numbers of people:
  – with different religions
  – by country of birth
  – speaking different languages
  – by country of birth of parents
■ Numbers of families/households:
  – of different sizes
  – with different numbers of dependent children
  – which are single parent families
  – with various numbers of vehicles
■ Numbers of people:
  – who left school at various ages
  – with different educational/technical qualifications
  – in different occupational groups
  – by working hours
  – unemployed
  – living in different types of dwelling

for the manager/marketer is to 'know your market or customer'. This applies as much in public sector agencies as in commercial organisations. The census provides valuable information about the numbers and characteristics of customers, or potential customers, in a geographical area. The census can be used to produce a 'profile' of an area, so that the manager has an overall view of the nature of the community being served. This might apply to the catchment area of a leisure facility or the areas from which a tourism destination draws its visitors. Nearly all the items of information listed in Figure 6.4 can be relevant to such a community profile or market profile.

3. Performance evaluation

The census can place a particular leisure or tourism operation into demographic perspective. For example, if a facility or enterprise is intended to serve a particular geographical area and is aimed at teenagers, the census will indicate how many teenagers live in that area. If, for example, 5,000 teenagers live in an area and the facility has 500 teenage customers then it is reaching 10 per cent of the potential market. This may be good or bad, depending on the level of competition and how specialised the product or service is.

4. Market segmentation

More sophisticated uses of the census involve analysing a large range of data by computer in order to classify geographical areas into 'types'. Residential areas can be classified, for example, into retirement areas, working-class family areas, affluent areas, and so on. In Britain, a system called 'ACORN' (A Classification Of Residential Neighbourhoods) has been developed to do this classification and it has been found that residents of different area 'types' have markedly different leisure participation patterns (Shaw, 1984; Williams *et al.*, 1988; Veal, 1993c). This is related to the ideas of *lifestyle* and *psychographics*, as referred to in Chapter 2.

Management data

Most leisure and tourism organisations generate routine data which can be of use for research purposes and many have *management information systems* specifically designed to produce data upon which assessments of the performance of the organisation can be based. Examples of such data, which may be available on an hourly, daily, weekly, monthly, seasonal or annual basis, are listed in Figure 6.5. It is usually advisable to explore fully the nature, extent and availability of such data, and their potential utilisation, before embarking on fresh data collection. For example, in Case study 3.1 in Chapter 3, the manager of a facility is concerned about declining levels of visits. Before initiating expensive procedures, such as surveys, to investigate the causes it would be advisable to study the *available visitor data* to see whether the decline was across all services, and whether it was taking place at all times or only at certain times of the day, week, season or year.

Figure 6.5
Management
data

- Visitor numbers (in various categories)
- Visitor expenditure/income (in various categories)
- Bookings and facility utilisation
- Customer enquiries
- Membership numbers and details
- Customer complaints
- Results of visitor/customer surveys
- Expenditure of the organisation (under various headings)
- Staff turnover/absenteeism, etc.

Documentary sources

Documentary sources lie somewhere between literature and management data as an information source for research. Typical examples are listed in Figure 6.6. Many of these sources are important for historical research, either for a primarily historical research project, or as background for a project with a contemporary focus. In some cases the documents are a focus of research in their own right – for example, some research on women and sport has examined the coverage of women's sport in the media (e.g. Rowe and Brown, 1994). As the links between cultural and media studies and leisure and tourism studies increase, so analysis of media content, including

Figure 6.6
Documentary
sources

- Minutes of committee/council/board meetings
- Correspondence of an organisation or an individual
- Archives (may include both of the above and other papers)
- Popular literature, such as novels, magazines
- Newspapers, particularly coverage of specific topics and/or particular aspects, such as editorials, advertising or correspondence columns
- Brochures and advertising material
- Diaries

television, is likely to increase (Tomlinson, 1990; Critcher, 1992). Approaches to analysing such data are addressed in Chapter 8.

Using secondary data

Some useful analysis can be done using secondary sources of data – in fact, there are certain forms of analysis which can only be done with such data. Four case studies are given at the end of the chapter by way of illustration.

Summary

This chapter is concerned with the use of secondary data or the secondary analysis of existing data – that, is, data which have been collected by others for other purposes. There are potential cost-saving and time-saving advantages to such a strategy and even an ethical dimension, which suggests that resources should not be expended on new data collection if adequate data already exist. The chapter reviews a number of sources of secondary data commonly used in leisure and tourism research, namely: national leisure participation surveys; tourism surveys; economic data on expenditure and employment; the census of population; management data; and documentary sources. The chapter concludes with four case studies demonstrating potential uses of secondary data in planning and man-agement situations, including: estimating demand for new facilities, analysing trends in seasonal data, assessing levels of resource utilisation and analysing a facility catchment area.

Test questions

1. What are the advantages and disadvantages of secondary data analysis?

2. What are some of the issues to be considered when using data from leisure participation surveys?

3. What are the names of the main surveys conducted in your country related to the following?

- Leisure participation
- Domestic tourism
- International tourism
- Household expenditure.

4. This chapter lists nine sources of 'management data'. What are they?

5. This chapter lists seven types of 'documentary' source. What are they?

6. What sorts of secondary data are used in the gross demand/market share approach to planning?

Exercises

1. Take a leisure activity of your own choice, and a community of your own choice and, using data from the General Household Survey, or equivalent, and data from the census, provide an estimate of the likely demand for the activity in the selected community, using the methodology outlined in Case study 6.1.

2. In relation to exercise 1, what would be the implications of a predicted increase of 15 per cent in the number of people aged 60 and over and a 15 per cent decrease in the number of people aged 25 and under, over the next five years?

3. Refer to the quarterly inbound tourism statistics for the last ten years and produce a trend line of the sort outlined in Case study 6.2.

4. Undertake an exercise similar to Case study 6.3 on a leisure facility for which you can obtain usage data.

5. Undertake an exercise similar to Case study 6.4 on a leisure facility for which you can obtain user/member address data.

6. Select an activity from the General Household Survey, or equivalent local survey, and provide a *profile* of the activity, indicating the overall level of participation and how participation is related to age, gender, occupation and education.

Further reading

International: Cushman *et al.* (2005a) includes data from leisure, time-use and some tourism surveys for 15 countries: Australia; Canada; Finland; France; Germany; Great Britain; Hong Kong; Israel; Japan; The Netherlands; New Zealand; Poland; Russia; Spain; and USA. See also: Hantrais and Kamphorst, 1987; Kamphorst and Roberts (1989).

General Household Survey: Office for National Statistics (formerly Office of Population Censuses and Surveys) (annual (b)); Veal (1984, 1993c); Gratton and Tice (1994); Gratton and Veal (2005).

Australian leisure participation surveys: Darcy (1994); Veal (1993a, 1993b, 2003b, 2005).

Tourism data sources: Burkart and Medlik (1981, Part III); Edwards (1991); Goeldner (1994).

Employment statistics: Corley (1982).

Economic data: Sports Industries Research Centre (annual); Henley Centre for Forecasting (quarterly)

On documentary sources: Kellehear (1993).

Case study 6.1 Estimating likely demand for a leisure facility

The problem

A developer or local council is considering whether to build a cinema on a particular site in a town centre, as part of a multi-purpose leisure complex (a cinema is used as an example, but the methodology could be applied equally to other types of facility). The town has a population of 100,000 and already has two 400-seat cinemas. The developer wants to know what demand exists in the area for such a facility. A range of approaches could be considered to investigate this question.

Possibilities

One approach to the problem would be to examine existing cinemas in the area to see whether they are over-used or under-used, that is whether demand is already being adequately met by existing facilities. This, however, may not give the full answer, since it might be found that a well-managed, well-located cinema is well used while another, perhaps poorly managed and poorly located, is poorly used. It might also be difficult to obtain commercially sensitive data from potential competitors.

Another approach might be to conduct an interview survey of local residents to ask them whether they would like to go to the cinema but do not do so at present because of lack of suitable facilities. Even if the time and money were available to conduct such a survey, the results could not be relied on as the main piece of information on which to base the decision because, while people's honesty and accuracy in recalling activities might be relied on in relation to activities which they have actually taken part in, asking them to predict their behaviour in hypothetical future situations is very risky.

A third approach would be to examine communities of similar population size and type to see what levels of cinema provision they have and how well they are used. Again this may be a time-consuming process and somewhat 'hit-and-miss' because it is not easy to find comparable communities and because some of the data required, being commercially 'sensitive', may not be readily available.

A fourth approach would be to use secondary data, namely the appropriate national survey (NS) and the Census, to provide an approximate estimate of likely demand for cinema seats in the area. The aim is to provide an estimate of the level of demand which a community of the size of the study area is likely to generate and compare that with the level of demand already likely to be catered for by existing cinemas, to see whether or not there is an excess of demand over supply.

The approach

The general approach used here has been called the gross demand/market share (GDMS) method (Veal, 2002: 177–82) and is represented diagrammatically in Figure 6.7.

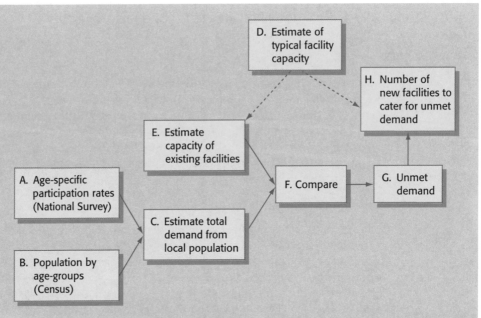

Figure 6.7 Estimating likely demand for a leisure facility – the gross demand/market share approach

A. Age-specific participation rates

One of the features of cinema attendance is that it varies considerably by age. Cinema is attended more by young people than by older people. If, for example, the study town contains a higher than average proportion of young people, it would be expected that it would produce a higher than average demand for cinema, and vice versa. The NS gives information on the percentage of people of different ages who go to the cinema, as shown in Table 6.8. It can be seen that teenagers are almost six times as likely to attend the cinema as the over 60s. The particular NS deals only with people aged 16 and over. Obviously children under that age do go to the cinema; but it may be that there is sufficient demand for an additional cinema even without taking account of the under 16s; so the under 16s can be ignored for the moment, only returning to them if necessary.

B. Population by age-groups

Suppose the census gives the population of the town as 100,000, and the population aged 16 and over as 80,000. In Table 6.9 the age structure of the national population aged 16 and over, is compared with that of the study town. Clearly the town has a much younger age profile than the national average with only just over half the proportion of over 55s and correspondingly larger proportions in the young age-groups. So it is clearly advisable to give consideration to the question of age structure.

Table 6.8 Cinema attendance by age

Age Group	% of age-group who go to the cinema in an average week (from national survey)
14–19 years	14.9
20–24	11.5
25–29	7.4
30–39	5.2
40–49	4.8
50–59	3.5
60+	2.5
Total/average	6.6

Source: hypothetical data

Table 6.9 Study town and national age structure compared

	National population – Census data	Study town population – Census data
Age Groups	%	%
14–19	12.5	19.5
20–24	11.9	19.0
25–29	10.6	14.2
30–39	20.1	21.1
40–49	14.2	9.0
50–59	11.8	7.7
60+	18.9	9.5
Total	100.0	100.0

Source: hypothetical data

C. Estimate total demand from local population

Table 6.10 indicates how demand for cinema attendance would be estimated: attendances are estimated for each age-group and summed to give a total of 6,543 attendances per week.

D. Estimate of typical facility capacity

For this exercise it is assumed that a typical 400-seat cinema auditorium requires 1,500 ticket sales a week to be viable (this is entirely hypothetical – in a real situation this information would be checked out with experts).

E. Estimate capacity of existing facilities

Two cinemas already exist in the town. If they have a seating capacity of 400 each, then they would accommodate some 3,000 visits a week.

Table 6.10   Estimating demand for cinema attendance

	% of age-group participating per week (X)	Town population (Y)	Estimated demand (visits per week)
Data source	National Survey	Census	X*Y/100
14–19 years	14.9	15,600	2,324
20–24	11.5	15,200	1,748
25–29	7.4	11,360	841
30–39	5.2	16,880	878
40–49	4.8	7,200	346
50–59	3.5	6,160	216
60+	2.5	7,600	190
Total/average	8.2	80,000	6,543

F. Compare
The total estimated demand is 6,500 visits per week, and the existing cinemas have a capacity of 3,000 per week.

G. Unmet demand
Unmet demand can therefore be estimated as about 3,500 visits per week.

H. Number of new facilities to cater for unmet demand
It would take two typical 400 seat cinemas to cater for the unmet demand – that is, it is estimated that a town can support four cinemas.

Comment

The gross demand/market share approach does not predict demand precisely – it merely indicates a 'ball park' demand figure. A well-managed and programmed cinema might draw far more demand than is estimated. The national survey attendance rates relate to average attendances across the country, so clearly there are places where higher attendance rates occur as well as places where lower rates occur. What the exercise indicates is that, on the basis of data to hand, 6,500 cinema attendances a week seems reasonably likely. This seems a very simple and crude calculation, but quite often investors – in the public and private sector – fail to carry out even this sort of simple calculation to check on 'ball park' demand figures; investments are made on the basis of personal hunch, and then surprise is expressed when demand fails to materialise.

Forecasting note: to provide a simple forecast of future demand, for, say, the year 2015 it would be necessary merely to insert population forecasts for the year 2015 into the second column of Table 6.10.

Economic note: while the exercise here has been outlined in terms of 'number of users or customers', use of expenditure data, such as that provided in Table 6.7, can convert the unit of analysis into expenditure.

Case study 6.2   Tourism trend analysis

Typically tourism statistics are produced on a quarterly basis, as in Table 6.11 (column A). Each quarterly figure of tourist arrivals reflects two factors: seasonal variation and longer-term trends. One way of examining the longer-term trend without the distraction of the seasonal variation is to produce a 'smoothed' series by calculating a 'moving average' (column B). The moving average consists of the average of the previous four quarters' figures. For example:

■ the moving average figure for Oct–Dec, 1999, is the average of the four figures for 1999;
■ the moving average figure for Jan–Mar, 2000 is the average of the figures from Apr–Jun, 1999 to Jan–Mar, 2000.

Table 6.11   Tourist arrivals, 1999–2004

Year	Quarter	A. No. of arrivals, millions	B. Moving average
1999	Jan–Mar	4.8	–
	Apr–Jun	5.5	–
	Jul–Sept	7.3	–
	Oct–Dec	6.5	6.0
2000	Jan–Mar	4.7	6.0
	Apr–Jun	5.8	6.1
	Jul–Sept	7.7	6.2
	Oct–Dec	6.9	6.3
2001	Jan–Mar	4.8	6.3
	Apr–Jun	6.0	6.4
	Jul–Sept	7.8	6.4
	Oct–Dec	7.2	6.5
2002	Jan–Mar	5.2	6.6
	Apr–Jun	6.0	6.6
	Jul–Sept	7.9	6.6
	Oct–Dec	6.4	6.4
2003	Jan–Mar	5.4	6.4
	Apr–Jun	5.8	6.4
	Jul–Sept	7.6	6.3
	Oct–Dec	6.4	6.3
2004	Jan–Mar	5.5	6.3
	Apr–Jun	6.4	6.5
	Jul–Sept	7.9	6.6
	Oct–Dec	6.8	6.7

Source: hypothetical; in practice arrivals are obtained from government arrivals/departures statistics

Figure 6.8
Tourism trends –
moving average

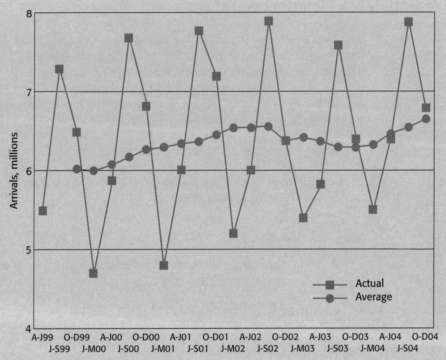

The calculations can be done very easily with a spreadsheet program. The effect is to present a 'smoothed' trend series, as shown graphically in Figure 6.8.

Case study 6.3   Facility utilisation

Managers often have information available on the use of facilities, but this is also often neglected as a source of data for research. As indicated in Case study 6.1, the level of utilisation of existing facilities is an important issue for managers and planners: this case study illustrates how existing data can be used to address this question.

Table 6.12 presents data which might be routinely collected on the level of use of particular areas of a leisure facility (e.g. various rooms or halls in an indoor leisure centre or various rides in a leisure park). The daily usage levels might be averaged over a number of weeks. For each of the areas it is necessary to estimate the daily capacity: this is a reasonable assessment of the number of users which would equate to the facility being deemed 'fully used' (see Veal, 2002: 125). The numbers of users

Table 6.12 Facility utilisation data

	Area A		Area B		Area C	
	Number	% utilisation	Number	% utilisation	Number	% utilisation
Capacity	300	100.0	120	100.0	500	100.0
Mon. usage	120	40.0	60	50.0	310	62.0
Tues. usage	150	50.0	40	33.3	210	42.0
Wed. usage	180	60.0	30	25.0	180	36.0
Thurs. usage	120	40.0	80	66.7	375	75.0
Fri. usage	100	33.3	95	79.2	430	86.0
Sat. usage	210	70.0	110	91.7	420	84.0
Sun. usage	250	83.3	40	33.3	310	62.0
Total for week	1,130	53.8	455	54.2	2,235	63.9

Figure 6.9
Facility
utilisation

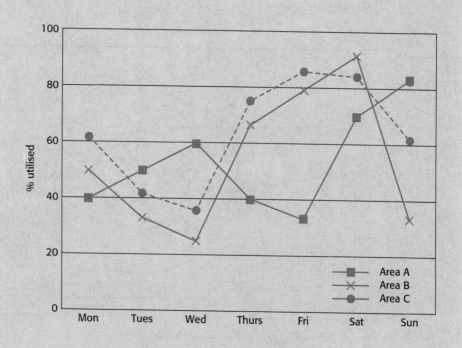

are related to the capacity in the form of percentages, and these are graphed in Figure 6.9. The graph shows a different pattern of use for Area A, compared with the other two areas. Area A is under-used on Monday, Thursday and Friday, while areas B and C are under-used between Sunday and Wednesday. This suggests the need for different programming and marketing policies for the various areas.

Case study 6.4   Facility catchment or market area

Leisure and tourism facilities often have available information on users' addresses which can be used to study the *catchment area* or *market area* – an important aspect of planning and management. Many leisure facilities, for example, have membership or subscriber lists. Hotels and resorts have details of home addresses of patrons. Figure 6.10 shows how such data can be plotted on a map to produce a visual representation of the catchment or market area of the facility. Such information can be used either to concentrate marketing to increase sales in the existing area, or to focus marketing outside the identified area in order to extend the catchment or market area.

When very large numbers are involved it may be necessary to sample membership or customer lists – for example selecting every fifth or tenth member or patron.

While this case study is used to illustrate the use of secondary data, catchment areas can also be based on survey data, which will be necessary if existing information on client addresses is not available (see Chapter 9, particularly discussion of user/site surveys).

Figure 6.10
Catchment/
market area

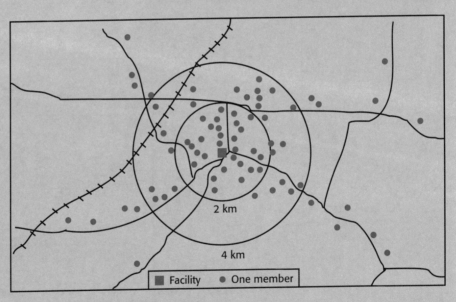

Source: membership/patron address records (hypothetical)

7 Observation

Introduction: the nature and purpose of observational research

The aim of this chapter is to draw attention to the importance of *looking* in research and to introduce some of the specific approaches of observational methods. It examines situations in which observation is particularly appropriate and outlines the main steps which should be taken in designing and conducting an observation-based project. Observation is a neglected technique in leisure and tourism research. While it is rarely possible to base a whole project on observation, the technique has a vital role to play, either formally or informally, in most research strategies.

Observation involves *looking*. It can take a number of forms, as indicated in Figure 7.1. Sometimes observational research is referred to as an *unobtrusive* method, since there is generally no involvement with the observed, who may not even be aware

Structured or systematic observation	Observation process is subject to written rules about what should be observed, how often, etc. – results of the observation typically being recorded on a form and invariably analysed quantitatively. Equivalent to the formal questionnaire survey in survey research.
Unstructured or naturalistic observation	No formal rules established and no formalised recording or analysis procedures. The observer seeks to describe the phenomenon of interest and develop explanations and understandings in the process. Equivalent to the informal, in-depth interview in survey research.
Contrived observation	The researcher intervenes to change the environment and observes what happens – for example, changing the design of children's play equipment. Observation and analysis may be structured or unstructured. In effect a form of experimental research.
Participant observation	The researcher is a participant in the milieu being studied – for example, the guided tour or the youth gang – rather than a separate, 'objective' researcher. May involve any of the above forms of observation. Discussed in Chapter 8.

Figure 7.1 Types of observational research

that they are being observed. However, the term 'unobtrusive method' also sometimes includes use of documentary sources, such as the media, organisational records and diaries (see Kellehear, 1993); in this book these sources are dealt with in the chapters on secondary data and qualitative methods – in this chapter we concentrate on direct visual engagement with leisure or tourism sites.

The chapter first presents an overview of possible situations where observational methods might be used and this is followed by a step-by-step examination of the observational research process. Looking can be done with the naked eye or with the help of sophisticated equipment. For example, time-lapse photography can be used to photograph an area automatically at set periods; aerial photography can be used to gain a panoramic view of a whole recreation or tourism area; and video can also be used. Technical aids to observation are considered briefly towards the end of the chapter.

Possibilities

A number of types of situation where observation is appropriate or necessary can be identified, as listed in Figure 7.2. These situations are discussed in turn below.

Children's play

There is some research which can only be tackled by means of observation. One example is children's play. Such research on play is concerned with such issues as: patterns of play in different environments; the types of equipment children of different ages prefer; whether boys have different patterns of play from girls; and whether there are differences in play patterns between children from different cultural backgrounds. It is clear that answers to such questions could not be found by interviewing children, particularly very young children. The obvious approach is to *observe* children at play and record their behaviour.

Usage of informal leisure/tourism areas

Structured observation methods can be used to estimate the level of use of informal recreation areas, such as beaches, urban parks or tourist sites, where there is no

Figure 7.2
Situations for
observational
research

- children's play
- usage of informal leisure/tourism areas
- spatial and functional use of sites
- user profile
- deviant behaviour
- consumer/*incognito* testing
- complementary research
- everyday life
- social behaviour

admission charge. In the absence of an entrance charge there are no ticket sales data and so managers and planners can only obtain estimates of their levels of use by observation. Further, in many cases, there are no formal constraints on capacity and usage patterns, such as formal seating or booking systems.

An indication of the level of use of sites may be required for a variety of reasons. For instance, a public agency might decide that it would be useful, for political or public relations reasons, to be able to state the total number of visitors which a facility serves in a week or a year – in order to justify the level of taxpayers' money being spent on maintaining it. In management terms it is often useful to be able to relate the costs of maintaining a site to the number of visits which it attracts, as one of a number of inputs into decisions on how much money should be spent on different sites. A single site manager might wish to compare levels of use over time to assess the impact of various marketing and other management measures. In order to obtain an estimate of use levels it is necessary to *observe* and *count* the number of users.

Where the bulk of users arrive at a facility by private car and a charge is made for parking, indications of use levels may be provided by parking income, but this does not account for non-vehicular use and in some cases parking charges do not apply outside of certain hours, or there may be season permit holders. To account for all vehicular use it may be possible to install automatic vehicle counters to count the number of vehicles entering and leaving the site, and thus give an approximation of use levels. The vehicle counter involves laying a rubber-coated pressure sensor across the roadway, attached to a recording device, which may be set up to transmit data to the manager or researcher's computer. Vehicle counts, however, provide information on the number of *vehicles* using a site but not the number of *people*. To obtain estimates of the numbers of people it is necessary to supplement the vehicle counts by direct observation for a period of the time to ascertain the average number of persons in vehicles and, at some sites, to estimate the numbers arriving by foot or bicycle, who would not be recorded by the mechanical counting device.

Although vehicle counters do not count pedestrians, devices are now available to count pedestrians using an electronic beam projected across pedestrian routes. Because pedestrians do not pass through the beam one at a time, and may pass in two directions, the calibration of the data is more complex than for vehicle counters.

Manual methods of counting usage levels are discussed in the section on 'main elements of observational research' below.

Spatial and functional use of sites

Observation is useful not only for gathering data on the number of users of a site but also for studying the way people make use of a site. This is particularly important in relation to the design and layout of leisure spaces, and their capacity. For instance, if people tend to crowd close to entrances and parking areas (which they often do in outdoor sites) then where those entrances and parking areas are positioned will affect the pattern of use of the site. This can be used as a management/design tool to influence the pattern of use of a site.

Similarly if, as has been found, people tend to locate themselves along 'edges' – such as walls, fences, banks, areas of trees and shrubs – then this tendency can be used to influence the pattern of use of a site, by determining the nature and location of such 'edges' (Ruddell and Hammitt, 1987). While this applies particularly to outdoor natural areas, it can also have some relevance in built up areas, such as shopping malls, and in buildings, such as museums.

Buildings and open spaces for public use are often designed with either little or no consideration as to how people will actually use them, or on the basis of untested assumptions about how they will be used. In reality it is often found that people do not actually behave as anticipated by the designers and some spaces are under-used while others are over-crowded, or spaces are not actually used for the activities for which they were designed or equipped. The pattern of movement of people around exhibitions can affect the information absorbed, depending on the relative prominence and attraction of exhibits, as demonstrated in Case study 7.1. Observation is the means by which these aspects of space utilisation can be discovered.

User profile

Questionnaire-based site surveys typically involve demographic and group composition data which combine to provide a 'user profile'. However, depending on the design

Case study 7.1 Observation of museum visitor behaviour

Source: Phillip L. Pearce (1988) Museums and visitor centres. Chapter 6 of *The Ulysses Factor: Evaluating Visitors in Tourist Settings.* New York, Springer-Verlag, 90–113

Approach:

Observation

Topic:

Visitors' spatial use of a museum

In a book chapter reviewing a number of issues related to visitors to museums and visitor centres, Pearce discusses the implications of visitors' decision to turn to the right on entering a museum and proceeding in an anti-clockwise direction, as opposed to turning left and proceeding in a clockwise direction. Research in the Telecom Museum in Victoria, Australia, as shown in Figure 7.3, shows that the two groups of visitors do indeed have different patterns of attention paid to the exhibits, as measured by the proportion of visitors who stop to view each exhibit. Further, those who turn right and proceed anti-clockwise have a higher level of attention throughout the exhibition – but this, it is argued, is likely to be due to the fact that they immediately encounter interactive exhibits, whereas those who turn to the left first encounter static, audio-visual exhibits. The methodology used is clearly simple, but possibly time-consuming, depending on how long visitors stay and the extent to which more than one group can be studied at the same time. But it clearly produces data which are likely to be of interest to, and readily understood and interpreted by, managers.

Figure 7.3
Visitor movement patterns in a museum

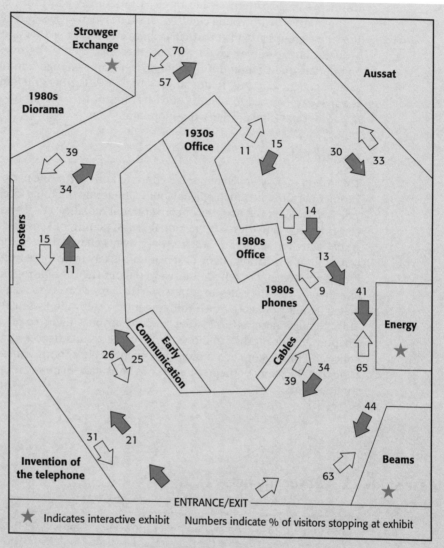

Source: adaptation of Pearce, 1988, Figs 5.2 and 5.3, pp. 100–1

of the questionnaire, and given that questionnaires in such situations are invariably quite brief, the information collected can miss vital features of the characteristics of the users of a site. For example, two music venues could have identical user age/ gender/group size profiles, but, because of the different type of music offered, could attract very different crowds, in terms of fashion, lifestyle and behaviour. Even at a single venue an overall profile based on averages and percentages may hide the fact that it is used by a number of distinct user-groups. Questionnaire-based profiles may also miss distinctive usage patterns. For example, a park survey may indicate that there are x per cent of mothers with young children, or single elderly users, but fail to pick up the fact that these groups attend at particular times and meet together and socialise. Of course a questionnaire survey could pick up these features if the questionnaire included appropriate questions and if the sample were large enough and the analysis sophisticated enough, but this is not always the case. Further, preliminary observational research can be used to identify such features of the user profile so that appropriate questions can be included in a questionnaire.

Deviant behaviour

The notion of *deviant* behaviour is a contested one, with one person's 'deviance' being another person's 'acceptable behaviour'. One term which has been used to cover this area is 'leisure on the margins of conventional morality' (Veal and Lynch, 2001: 335), covering such activities as recreational drugs; graffiti and vandalism; various types of sexual activity; gambling; and rowdy crowd behaviour in leisure settings. Deviant behaviour is a situation where observation is likely to be more fruitful than interviews. People are unlikely to tell an interviewer about their litter-dropping habits, their lack of adherence to the rules in a park, or their beer can throwing habits at a football match. Finding out about such things requires observation – usually of a covert nature! This of course raises ethical issues, such as people's rights to privacy, as discussed in Chapter 3. Case study 7.2 shows parts of the results from a study of riots between police and biker gangs at a motor-sport event in New South Wales in the 1980s, indicating that the safety of the researchers can be at stake in observational research in some environments.

Case study 7.2   Observing riots

Chris Cuneen, Mark Findlay, Rob Lynch and Vernon Tupper (1989) *The Dynamics of Collective Conflict: Riots at the Bathurst 'Bike Races*. North Ryde, NSW: Law Book Co.

Approach:

Naturalistic observation

Topic:

Crowd behaviour

In their book, Cuneen *et al.* present the results of their study of a series of violent conflicts, including pitched battles, which took place between police and fans at the annual Bathurst Motorcycle Grand Prix meetings in New South Wales in the mid-1980s. They use a variety of research methods, including observation, interviews, historical research and analysis of press and television reports, in an attempt to understand the origins and nature of the conflicts between the two groups and the role of the media, which reported the events and created images and interpretations for the consumption of the public and politicians. While media reports portrayed the fans as 'mindless hooligans' on the rampage, detailed research revealed a history of suspicion between police and 'bikies' and a picture of excessive and escalatory police response to the carnivalesque behaviour of the crowd. There was no single explanation of the riots – the meaning and interpretation of the events depended on who was doing the interpretation – the police, the fans, the press or politicians. Figure 7.4 presents the results of detailed observation of the layout of the site and the parties involved in one of the pitched battles. Clearly it would be difficult to describe the scene entirely verbally – visual presentation of the results of the observational exercise is the obvious approach to adopt.

Figure 7.4
Pattern of conflict at the Bathurst 'Bike Races, Easter Saturday, 1995

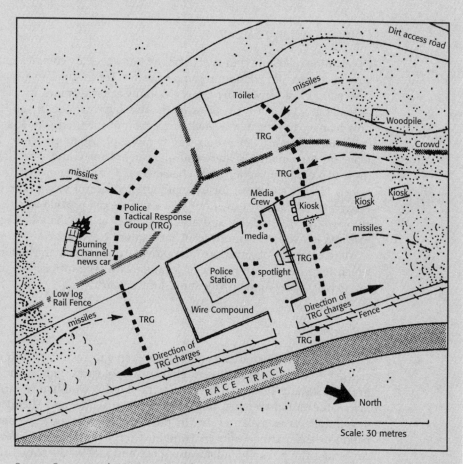

Source: Cuneen *et al.*, 1989, 95. (See also Cuneen and Lynch, 1988)

TRG = Tactical Response Group (special police squad)

Consumer/*incognito* testing

Consumer or *incognito* testing, sometimes referred to as *mystery shopping*, is another potentially fruitful but under-exploited use of observation. While interviews are one way of obtaining information on the quality of the experience enjoyed by users of a leisure or tourism facility or product, an additional means is for a researcher to play the role of *incognito* user/customer/observer. Such an observer would be required to make use of facilities or services on offer, armed with a checklist of features to observe – such as cleanliness, information availability and clarity, staff performance – and would make a report after using the facilities or services. Such an approach draws on the expertise of the observer to assess quality of services and to record details, for example related to safety, which might not be noticed by 'real' users. Again, ethical and industrial relations issues may arise in such a study because of the element of deception involved in playing the part of a customer.

Complementary research

Observation involving counts of users can be a necessary complement to interview surveys to correct for variation in sampling rates. For instance in a typical tourist attraction, park or beach, two interviewers, working at a steady rate, may be able to interview virtually all (100 per cent) users in the less busy periods in the early morning but only manage to interview a small proportion of the users (say 5 per cent) during the busy lunch hour and afternoon. The final sample would therefore, in this case, over-represent early morning users and under-represent mid-day and afternoon users. If these two groups have different characteristics the differential rate of sampling may have a biasing effect on, for example, the balance of views expressed by the users. Observational counts of the hourly levels of use can provide data to give an appropriate *weight* to the mid-day and afternoon users at the analysis stage. The process of *weighting* is described in more detail in Chapter 12.

More informal observation may provide complementary material for any study which is focussed on a particular location or a type of location in order to set the research in context and provide some 'local colour'.

Everyday life

The idea of simply observing *everyday life* as an approach to studying a society is associated with Britain's Mass Observation anthropological study of the British way of life in the 1930s and 1940s and with the work of Irving Goffman (1959). An anthology of Mass Observation sketches, published in 1984 (Calder and Sheridan, 1984) includes descriptions of everyday events in pubs, on the Blackpool promenade and in the period of the wartime blitz in London. Goffman's work was more theoretical and concerned the ways individuals use space and interact in public and private places. An anthology of work in the Goffman style (Birenbaum and Sagarin, 1973) includes observational studies of such leisure activities as pinball, bars, card games and restaurants.

Social behaviour

Observation has been used in sociological research to develop ideas and theories about social behaviour in specific milieux and generally. The research of Fiske (1983) and Grant (1984) on the use of beaches and Marsh and his colleagues (1978) on soccer fans are examples of this approach. These researchers use an interactive, inductive process to build explanations of social behaviour from what they observe. Very often a key feature of such studies is the way the researchers seek to contrast what they have observed with what has apparently been observed by others, particularly those with influence or authority, such as officials, police and the media. Observational research can challenge existing stereotypical interpretations of events.

Main elements of observational research

Observation seems to be essentially a simple research method with little 'technique' to consider. However, as with any research method, careful thought must go into design, conduct and analysis stages of a project. In structured observation what is mainly required from the researcher is precision, painstaking attention to detail, and patience. In unstructured observation the same skills and attributes are required but, in addition, there is a need for a creative 'eye' which can perceive the significance and potential meanings of what is being observed and relate this to the research question. The main tasks in planning and conducting an observational project are as set out in Figure 7.5.

As with the 'elements of the research process' outlined in Chapter 3, it is difficult to produce a list of steps which will cover all eventualities. In particular, if the approach is unstructured rather than structured, then a number of the steps discussed here, particularly those concerning counting, may be redundant.

Step 1: Choice of site(s)

In the case of consultancy research the sites to be studied may be fixed; but where there is an element of choice some time should be devoted to inspecting and choosing sites which will not only offer the appropriate leisure/tourism behaviour but will also provide suitable conditions for observation.

Figure 7.5
Steps in an observation project

1. Choice of site(s)
2. Choice of observation point(s)
3. Choice of observation time-period(s)
4. Continuous observation or sampling
5. Count frequency
6. What to observe
7. Division of site into zones
8. Recording observational information
9. Conducting the observation
10. Analysing data

Step 2: Choice of observation point(s)

Choice of observation points within a site is clearly important and needs to be done with care. Some sites can be observed in their entirety from one spot. In other cases a circuit of viewing spots must be devised. For structured observation – for example involving counting the number of people present or passing a point over a period of time – it may be vital to conduct the observation from the same point(s) in various study periods, but for unstructured observation this may not be a consideration, indeed, exploring and observing from different locations within a site may be necessary.

When unstructured, but intensive observation of people's behaviour is involved, it may be necessary to choose observation points which are unobtrusive to avoid attracting attention, particularly in a confined space with relatively few people. This is related to the issue of the method of recording observations, as discussed in Step 8 below, since some forms of formal recording are more 'obvious' than others.

Step 3: Choice of observation time-period(s)

The choice of time-period is important because of variations in use of a facility, either by time of the year, day of the week, time of day or weather conditions, according to external social factors such as public holidays, or internal factors, such as the type of music – and hence of patron – on particular nights in a club. Observation to cover all time-periods may be very demanding in terms of resources, so some form of sampling of time-periods will usually be necessary.

Step 4: Continuous observation or sampling?

The question of whether to undertake continuous observation or to sample different time periods is related to the resources available and the nature of the site and the overall design of the project. The issue is particularly important if one of the aims of the research is to obtain an accurate estimate of the number of visitors to the site, when the terminology used to refer to the two approaches is *continuous counts* versus *spot counts*. It could, for example, be very expensive to place observers at the numerous gates of a large urban park for as much as 100 hours in a week to count the number of users during all the time the park is open. Even if that were possible it is unlikely that resources would be available to cover a whole year – except using automatic mechanical devices. A sampling approach must be adopted in most observation projects. Having decided to sample, it is of course necessary to decide how often to do this. This is discussed further under Step 5.

If counting is being undertaken there is also a decision to be made as to whether to count the number of people *entering* or *leaving* the site during specified time periods or the number of people *present* at particular points in time. Counting the number of people present is, of course, a form of spot count. Counting the number of people entering or leaving over a period of time generally constitutes continuous counting, but if the time periods are relatively short – for example half an hour or an hour – then the results can be seen as a form of spot count. Counting the number of people present at particular points in time is generally less resource-intensive since it can be done by one person regardless of the number of entrances to the site, and can provide information on the spatial use of the site at the same time. Thus one person, at specified times, makes a circuit of the site and records the numbers of people present in designated zones (see Step 7).

When unstructured observation is being undertaken it is more likely that continuous observation will be adopted since the aim will generally be to observe the dynamics of events and behaviour at the site. However, the question of when to undertake such observation in order to cover all aspects of the use of the site still needs careful consideration.

Step 5: Count frequency

When the study involved counts of users, how often should the counts be undertaken? This will depend to a large extent on the rate of change in the level of use of the site. For example, the seven counts in Figure 7.6 are clearly insufficient since, if the broken line is the pattern of use observed in a research project, but the unbroken line is the true pattern, the research would have inaccurately represented the true situation. There is little advice that can be given to overcome this problem, except to sample frequently at the beginning of a project until the basic patterns of peaks and troughs in usage have been established; subsequently it may be possible to sample less often.

Step 6: What to observe

One approach to observing the spatial behaviour of visitors within a facility is to record people's positions directly as indicated in Figure 7.7. In addition to observing numbers of people and their positions, it is possible to observe and record different types of activity. It is also possible, to a limited extent, to record visitor characteristics. For

Figure 7.6
Counts of
site use

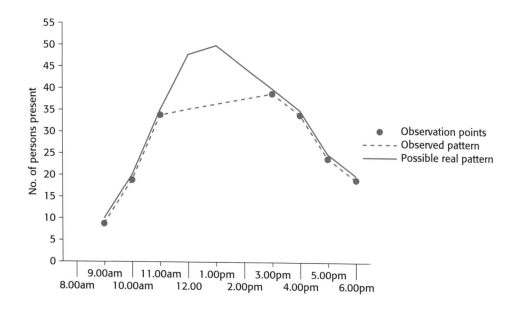

Figure 7.7
Mapping
observed data:
use of a park

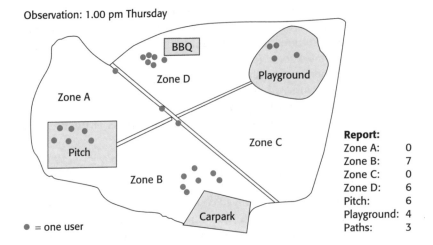

Observation: 1.00 pm Thursday

BBQ

Zone D

Playground

Zone A

Pitch

Zone C

Zone B

Carpark

● = one user

Report:

Zone A:	0
Zone B:	7
Zone C:	0
Zone D:	6
Pitch:	6
Playground:	4
Paths:	3

instance men and women could be separately identified. It is also possible to distinguish between children and adults and to distinguish senior citizens, although, if a
number of people are involved as counters, care will need to be taken over the dividing
line between such categories as child, teenager, young adult, adult and elderly person.
It is also possible, again with care, to observe the size of parties using a site, especially if
they are observed arriving or leaving at a car park.

These additional items of information would of course complicate the recording
sheet and symbols would be necessary to record the different types of person on a map.
Care needs to be taken not to make the data collection so complicated that it becomes
too difficult for the observers to observe and collect and leads to inaccuracies. This is
one of those situations where it is necessary to consider carefully *why* the data are being
collected and not to get carried away with data collection for its own sake.

In addition to observing people statically, or as they arrive at an entrance, it is also
possible to observe visitors' movements through a site, and illustrate the results graphically. A simple example is shown in Figures 7.3 and 7.8. Of course care must be taken
not to give offence by letting visitors become aware that they are being 'followed', but
routes taken by visitors can be revealing for management.

Car registration numbers can be a useful source of information. First, they can provide information on where people have travelled from. Second, number plates can be
used to trace the movement of vehicles within an area – for instance within a national
park with a number of stopping points.

Step 7: Division of site into zones

In large sites it is advisable to divide the site into areas or zones and record the number
of people and their activities within those zones, as indicated in Figures 7.7 and 7.8.
The zones should be determined primarily by management concerns – for example, in
a park: the children's playground, the sports areas, the rose garden. But they should
also be designed for ease of counting; ideally zones should be such that they can be
observed from one spot and should be clearly demarcated by natural or other features.

Figure 7.8
Flows within
a site

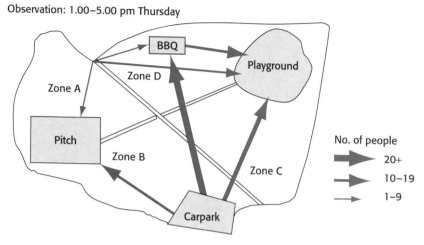

Observation: 1.00–5.00 pm Thursday

Step 8: Recording observational information

Figure 7.9a provides an example of a counting sheet used in a structured observation project requiring counts of use in a study area with six zones and the possibility of a variety of activities. The data collected using such a form are ideal for storage, manipulation and presentation in graphic form using a spreadsheet computer program as discussed in Step 10 below. An alternative to this sort of form is to record data on copies of maps of the site, using numerals or dots, as in Figure 7.7 (with symbols for different types of activity).

Figure 7.9b is an example of a recording sheet for an unstructured observation exercise. There are fewer zones since the observation is likely to be more intensive and time-consuming. In each zone space is provided for free-form notes. The amount of space to reserve on the sheet depends on the length of time spent and the detail of the observation; it is possible that a whole page, or even more, may be required per zone per time-period.

Step 9: Conducting the observation

In the case of a structured observational project, if the project has been well planned then the actual conduct should be straightforward. The main danger in a major project involving a lot of counting can be boredom, leading to inaccuracies in observing and recording data. It is therefore advisable to vary the work of those involved with, where appropriate, data collectors being involved in alternate spells of behavioural observation and counting and, where possible, being switched between sites. Counting can be done manually or using a hand-held mechanical counter.

In the case of unstructured observational projects, more demands are placed on the observer. Such a project is, in effect, a visual form of the qualitative type of research discussed in Chapter 8. The observer is required to observe and describe what is going on at the site, but must also engage directly with the research questions of the project in order to determine what to observe and what aspects of the observed scene should be described and recorded.

Figure 7.9
Examples of
observation
recording sheets

a. Structured

Site	Observer	Date		Start time		Finish time	
	Zone:						
Activity	A	B	C	D	E	F	G
Walking							
Sitting							
Playing sport							
Children playing							
Eating							
Total							

b. Unstructured

Site	Observer	Date	Start time	Finish time
Zone A				
Zone B				
Zone C				
Zone D				

Step 10: Analysing data

In some cases of structured observation, visual presentations of the sort provided in Figures 7.7 and 7.8 constitute the analysis. In other cases data must be analysed and processed to present useable results. Three examples are presented here: presentation of usage patterns over the course of a day; estimating usage numbers from spot count data; weighting; and analysis of unstructured data.

Usage patterns

Consider the set of counts shown in Table 7.1, which relate to the numbers of people present in a park, which opens at 8 am and closes at 7 pm. This pattern is illustrated graphically in Figure 7.10. Again, this presentation may be sufficient for the project in hand, but it can be taken further, including converting the sample counts into an estimate of overall use numbers.

Estimating usage numbers

Table 7.2 sets out a process to estimate usage numbers from spot count data. It is estimated in the example that there is an average of 94.3 people in the park, over a

Table 7.1 Observed use of a park

	Walking	Sitting	Playing sport	Kids playing	Total
			No. of people observed		
8 am	5	1	0	2	8
9 am	52	6	5	5	64
10 am	44	19	10	7	75
11 am	28	25	12	11	76
12 am	31	40	25	13	109
1 pm	32	56	32	17	137
2 pm	37	46	23	22	128
3 pm	38	45	12	22	117
4 pm	39	40	33	32	144
5 pm	40	33	27	15	115
6 pm	42	20	12	12	86
7 pm	45	15	4	9	73
Total	429	349	192	162	1,132
Average	35.8	29.1	16.0	13.5	94.3

Figure 7.10
Park usage
pattern

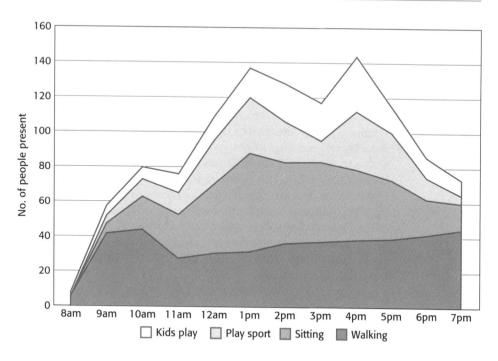

twelve-hour period, giving a total of 1,132 *visitor-hours*. The number of visitor-hours is a valid measure of use in its own right and could be used to compare different sites or to compare the performance of the same site over time. But, for example, twelve visitor-hours could result from:

Table 7.2 Estimating user numbers from count data

	Data	Source	Result
A	Average no. of users present	Counts (Table 7.1)	94.3
B	No. of hours open	Table 7.1	12 hours
C	No. of user-hours	A × B	1,131.6
D	Average length of stay	User survey	0.5 hours
E	No. of users	C/D	2,263

- one person visiting the park and staying all day;
- two people staying six hours each;
- twelve people staying one hour each; or
- twenty-four people staying half an hour each.

So if an estimate is required of the number of different *persons* visiting the park over the course of the day, additional information, on the *length of stay*, is necessary – this would usually be obtained from a questionnaire-based user survey, although it might possibly be obtained from detailed observation of a sample of groups. In the example in Table 7.2, the length of stay is 0.5 hour, so every user-hour represents two users, giving a total of 2,264 users for the day. Thus the number of visitors is equal to the number of visitor-hours divided by the average length of stay.

Weighting

Details of user characteristics obtained from observation can be used as a check on the accuracy of sampling in interview surveys and may be used to 'weight' the results of such surveys so that the final result is a better reflection of the characteristics of the users of the facility. This is similar to the 'time of day' correction discussed above, but relates to the personal characteristics of users, rather than their time of use of the facility. For instance, if it was found by observation that half the users of a site were women but in an interview survey only a third of those interviewed were women, the women in the sample could be given a greater weighting at the analysis stage so that their views and attitudes would receive due emphasis. The details of weighting are described more fully in Chapter 12.

Unstructured analysis

The raw form of the data from unstructured observation is likely to comprise a set of notes, possibly with some numbers, and probably with some diagrams. The immediate task for the researcher is therefore to ensure that these notes are in a readable form for future reference; this may involve writing or typing them out to provide a narrative. In the process of doing this, analysis may start: for example, the absence of a particular group of users on one occasion and their presence on another may be linked to a absence or presence of another group or some other change in the environment. The result is therefore likely to be an extended set of notes which can be seen as comparable with sets of notes or transcripts from qualitative research, as discussed in Chapter 8. Similar approaches to analysis are therefore appropriate, including identification of themes and patterns. The inductive interactions between data collection, data analysis and theory development which apply to qualitative research generally also apply to unstructured observational research. The *NVivo* software described in Chapter 8 for analysing informal interview transcripts might also be used to analyse notes from observational research.

Photography and video

Aerial photography

The use of aerial photography is well developed in geography and geology, where a whole sub-discipline of *remote sensing* has developed using a variety of techniques. It can also be an effective technique in leisure and tourism studies. Where large areas are concerned – such as coastlines and estuaries, where access is difficult and recreational use of the site is very scattered, aerial photography may be the only way of obtaining estimates of levels and patterns of use. In harbours and estuaries it is probably the best means of obtaining estimates of numbers of craft using the area since, as they are generally moving about, it can be difficult to count manually on a crowded waterway. Needless to say a good quality camera is needed for such work. Generally slides are the best medium because they can easily be projected on a large screen for the subsequent laborious task of counting.

Still photography

The value of ordinary, land-based, photography as an adjunct to direct observation should not be overlooked. Digital photography and editing software have made the incorporation of photographs into research increasingly easy. The level of crowding of a site, its nature and atmosphere can be conveyed to the reader of a report with the aid of photographs. Particular problems, for instance of erosion, or design faults, can be conveyed better visually than verbally – a picture paints a thousand words. A 'photo-essay' can be composed around a number of themes or messages to convey simple research findings.

Video

Video can be used to record patterns of use of a site, but is likely to be used for illustrative rather than analytical purposes. The medium can provide a useful illustration of 'before' and 'after' situations, to illustrate the nature of problems on a site and the effect of measures taken to ameliorate the problems – for example congestion, erosion or littering.

Time-lapse photography

Time-lapse photography lies somewhere between still photography and video. A time-lapse camera can be set up to take pictures of a scene automatically, say, every ten seconds or every minute. The resultant sequence of pictures can then be projected as a film or video to show the speeded up pattern of use of the area viewed. This is the technique used in wildlife documentaries which show a plant apparently growing before your eyes, but it can also be used to show the changing pattern of use of a leisure or tourism site.

Just looking

Finally we should not forget just how important it is to use our eyes in research, even if the research project does not involve systematic observational data collection. Familiarity with a leisure activity or a leisure or tourism site helps in the design of a good research project and aids in interpreting data. Many studies have been based just on informal, but careful, observation. All useful information is not in the form of numbers. Careful observation of what is happening in a particular leisure or tourism situation, at a particular facility or type of facility or among a particular group of people can be a more appropriate research approach in some circumstances than the use of questionnaires or even informal interviews. The good researcher is all eyes.

Summary

This chapter is concerned with the neglected technique of observation – *looking* – as a tool for research in leisure and tourism. It is noted that observation can be formalised or structured, involving counting of leisure and tourism site users and strict time and space sampling methods, or it can be informal or unstructured. In general observation is non-intrusive in the study site, but 'contrived observation', as in the experimental method, is also possible. Participant observation is a further type of observational research, but is dealt with in Chapter 8. Observational research spans the quantitative/qualitative methodological spectrum and can generate both quantitative and qualitative data and therefore involve both quantitative and qualitative analysis methods. A number of leisure and tourism situations are described in which observation methods might be used, including: children's play; the usage of informal leisure/tourism areas where no entrance fee is required and capacity and use patterns are not constrained by factors such as formal seating or booking systems; spatial and functional patterns of use of sites; user profiles; studying deviant behaviour; consumer/*incognito* testing; research which is complementary to research conducted using other methods; everyday life; and social behaviour. The chapter outlines the observational research process in ten steps: choice of study site(s); choice of observation point(s); choice of observation time period(s); deciding on continuous observation or sampling; deciding on the number and length of sampling periods; deciding what to observe; division of the study site(s) into zones; recording observational information; conducting the observation; analysing data. Finally, brief consideration is given to audio-visual equipment, such as still, video and time-lapse cameras in observational research.

Test questions

1. Four types of observational research are identified at the beginning of the chapter. What are they?

2. In total, eight leisure or tourism situations are described where observation is a suitable, and sometimes the *most* suitable, form of research. Name three of these situations and explain in each case why observation is a suitable research method.

3. What is the difference between spot counting and continuous counting?

4. In what forms can data from observational research be presented?

5. How can observational research findings assist in regard to weighting of survey data?

Exercises

1. Select an informal leisure or tourism site, position yourself in an unobtrusive location, but where you can seen what is going on. Over a period of two hours, record what happens. Write a report on: how the site is used; who it is used by; how many people use it; what conflicts there are, if any, between different groups of users; and how the design aids or hinders the activity which people engage in on the site.

2. Establish a counting system to record the number of people present in a leisure or tourism site at hourly intervals during the course of a day. Estimate the number of visitor-hours at the site for the day.

3. In relation to exercise 2: conduct interviews with three or four visitors each hour, and ask them how long they have stayed, or expect to stay, at the site. Establish the average length of stay and, using this information and the data from exercise 2, estimate the number of persons visiting the site in the course of the day.

4. Use photographs to record examples of neglect or damage to leisure or tourism sites known to you.

Further reading

General/methodological: Tyre and Siderelis (1978); Burch (1981); Ely (1981); TRRU (1983); Kellehear (1993); Adler and Adler (1994). Distinction between structured and unstructured observation: Bryman and Bell (2003), chapter 8.

Examples of leisure/tourism studies using observation:
General: Birenbaum and Sagarin (1973)
Mystery shopping: general; Dawson and Hillier (1995); *travel agents*: Hudson *et al.* (2001)
Children's play: Child (1983)
Sporting crowds/riots: Cuneen *et al.* (1989); Football: Marsh *et al.* (1978)
Beach use: Douglas *et al.* (1977); Fiske (1983); Grant (1984)
Countryside recreation: Glyptis (1981a, 1981b); Van der Zande (1985); Keirle and Walsh (1999)
Parks: Gold (1972)
Museums: Bitgood, *et al.* (1988); Pearce (1988) – Case study 7.1.

8 Qualitative methods

Introduction: qualities and uses

In this chapter methods of research which involve the collection and analysis of *qualitative* information rather than numerical data are addressed. The chapter discusses the advantages and features of qualitative methods, their role in research and the range of specific methods available, including in-depth interviews, group interviews/focus groups, participant observation, biographical methods and ethnographic approaches. The analysis of *texts*, which can be undertaken quantitatively as well as qualitatively, but has generally been associated with the qualitative tradition, is also discussed. Manual methods of qualitative data analysis are briefly outlined, followed by an introduction to analysis using the *NVivo* computer package.

The term 'qualitative' is used to describe research methods and techniques which use, and give rise to, qualitative rather than quantitative information. In general the qualitative approach tends to collect a great deal of 'rich' information about relatively few cases rather than the more limited information about each of a large number of cases which is typical of quantitative research. It is, however, possible to envisage qualitative research which actually deals with large numbers of cases. For example, a research project on sports spectators, involving observation and participation in spectator activity could involve information relating, collectively, to tens of thousands of people.

Qualitative methods can be used for pragmatic reasons, in situations where formal, quantified research is not necessary or is not possible, but there are also theoretical grounds for using such methods. Much quantitative research necessarily tends to impose the *researcher's* view on a situation; the researcher decides which are the important issues and which questions are to be asked and determines the whole framework within which the discourse of the research is conducted. Qualitative research is generally based on the belief that the people personally involved in a particular (leisure or tourism) situation are best placed to describe and explain their experiences or feelings in their own words, that they should be allowed to speak without the intermediary of the researcher and without being overly constrained by the framework imposed by the researcher – a sort of *cinema vérité* or *vox populi* style of research.

For many years, qualitative approaches were seen as problematical within the social sciences. Most social scientists sought to emulate the positivist methods of the natural sciences, as discussed in Chapter 2. This was reflected in early leisure and tourism studies. For example, in the earliest research methods text in the field, published in 1987, Kraus and Allen discussed only the classical 'scientific' model of research. They recognised the existence of qualitative as well as quantitative methods, but cautiously stated:

> Both forms of research represent important and valid approaches. However, there is a widely held view that the most significant kinds of research studies are those that are based on quantitative analysis, and that science must rely on actual measurement of scientific data. As a result, researchers tend to use quantitative measures wherever possible.
>
> (Kraus and Allen, 1987: 24–5)

They further stated that qualitative research methodology is 'less easily described', so there was no guidance on qualitative methods in their text. Nevertheless, they were of the opinion that: 'in such an individualistic and diversified field as recreation and leisure, there ought to be a place for research of a more intuitive or descriptive nature' (Kraus and Allen, 1987: 25).

A shift in attitudes towards qualitative methods in leisure studies took place across the Anglophone world during the 1980s, and this was reflected in the publication of Karla Henderson's *Dimensions of Choice: A Qualitative Approach to Recreation, Parks and Leisure Research* (Henderson, 1991). The shift was also reflected in the second edition of Kraus and Allen's book, published in 1998, in which they devoted a whole chapter to qualitative methods and one to documentary methods. The 'naturalistic perspective' was discussed alongside the scientific model and the above observations were modified to state:

> Quantitative research has tended to be more highly regarded than qualitative methods in varied scholarly disciplines, in part because this has been the approved method of investigation in the physical and natural sciences. However, a strong case can be made that, in such an individualistic and diversified field as recreation and leisure, there ought to be a place for research of a more deeply probing, intuitive, or philosophical nature.
>
> (Kraus and Allen, 1998: 36)

The divide between qualitative and quantitative methods was stronger in North America than in the UK, indeed, it has been argued that qualitative methods played a significant role in British leisure research from its beginnings in the 1970s (Veal, 1994).

The shift from an almost exclusively quantitative approach to a mix of quantitative and qualitative methods also took place in tourism studies. Ritchie and Goeldner's (1994) *Travel, Tourism and Hospitality Research* and Ryan's (1995) *Researching Tourist Satisfaction* both included chapters on qualitative methods, although the overall emphasis of the texts was quantitative. The evolution of qualitative research from the 1970s to the 1990s has been described by Riley and Love (2000). More recently, in 2004, a book of readings on *Qualitative Research in Tourism* (Phillimore and Goodson, 2004a) was published, with various contributions arguing strongly for a critical/interpretive approach to tourism research using qualitative approaches, and the editors providing another view of the evolutionary story (Phillimore and Goodson, 2004b).

Thus, in recent decades qualitative methods have become widely accepted and are no longer seen as exceptional and in need of special justification. In leisure studies qualitative studies are now at least as common in the literature as quantitative studies, and in tourism studies they are commonplace.

Merits of qualitative methods

Kelly (1980), in making a plea for more qualitative leisure research a quarter of a century ago, suggested that qualitative research has the following advantages over quantitative research.

1. The method corresponds with the nature of the phenomenon being studied – that is, leisure is a qualitative experience.
2. The method 'brings people back in' to leisure research. By contrast, quantitative methods tend to be very impersonal – *real* people with names and unique personalities do not feature.
3. The results of qualitative research are more understandable to people who are not statistically trained.
4. The method is better able to encompass personal change over time – by contrast much quantitative research tends to look only at current behaviour as related to current social, economic and environmental circumstances, ignoring the fact that most people's behaviour is heavily influenced by their life history and experience.
5. Reflecting his first point, Kelly argues that leisure, including tourism, involves a great deal of face-to-face interaction between people – involving symbols, gestures, etc. – and qualitative research is well suited to investigating this.
6. Kelly argues that qualitative techniques are better at providing an understanding of people's needs and aspirations, although some researchers in the psychological field in particular might disagree with him.

In this book it has been argued that different methods are not inherently good or bad, but just more or less appropriate for the task in hand. Thus Kelly's comments relate to particular types of research with particular purposes. A similar list of claims could of course be made about the merits of various forms of quantitative research, as indicated in a number of chapters in this book.

Peterson (1994), speaking from a market researcher's perspective, lists the potential uses of qualitative research as:

1. to develop hypotheses concerning relevant behaviour and attitudes;
2. to identify the full range of issues, views and attitudes which should be pursued in larger-scale research;
3. to suggest methods for quantitative enquiry – for example in terms of deciding who should be included in interview surveys;

4. to identify language used to address relevant issues (thus avoiding the use of jargon in questionnaires);

5. to understand how a buying decision is made – questionnaire surveys are not very good at exploring *processes*;

6. to develop new product, service or marketing strategy ideas – the free play of attitudes and opinions can be a rich source of ideas for the marketer;

7. to provide an initial screening of new product, service or strategy ideas;

8. to learn how communications are received – what is understood and how – particularly related to advertising.

The qualitative research process

Qualitative methods generally require a more flexible approach to overall research design and conduct than other approaches. Most quantitative research tends to be *sequential* in nature; the steps set out in Chapter 3 tend to be distinct and follow in a pre-planned sequence. This is inevitable because of the nature of the typical quantitative core data collection task. Much qualitative research involves a more fluid relationship between the various elements of the research – an approach which might be called *recursive*. In this approach hypothesis formation evolves as the research progresses; data analysis and collection take place concurrently; and writing is also often an evolutionary, on-going, process, rather than a separate process which happens at the end of the project. The two approaches are represented diagrammatically in Figure 8.1. Although these two approaches are presented here in the context of a contrast between quantitative and qualitative methods, in fact quantitative and qualitative methods can

Figure 8.1
Sequential
and recursive
approaches
to research

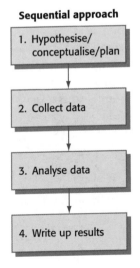

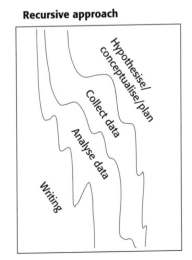

both involve sequential and recursive approaches. Thus, it is possible for an essentially quantitative study to involve a variety of data sources and a number of small-scale studies, which build in an iterative way. On the other hand, it is also possible for an essentially qualitative study to be conducted on a large scale, with a single data source – for example, a nation-wide study of council leaders, involving fairly standardised in-depth interviews.

An important philosophical perspective in the analysis of qualitative data is the concept of *grounded theory* developed by two sociologists, Barney Glaser and Anselm Strauss (1967). Grounded theory is concerned with the generation of theory from research, as opposed to research that tests existing theory. In this paradigm, theories and models should be *grounded* in real empirical observations rather than being governed by traditional methodologies and theories. In the generation of theory the researcher approaches the data with no pre-formed notions in mind, instead seeking to uncover patterns and contradictions through close examination of the data. To achieve this the researcher needs to be very familiar with the data, the subjects and the cultural context of the research. The process is a complex and personal one.

The range of methods – introduction

Qualitative techniques commonly used in leisure and tourism research and which are discussed in more detail in this chapter include: in-depth interviews; group interviews or focus groups; participant observation; textual analysis; biographical methods; and ethnography. The basic characteristics of these approaches are summarised in Figure 8.2.

While data collection and data analysis are, in practice, difficult to separate in qualitative research, the discussions of individual methods below concentrate on data collection. Since analysis procedures tend to have common characteristics across the range of qualitative data collection methods, analysis is dealt with in the second part of the chapter.

In-depth interviews

Nature

An in-depth interview is characterised by its length, depth and structure. In-depth interviews tend to be much longer than questionnaire-based interviews, typically taking at least half an hour and sometimes several hours. The method may involve interviewing people more than once. As the name implies, the in-depth interview seeks to probe more deeply than is possible with a questionnaire-based interview. Rather than just asking a question, recording a simple answer, and moving on, the in-depth interviewer typically encourages respondents to talk, asks supplementary questions and asks respondents to explain their answers. The in-depth interview is

In-depth interviews	■ Usually conducted with a relatively small number of subjects. ■ Interview guided by a checklist of topics of rather than formal questionnaire. ■ Interviews often tape-recorded and verbatim transcript prepared. ■ Interviews typically take at least half an hour and may extend over several hours. ■ Repeat interviews possible.
Group interviews/ focus groups	■ Similar to in-depth interviews but conducted with a group. ■ Interaction between subjects takes place as well as between interviewer and subject.
Participant observation	■ Researcher gathers information by being an actual participant with the subjects being studied. ■ Researcher may be known by the subjects as a researcher or may be *incognito*.
Textual analysis	■ Analysis of the content of 'texts', including print and audio-visual media.
Biographical research	■ Focusses on individual full or partial life histories. ■ May involve in-depth interviews but also documentary evidence and subjects' own written accounts.
Ethnography	■ Utilises a number of the above techniques rather than being a single technique – borrowed from anthropology.

Figure 8.2 Qualitative methods: summary

therefore less structured than a questionnaire-based interview – every interview in a study, although dealing with the same issues, will be different.

Purposes and situations

In-depth interviews tend to be used in three situations.

1. The subjects of the research may be relatively few in number so a questionnaire-based, quantitative style of research would be inappropriate.
2. The information likely to be obtained from each subject is expected to vary considerably, and in complex ways. An example would be interviews with the management staff of a recreation or tourism department of a local council, or interviews with the coaches of different national sports teams. Each of these interviews would be different and would be a 'story' in its own right. In reporting the research it would be the unique nature and structure of each of these 'stories' which would be of interest – data on 'what percentage of respondents said what' would not be relevant.
3. A topic is to be explored as a preliminary stage in planning a larger study, possibly a quantitative study, such as a questionnaire-based survey.

Checklist

Rather than a formal questionnaire the 'instrument' used in in-depth interviews is often a *checklist* of topics to be raised. For example, a formal questionnaire might ask a question: 'Which of the following countries have you ever visited on holiday?' The informal interview checklist might simply include the words 'countries visited'. The interviewer would shape the question according to the circumstances of a particular interview. If the interviewer is interested, for example, in the influence of childhood holiday experiences on adult visit patterns, in some interviews it may be necessary to ask a specific question such as: 'What overseas holiday trips did you take as a child?' In other interviews the interviewee might volunteer detailed information on childhood trips in response to the interviewer's initial question. It is then not necessary to ask the separate question about childhood trips. Thus in-depth interviews vary from interview to interview; they take on a life of their own. The skill on the part of the interviewer is to ensure that all relevant topics are covered – even though they may be covered in different orders and in different ways in different interviews.

The design of the checklist should nevertheless be as methodical as the design of a formal questionnaire – in particular, the items to be included on the checklist should be based on the conceptual framework for the study and the resultant list of data needs, as discussed in Chapter 3. An example of a checklist is included as Appendix 8.1. The example given is in the form of a fairly terse list of topics. An alternative would be to include fully worded questions, as would appear in a questionnaire; this may be necessary when interviewers other than the researcher are being used. The problem with fully worded questions is that actually turning to the clipboard and reading out lengthy questions can interrupt the flow and informality of the interview.

The interviewing process

Conducting a good in-depth interview could be said to require the skills of a good investigative journalist. As Dean and his colleagues put it:

> Many people feel that a newspaper reporter is a far cry from a social scientist. Yet many of the data of social science today are gathered by interviewing and observation techniques that resemble those of a skilled newspaper man at work on the study of, say, a union strike or a political convention. It makes little sense for us to belittle these less rigorous methods as 'unscientific'. We will do better to study them and the techniques they involve so that we can make better use of them in producing scientific information.
>
> (Dean *et al.*, quoted in McCall and Simmons, 1969: 1)

An important skill in interviewing is to avoid becoming so taken up in the conversational style of the interview that the interviewee is 'led' by the interviewer. The interviewer should avoid agreeing – or disagreeing – with the interviewee or suggesting answers. This is more difficult than it sounds because in normal conversation we tend to make friendly noises and contribute to the discussion. In an in-depth interview we are torn between the need to maintain a friendly conversational atmosphere and the need *not* to influence the interviewee's responses.

Some of the carefully planned sequencing of questions which is built into formal questionnaires must be achieved by the interviewer being very sensitive and quick thinking. For example, having discovered that the respondent does not go to the theatre, the interviewer should not lead the respondent by saying: 'Is this because it is too expensive?' Rather, the interviewee should be asked a more open question, such as: 'Why is that?' If the interviewee does not mention cost, but cost is of particular interest in the study, then the respondent might be asked a question such as: 'What about seat prices?' But this would be only *after* the interviewee has given his or her own unprompted reasons for not attending the theatre.

Whyte (1982) lists a sort of hierarchy in interviewer responses which vary in their degree of *intervention* in the interview. Whyte also sees this as the interviewer exercising varying degrees of *control* over the interview. Beginning with the least intrusive style of intervention, Whyte's list is as shown in Figure 8.3. It should be noted that, except for the sixth of these responses, the interviewer is essentially drawing on what the subject has already said and is inviting her or him to expand on it.

An important skill in interviewing of this sort is not to be afraid of silence. Some questions puzzle respondents and they need time to think. The interviewer does not have to fill the space with noise under the guise of 'helping' the interviewee. The interviewee should be allowed time to ponder. The initiative can be left with the respondent to ask for an explanation if a question is unclear. While it is pleasant to engender a conversational atmosphere in these situations, the in-depth interview is in fact different from a conversation. The interviewer is meant to listen and encourage the respondent to talk – not to engage in debate!

Recording

Tape-recording of in-depth interviews is common, although in some cases it might be felt that such a procedure could inhibit respondents. If tape-recording is not possible then notes must be taken during the interview or immediately afterwards. There can be great value in producing complete *verbatim* (word for word) transcripts of interviews. This is a laborious process – one hour of interview taking as much as six hours to transcribe. Such transcripts can, however, be used to analyse the results of interviews in a more methodical and complete manner than is possible with notes.

1.	'Uh-huh'	A non-verbal response which merely indicates that the interviewer is still listening and interested.
2.	'That's interesting'	Encourages the subject to keep talking or expand on the current topic.
3.	Reflection	Repeating the last statement as a question – e.g. 'So you don't like sport?'
4.	Probe	Inviting explanations of statements – e.g. 'Why don't you like sport?'
5.	Back tracking	Remembering something the subject said earlier and inviting further information – e.g. 'Let's go back to what you were saying about your school days.'
6.	New topic	Initiating a new topic – e.g. 'Can we talk about other leisure activities – what about entertainment?'

Figure 8.3 Interviewing interventions – Whyte

Focus groups

Nature

The idea of interviewing groups of people together rather than individually is becoming increasingly popular in market and community research. In this technique the interviewer becomes the *facilitator* of a discussion rather than an interviewer as such. The aim of the process is much the same as in an in-depth interview, but in this case the 'subjects' interact with each other as well as with the researcher.

Purposes

The technique can be used:

■ when a particular group is important in a study but is so small in number that members of the group would not be adequately represented in a general community survey – for example members of minority ethnic groups or people with disabilities;

■ when the interaction/discussion process itself is of interest – for example in testing reactions to a proposed new product, or when investigating how people form political opinions;

■ as an alternative to the in-depth interview, when it may not be practical to arrange for individual in-depth interviews but people are willing to be interviewed as a group – for example some youth groups or members of some ethnic communities.

Methods

A group will usually comprise between five and twelve participants. They may be chosen from a 'panel' of people who make themselves available to market researchers for this sort of exercise, or they may be chosen because they are members of a particular group of interest to the research – for instance local residents in a particular area, members of a sports club, or a group of people on a holiday package. The members of the group may or may not be known to one another.

The usual procedure is to tape-record the discussion and for the researcher to produce a summary from the recording.

Many of the same considerations apply here as in the in-depth interview situation: the process is informal but the interviewer (or convenor or discussion leader) still has a role in guiding the discussion and ensuring that all the aspects of the topic are covered. In addition, in the group interview, the interviewer has the task of ensuring that everyone in the group has their say and that the discussion is not dominated by one or two vociferous members of the group.

Participant observation

Nature

In participant observation the researcher becomes a participant in the social process being studied. The classic study of this type is Whyte's *Street Corner Society* (1955), in which the researcher spent several years living with an inner city US Italian community. Smith's (1985) study of pubs in England is a direct leisure example as is Wynne's (1986) study of community involvement with recreation facilities.

Purposes

In leisure and tourism elements of 'participant observation' are common in many types of research. For instance, a researcher involved in studying the use of a park or resort can easily spend periods as a user of the facility. This is, however, a very minimalist view of participant observation. Traditionally the process has involved much more interaction of the researcher with the people being researched. In many cases some sort of participant observation is the only way of researching particular phenomena – for instance it would be difficult to study what really goes on in a drug sub-culture or in some youth sub-cultures using a questionnaire and clip-board. Becoming part of the group is the obvious way of studying the group.

Methods

Participant observation raises a number of practical/tactical problems. For example, in some cases actually gaining admittance to the social setting of interest may be a problem – for instance where close-knit groups are involved. Having gained admittance to the setting, the question arises as to whether to pose as a 'typical' member of the group, whether to adopt a plausible 'disguise' (e.g. a 'journalist' or 'writer') or whether to admit to being a researcher.

Selection of informants is an issue to be addressed by the participant observer in the same way that sampling must be considered by the survey researcher. The members of the study group who are most friendly and talkative may be the easiest to communicate with, but may give a biased picture of the views and behaviour of the group.

In addition there are practical problems to be faced over how to record information. When the researcher's identity has not been revealed, the taking of notes or the use of a tape-recorder may be impossible. Even when the researcher has identified her or himself as such, or has assumed a plausible 'identity', the use of such devices may interfere with the sort of natural relationship which the researcher is trying to establish. The question of the researcher's relationship with informants also raises ethical questions, which are discussed in Chapter 3.

Recording of information can present problems, especially if the researcher is *incognito*, or simply wishes to avoid introducing the distancing and inhibitions which the presence of a notebook may entail. The taking of regular and detailed notes is, however, the basic data recording method. This may be supplemented by photographs and even video and tape-recordings in some instances.

Analysing texts

Nature

The analysis of texts, such as plays and novels, is the very basis of some disciplines in the humanities, such as English, media studies and cultural studies. As researchers from these disciplines have turned their attention to leisure and tourism issues, and as the relationships between leisure, tourism and 'cultural products' have become recognised, the approach is playing an increasingly important role in leisure and tourism research. The term *text* is now used to embrace not just printed material, but also pictures, posters, recorded music, film and television. Indeed, virtually any cultural product can, in the jargon, be *read* as *text*. The trend is reflected in the increasing use of the term *gaze* to describe the activity of both leisure and tourism researchers and the subjects of their research. John Urry, in his book *The Tourist Gaze* (1990) states the following.

> Tourism research should involve the examination of texts, not only written texts but also maps, landscapes, paintings, films, townscapes, TV programmes, brochures, and so on . . . Thus, social research significantly consists of interpreting texts, through various mainly qualitative techniques, to identify the discursive structures which give rise to and sustain, albeit temporarily, a given tourist site.
> (Urry, 1990: 238–9)

It is not proposed to outline analysis techniques in detail here, since approaches are very varied, including the qualitative, literary 'reading' of texts, the *interpretation* of texts sometimes referred to as *hermeneutics*, and the highly quantified form of analysis known as *content analysis*. The approach here is, rather, to introduce some examples of work in this area.

Novels and other literature

Sönmez *et al.* (1993) examine the concept of leisure as portrayed in the novels of Kenyan author Ngugi wa Thiong'o. The analysis provides a perspective on a non-Western view of leisure and its place in a culture faced with the upheaval of the colonial and post-colonial experience. In two papers, Hultsman and Harper (1992, and Harper and Hultsman, 1992) analyse a collection of 1930s essays on life in the 'Old South' of the United States to reveal new insights into leisure and class at that time. One chapter in Paul Barry's (1994: 414–44) biography of Kerry Packer provides a fascinating insight into one, very rich, man's approach to 'serious leisure' (Stebbins, 1992) – in this case polo – illustrating the value of biographies as a source of material on leisure. The relationship between tourism and literature is explored in Anderson and Robinson (2002).

Mass media coverage

Media coverage of selected topics can be studied quantitatively by measuring the column centimetres devoted to the topic in newspapers or the time devoted to the topic on television. Examples are the studies by Brown (1995) and Rowe and

Brown (1994), of press coverage of women's sport in Australian newspapers, Toohey's (1990) analysis of the television coverage of the Barcelona Olympic Games and the study by Cuneen *et al.* (1989) involving an analysis of the verbal and pictorial press coverage of a sporting event.

Film

MacCannell (1993) provides an extensive analysis of the tourist film *Cannibal Tours*, upon which he builds a detailed theoretical interpretation of the role of tourism in the modern world. Rojek (1993) provides an analysis of Disney films and their role in contemporary culture, in his paper 'Disney culture'.

Material culture

In his paper on 'The interpretation of documents and material culture', Hodder (1994) devotes relatively little space to documents, but concentrates on the idea of studying 'material culture' or artefacts. Among the latter he includes dress fashions, national flags and the archaeological study of garbage. The scope for the direct study of leisure-related cultural products is enormous. Among examples in the research literature are the study of the theme parks of the Disney Corporation (Rojek, 1993; Klugman *et al.*, 1995), postcards (Cohen, 1993), American musicals (Dyer, 1993) and heavy metal rock music (Straw, 1993).

Biographical research

Nature

Biographical research covers a range of research methods which involve researching all or a substantial part of individuals' or groups of individuals' lives. The most common example of such research is the conventional biography or autobiography, but the biographical approach includes a number of other research approaches and outputs, including: oral history; memory work; and personal domain histories. Detailed guidance on the conduct of biographical research is not given in this book, but a brief overview of the field is given here and sources of further information are provided in the further reading section.

Biography/autobiography

There are many published accounts of lives of business leaders which, while often read for entertainment, also provide insight into how business and business leaders operate. Perhaps the best-known is the autobiography of Lee Iacocca (1984), the CEO of Chrysler during a turbulent period. In the case of Walt Disney, there is an enormous literature in which the biography of Walt Disney himself and the story of the corporation are intertwined (e.g. Bryman, 1995; Foglesong, 2001; Project on Disney, 1995).

In Australia, *The Rise and Fall of Alan Bond* (owner of breweries and television stations among other things) and the *Rise and Rise of Kerry Packer* (owner of television stations, magazines and casinos), both by Paul Barry (1990, 1994), are notable examples of leisure-related business biographies.

Oral history

Oral history involves tape-recording eye-witness accounts of events and typically storing the tapes and/or a transcription of them in an archive as a source for research. While such accounts range more widely than the interviewees' own lives, they are nevertheless personal accounts. An example is Parker's (1988) study of a British mining community during the miners' strikes of the 1980s – the book includes accounts by miners, Coal Board employees, police and community members.

Memory work

Memory work is a structured way of eliciting subjects' memories of events; it can be seen as a focus group aided by individual writing. Participants are asked to write a short account of an experience related to the research topic – for example, holiday experiences (Small, 2004). The written accounts are read aloud in focus group settings and discussed, and may be followed up with further writing and/or interviewing.

Personal domain histories

In the 1980s, a technique termed 'personal leisure histories' was developed by Hedges (1986) to study the ways in which significant changes in life circumstances (marriage, birth of a child, change of job, health issues, etc.) impacted on patterns of leisure participation. While no known example exists, it seems clear that such a technique might be used to focus on more specific domains of life, such as holidays, sport or consumption activities, hence the use of the term personal *domain* histories.

Ethnography

The ethnographic style of research is not one technique but an approach drawing on a variety of techniques. Generally, as applied to leisure and tourism research, it seeks to see the world through the eyes of those being researched, allowing them to speak for themselves, often revealed through extensive direct quotations in the research report. Often also, the aim is to debunk conventional, establishment, 'common sense' views of 'social problems', 'deviants', sexual and ethnic stereotypes, and so on. In leisure studies the approach has become particularly associated with 'cultural studies', for example of youth sub-cultures and ethnic groups.

It is better to read the results of the research than read about the methodology *per se*. Examples are Hall and Jefferson (1976) on youth sub-cultures, Griffin *et al.* (1982) on women and leisure and Hollands (1985) on unemployed youth.

Analysis of qualitative data

Introduction

This section of the chapter addresses the task of analysing qualitative data. As indicated earlier in the chapter, it is sometimes difficult to separate the collection and analysis processes for qualitative data, at least in a temporal sense; but there is nevertheless a clear difference between certain data collection activities, such as interviewing someone with a tape-recorder, and certain analysis activities, such as poring over typed interview transcripts.

Traditionally qualitative data have been analysed by manual means, and this continues, but in recent years computer software has become available to aid the process. Computers replicate and speed-up some of the more mechanical of the manual processes, but, of course, the task of interpretation remains with the researcher. This section begins by discussing the question of data storage and confidentiality; it then goes on to consider manual analysis methods and computer-based methods in turn. Since the most common form of qualitative data is interview or focus group transcripts or notes, the following discussions are based on this form of data. Most of the procedures nevertheless apply, in adapted form, to other forms of data, such as printed materials from organisational archives and the media.

In Chapter 3, it was noted that the development of a conceptual framework and research questions or hypotheses is the most difficult and challenging part of a research project. In quantitative research involving primary data collection this work must mostly be done in advance of data collection because of the formal, once-off nature of the data collection process. It is therefore based primarily on reading of the literature. In the case of qualitative research this challenging work may be spread throughout the research process, as indicated in Figure 8.4. This is another way of viewing the induction/deduction distinction discussed in Chapter 2.

Data storage and confidentiality

Regardless of whether qualitative data are analysed manually or by computer, consideration should be given to the security and confidentiality of transcripts and tapes, particularly if sensitive material is involved. This raises ethical issues, as discussed in Chapter 3. As a precaution, research material should ideally not be labelled with real names of organisations or people. Fictitious names should be created. If it is felt that it will be necessary to relate tapes and transcripts back to original respondents at some later date, for example for second interviews, a key relating fictitious to real identities should be kept in a separate, secure place. Of course actual names mentioned by respondents on tapes cannot easily be erased, and it is a matter of judgement as to whether it is necessary to disguise such names in transcripts – in most cases they should be disguised in any quotations of the material in the research report. In some cases, however, it is necessary to create transcripts which are, in a way, less anonymous than the original. For example, an interviewee might say: 'I find it difficult to get on with John' – the transcript might change 'John' to 'David', but may need to identify John/David's position – for example: 'I find it difficult to get on with David [Supervisor]'.

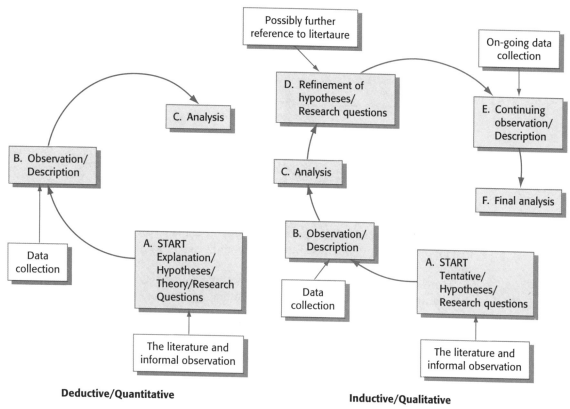

Figure 8.4 Circular model of the research process in quantitative and qualitative contexts

Case study example

A case study of some in-depth interview data is used to illustrate qualitative data analysis – both manual and by computer. Figure 8.5 presents a very simple conceptual framework for studying leisure activity choice. It is based on a model presented by Brandenburg *et al.* (1982) and further developed in Veal (1995) and suggests that individuals' choice of leisure activity is influenced by background characteristics and experiences, present constraints and personal factors, but also by key events which trigger participation. While this example is expressed in terms of leisure as a whole, the framework would be suitable for analysis of a sector of leisure, such as sport, or holiday-taking, or the arts. Thus the activity choices, X, Y, Z, could relate to the whole range of leisure activities or a restricted sector. The model could be explored quantitatively, for example, by means of a questionnaire, but that would be likely to require prior definition of the three sets of influences and a set of key events. Further, since any one of the three groups could involve a substantial list of items (e.g. Background/ experience: parental influence, school experience, higher education experience, geography/climate, activities experienced), the analysis task would be daunting. A qualitative

Figure 8.5
Outline
conceptual
framework for a
qualitative study
of leisure choice

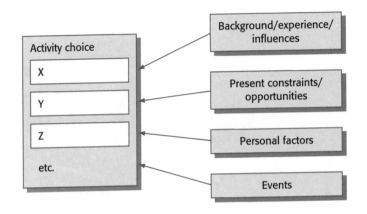

approach would enable the various factors and influences to be identified and analysed in a more exploratory manner. Interviews could be conducted using a checklist of the sort presented in Appendix 8.1.

Figure 8.6 contains short extracts from three interviews with individuals about their leisure choices. The comments in the first column are explained below. These transcripts are used to illustrate manual and computer analysis of texts. The aim is to illustrate the mechanics of analysis in a way which could be readily replicated by the

---

Mark (Age 22, Male, Student, Income £8K)

Q. What would you say is your most time-consuming leisure activity outside of the home at present?

Act.: Sport – football
Constraint:
Commitments,
Need to keep fit,
Time, Money

Well, I would say it's playing football, at least during the season. While the football's on, because of training twice a week and needing to be fairly serious about keeping fit I don't do much else: I probably only go to a pub once – or at most twice – a week. I don't have the time or the money to do much more.

Q. How were you introduced to football?

Influence: Parent +

Teacher + +

Event: Coaching clinic

Oh, I've always played . . . since I could run around I suppose. My dad says he spotted my talent – so-called – when I was a toddler, but it was one of the teachers at primary school that really encouraged me. He persuaded my mum to take me to a coaching clinic when I was about 8 or 9, then I got into the local under-11s.

Q. Why do you think you are attracted to football?

Personal: Competitive,
Team oriented, Active

Well, I'm pretty competitive – so I like sport generally. I like the team-spirit thing with football – I don't think I could do an individual sport where you didn't have a team around you. You make good friends. And it's fast and you're involved the whole time . . . I get bored playing cricket where you're standing around half the time.

Figure 8.6 Interview transcript extracts

Donna (Age 27, Female, FT Employed, Income £19K)

Q. What would you say is your most time-consuming leisure activity outside of the home at present?

Act.: Socialising

Just socialising I would say . . . you know, going out for a meal or a drink with friends . . . I go to the gym once or twice a week . . . and I like to swim a bit in the summer, but they don't take up much time overall.

Q. When did you first start going out socially on a regular basis?

Event: Earning money
Influence: Peers

I was about 16, I guess: the parents were a bit restrictive, but once I started earning a bit of money at weekends I managed to go out at least twice a week – to parties and to the cinema and stuff . . . my mum and dad didn't have any money to give me, so it wasn't until I started to work part-time that I could go out, sort of regularly. I've always had a fairly close-knit group of friends, girlfriends, about the same age as me, who've always gone out together . . . even with boyfriends – and one husband – arriving on the scene and disappearing from time to time!

Q. What limits the number of times you go out socialising in a week?

Constraint: Time, Money

Time and money! But mostly it's time these days – 'cos we don't always spend a lot.

Q. What are the essential ingredients for a good night out?

Personal: Social – informal

Constraint: Time

It's all about people . . . people you know and people you might meet! Things like good food – and drink – or good music are important, but the enjoyment comes from doing it with your friends and knowing they have the same sorts of tastes and the same sense of fun. I am serious enough at work, I couldn't imagine myself spending a lot of time with some team sport with serious training and all that: I just don't have the time – or the inclination!

Lee (Age 23, Male, FT Employed, Income £22K)

Q. What would you say is your most time-consuming leisure activity outside of the home at present?

Event: Girlfriend
Personal: Anti-routine

It varies. I don't have any set pattern. Up until a couple of weeks ago I was going out with this girl and, apart from going round each other's house, we spent a lot of time going out, one way or another – to the pub, cinema, walking, shopping – it varied. Now that's stopped, it's still a bit of a mixture, but with various friends. I hate routine, so I don't get involved with anything regular.

Q. So what single thing – from among the mixture of things you do – would you say you spent most time doing in the last week?

Act.: Cinema

In the last week? Well, I haven't been out that much: it would have to be the movies: I went twice and one of them was one of those late-night double billers – about four hours.

Q. Are you a movie buff?

Event: Good review

I wouldn't go that far, but I like movies. I read reviews and that. The movie I saw on Tuesday had a lot of hype and I saw two or three good reviews. For once, the hype was justified: it was really good. Really good: better than the reviews – and that doesn't happen often.

Figure 8.6 *(continued)*

student. The length of the transcripts extracts and their number has therefore been limited. The substantive outcomes are therefore incidental and not particularly meaningful taken in isolation. In a complete research exercise full transcripts, running to many pages, would be involved and, although we are dealing with qualitative research, the number of interviews/transcripts in a study of this type would normally be more than three.

Manual methods of analysis

Introduction

There are various ways of analysing interview transcripts or notes. The essence of any analysis procedure must be to return to the terms of reference, the conceptual framework and the research questions or hypotheses of the research, as discussed in Chapter 3. The information gathered should be sorted through and evaluated in relation to the concepts identified in the conceptual framework, the research questions posed or the hypotheses put forward. In qualitative research, those original ideas may be tentative and fluid. Questions and/or hypotheses and definitions and operationalisation of concepts may be detailed or general; the more detailed and specific they are, the more likely they will be to closely influence the analysis. Conversely, the more general and tentative they are the more likely it is that the data analysis process will influence their development and refinement. Data gathering, hypothesis formulation and the identification of concepts is a two-way, evolving process. Ideas are refined and revised in the light of the information gathered, as described in relation to the *recursive* approach and *grounded theory* approach discussed above.

In addition to the problem of ordering and summarising the data conceptually, the researcher is faced with the very practical problem of just how to approach the pile of interview notes or transcripts.

Reading

The basic activity in qualitative analysis is *reading* of notes, transcripts, documents or *listening* or *viewing* audio and video materials. In what follows, it is assumed that the material being analysed is text – while practical adaptations are necessary for audio and video material, the principles are the same. The reading is done initially in light of initial research questions and/or hypotheses and/or those which have evolved during the data collection process.

Emergent themes

A typical approach to qualitative analysis is to search for *emergent themes* – the equivalent of *variables* in quantitative research. The themes may arise from the conceptual framework and research questions, and therefore be consciously searched for in a deductive way, or they may emerge unprompted in a more inductive way. Typically, both processes will be at work.

Themes which emerge from the transcripts are 'flagged' in the left-hand margin of the transcripts in Figure 8.6. The researcher's judgement of the strength with which the views are expressed is indicated here with one or more plus or minus signs. It is clear that other themes might be identified and alternative terms might be used for the items which are identified, illustrating the personal and subjective nature of qualitative analysis.

The 'developed' conceptual framework presented in Figure 8.7 shows how some of the themes/concepts/factors and relationships emerging from the interviews might begin to be incorporated into the conceptual framework. On the basis of information from short abstracts from three interviews, the conceptual framework is *developed* but not *fully* developed; it represents work in progress.

Figure 8.7
Developed conceptual framework for qualitative study of leisure choice

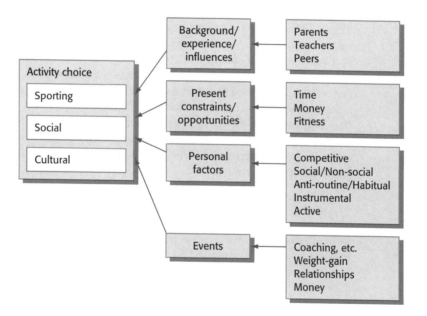

Mechanics

The initial steps in qualitative analysis involve fairly methodical procedures to classify and organise the information collected.

Analysis can be done by hand on hard-copy transcripts, which should have a wide margin on one side to accommodate the 'flagging' of themes as discussed above. Colour coding can be used in the flagging process and 'Post-it' notes can also be used to mark key sections.

Standard word processing packages can be of considerable assistance in the analysis process. The space for flagging can then be secured using the 'columns' or tables facility in the word processor. Word processing packages also have facilities for:

- adding 'comments' and for blocking text with colour, underlining or bold;
- 'searching' to locate key words and phrases;
- coding and cross-referencing using indexing or cross-referencing procedures.

It can be seen, therefore, that standard word processing packages have a number of features to aid text analysis although obviously not as many as the specialist packages discussed later in this chapter.

It can be useful to number the paragraphs in a transcript, or use the line numbering facility available in word-processing packages. This can facilitate a *cataloguing* process, which might result in something like the following:

Constraint – time: Mark: p. 2, para. 3
                      Anna: p. 7, para. 4
Constraint – money: Mark: p. 2, para. 3

This is often necessary to keep track of topics across a number of interviews, but also because topics are typically covered several times in the same interview. A particular focus of the analysis may be related not to particular substantive topics raised by the interviewer, and therefore related to particular questions, but to, for example, underlying attitudes expressed by interviewees, which might arise at any time in an interview.

The catalogue becomes the basis for further analysis and writing up the results of the analysis: being able to locate points in the transcripts where themes are expressed enables the researcher to check the wording used by respondents and explore context and related sentiments and facilitates the location of suitable quotations to illustrate the write-up of the results.

Analysis

In qualitative data analysis it is possible to use techniques and presentation methods that are similar to those used in quantitative analysis. For example, in Figure 8.8 an analysis similar to a cross-tabulation is shown, with twelve hypothetical interviewees 'plotted' on a two-dimensional space based on two variables derived from the interviews referred to above. The placing of the respondents depends on a qualitative assessment based on the interview transcripts. It can be seen that, in the example, the respondents fall into four groups. Given that this is a qualitative survey and the sample of interviewees is unlikely to be statistically representative, the *numbers* in each group are not important, but simply the identification of the existence of four groups. Such a grouping would provide the basis for further analysis of the transcripts (see Huberman and Miles 1994: 437).

Thus analysis of qualitative data has certain parallels with quantitative analysis, with themes corresponding to variables and relationships explored in ways which parallel cross-tabulation and correlation. But they are parallels only, not equivalents. Whereas quantitative analysis generally seeks to establish whether certain observations and relationships are generally true in the wider population on the basis of probability, qualitative analysis seeks to establish the existence of relationships on the basis of

Figure 8.8
'Cross-
tabulation' of
qualitative data

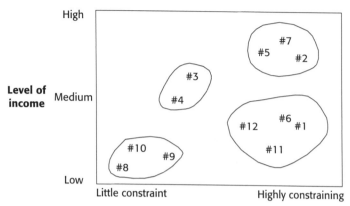

Numbers refer to individual interviewees

what individual people say and do. If only one person or organisation in the study is shown to behave in a certain way as a result of certain forces, this is a valid finding for qualitative research – the question of just how widespread such behaviour is in the wider society becomes a matter for other types of research.

Detailed analysis may be less important when the purpose of in-depth or informal interviews is to provide input into the design of a formal questionnaire. In that case the interviewer will generally make a series of notes arising from the interview which are likely to be of relevance to the questionnaire design process, and can also provide input to the design process from memory, as long as the questionnaire design work is undertaken fairly soon after the interviews.

Qualitative analysis using computer software – introduction

When the researcher is faced with a substantial number of lengthy documents to analyse, the decision may be made to ease the laborious process of coding and analysing by making use of one of the computer-aided qualitative data analysis software (CAQDAS) packages now available. As with statistical packages, it takes time to learn how to use qualitative analysis packages and to set up a system for an individual project, so a decision has to be made, on the basis of the size and complexity of the documentary material to be analysed, as to whether that investment of time will result in a net time saving, compared with manual analysis. Consideration should, however, be given to the fact that, once an analysis system has been set up, more analysis can be relatively quickly undertaken, possibly resulting in better quality of output than may have been possible using manual methods. Further, looking to the future, a computerised analysis system can more easily be returned to at future dates for additional interrogation. Finally, even if the amount of data in a given project does not justify setting up a computerised analysis system, a smaller project may be an easier vehicle for learning to use and gain experience with a package.

It has been noted above that standard word-processing packages such as *Word* offer facilities which can aid in sorting and locating material in transcripts. The standard word-processing package is, however, limited in its capabilities for this purpose. A number of purpose-designed CAQDAS packages are now on the market. One of the most commonly used, and which is demonstrated here, is *NVivo*, part of a stable of packages from QSR (Qualitative Solutions and Research Pty Ltd), which includes N6, an updated version of the well-known *NUD*IST*, and *XSight* designed for market researchers. Details of the packages can be found on the QSR website, the address for which is given at the end of the chapter.

NVivo

Introduction

NVivo is one of the most widely used CAQDAS packages. The reasons for its popularity include its ability to assist in shaping and understanding data and its capacity to help form and test theoretical assumptions about the data. *NVivo* is also able to index and coordinate the analysis of text stored as computer files, including primary textual material, such as interview transcripts and field notes, as well as other material such as newspaper clippings and company reports.

Running *NVivo* software

The transcripts on leisure choice presented in the manual analysis section above are used to demonstrate operation of *NVivo* here. An ideal way for readers to engage with this section is to replicate the processes outlined on a computer. In what follows it is assumed that *NVivo* has been installed on a computer and an *NVivo* icon is displayed on the computer 'desktop'.

It is not possible in a short summary such as this to present all the features of *NVivo* – this is done in the tutorials and 'Help' built into the package, the manuals which accompany the software, and in other specialist texts, such as those by Gibbs (2002) and Bazeley and Richards (2000). Details of support materials are provided on the QSR website (see end of this chapter). Here just seven *NVivo* procedures, considered to be sufficient to get someone started with the package, are outlined. They are:

■ Starting up

■ Creating a project

■ Creating documents

■ Document attributes

■ Setting up a coding system

■ Coding text

■ Analysis

Typically, in order to move from step to step in any process, the user of *Nvivo* is required to click on such buttons as 'Next', 'Finish' or 'OK'. These instructions are indicated below in square brackets: [Next], [Finish], etc.

Starting up

Clicking on the *NVivo* icon, opens the *Nvivo* 'Launch pad' window, as shown in Figure 8.9. The user is provided with the opportunity to:

- Create a [new] Project
- Open a [existing] Project
- Open an *NVivo* tutorial [on how *Nvivo* works]
- Exit *NVivo*

Figure 8.9
NVivo: Launch Pad

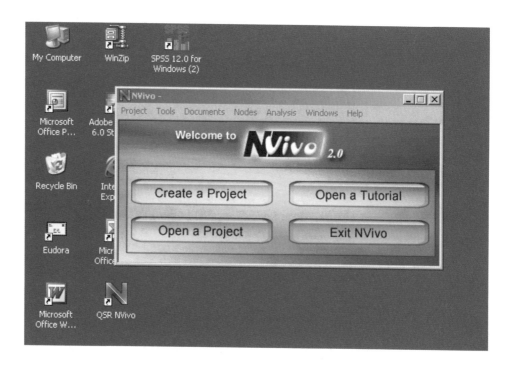

Creating a project

To demonstrate the system, we start with **Create a project**. This involves creating a named location for a research project, into which the documents to be analysed, such as interview transcripts, will later be added – rather like setting up a normal Windows 'folder' for storing files. The basic procedure is outlined in Figure 8.10.

Figure 8.10
NVivo: Create project

- Click on **Create a New Project** to reveal the **New Project Wizard**: this offers the user a **Typical** or **Custom** set up – we will deal only with the Typical set up here. [Next]
- A dialog box is presented requesting a **Name** and **Description**. Type in 'Leisure Choice' as the Name and 'Leisure Choice Project' as the *Description*. [Next]
- *NVivo* confirms the project name and description and indicates that the details will be stored in a folder located at: C:\QSR Projects\Leisure Choice. [Finish]

    (Note: If you wish to save your project details onto a floppy disk, as is sometimes necessary in a computer laboratory environment, use the 'Custom' set-up, where an alternative file location – e.g. A:Leisure Choice – can be specified)

- The *NVivo* 'Project Pad' now appears on the screen, as shown below.

    (Note: This screen can also now be obtained by clicking on 'Open a Project' in the Launch Pad and selecting Project Name 'Leisure Choice').

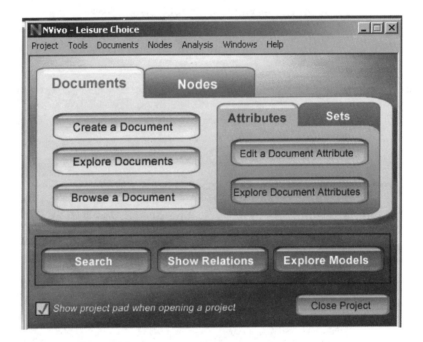

Creating documents

Each of the interview transcripts in Figure 8.6 becomes a separate document for *NVivo* analysis purposes. Documents must be saved in Rich Text Format (suffix .rtf), which can easily be done in word-processing packages such as *Word* by saving a copy of the document using *Save as* and selecting Rich Text Format in *File type* – a copy of the file will automatically be saved with a suffix: .rtf. The text should be as plain as possible: *Italic* and **bold** and *Word* style headings can be used, but more complex formatting, such as tables and columns, should not be used.

For this demonstration, therefore, three files were created, containing the questions and answers, but not the annotations, from Figure 8.6. These were named: Int_Mark.rtf; Int_Donna.rtf; and Int_Lee.rtf.

Figure 8.11
NVivo: Create
document

1. In the Project Pad, click on **Create a Document**. The **New Document Wizard: Creation** dialog box appears and offers a range of options – for this demonstration, select the first option: **Locate and import readable external file(s)**. [Next]
2. Locate the first text file – in this case Int_Mark.rtf – on the hard disk or floppy disk. [Open]
3. The **New Document Wizard: Obtain Name** box offers a range of ways of providing a name and description for the file. In this case, select the first option: **Use the source file name as document name, and first paragraph as description**. [Finish] This means that *NVivo* will refer to this document by the name of: 'Int_Mark.rtf' and, when appropriate, will also use the more detailed Description: 'Mark (Age 27, Male, Student, Income £8K)'.
4. Repeat this process for each the other two interview files.
5. Returning to the Project Pad, click on **Explore Documents** to reveal the three files listed, as shown below.

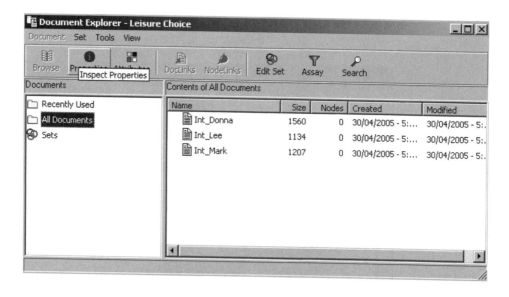

These can be stored on hard disk, floppy disk or CDROM. Copies can be downloaded from the book website, details of which are provided at the end of this chapter.

The three documents must be loaded into the 'Leisure Choice' *NVivo* project system, as shown in Figure 8.11.

Document attributes

Attributes of documents can be recorded rather like variables in a quantitative study. This can aid analysis. For example, if one attribute of the interview transcripts is 'Gender of interviewee', results can be divided into male and female for some analysis purposes. We have four items of information for each respondent: age; gender; employment status; and income (see Figure 8.6) and these can be recorded as attributes, as shown in Figure 8.12.

Figure 8.12
NVivo:
Document
attributes

1. In the Project Pad, select **Documents** and click on **Edit a Document Attributes**.
2. **Create new Attribute** is highlighted. In the **Type the new attribute name** box, type *Age*, then specify **value type** – in this case 'Number'. [Apply]
3. Repeat for *Gender* (Value type: String), *Empstat* (Value type: String) and *Income* (Value type: Number). 'Descriptions' can be added in the space provided if you wish – e.g. 'Annual salary, £'000s'. [Close]

   This defines the Attributes to be used – similar to defining variables in SPSS. Values for each interviewee/transcript must now be recorded.
4. In the Project Pad, select **Documents** and click on **Explore document attributes**.
5. A spread-sheet-style table is presented, with document names down the side and attributes across the top – as below, but with the table spaces blank.
6. To enter the attribute data, in each space right-click, then click on **New Value** and enter the value [OK], as shown below. Once started, values which have already been used appear in the dialog box – clicking on these values removes the necessity to re-type frequently used values – e.g. male and female – when a number of documents is involved.

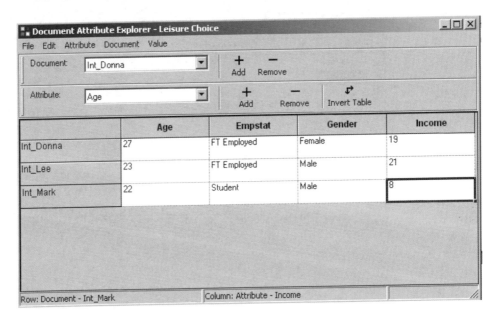

Setting up a coding system

Documents such as interview transcripts must be *coded* before they can be analysed. This involves setting up a *coding system*. A coding system can be developed and evolve as the research progresses, but it has to start somewhere. In the section on manual coding above, the 'flagging' process is similar to the coding process involved here. On the basis of an initial conceptual framework (Figure 8.5) and reading just short extracts from three interviews, it was possible to develop a coding system which is displayed in the notes in Figure 8.6 and reflected in the more developed conceptual framework in Figure 8.7. In a full-fledged project the researcher would go on to read and code the full interview transcripts of the three example interviewees and other interviewees as well, and would apply the flagging/coding system to the other texts read and would further develop the system in an inductive way. Coding systems using *NVivo* are developed in the same way. In the example below, the codes developed in the manual process are entered into the *NVivo* Leisure Choice project to demonstrate the beginnings of an *NVivo*-based coding process.

The grouping of related concepts, as shown in Figure 8.7, are referred to in *NVivo* as **trees** and **tree nodes**. Free-floating concepts, which have not been linked to any tree structure are referred to as **free nodes**. The procedures in Figure 8.13 describe the process for entering coding information from Figure 8.7 into the *NVivo* project file.

Figure 8.13
NVivo: Setting up a coding system

1. In the Project Pad, click on **Nodes**, then on **Create a Node**, then the **Tree** tab: the **Create Node** dialog box is displayed, as shown below.
   The **Create Node** dialog box now appears as follows:

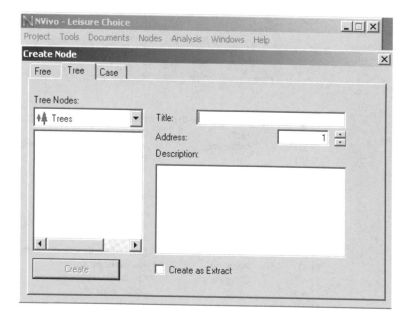

2. Type *Main activity* in the **Title** box and *Main activity choice* in the **Description** box [Create]: *(1) Main activity* appears in the left-hand box under **Trees**.
3. Double click on *Main activity* and it moves up into the **Tree Nodes** box.
4. In the **Title** box Type *Activity type*; check that **Address** is 1; and in the **Description** box, key in *Activity type chosen* [Create]: *(1 1) Activity type* now appears under *(1) Main activity*.
5. Double click on *Activity type (1 1)* and it moves up into the **Tree Nodes** box.

Figure 8.13
(continued)

6. In the **Title** box, type *Sport*; check that **Address** is 1; and in the **Description** box type *Sport and physical recreation* [Create]: *(1 1 1) Sport* now appears under *(1 1) Activity*.

7. Repeat step 6 for the following (**Address** will automatically update):

Node (1 1 2):   Title: *Social*   Description: *Informal social activities*
Node (1 1 3):   Title: *Culture*   Description: *Cultural activities*
Node (1 1 4):   Title: *Friends*   Description: *Activities with friends*

The **Create Node** dialog box now appears as follows:

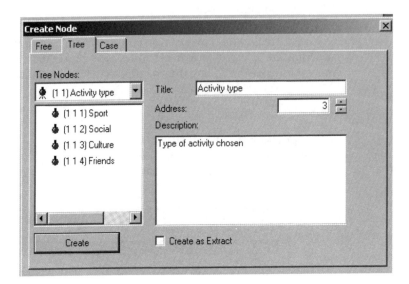

8. Restore (1 1) Main activity to the **Tree Nodes** box and repeat steps 6–8 for:

Node	Title	Description
(1 2)	**Influence**	**Influence/background/experience**
(1 2 1)	Parents	Parental influence
(1 2 2)	Teachers	Teacher influence
(1 2 3)	Peers	Peer influence
(1 3)	**Present**	**Present constraints**
(1 3 1)	Time	Availability of time
(1 3 2)	Money	Availability of money
(1 3 3)	Fitness	Need to be fit
(1 3 4)	Commitments	Commitments – work, study, etc.
(1 4)	**Personal**	**Personal attitudes**
(1 4 1)	Competitive	Competitive outlook
(1 4 2)	Social	Social outlook
(1 4 3)	Routine	Anti-routine
(1 4 4)	Active	Desire to be physically active
(1 4 5)	Team	Team-oriented
(1 5)	**Events**	**Key events**
(1 5 1)	Coaching	Coaching, tuition, etc.
(1 5 2)	Money	Change in financial situation
(1 5 3)	Relationships	Change in key personal relationships
(1 5 4)	Reading	Reading something, e.g. review, book

9. A rudimentary coding system has now been created. It can be examined and edited by clicking on **Explore Nodes** in the Project Pad – as shown in the **Node Explorer** below.

Figure 8.13
(continued)

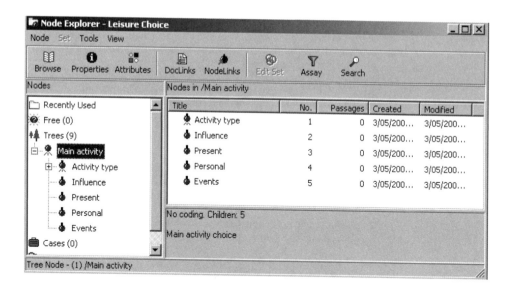

Figure 8.13
(continued)

Coding text

Once a coding system has been set up documents, such as interview transcripts, can be coded. This process is outlined in Figure 8.14.

Analysis

Software packages invariably include a large range of procedures which it is imposs-ible to cover in a short summary such as this. Here we cover five very basic analysis procedures/ issues which will be sufficient to get the researcher started. These are:

1. Search
2. Dealing with search results
3. Search and code
4. Selective search
5. Models – conceptual frameworks

1. Search

One of the simplest forms of analysis is simply to obtain a listing of all the sections of text coded in a certain way. Thus a listing of all passages coded with 'Time' as a current constraint would be obtained as shown in Figure 8.15.

Figure 8.14
NVivo: Coding text

1. In the project pad, click on **Documents** and **Browse a Document**. The list of document files is presented. Select **Int_Mark** [OK]. Mark's interview transcript is presented.
2. Block in: '**playing football**', then click on **Coder** at the bottom right of the screen and click on **Activity type**, then **Sport** then on **Code**.
3. Block in: '**While the football's on, because of training twice a week and needing to be fairly serious about keeping fit I probably only go to a pub once – or at most twice – a week**'. Click on **Coder** at the bottom right of the screen and click on **Present** then on **Commitments** and then on **Code**.
4. To provide a visual display of the results of coding, click on **View** and select **Coding stripes**. The 'coding stripe' appears to the right.
5. Repeat this process for:
   '**needing to be fairly serious about keeping fit**': code it **Present** and **Fitness**.
   '**I don't have the time or the money to do much more**': code it twice: **Time** and **Money**.
6. This process can be repeated for the other parts of Mark's interview abstract, using the notes in Figure 8.6.
7. The screen should now appear as in the **Document Browser** below.
8. This process can be repeated for the other two interview transcripts.

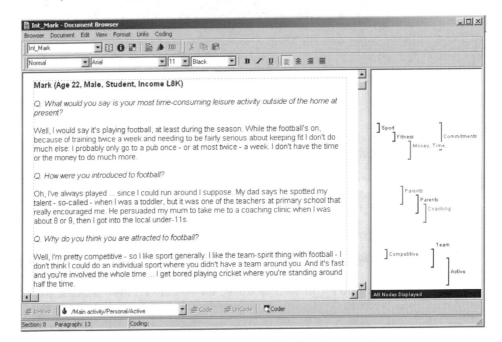

Rather than searching for a named node it is possible to search for any item of specified text – for example, suppose it is noticed that remarks about *friends* are cropping up in the transcripts. Occurrences can be listed as indicated in step 9 of Figure 8.15.

2. Dealing with search results

Search results are not just displayed on the screen but are stored as *new nodes*. This can be seen as shown in Figure 8.16.

Figure 8.15
NVivo: Search

1. In the Project Pad, select **Search**. The **Search Tool** dialog box is displayed, as shown below. This has three sections: **Find; In this Scope;** and **And Spread Finds**.

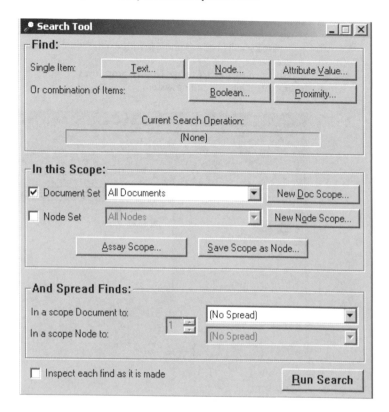

2. In **Find:** double click on **Node** to reveal the **Single Node Lookup** dialog box.
3. Click on **Choose** and, in the **Choose Node** box, select the **Trees** then *(1) Main activity* then *(1 3) Present* then *(1 3 1) Time*.
4. Still in the **Single Node Lookup** dialog box:
   a. the **Return** box indicates how the results of the search will be stored – keep the default **All finds as a node**
   b. the **Name** box indicates the name of the folder/file in which the results will be stored – keep the default **/Search Results/Single Node Lookup**. Click on OK to return to the **Search Tool** dialog box.
5. **In this Scope:** indicates the type of documents which will be searched – keep the default **All Documents**.
6. **And Spread Finds**: indicates the spread of text to be retrieved around each 'find' of the search – for example, a number of characters either side of the find, or the surrounding paragraph – set the number to 40 for this exercise.
7. Click **Run Search**.
8. The results of the search are placed in a new 'Search Results' node (see 'Dealing with search result' below). You are given two options to view the results: **Show Node in Explorer** or **Browse Node**. Select the latter – the results are displayed in the **Search Results/Single Node Lookup- Node Browser** as shown below.
9. Searching need not be dependent on pre-set nodes. For example, occurrences of the word *friends* could identified and listed by select **Text** instead of **Node** in step 2 above and entering the search text *friends* rather than specifying a node.

Figure 8.16
NVivo: Dealing
with search
results

1. In the **Project Pad**, select **Nodes** and click on **Explore Nodes**.
2. In the **Node Explorer:** click on **Trees** and it will be seen that, in addition to the **Main activity** group of nodes, there is now one or more **Search Results** nodes, as shown below.
3. Right click on any **Search Result** to:
   - view (**browse**) it;
   - delete if it will not be required in future – this is recommended to avoid confusion with later searches;
   - rename it (**Inspect/Change Node's properties**)
4. Incorporate it into the coding system.

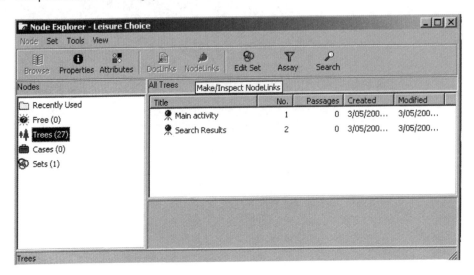

3. Search and code

The results of a search can be used to add further coding to the document. Having searched for occurrences of the word *friends* and decided that this should be identified as a node in its own right, the transcripts can be automatically coded as shown in Figure 8.17.

4. Selective search

Suppose we would like to list all instances of *time* as a constraint being mentioned by female respondents only – the equivalent to a cross-tabulation in quantitative analysis. This can be achieved as shown in Figure 8.17.

5. Models – conceptual frameworks

One of the principles of qualitative analysis is the inductive development of theory as the research progresses. The sort of conceptual framework presented in Figure 8.7 is just a starting point. New concepts and elements of the conceptual framework can be expected to emerge as the analysis progresses – the *friends* example above is a simple example. *NVivo* refers to the conceptual framework as a *Model* and includes a procedure to produce a diagrammatic presentation of the model as it develops. The procedure for doing this is shown in Figure 8.18.

Figure 8.17
NVivo: Search
and code +
Selective search

Search and code

1. Conduct a search for occurrences of the text *friends* as suggested in Figure 8.15, step 9. In the **Search complete** box select just the **Show Node in Explorer** option.
2. In the **Node Explorer** the search result appears as **Single Text Lookup** under **Search Results.**
3. Right click on **Single Text Lookup** and change its name to *friends* via **Inspect/Change Node's properties**.
4. Suppose we decide that *friends* should become a node within the system, similar to, but slightly different from, *peers*. To do this, click on **Trees** and **Main activity** to reveal the list of factors and cut and paste the **friends** node onto **Influence.** Now **friends** is listed under **Influence** and becomes part of the 'Main activity' coding system.
5. The result can be seen by going to **Browse a document** and inspecting one of the transcript files. Viewing 'coding stripes' will show that the mentions *friends* in the document have been automatically coded.

Selective search

1. In the Project Pad, select **Search**.
2. In the **Search Tool** window: in **Find Single item** click on **Node**.
3. In the **Single Node Lookup** dialog box select Present then **Money** [OK].
4. Back in the **Search Tool** window: in **Find Single item** click on **Attribute Value**.
5. In **Attribute Value Lookup** dialog box: select **Document Attributes** then **Gender** then **Female** [OK].
6. Back in the **Search Tool** window: Click on **Run Search**.
7. It will be found that, although *time* is mentioned in both Mark's and Donna's transcripts, the search lists only results from Donna.

Figure 8.18
NVivo: Model
diagram

1. In the Project Pad select **Explore Models** then **Tools** then **Add to Model.**
2. Select **Node** the **Main activity**. The computer presents a message: **'(1) Main activity: This model has descendants. Do you want to add them?'** Select **Yes.**
3. The model appears on the screen as shown below: the layout may be cramped but can be rearranged by selecting and 'dragging' the points on the diagram as desired.

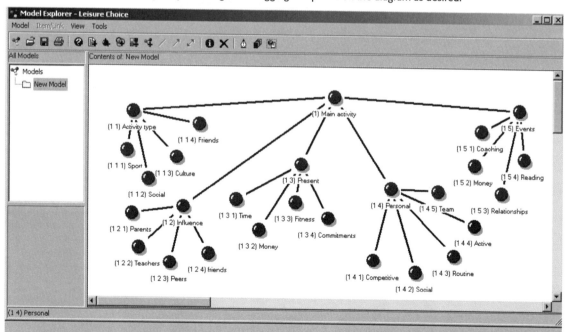

Summary

This chapter introduces the role of qualitative approaches in leisure and tourism research. One of the basic assumptions of qualitative research is that reality is socially and subjectively constructed rather than objectively determined. In this perspective researchers are seen as part of the research process seeking to uncover meanings and an understanding of the issues they are researching. In general, qualitative research involves the collection of a large amount of 'rich' information concerning relatively few people or organisations, or more limited information from a large number of people or organisations.

Qualitative methods generally require a more flexible, recursive, approach to overall research design and conduct than in contrast with the more linear, sequential approach used in most quantitative research. Hypothesis formation evolves as the research progresses; data collection and analysis take place concurrently and writing is also often an evolutionary process, rather than a separate process which happens at the end of the project.

There is a range of qualitative methods available to the researcher, including in-depth interviews, group interviews, focus groups, participant observation, textual analysis, biographical methods and ethnographic methods. The chapter outlines the nature and techniques involved in using each of these methods.

The second half of the chapter deals with the collection and analysis of qualitative data. First the issue of storage of qualitative data is discussed – since interviewees may speak frankly and at length on sensitive topics, it is an important ethical issue to ensure confidentiality, in the security of data storage as well as in the way interviewees are identified in research. The rest of the chapter is divided into two sections dealing respectively with manual and computer-aided analysis methods.

Manual methods of data analysis involve 'flagging' issues or themes which emerge in texts such as interview transcripts. Such issues or themes may relate to an existing draft conceptual framework, research questions and/or hypotheses or, in a 'grounded theory', inductive approach, they may be used to build up a conceptual framework from the data. Since texts are invariably available as word-processed files, it is noted that certain features of word-processing packages, such as 'search' and 'list' or 'index' can be used to assist in the 'flagging' process. this provides a link to the custom-made Computer Aided Qualitative Data Analysis Software (CAQDAS) packages.

The chapter introduces the *NVivo* package, covering the setting up of a project file and a coding system, coding of data and some elementary analysis procedures. While the package has a large range of capabilities – including the handling of data other than interview transcripts – just a limited range of seven analysis procedures is presented in this short outline; but it is believed this is adequate for the qualitative researcher to make a start with computer-aided data analysis.

Test questions

1. Outline some of the merits of qualitative data.

2. Explain the difference between sequential and recursive approaches to research.

3. Outline Whyte's levels of interviewer intervention in an in-depth/informal interview.

4. In-depth interviews involve an interviewer: what is the equivalent in a focus group?

5. Name three types of biographical research.

6. Why is the storage of qualitative data an ethical issue?

7. What are the two major activities involved in manual analysis of qualitative data?

8. What word-processing procedures might be used in 'manual' analysis of qualitative data?

9. What is the difference between a 'node' and a 'document' in *NVivo*?

10. What is the difference between a 'tree node' and a 'free node' in *NVivo*?

Exercises

1. Download from the book website (www.business.uts.uts.edu.au/lst/****) the three tran-script files for the 'Leisure choice' project used above – or type them out from Figure 8.6 – and replicate the coding and analyses presented above. This can be done manually or by using *NVivo*.

2. Run the *NVivo* tutorials included with the package, particularly exploring features of *NVivo* not presented in this chapter.

3. Select an example of a quantitative and a qualitative research report from a recent edition of one of the leisure or tourism journals and consider whether the qualitative research project could have been approached using quantitative methods and whether the quantitative project could have been approached using qualitative methods.

4. Use the checklist in Appendix 8.1 to interview a willing friend or colleague. Assess your performance as an interviewer.

5. If you are studying with others, organise yourselves into groups of five or six and organise a focus-group interview, with one person as facilitator, choosing a topic of mutual interest, such as 'the role of education and qualifications in the leisure/tourism industries' or 'holiday choice processes', or 'fitness versus the enjoyment of sport'. Take turns in acting as convenor and assess each others' skills as convenor.

6. Using the issues of a newspaper for one week, provide a qualitative and quantitative analysis of the coverage of a topic of interest, such as: the environment, ethnic minorities, women and sport or overseas locations.

7. Arrange to view a copy of *Cannibal Tours* and discuss the film in the light of MacCannell's (1993) essay on the film. Or, view any Disney cartoon film and discuss it in relation to Rojek's (1993) paper.

Further reading

Qualitative methods generally: Burgess (1982); Lofland and Lofland (1984); Silverman (1993); Denzin and Lincoln (1994).

In leisure studies: Kelly (1980); Kamphorst *et al.* (1984); Godbey and Scott (1990); Henderson (1990, 1991).

In tourism studies: Cohen (1988); Peterson (1994); Walle (1997); Riley and Love (2000); Davies (2003); Phillimore and Godson (2004a).

Examples in leisure studies: Marsh *et al.* (1978); Griffin *et al.* (1982); Hollands (1985); Wynne (1986); Cuneen *et al.* (1989); Walker (1988).

Examples in tourism studies: Palmer and Dunford (2002); Jordan and Gibson (2004).

Informal/in-depth interviews: example: Rapoport and Rapoport (1975); Moeller *et al.* (1980a, 1980b); Dunne (1995).

Participant observation: Campbell (1970); Glancy (1986).

Focus groups: Calder (1977); Reynolds and Johnson (1978); Krueger (1988); Stewart and Shamdasani (1990); Morgan (1993); Greenbaum (1998, 2000).

Biographical methods: Bertaux (1981); Project on Disney (1995); Atkinson (1998); Roberts (2002); in tourism: Ladkin (2004); personal domain histories: Hedges (1986); memory work in tourism: Small (2004).

Grounded theory: general: Glaser and Strauss (1967); in tourism: Connell and Lowe (1977); Strauss (1987); Strauss and Corbin (1994).

Web-site for the software package *NVivo*: www.qsrinternational.com – includes a downloadable bibliography on qualitative data analysis sources.

Analysis of qualitative data generally: Miles and Huberman (1994).

Use of computer software packages in qualitative data analysis is outlined by Miles and Weitzman (1994) and Richards and Richards (1994).

Use of NVivo software: Gibbs (2002); Bazeley and Richards (2000); Morse and Richards (2002).

Appendix 8.1   Example of a checklist for in-depth interviewing

This is part of a checklist devised in connection with a study of people's use of leisure time and attitudes towards leisure.

CURRENT ACTIVITIES	HOW OFTEN? WHY?	
EXPLORE EACH ONE – COMPARE	WHERE? WHO WITH? MEANING/IMPORTANCE TYPE OF INVOLVEMENT	– HOME/AWAY FROM HOME
ACTIVITIES WOULD LIKE TO DO	WHY NOT?	
MEANING OF 'LEISURE' TO YOU		
CONSTRAINTS:	HOME WORK FAMILY ROLES BEING A WOMAN/MAN BEING A PARENT MONEY/COSTS CAR/TRANSPORT	– TIME/ENERGY/COLLEAGUES
PAST ACTIVITIES	AT SCHOOL	
WHY CHANGES?	AT COLLEGE/UNIV. WITH FAMILY	
FACILITIES	LOCALLY CITY	FAVOURITE USE/NON-USE WHY?
CLUBS/ASSOCIATIONS PERSONALITY		
SKILLS		
DISLIKES	ASPIRATIONS	

9 Questionnaire surveys

Introduction

This chapter presents an overview of the range of types of questionnaire survey and questionnaire design. Questionnaire surveys involve the gathering of information from individuals using a formally designed schedule of questions called a *questionnaire* or *interview schedule*. The technique is arguably the most commonly used in leisure and tourism research.

The first part of the chapter discusses the merits of questionnaire methods and the distinction between interviewer-completion and respondent-completion questionnaire surveys, followed by an overview of the characteristics of: the household questionnaire survey; the street survey; the telephone survey; the postal or mail survey; on-site or user surveys; and captive group surveys.

The second half of the chapter considers the factors which must be taken into account in designing questionnaires for leisure and tourism studies. First, the relationships between research problems and information requirements are examined. This is followed by consideration of the types of information typically included in leisure and tourism questionnaires, the wording of questions, coding of questionnaires for computer analysis, the ordering and layout of questions and the problem of validity. Finally some consideration is given to fieldwork arrangements and conducting a pilot survey.

Roles and limitations

Questionnaire surveys usually involve only a proportion, or *sample*, of the population in which the researcher is interested. For example, the national surveys discussed in Chapter 6 are based on samples of only a few thousand to represent tens of millions of people. How such samples are chosen, how the size of the sample is decided and the implications of relying on a sample to represent a population, are discussed in Chapter 10.

Questionnaire surveys rely on information from respondents. The accuracy of what respondents say depends on their own powers of recall, on their honesty and, fundamentally, on the format of the questions included in the questionnaire. There has been very little research on the validity or accuracy of questionnaire data in leisure and tourism studies, however, some research has suggested that respondents exaggerate levels of participation, at least in some activities (see Bachman and O'Malley 1981; Chase and Godbey, 1983; Chase and Harada, 1984). It has been suggested that interviewees are affected by the desire to be helpful and friendly towards the interviewer – at least in a face-to-face situation – so that, for example, if the interview is about sport or the arts, respondents will tend to exaggerate their interest in and involvement with sport or the arts, just to be helpful and positive. John Clarke and Chas Critcher warn against attempts to assess complex concepts such as satisfaction using over-simplified, leading questions in questionnaires. The conclusion of their discussion does not follow clearly from their argument since it shifts from the study of attitudes to the measurement of activities, but it is nevertheless worth repeating.

> There is always a gap between what people say and what they actually do and no study of work or leisure can afford to take what people say at face value, especially when the answers are contained in the questions. (Clarke and Critcher, 1985: 27)

This warns against poor questionnaire design but also suggests that the researcher and the user of research results should always bear in mind the nature and source of the data and not fall into the trap of believing that, because information is presented in numerical form and is based on large numbers, it represents immutable 'truth'.

Questionnaire surveys usually involve substantial numbers of 'subjects' (the people being surveyed), ranging from perhaps fifty or sixty to many thousands. This, together with the complexity of some forms of quantitative analysis, means that computers are invariably used to analyse the results. The practical implications of this are considered in the second half of the chapter which deals with questionnaire design.

The term 'questionnaire survey' is used deliberately in this chapter to emphasise that the words 'survey' and 'questionnaire' mean two different things. There is a tendency in common parlance – and unfortunately in some research literature – to use the term 'survey' synonymously with 'questionnaire'. Thus, for example, researchers have been known to make statements such as: '1,000 surveys were distributed'. This is inappropriate; only *one* survey was involved – a 1,000 *questionnaires* were distributed. The written schedule of questions is the questionnaire: a *survey* is the *whole process* of designing and conducting a study involving the gathering of information from a number of subjects.

Merits of questionnaire methods

Compared with the qualitative techniques discussed in Chapter 8, questionnaire surveys usually involve quantification – the presentation of results in numerical terms. This has implications for the way the data are collected, analysed and interpreted. In Chapter 8 a list of merits of qualitative methods, as put forward by Kelly, was presented. The merits of questionnaire surveys can be similarly examined. Some of the qualities of questionnaires surveys which make them useful in leisure and tourism research are set out below.

1. Contemporary leisure and tourism are often mass phenomena, requiring major involvement from governmental, non-profit and commercial organisations, which

rely on quantified information for significant aspects of their decision making. Questionnaire surveys are an ideal means of providing some of this information.

2. While absolute 'objectivity' is impossible, questionnaire methods provide a 'transparent' set of research procedures. Just how information was collected and how it was analysed or interpreted is clear for all to see. Indeed, data from questionnaire surveys can often be re-analysed by others if they wish to extend the research or provide an alternative interpretation.

3. Quantification can provide relatively complex information in a succinct, easily understood, form.

4. Methods such as longitudinal surveys and annually repeated surveys provide the opportunity to study change over time, using comparable methodology.

5. Leisure and tourism encompass a wide range of activities, with a range of characteristics, such as frequency, duration and type of participation, expenditure, location, level of enjoyment. Questionnaires are a good means of ensuring that a complete picture of a person's patterns of participation is obtained.

6. While qualitative methods are ideal for exploring attitudes, meanings and perceptions on an individual basis, questionnaire methods provide the means to gather and record simple information on the incidence of attitudes, meanings and perceptions among the population as a whole.

Comparison of this list and the one referring to qualitative methods at the beginning of Chapter 8 reinforces the view that each method has its merits and appropriate uses – the 'horses for courses' idea. Questionnaire surveys have a role to play when the research questions indicate the need for fairly structured data and generally when data are required from samples which are explicitly representative of a defined wider population. Examples of the role of questionnaire surveys versus other methods are shown in Figure 9.1.

Interviewer-completion or respondent-completion?

Questionnaire surveys can take one of two forms: they can be interviewer-completed or respondent-completed. When interviewer-completed the questionnaire provides the *script* for an interview; an interviewer reads the questions out to the respondent and records the respondent's answers on the questionnaire – the classic 'clipboard' situation. When the questionnaire is respondent-completed respondents read and fill out the questionnaire themselves. It should be noted that some commentators on research methods draw a distinction between 'interview methods' and 'questionnaire methods'; this is misleading because the interviewer-completed questionnaire survey clearly involves an interview.

Each approach has its particular advantages and disadvantages, as summarised in Figure 9.2.

Interviewer-completion is more expensive in terms of interviewers' time (which usually has to be paid for) but the use of an interviewer usually ensures a more accurate and complete response. Respondent-completion can be cheaper and quicker but often

Organisation	Topic	Questionnaire Survey	Qualitative Methods	Other Methods
Political party	Voting intentions of electors	■ Party's current level of support vis-à-vis other parties – telephone survey	■ Concerns and attitudes of different types of voter – focus groups	■ Past voting patterns – marginal seats – previous election voting returns ■ Overall characteristics of electors in different seats – census data
Leisure facility management	How to increase number of visitors	■ Information on what types of people use which services and when – user survey ■ Information on socio-demographic characteristics of users vs non-users and perceptions of facility – community survey	■ The experience of visiting the facility – quality, atmosphere, service – observation and/or focus groups	■ Information on relative popularity of different activities/services – ticket sales and utilisation data
Tourism Commission	Data for Tourism Strategic Plan	■ Accommodation used, sites visited, expenditure patterns and socio-demographic characteristics of visitors from different places	■ Quality of visitor experience – in-depth interviews or focus groups with visitors ■ Resident attitudes towards tourists and tourist development – focus groups ■ Visitor survey	■ Arrival and departure data (if national study)
Individual researcher	The role of the holiday in leisure (Case study 3.1)	■ Socio-demographic characteristics and numbers of those who do and do not take holidays – measures of income, health and attitudes	■ Meanings and importance of holidays and local leisure in individuals' lifestyle – in-depth interviews	–

Figure 9.1 The use of questionnaire surveys *vs* other methods – examples

Figure 9.2
Interviewer-completion *vs* respondent-completion

	Interviewer-completion	Respondent-completion
Advantages	More accuracy Higher response rates Fuller and more complete answers Design can be less 'user-friendly'	Cheaper Quicker Relatively anonymous
Disadavantages	Higher cost Less anonymity	Patchy response Incomplete response Risk of frivolous responses More care needed in design

results in low response rates, which can introduce bias in the results because those who choose not to respond or are unable to respond, perhaps because of language or literacy difficulties, may differ from those who do respond. When designing a questionnaire for respondent-completion, greater care must be taken with layout and presentation since it must be read and completed by 'untrained' people. In terms of design, respondent-completion questionnaires should ideally consist primarily of 'closed' questions – that is, questions which can be answered by ticking boxes. 'Open-ended' questions – where respondents have to write out their answers – should be avoided, since they invariably achieve only a low response. For example, in an interview, respondents will often give expansive answers to questions such as 'Do you have any comments to make on the overall management of this facility?' But they will not as readily write down such answers in a respondent-completion questionnaire.

There may, however, be cases when respondent-completion is to be preferred, or is the only practicable approach – for example when the people to be surveyed are widely scattered geographically (which would make face-to-face interviews impossibly expensive and a mail or postal survey involving respondent-completion is an obvious choice), or when it is felt that, on sensitive matters, respondents might prefer the anonymity of the respondent-completed questionnaire. Some of the issues connected with respondent-completion questionnaires are discussed more fully in the section on mail surveys.

Types of questionnaire survey

Questionnaire surveys in the leisure and tourism field can be divided into six types:

Household survey	people are selected on the basis of where they live and are interviewed in their home.
Street survey	people are selected by stopping them in the street, in shopping malls, etc.
Telephone survey	interviews are conducted by telephone.
Mail survey	questionnaires are sent and returned by mail.

Type	Self- or Interviewer-completion	Cost	Sample	Possible Length of Questionnaire	Response Rate
Household	Either	Expensive	Whole population	Long	High
Street	Interviewer	Medium	Most of population	Short	Medium
Telephone	Interviewer	Medium	People with telephone	Short	High
Mail	Respondent	Cheap	General or special	Varies	Low
On-site	Either	Medium	Users only	Medium	High
Captive	Respondent	Cheap	Group only	Medium	High

Figure 9.3   Types of questionnaire survey – characteristics

E-surveys	surveys making use of the Internet and email.
User/on-site/visitor survey	users of a leisure or tourism facility, site or destination are surveyed on-site.
Captive group survey	members of groups, such as classes of school children, members of a club or employees of an organisation, are surveyed.

Each of these is discussed in more detail below and some of their basic characteristics are summarised in Figure 9.3.

The household questionnaire survey

Nature

Much of the quantified data in the field of leisure and tourism derive from household questionnaire surveys. While academics draw on the data extensively, the majority of such surveys are commissioned by government and commercial leisure and tourism organisations for policy or marketing purposes. The advantage of household surveys is that they are generally representative of the community – the samples drawn tend to include all age-groups, above a certain minimum, and all occupational groups. They also generally represent a complete geographical area – a whole country, a state or region, a local government area or a neighbourhood. Household surveys are therefore designed to provide information on the reported leisure or tourism behaviour of the community as a whole or a particular group drawn from the whole community – for example the older population aged 65 and over, or young people aged 15–24.

While some household leisure/tourism surveys are specialised, many are broad-ranging in their coverage. That is, they tend to ask, among other things, about participation in a wide range of leisure activities, holiday-taking patterns or buying habits. This facilitates exploration of a wide range of issues which other types of survey cannot so readily tackle.

Conduct

Normally household questionnaire surveys are interviewer-completed. However, it is possible for a questionnaire to be left at a respondent's home for respondent-completion and later collection, in which case the field-worker then has the responsibility of checking that questionnaires have been fully completed and perhaps conducting an interview in those situations where respondents have been unable to fill in the questionnaire, either because they have been too busy, have forgotten, or have lost the questionnaire, or because of literacy or language problems or infirmity.

Being home-based, this sort of survey can involve quite lengthy questionnaires and interviews. By contrast, in the street, at a leisure or tourism facility, or over the telephone, it can be difficult to conduct a lengthy interview. Leisure participation surveys in particular, with their huge range of possible activities, often involve a very complex questionnaire which is difficult to administer 'on the run'. With the home-based interview it is usually possible to pursue issues at greater length than is possible in other settings. An interview of three quarters of an hour in duration is not out of the question and 20–30 minutes is quite common.

A variation on the standard household questionnaire interview survey is to combine interviewer-completed and respondent-completed elements. This often happens with leisure surveys: the interviewer conducts an interview with one member of the household about the household – how many people live there, whether the dwelling is owned or rented, perhaps information on recreational equipment, or anything to do with the household as a whole. Then an individual questionnaire is left for each member of the household to complete, concerning their own leisure behaviour. The interviewer calls back later to collect these individual questionnaires.

The potential length of interviews, the problems of contacting representative samples and, on occasions, the wide geographical spread of the study area, mean that household surveys are usually the most expensive to conduct, per interview. Costs of the order of £20 or £25 per interview are typical, depending on the amount of analysis included in the price. When samples of several thousands are involved, the costs can therefore be substantial.

Omnibus surveys

While considering household surveys, mention should be made of the *omnibus* survey. Omnibus surveys are single surveys conducted by a market research or survey organisation for several clients, each of which contributes their own particular questions to the questionnaire. In an omnibus survey the main costs of the survey, which lie in sampling and contacting respondents, are therefore shared by a number of clients. The cost of collecting fairly standard demographic and socio-economic information – such as age, gender, family structure, occupation and income – is also shared among the clients. With regular omnibus surveys many of the procedures, such as sampling and data processing, have become routinised, and interviewers are in place throughout the country already trained and familiar with the type of questionnaire and the requirements of the market research company – these factors can reduce costs significantly.

The British *General Household Survey* is an omnibus survey of 20,000 people run by the Office of National Statistics, the clients being government departments and agencies. In the years when leisure questions are included, the clients for those questions are the various national leisure/recreation agencies, such as the Sports Council and the Countryside Agency.

Time-budget studies

Time-budget studies are designed to collect information on people's use of time. Such information is usually collected as part of a household survey, but in addition to answering a questionnaire, respondents are asked to complete a diary, typically covering a period of between two and four days. Respondents are asked to record their activities during their waking hours, including starting and stopping times, together with information on where the activity was done, with whom, and possibly whether the respondent considered it to be paid work, domestic work or leisure.

Coding and analysis of such data presents a considerable challenge, since every possible type of activity must be given a code and information processed for, say, 60 or 70 quarter hour periods each day. Space does not permit a detailed treatment of this specialised topic here, but it can be followed up in the literature indicated in the further reading section.

The street survey

Nature

The street survey involves a relatively short questionnaire and is conducted, as the name implies, on the street – usually a shopping street or tourist area – or in squares or shopping malls, where a cross-section of the community might be expected to be found. In the case of surveys of tourists to an area, locations where tourists are known to congregate, such as the environs of major attractions, or restaurant or tourist accommodation areas, are used. Transport locations, such as airports or bus stations, can be seen as similar, although they also have some of the characteristics of the site or user survey, as discussed below.

Conduct

Stopping people in such environments for an interview places certain limitations on the interview process. First, an interview conducted in the street cannot generally be as long as one conducted at someone's home – especially when the interviewee is in a hurry. Of course there are some household interviews which are very short because the interviewee is in a hurry or is a reluctant respondent and there are street interviews which are lengthy because the respondent has plenty of time. As a general rule, however, the street interview must be shorter. Both in the home and street interview situation, before committing themselves to an interview, potential respondents often ask 'How long will it take?' In the home-based situation a reply of '15–20 minutes' is generally acceptable but in the street situation anything more than '5 minutes' would generally lead to a marked reduction in the proportion of people prepared to cooperate. The range of topics/issues/activities which can be covered in a street interview is therefore restricted and this must be taken into account in designing the questionnaire.

The second limitation of the street survey is the problem of contacting a representative sample of the population. Certain types of people might not frequent shopping areas at all, or only infrequently – for instance people who are housebound for various reasons or people who have other people to do their shopping. Some types of tourist – for example business tourists or those visiting friends or relatives – may not be found in the popular tourist areas. Such individuals might be of particular importance in some studies, so their omission can significantly compromise the results. There is little that can be done to overcome this problem; it has to be accepted as a limitation of the method. The other side of this coin is that certain groups will be over-represented in shopping streets – notably full-time home/child carers, the retired and the unemployed in suburban shopping areas, or office workers in business areas. It might also be the case that certain areas are frequented more by, for example, young people than old people or by men rather than women, so any sample would be representative of the users of the area, but not of the local population or visitor population as a whole.

Quota sampling

The means used to attempt to overcome the problem of unrepresentative samples is the technique of *quota sampling,* in which the interviewer is given a 'quota' of different types of people – for example, by age, sex, occupation – to interview. The proportions in each category in the target population must be known in advance – for example by reference to the Population Census (see Chapter 6) or, in the case of tourists, by reference to the official Short-term Arrivals and Departure data (see Chapter 6). When the survey is complete, if the sample is still not representative with regard to the key characteristics, further adjustments can be achieved through the process of *weighting,* discussed in Chapter 10.

The telephone survey

Nature

The telephone survey is particularly popular with political pollsters because of its speed and the ease with which a widespread sample of the community can be contacted. It is also used extensively in market and academic research for the same reasons.

An obvious limitation of the technique is that it excludes non-telephone subscribers – generally low income groups and some mobile sections of the population. With telephones in the great majority of homes in developed countries this is not now as serious a problem as it was in the past. In the case of fairly simple surveys like political opinion polls, where the researcher has access to previous survey results using telephone and face-to-face interviews, this problem may be overcome by the use of a correction factor – for instance it might be known that non-telephone subscribers always add x per cent to the Labour vote. In certain kinds of market research the absence of the poorer parts of the community from the survey may be unimportant because they do not form a significant part of the market. For much public policy and academic research, however, this can be a significant limitation.

An emerging problem is the case of households which do not have land-line telephones, relying only on mobile phones, which are not listed. This is likely to involve mainly young people, who are an important target of much survey work. Again, it may be possible to correct for this statistically if the characteristics of this group are known.

Conduct

Length of interview can be a limitation of telephone surveys – but not as serious as in the case of street interviews; telephone interviews of 10 or 15 minutes are acceptable.

The technique has its own unique set of problems in relation to sampling. Generally the numbers to be called are selected at random from the telephone directory. Market research companies generally use equipment and software – Computer Assisted Telephone Interviewing (CATI) – which will automatically dial random telephone numbers as required. CATI systems also enable the interviewer to key answers directly into a computer, so dispensing with the printed questionnaire. This speeds up the analysis process considerably and cuts down the possibility of error in transcribing results from printed questionnaire to computer. It explains how the results of overnight political opinion polls can be published in the newspapers the next morning.

If a representative cross-section of the community is to be included then it is necessary for telephone surveys to be conducted in the evenings and/or at weekends if those who have paid jobs are to be included.

A limitation of the telephone interview is that respondents cannot be shown such things as lists. This is particularly relevant to leisure and tourism surveys. In leisure participation surveys respondents are frequently shown lists of activities and asked if they have participated in them. Such lists can include 20 or 30 items, which can be tedious to read out over the telephone. Similarly in tourism studies respondents may be shown a list of places and asked which they have visited. Surveys which involve long checklists – for example attitude dimensions – are also not easily conducted by telephone.

It can be argued that telephones have an advantage over face-to-face interviews in that respondents may feel that they are more anonymous and may therefore be more forthcoming in their opinions. But it could also be argued that the face-to-face interview has other advantages in terms of eye-contact and body language which enable the skilled interviewer to conduct a better interview than is possible over the telephone.

The main advantage of the telephone survey is that it is quick and relatively cheap to conduct. However, in some countries there is growing reluctance on the part of the public to cooperate with telephone surveys, resulting in the need to make a number of calls to contact cooperative respondents, thus raising the costs and raising questions about representativeness.

The mail survey

Nature

There are certain situations where the mail or postal method is the only practical survey technique to use. The commonest example is where members or customers of some national organisation are to be surveyed. The costs of conducting face-to-face interviews with even a sample of the members or customers would be substantial – a mail survey is the obvious answer. The mail survey has the advantage that a large sample can be included. In the case of a membership organisation, there may be advantages in surveying the whole membership, even though this may not be necessary in statistical terms. It can however be very helpful in terms of the internal politics of the organisation for all members to be given the opportunity to participate in the survey and to 'have their say'.

The problem of low response rates

The most notorious problem of postal surveys is low response rates. In many cases as few as 25 or 30 per cent of those sent a questionnaire bother to reply. There are even notorious instances, for example in community surveys on local government planning strategies, of only 3 or 4 per cent response rates. Surveys with only 30 per cent response rates are regularly reported in the research literature, but questions must be raised as to their validity when 70 per cent of the target sample is not represented.

What affects the response rate? Seven different factors can be identified, as listed in Figure 9.4. The various factors and measures listed in Figure 9.4 are discussed in detail below.

1. The interest of the respondent in the survey topic

A survey of a local community about a proposal to route a six-lane highway through the neighbourhood would probably result in a high response rate, but a survey of the same community on general patterns of leisure behaviour would probably result in a low response rate. Variation among the population in the level of interest in the topic can result in a biased, that is unrepresentative, response. For example a survey on sports facility provision might evoke a high response rate among those interested in sport and a low response rate among those not interested – giving a false impression

Figure 9.4
Factors affecting mail survey responses

1. The interest of the respondent in the survey topic
2. The length of the questionnaire
3. Questionnaire design/presentation/complexity
4. The style, content and authorship of the accompanying letter
5. The provision of a postage-paid reply envelope
6. Rewards for responding
7. The number and timing of reminders/follow-ups

of community enthusiasm for sports facility provision. To some extent this can be corrected by weighting (see Chapters 10 and 12 if the bias corresponds with certain known characteristics of the population. For example, if there was a high response rate from young people and a low response rate from older people, information from the Census on the actual proportions of different age groups in the community could be used to weight the results.

2. Length of the questionnaire

It might be expected that a long questionnaire would discourage potential respondents. It can, however, be argued that other factors, such as the topic and the presentation of the questionnaire, are more important than the length of the questionnaire – that is, if the topic is interesting to the respondent and is well presented then length is not an issue.

3. Questionnaire design/presentation/complexity

More care must be taken in design and physical presentation with any respondent-completed questionnaire. Type-setting, colour coding of pages, graphics and so on may be necessary. Leisure and tourism surveys often present awesome lists of activities which can make a questionnaire look very complicated and demanding to complete.

4. The accompanying letter

The letter from the sponsor or researcher which accompanies the questionnaire may have an influence on people's willingness to respond. Does it give a good reason for the survey? Is it from someone, or the type of organisation, whom the respondent trusts or respects?

5. Postage-paid reply envelope

It is usual to include a postage-paid envelope for the return of the questionnaire. Some believe that an envelope with a real stamp on it will produce a better response rate than a business-reply-paid envelope. Providing reply envelopes with real stamps is more expensive because, apart from the time spent in sticking stamps on envelopes, stamps are provided for both respondents and non-respondents.

6. Rewards

The question of rewards for taking part in a survey can arise in relation to any sort of survey but it is a device used most often in postal surveys. One approach is to send every respondent some small reward, such as a voucher for a firm's or agency's product or service, or even money. A more common approach is to enter all respondents in a draw for a prize. Even a fairly costly prize may be money well spent if it results in a substantial increase in the response rate. When the cost of the alternative household surveys involving face-to-face interviews are considered, a substantial prize which results in a significant increase in responses may be considered good value. It could however be argued that the introduction of rewards causes certain people to respond for the wrong reasons and that it introduces a potential source of bias in responses. It might also be considered that the inclusion of a prize or reward 'lowers the tone' of the survey and places it in the same category as other, commercial, junk mail that comes through people's letter boxes every day.

7. Reminders/follow-ups

Sensible reminder and follow-up procedures are perhaps the most significant tool available to the researcher. Typically, a postcard reminder might be sent one week or ten days after the initial mailing. After two weeks a letter accompanied by a second copy of the questionnaire ('in case the first has been mislaid') should be sent. A final reminder card can be sent a week or so after that. The effects of these reminders and follow-ups can be seen in Figure 9.5, which relates to a survey of residents' recreational use of an estuary. It can be seen that the level of responses peaked after only three days and looked likely to cease after about sixteen days, giving a potential response rate of just 40 per cent. The surges in responses following the sending of the postcard and the second copy of the questionnaire can be seen and the net result was a 75 per cent response rate, which is very good for this type of survey. The need for follow-ups must be considered when budgeting for a postal survey, since postage and printing costs are often the most significant item in such budgets.

The sending out of reminders necessitates being able to identify returned questionnaires, so that reminders are not sent to those who have replied. This means that questionnaires or envelopes must have an identifying number which can be matched with the mailing list. Some respondents resent this potential breach of confidentiality

Figure 9.5
Mail survey response pattern
Source: Based on data from Robertson and Veal (1987)

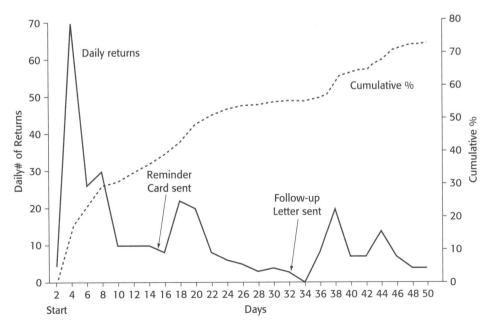

but it cannot be avoided if only non-respondents are to be followed up. Anonimity can be partially maintained if the identifier is placed on the envelope and not on the questionnaire. There is often a further advantage to being able to identify responses; they can be used to check the representativeness of the response. For instance, the questionnaire may not include respondents' addresses, but the geographical spread of the response can be examined if the identity of the responses is known, and any necessary weighting can be carried out.

E-surveys

Standard 'hard copy' mail has been the traditional medium for mail surveys and is still popular, but e-mail and the Internet are rising rapidly in popularity, resulting in an emerging category – the e-survey. A number of formats exist, as follows.

- E-mail is used to transmit a letter of request and an attached copy of a questionnaire to potential respondents, thus saving in postage costs.
  - Respondents then print out the attached questionnaire, fill it out and mail back to the researcher, or
  - the questionnaire is completed using a word-processor or spreadsheet and e-mailed back to the researcher.
- Fully electronic – involves the respondent logging into a specified Internet site and completing the questionnaire on-line. This has the advantage to the researcher that the data are delivered in electronic form and can be instantly analysed using appropriate software.

Commercial organisations offer e-survey services in which the customer specifies the questions to be included and can download the results on demand. Such on-line surveys can also simplify completion for the respondent when 'filter' questions are involved, which means that parts of the questionnaire are irrelevant to some users. One of the best-known e-surveys allows taxpayers to complete their income tax return on-line.

The disadvantage of the e-survey is that it is confined to those with access to the Internet and, while the sending of reminders is cheap, the problem of low response rates may still be a problem for some surveys because they may be seen as part of the increasing volume of 'junk mail' received via email.

User/On-site/Visitor surveys

Nature

The terms *on-site*, *site*, *user* or *visitor* survey are used to refer to this type of survey. *On-site* and *site survey* tend to be used in the context of outdoor recreation studies, *user survey* in the context of indoor recreation facilities, and *visitor survey* when tourists or daytrippers are involved, or types of facility where visits are relatively infrequent, such as museums or zoos. A fourth term, *audience survey*, is used in the arts environment, for example for surveys of theatre audiences. Researchers with a background in transport tend to use the term *intercept* survey. The term user survey is utilised in this chapter to cover all these situations.

The user survey is the most common type of survey used by managers in leisure and tourism. Surveys of tourists and local users are carried out at recreation or leisure facilities and surveys of tourists are carried out at hotels and en route on various types of transport, particularly international air trips. General surveys of visitors to a tourist area often take the form of street surveys. Visitors are interviewed in the street, in squares/plazas or in seafront areas – anywhere where tourists are known to congregate. In this case the 'facility' is the tourist town or area, so the 'street survey' and the 'site survey' overlap and consideration must be given to the features of both types of survey. In general, the site survey is more controlled than the street survey; interviewers are seen by respondents to be part of the management of the facility and usually it is possible to interview users at a convenient time when they are not 'in a rush', as they may be in the street or shopping mall.

Conduct

User surveys can be conducted by interviewer or by respondent-completion. Unless carefully supervised, respondent-completion methods can lead to a poor standard in the completion of questionnaires and a low response level. And as with all low response levels this can be a source of serious bias in that those who reply may be unrepresentative of the users or visitors as a whole.

The usual respondent-completion survey involves handing users a questionnaire on their arrival at the site and collecting them on their departure, or conducting the whole procedure upon departure. Where respondent-completion is thought to be desirable or necessary then sufficient staff should be employed to check all users leaving the site, to ask for the completed questionnaires, to provide replacements for questionnaires which have been mislaid, and to assist in completing questionnaires, including completion by interview if necessary.

Conducting user surveys by interview is generally preferable to respondent-completion for the reasons discussed earlier in this chapter. The use of interviewers obviously has a cost disadvantage, but, depending on the length of the interview, costs per interview are usually comparatively low. Typically a user-survey interview will take about five minutes. Given the need to check through completed questionnaires, the gaps in user traffic and the need for interviewers to take breaks, it is reasonable to expect interviewers in such situations to complete about six interviews in an hour. Such estimates are of course necessary when considering project budgets and timetables.

The survey methods considered so far have been fairly multi-purpose – they could be used for market research for a range of products or services, by public agencies for a variety of policy-oriented purposes, or for academic research. User surveys are more specific. While academics conduct user surveys as a convenient way of gathering data on particular leisure or tourism activities, the more usual use of such surveys is for policy, planning or management purposes. User surveys are the type of survey which readers of this book are most likely to be involved with; they are the most convenient for students to 'cut their teeth' on, and they are the most common surveys for individual managers to become involved in. For these reasons the roles of user surveys are considered in some detail below.

The uses of user surveys

What can user surveys be used for? The most obvious use is to provide direct feedback to management on a range of issues, including the following.

Catchment area

What is the *catchment* or *market* area of the facility or service? That is, what geographical area do most of the users come from? This can be important in terms of advertising policy. Management can concentrate on its existing catchment area and focus its advertising and marketing accordingly or it can take conscious decisions to use marketing to attempt to extend its catchment area. But in order to do this it is necessary to establish the catchment area. In some cases this information is already available from membership records, but in many cases it can only be discovered by means of a survey.

User profile

What is the socio-economic/demographic profile of the users? It might be thought that a management capable of observation would be able to make this assessment without the need for a survey. This depends on the type of facility, the extent to which management is in continuous contact with users and the variability of the user profile. For example, a restaurant, hotel or resort manager might be very well informed on this but managers of beaches, urban parks, national/state parks or theatres might, for various reasons, be less well informed, or even mis-informed.

Profile information can be used in a number of ways. Similarly to the data on catchment area, it can be used to concentrate or extend the market. Very often the commercial operator will opt to concentrate – to focus on a particular client group and maximise the market share of that group. In the case of a public sector facility the remit is usually to attract as wide a cross-section of the community as possible, so the data would be used to highlight those sections of the community not being catered for and therefore requiring marketing attention.

User opinions

What are the opinions of users? These data are invariably collected in user surveys and are usually of great interest to managers, but the interpretation of such data it is not without its difficulties (Veal, 1988). If management is looking for pertinent criticisms current users may be the wrong group to consult. Those who are most critical are likely no longer to be using the facility. Those using the facility may be reluctant to be very critical because it undermines their own situation – if the place is so poor why are they there? Those who are prepared to be critical may not be the sorts of clients for whom the facility is designed. As Lucas has said:

> It seems misleading to give equal weight to evaluations by people who are seeking a different type of area or experience. By analogy, a Chinese restaurant would do well to ignore the opinion about the food by someone who ate there by mistake while seeking an Italian restaurant.
>
> (Lucas, 1970: 5)

In some situations people have little choice between facilities so criticisms are perhaps more easily interpreted. For example, parents' comments about the suitability of a local park for children's play can be particularly pertinent when it is the only play area available in the neighbourhood.

When opinion data have been collected it is often difficult to know precisely what to do with the results. Very often the largest group of users has no complaint or suggestion to make – either because they cannot be bothered to think of anything in the interview situation or because of the 'respondent selection' process referred to above. Often the most common complaint is only raised by as few as 10 per cent of users. If this is the most common complaint, then logically something ought to be done about it by the management – but it could also be said that 90 per cent of the users are not concerned about that issue, so perhaps there is no need to do anything about it! Very often therefore, management can use survey results to suit their own needs. If they want to do something about X, they can say that X was complained about by more users than anything else: if they do not want to do anything about X they can say that 90 per cent of users are satisfied with X the way it is.

Managers mostly want to enhance and maximise the quality of the experience enjoyed by their visitors: it may not be criticism of specific features that is important but users' overall evaluation of the experience. Thus users can be asked to rate a facility or area using a scale such as: Very good/good/fair/poor/very poor or Very satisfied/satisfied/dissatisfied/very dissatisfied. The results of such an evaluation can be used to compare users' evaluation of one facility with another – for example in a system of parks. Or they could be used to examine the same facility at different times to see if satisfaction has increased or declined. This can be important in evaluation research of the sort discussed by Hatry and Dunn (1971) and discussed in Case study 3.3 (pp. 92–4).

Non-users

User surveys by definition involve only current users of a facility or current visitors to an area. This is often cited as a limitation of such surveys, the implication being that non-users may be of more interest than users if the aim of management is to increase the number of users or visitors. Caution should however be exercised in moving to consider conducting research on non-users. For a start the number of non-users or non-visitors is usually very large. For example, in a city of a million population, a facility which has 5,000 users has 995,000 non-users! In a country with a population of 50 million, a tourist area which attracts a million visitors a year has 49 million non-visitors, and if management is interested in international visitors, they have around 6 billion non-visitors! The idea that all non-users are potential users, and should therefore be researched, is therefore somewhat naive.

The user survey can assist in focussing any research which is to be conducted on non-users. For example, in the case of a local recreation facility the user survey defines the catchment area and, unless there is some reason for believing that the catchment area can or should be extended, the non-users to be studied are those who live within that area. Similarly the user profile indicates the type of person currently using the facility, and again, unless there is a conscious decision to attempt to change that profile, the non-users to be studied are the ones with that profile living within the defined catchment area. Comparison between the user profile and the profile of the population of the catchment area, as revealed by Census data, will indicate the numbers and characteristics of non-users in the area. Thus user surveys can reveal something about non-users!

Captive group surveys

Nature

The 'captive group' survey is not referred to in other research methods texts. It refers to the situation where the people to be included in the survey comprise the membership of some group where access can be negotiated *en bloc*. Such groups include school children, adult education groups, clubs of various kinds and groups of employees – although all have their various unique characteristics.

Conduct

A roomful of cooperative people can provide a number of respondent-completed questionnaires very quickly. Respondent-completion is less problematic in 'captive' situations than in less controlled situations because it is possible to take the group through the questionnaire question by question and therefore ensure good standards of completion.

The most common example of a captive group is school children: the easiest way to contact children under school leaving age is via schools. The method may, however, appear simpler than it is in practice. Research on children for education purposes has become so common that education authorities are cautious about permitting access to children for surveys. Very often permission for any survey work must be obtained from the central education authority – the permission of the class teacher or head teacher is not sufficient.

The most economical use of this technique involves using a respondent-completed questionnaire, but interview methods can also be used. The essential feature is that access to members of the group is facilitated by their membership of that group and the fact that they are gathered together in one place at one time. It is important to be aware of the criteria for membership of the group and to compare that with the needs of the research. In some cases an apparent match can be misleading. For example attendees at a retired people's club meeting does not include all retired people – it excludes 'non-joiners' and the house-bound. While schools include all young people, care must be taken over their catchment areas, compared with the study area of the research, and with the mix of public and private schools.

Questionnaire design

Introduction: research problems and information requirements

The important principle in designing questionnaires is to take it slowly and carefully and to remember why the research is being done. Very often researchers move too quickly into 'questionnaire design mode' and begin listing all the things 'it would be interesting to ask'. In many organisations a draft questionnaire is circulated for comment and everyone in the organisation joins in. The process begins to resemble Christmas tree decorating – nobody must be left out and everybody must be allowed to contribute their favourite bauble. This is not the best way to proceed!

The decision to conduct a questionnaire survey should itself be the culmination of a careful process of thought and discussion, involving consideration of all possible techniques, as discussed in Chapter 3. The concepts and variables involved, and the relationships to be investigated, possibly in the form of hypotheses, theories, models or evaluative frameworks – should be clear and should guide the questionnaire design process, as illustrated in Figure 9.6. It is not advisable to *begin* with a list of questions to be included in the questionnaire. The starting point should be an examination of the management, planning, policy or theoretical questions to be addressed, followed by the drawing up of a list of information required to address the problems. This is outlined in Chapter 3 as elements 1–5 of the research process. Element 6, deciding the research strategy, involves determining which of the listed information requirements should be met by means of a questionnaire survey. Questions should be included in the questionnaire only if they relate to requirements listed in element 5. This means that every question included must be linked back to the *research questions*.

In designing a questionnaire, the researcher should of course have sought out as much previous research on the topic or related topics as possible. This can have an effect on the overall design of a project as discussed in Chapter 3. More specifically, if it is decided that the study in hand should have points of comparison with other studies, then data will need to be collected on a similar basis. Questionnaires from previous studies therefore become part of the input into the questionnaire design process.

Figure 9.6
Questionnaire
design process

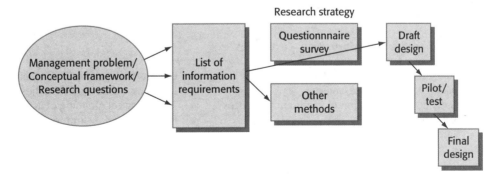

Types of information

Generally the information to be gathered from questionnaire surveys can be divided into three groups:

1. Respondent characteristics   Who?
2. Activities/behaviour   What?
3. Attitudes/motivations   Why?

Figure 9.7 lists some of the more common types of information collected under these three headings. The items covered are necessarily general in nature and do not cover all the specialised types of information which can be collected by questionnaire surveys.

Respondent characteristics
- Gender
- Age
- Economic status
- Occupation/social class (own or 'head of household')
- Previous employment history
- Income (own or household)
- Education/qualifications

- Marital/family status
- Household type/family size
- Life-cycle
- Ethnic group/country of birth
- Residential location
- Mobility – driving licence, access to private transport
- Party/group size/type (site/visitor surveys)

Activities/behaviour
a. Site/visitor surveys
- Activities while on site or in the area
- Use of site attractions/facilities
- Frequency of visit
- Time spent on site
- Expenditure per head – amounts/purposes
- Travel-related information
- Trip origin (where travelled from)
- Trip purpose
- Home address
- Travel mode
- Travel time
- Accommodation type used

b. Household surveys
- Leisure activities (including holidays) – what, where, how often, time spent, when, who with?
- Use of particular facilities/sites
- Travel mode to out-of-home leisure
- Expenditure patterns
- Past activities (personal leisure histories)
- Planned future activities

Attitude/motivation information – examples
a. Site/visitor surveys
- Reasons for choice of site/area
- Meaning/importance/values
- Satisfaction/evaluation of experience/services
- Comments on facility
- Future intentions/hopes

b. Household surveys
- Leisure/travel aspirations/needs
- Evaluation of services/facilities available
- Psychological meaning of activities/satisfactions
- Reactions to development/provision proposals
- Values – re environment, etc.

Figure 9.7   Range of information in leisure and tourism questionnaires

Some of these items of information require more intrusive questions than others – for example income. And some can be difficult to ascertain accurately – for example occupation or details of expenditure while on a tourist trip. They are not therefore all equally suitable for all survey situations.

The items of information discussed here are often referred to as *variables* – that is, they are characteristics or behaviour patterns which *vary* from one individual to another. The term variable is widely used in research generally and in particular in computer analysis of data, as discussed in Chapters 11 and 12.

Wording of questions

Principles

In wording the questions for a questionnaire the researcher should:

- Avoid jargon
- Simplify wherever possible
- Avoid ambiguity
- Avoid leading questions
- Ask only one question at a time (ie. avoid multi-purpose questions).

Examples of good and bad practice in question wording are given in Figure 9.8.

Pre-coded vs open-ended questions

As illustrated in Figure 9.9, an *open-ended* question is one where the interviewer asks a question without any prompting of the range of answers to be expected, and writes down the respondent's reply verbatim. In a self-completed questionnaire a line or space is left for respondents to write their answers. A closed or pre-coded question is one where the respondent is offered a range of answers to choose from, either verbally

Principle	Bad example	Improved version
Use simple language	What is your frequency of utilisation of retail travel outlets?	How often do you use travel agents?
Avoid ambiguity	Do you play sport very often?	Have played any of the following sports within the last four weeks? (present list)
Avoid leading questions	Are you against the extension of the airport?	What is your opinion on the extension of the airport? Are you for it, against it or not concerned?
Ask just one question at a time	Do you use the local arts centre, and if so what do you think of its facilities?	1. Do you use the local arts centre? Yes/No 2. What do you think of the facilities in the local arts centre?

Figure 9.8 Question-wording: examples of good and bad practice

Figure 9.9
Open-ended
vs pre-coded
questions –
example

Open-ended
What is the main constraint on your ability to study?

_____

Pre-coded/closed
Which of the following/items listed on the card is the main constraint on your ability to study? (show card – if interviewer-completed)

A.	My job	$\square_1$
B.	Timetabling	$\square_2$
C.	Child care	$\square_3$
D.	Spouse/partner	$\square_4$
E.	Money	$\square_5$
F.	Energy	$\square_6$
G.	Other _____	$\square_7$

Card shown to respondent:

> A. My job
> B. Timetabling of the course
> C. Child care
> D. Spouse/partner
> E. Money
> F. Energy
> G. Other _____

or from a show card or, in the case of a self-completed questionnaire, having the range of answers set out in the questionnaire and (usually) being asked to tick boxes.

In the open-ended case there is no prior list. In the closed/pre-coded case there is a list which is shown to the respondent. A third possibility, in an interviewer-administered survey, is a combination of the two, where the question is asked in an open-ended manner, but no card is shown to the respondent, but the questionnaire includes a pre-coded list where the answer is recorded. If respondents answer 'other' it is usual to write in details of what the 'other' is.

The advantage of the open-ended question is that the respondent's answer is not unduly influenced by the interviewer or by the questionnaire wording and the verbatim replies from respondents can provide a rich source of varied material which might have been hidden by categories on a pre-coded list. Figure 9.10 gives an example of the range of responses which can result from a single open-ended question.

Pre-coded groups are often used when asking respondents about quantified information, such as age, income, expenditure, because of convenience and saving any embarrassment respondents may have about divulging precise figures. There is, however, an advantage in using the open-ended approach for such data – obtaining actual figures rather than group codes. Recording the actual number permits the flexible option of grouping categories in alternative ways when carrying out the analysis. It also enables *averages* and other measures to be calculated and facilitates a range of statistical analysis which is not possible with groups. The actual figure is therefore often more useful for analysis purposes.

Question: Do you have any complaints about this (beach/picnic) area?
(Site survey in a beachside National Park with boating and camping. Number of responses in brackets)

Sand bars (22)
Parking (5)
Wild car driving (1)
Lack of beach area (1)
Too few shops (1)
Too few picnic tables (4)
No timber for barbecue (2)
Need more picnic space (3)
Need boat hire facilities (1)
Need active recn facilities (1)
Litter/pollution (74)
Urban sprawl (1)
Need wharf fishing access (1)
Lack of info. on walking trails (1)
Not enough facilities (3)
Slow barbecues (2)
Uncontrolled camping (1)
Lack/poor toilets (9)
Amenities too far from camp site (1)
Too much development (4)
(Speed) boats (44)
Need more trees for shade (1)
Yobbos drinking beer on beach (1)
Spear fishermen (1)
Water skiers (2)
Against nudism (3)
Loud music (1)
Dumped cars (1)
Traffic (1)
Poor roads (1)
Sand flies (1)
More barbecues (1)
Shells/oysters (1)
Need outdoor cafes (1)
Need more food places (1)
Water too shallow (1)

Uncontrolled boats (23)
Jet skis (39)
Surveys (1)
Should be kept for locals (1)
Seaweed (3)
Need showers (1)
Administration of National Park (1)
Maintenance & policing of Park (1)
Trucks on beach (2)
Anglers (1)
Crowds/tourists (26)
Having to pay entry fee (6)
Houses along waterfront (2)
Unpleasant smell (drain) (2)
Sales people (1)
Need electric barbecues (1)
Dogs (21)
No access to coast (1)
Park rangers not operating in interest of
the public (1)
Behaviour of others (20)
Access – long indirect road (1)
Need more shops (2)
Navigation marks unclear (1)
Need more taps (1)
Need more swings (1)
No first-aid facilities (1)
Need powered caravan sites (1)
Allow dogs (1)
Private beach areas (1)
Lack of restaurant (1)
Need rain shelters (1)
Can't spear fish (1)
No road shoulders for cyclists (1)
Remove rocks from swim areas (1)
Dangerous boat ramp pollutant activities (1)

Source: Robertson and Veal, 1987

Figure 9.10   Example of range of replies resulting from an open-ended question

Open-ended questions have two major disadvantages. First, the analysis of verbatim answers to qualitative questions for computer analysis is laborious and may result in a final set of categories which are of no more value than a well-constructed pre-coded list. In the case of the answers in Figure 9.10, for example, for detailed analysis it may be necessary to group the answers into, say, six groups – this would be time-consuming and would involve a certain amount of judgement in grouping individual answers, which can be a source of errors. This process is discussed in more detail under coding below.

The second disadvantage of the open-ended approach is that, in the case of respondent-completed questionnaires, response rates to such questions can be very low: people are often too lazy or too busy to write out free-form answers. When to use open-ended or closed questions is therefore a matter of judgement.

Common questions

The case studies at the end of this chapter give examples of typical questions used in household and site surveys, with interviewer-completed and respondent-completed examples. Case study 9.1 is a questionnaire used to assess students' attitudes to campus social life – it is labelled as a site/street survey since it would be administered to students on-campus, it partly resembles a site or user survey, but since not all students may make use of the services being examined, it resembles a survey conducted in a street or shopping centre. It is presented as respondent-completed, but completion would probably best be conducted 'under supervision' – that is completed and handed back to a survey worker at the time, rather than being handed out for later return, which would inevitably produce a low response rate. If the cooperation of the university authorities was obtained so that the questionnaire could be handed out and completed in class time, it would become a 'captive group' survey. Case study 9.2 is an interviewer-completed questionnaire for a household survey on short-stay holidays, while Case study 9.3 is an interviewer-completed questionnaire for a site survey of park users.

Annotations in the margins of these example questionnaires indicate the type of question involved ('multiple response' is explained in Chapter 11). The examples cannot, of course, cover all situations, but they give a wide range of examples of questions and appropriate formats. Below are some comments on some of the more common questions used, beginning with a number of respondent characteristics.

Age

Any examination of leisure participation and tourism data will show the importance of age in differentiating leisure and tourism behaviour and attitudes; it is therefore one of the data items most commonly included in questionnaires. The main decision to be made is whether to use pre-coded groups or ask for respondents' actual age. The advantages and disadvantages of the two approaches are discussed above, under pre-coded *vs* open-ended questions. If using pre-coded groups, ensure that there are no overlapping age-categories. For example, in the following it would not be clear into which group a 14 year-old respondent would fall.

A   0–14
B   14–19

Note that, to ensure comparability with census data, age groups should be specified as: 15–19, 20–24, 25–29, etc., *not* 16–20, 21–25, 26–30 etc.

Economic status/occupation/socio-economic group/class

A person's economic and occupational situation clearly impinges on leisure and tourism behaviour. Information on such matters is important for marketing and planning and also in relation to public policy concerns with equity. Economic status is a person's situation vis-à-vis the formal economy, as listed in Figure 9.11. In contemporary developed economies, only about half the population is engaged in the paid workforce.

Occupation is generally used to denote a person's type of paid work, so it is generally asked only of those identified from the economic status question as being in paid work. Others are sometimes asked what their last paid job was or what the occupation of the 'main breadwinner' of the household is. Such questions can, however, become complex because of full-time students living with parents or independently, single parents living on social security and so on. In a household survey it may be possible to pursue these matters, but in other situations, such as site surveys, it may not be appropriate because it would seem too intrusive. For those in paid work the sorts of question asked are:

- What is your occupation?
- What sort of work do you do?
- Which of the groups on this card best describes your occupation?

Figure 9.11
Economic status/ occupational/ socio-economic groupings

Economic status
- In full-time paid work
- In part-time paid work
- Full-time home or child carer
- In full-time education
- Retired
- Unemployed/looking for paid employment
- Other

Market research occupation/SEG classification
AB Managerial, administrative, professional (at senior or intermediate level)
C1 Supervisory or clerical (i.e. white collar) and junior managerial, administrative or professional
C2 Skilled manual
DE Semi-skilled, unskilled and casual workers and those entirely dependent on state pensions

Census occupation/SEG classification
- Professional
- Employers, managers
- Other self-employed
- Skilled workers and foremen
- Non-manual
- Service, semi-skilled and agricultural
- Armed forces
- Unskilled

Sufficient information should be obtained to enable respondents to be classified into an appropriate occupational category. Market researchers and official bodies, such as the Office for National Statistics and the Australian Bureau of Statistics, tend to use slightly different classifications, as shown in Figure 9.11. Such groupings, along with economic status, are often referred to as a person's *socio-economic group* or SEG. This is closely related to the idea of *class* or social class. Space does not permit a discussion of this complex concept here, but sources are given in the list of further reading at the end of the chapter.

Because people can be vague in response to an open-ended question on occupation it is wise to include a supplementary question to draw out a full description. For example 'office worker', 'engineer' or 'self-employed' are not adequate answers because they can cover such a wide variety of grades of occupation. A supplementary question could be: 'what sort of work is that?' In a household survey it may be possible to ask additional questions to be absolutely sure of the respondent's occupation. Such questions would check on the industry involved and the number of staff supervised by the respondent.

Income

A typical wording of a question on income would be:

■ What is your own personal gross income from all sources before taxes? or

■ Which of the groups on the card does your own personal gross income from all sources fall into?

Gross income is normally asked for, since it can be too complicated to gather information on income net of taxes and other deductions. Since there is often a major difference between gross and net income, this makes the variable a somewhat imprecise one. A further problem with income as a variable is that personal income is not a particularly useful variable for those who are not income recipients or who are not the main income recipients of the household. This can be overcome if all members of the household are being interviewed or if the respondent is asked about the 'main income earner' in the household. However, many teenage children, for example, do not know their parents' income and it might be seen as improper to ask them. Income is a sensitive issue and, in view of the limitations discussed above, is often excluded in site or visitor surveys.

Marital status

Since legal marital status fails to indicate the domestic situation of increasing numbers of people, the usefulness of this variable is declining. In terms of leisure and tourism behaviour, whether or not a person has responsibility for children is likely to be a more important variable. Usual categories for marital status are:

■ Married

■ Single – never married

■ Widowed/divorced/separated.

Respondents who are not formally married but living in a *de facto* relationship can then decide for themselves how they want to be classified, or a separate category can be created.

Household type and group type

Household type is a useful variable for many leisure and tourism studies but, except in the household interview situation, the data may be difficult to collect, because a number of items of information are required. In a household interview it is possible to ask 'Who lives here?' A simplified version would be to ask about the number of children of various ages in the household. Classifying the information into 'household type' must be done subsequently. Typical categories are as set out in Figure 9.12.

In the case of user/site surveys it is more usual to ask about the size of the party or group and its composition – for example, how many children and adults of various ages are present. Clearly such information is important for planning, marketing, managing and programming facilities. A typical categorisation of groups is as shown in Figure 9.12.

Lifecycle

Some researchers have argued that individual variables, such as age and marital status, are not good predictors of leisure and tourism behaviour; rather, we should examine the composite variable *lifecycle* (Rapoport and Rapoport, 1975). As with household type, a person's stage in the lifecycle is not based on a single question but built up from a number of items of information, including age, economic status and marital/family status. A possible classification is as set out in Figure 9.13. Life*style*, as discussed in Chapter 2, is a further development of this idea, but generally involves collection of a considerable amount of additional data.

Ethnic group

Ethnic group is included in leisure and tourism surveys because ethnically based cultures influence leisure and tourism behaviour and also because of policy concerns for equity between social groups. Everyone belongs to an ethnic group – that is, a social group that shares religious, language and other cultural values and practices and experiences – including leisure and tourism. Ethnicity therefore becomes important in leisure and tourism policy, planning and management, particularly as regards minority groups whose needs may not be met by mainstream facilities and services. A common approach to ethnicity in the past was to ask the respondent's country of birth, since most ethnic minority groups were migrant groups. But this of course does not identify members of ethnic minority groups not born overseas. Parents' place of birth identifies the second generation of migrant groups but not third and subsequent generations. Country of birth has therefore become less and less useful as an indicator of ethnic group membership. Observation is an obvious solution but is not reliable for many groups. The solution is to ask people what ethnic group they consider they belong to. While this may cause offence to some, it is the most satisfactory approach overall.

Figure 9.12
Household type
and group type

Household type – Household survey

Question format:

Can you please tell me who lives here?

Person	Relationship to Respondent	Gender M/F	Age	Occupation
1	Respondent			
2				
3				
4				
5				
6				

Group classification:
A. Single parent and 1 dependent child
B. Single parent and 2 or more dependent children
C. Couple and 1 dependent child
D. Couple and 2 or more dependent children
E. Couple, no children
F. Related adults only
G. Unrelated adults only
H. Single person
I. Other.

Visitor groups – Site survey

Question format:
a. How many people are there in this group, including yourself?   ____
b. How many children aged under 5 are there in the group?   ____
c. How many children age between 5 and 15 are there?   ____
d. How many people aged 60 or over are there?   ____

Group classification:
A. Youngest member aged 0–4
B. Youngest member aged 5–15
C. Lone adult
D. Two adults (under 60)
E. Older couple (60 and over)
F. 3–5 adults
G. 6 + adults.

Figure 9.13
Lifecycle stages

A. Child/Young single – dependent (on parents)
B. Young single – independent
C. Young married/partnered – no children
D. Parent – dependent children
E. Parent – children now independent
F. Retired – up to 70
G. Retired – over 70

Residential location/trip origin

Where a person lives can be a significant determinant of access to leisure facilities and is a reflection of socio-economic position and related patterns of consumption (Shaw, 1984; Zukin, 1990). And residential location and trip origin are the basis of catchment area analysis for individual facilities. In the case of a household survey the residential location would be known by the interviewer and some sort of code – for street, suburb, local government area, county, as appropriate – can be recorded on the questionnaire. In the case of site/visitor surveys, in order to study the catchment area of the facility, it is necessary to ask people where they live or where they have travelled from. How much detail is required? In some surveys the suburb/town is sufficient. In other cases it is necessary to know the street. The number of the dwelling in the street is rarely necessary. For overseas visitors the country is usually adequate information. In Case study 6.4, an example is given of the use of home-location data to show the catchment area of a facility. In that example the information came from membership records, but the information could equally well arise from a questionnaire survey of users.

Market research firms often record full addresses and/or telephone numbers of survey respondents in order to undertake subsequent quality checks on interviewers, to ensure that the respondents have in fact been interviewed.

Housing information

Information on the type of dwelling in which respondents live is usually collected in household surveys because it can easily be gathered by observation. The information is clearly relevant in leisure research because of the implications of dwelling type for access to private recreational space. Whether or not people own their own home is an important socio-economic variable. Typical categories for these items of information are shown in Figure 9.14.

Transport

Because mobility is such an important factor in leisure behaviour, leisure questionnaires often include questions on ownership of and access to vehicles. People are sometimes

Figure 9.14
Housing
information

Type of Dwelling
A. Separate house
B. Semi-detached house
C. Terrace house
D. Flat/maisonette
E. Caravan, houseboat
F. Other

Tenure
A. Owned outright
B. Being purchased
C. Rented
D. Other

asked if they possess a current driver's licence. In the case of site surveys, the mode of transport used to travel to the site is often asked. If people claim to have used two or more modes of transport, the various modes can all be recorded or respondents can be asked to indicate the one on which they travelled the furthest.

Leisure activities

The problem of devising questions to gather information on leisure activities in leisure participation surveys is a difficult one. The difficulties centre on two main issues:

■ whether to use an open-ended or pre-coded format,

■ the time-period for participation.

An open-ended format question simply asks respondents to list the activities they have engaged in during their leisure time or free time over a specified period. Without any prompting of the range of activities intended to be included respondents might have difficulty in recalling all their activities, and in any case may not understand the full scope of the word 'leisure' or 'free time'. The word 'leisure' has different connotations for different people. Without explanation, some people might assume that having a cup of coffee and chatting with a friend was not leisure, or that knitting or gardening was not leisure. Using the word 'free time' might help a little, but it is still open to variation in interpretation.

Although providing people with checklists of activities to choose from may be unwieldy, it at least ensures that all respondents consider the same range of options. The disadvantage of the checklist is that the length of the list may be daunting to some respondents, particularly the less literate. In the case of an interviewer-completed questionnaire the main problem may be the time it takes to read out the list and the problem of patience and tedium which it may entail. The General Household Survey compromises by offering a checklist of about a dozen 'types' of leisure activity, such as home-based activities, outdoor recreation, arts and entertainment, as an *aide-mémoire* for the respondent.

The time-period for recalling activities is crucial to the nature of the findings. Table 9.1 shows the results from a 2001 survey in which respondents were asked about attendance at arts events in the previous four weeks, but if they had not participated in the previous four weeks they were asked if they had participated in the last year. The results are plain to see (for similar data for Australia, see Darcy, 1994). The time-period used to measure participation affects the absolute levels of participation recorded and also the apparent relative popularity of activities. The shorter the time-period used the more accurate the results are likely to be, but shorter time-periods exclude large proportions of participants in those activities which are engaged in relatively infrequently.

In addition to asking whether they have participated in an activity respondents can also be asked *how often* they have participated and *how much time* was spent on the activity. This can lead to very lengthy interviews for people who have engaged in a wide range of activities. To avoid this, in some surveys a particular leisure occasion, say the last trip to the countryside, is explored in more detail – where the respondent went,

Table 9.1 Attendance at arts events, England, 2001

	% of persons aged 16+ attending in last:	
	12 months	**4 weeks**
Film at a cinema or other venue	55	19
Play or drama	27	5
Carnival, street arts or circus	23	4
Art, photography or sculpture exhibition	19	6
Craft exhibition	17	4
Pantomime	13	–
Cultural festival	10	2
Event connected with books or writing	8	2
Event including video or electronic art	7	2
A musical	24	4
Pop or rock concert	18	4
Classical music concert	10	3
Opera or operetta	6	1
Jazz concert	5	2
Folk or country and western concert	3	–
Other music	9	–
All types of live dance performance	12	–
Contemporary dance	3	–
Ballet	2	–
Other dance	7	–
Sample	6,042	6,042

– = zero/not asked

Source: Skelton *et al.*, 2002

with whom, what day of the week and what time of day, what specific activities were engaged in, and so on.

In local surveys or surveys with an interest in specific policy areas, it may be of interest to explore the use of specific, named, leisure facilities or tourist attractions – for example visits to particular national parks or sports centres – using a variety of approaches to measuring use.

In the case of site/user surveys there is usually little problem in asking about activities. Many leisure sites offer opportunity for more than one activity – for example, swimming, picnicking and sunbathing, at the beach – so it is usual to ask people what activities they plan to engage in or have engaged in during their visit. Use of specific facilities – such as refreshment facilities – may also be explored.

Tourism activity

In the case of household questionnaire surveys concerned with tourism, the 'activity' question concerns trips taken away from the home area over a specified time-period. As with local leisure activities, a major consideration is the recall time-period. For major holidays a one-year recall period is not out of the question, but for short breaks, asking about trips during that length of time may lead to inaccuracies in recall, so a shorter time-period of, say, three months may be adopted.

A second time-period issue concerns the definition of tourist 'trip'. The definition used in a survey may follow an accepted definition of tourism, for example a trip involving a stay away from home of one night or more. However, in some local tourism studies *day-trips* may also be of interest.

In addition to indicating trips taken, household tourism questionnaires also generally include questions on where the respondent has been on the trip, length of stay, travel mode and type of accommodation used. Tourism surveys are usually much more concerned with economic matters than leisure surveys, so questions on the cost of the trip and of expenditure in various categories are often included. For site surveys in a tourism context, including *en route* surveys, the activity questions asked of tourists and locals will generally be identical.

Measuring leisure and tourism activity

Clearly leisure and tourism activity encompasses a wide range of variables. The variety of possible measures of leisure and tourism activity is indicated in Figure 9.15. In any study consideration should be given as to which types of measure are necessary.

Media use

Questionnaires often include questions on media use because such information can be used when considering advertising policy. To obtain accurate information in this area would require a considerable number of questions on frequency of reading/viewing/listening and, in the case of electronic media, the type of programmes favoured. When the research is concerned with small-scale local facilities or services, television advertising is generally out of the question because of cost, so information on television watching need not be gathered. Similar considerations may apply to magazine and national newspaper reading. For many surveys therefore, two questions are involved (show cards would usually be used):

'What (local) newspapers do you read regularly – that is at least weekly?'
'What (local) radio stations do you listen to regularly – that is at least twice a week?'

Attitudes/opinions

Attitudes and opinions are more complex aspects of questionnaire design. A range of techniques exists to explore people's opinions and attitudes, as listed in Figure 9.16. The first three formats, direct, open-ended questions, checklists and ranking, are straightforward, but the other formats presented merit some comment.

Likert scales

Scaling techniques are sometimes known as 'Likert scales' after the psychologist who developed their use and analysis. In this technique respondents are asked to indicate

Measure	Definition	Leisure example	Tourism example
A. The participation rate	The proportion of a defined population which engages in an activity in a given period of time	6 per cent of the adult population of community X go swimming at least once a week	5 per cent of the adult population of country X make an overseas trip each year
B. Number of participants	Number of people in a defined community who engage in an activity in a given period of time (A × pop'n. or C ÷ frequency of visit)	20,000 people in community X swim at least once a week	700,000 residents of country X visit country Y in a year
C. Volume of activity (visits)	The number of visits made or games played in an activity by members of a defined community or to a defined geographical area for an activity in a specified time period (B × visits/games per time period)*	There are 1.2 million visits to swimming pools in community X (one million by local residents) in a year	850,000 trips are made to country Y by residents of country X in a year
D. Time	The amount of leisure time available to the individual in a defined community, over a specified period – or time spent on specific activity (C × time per visit)	The average retired person has 5 hours leisure time per day/or spends an average of 3 hours watching television per day	The average tourist visiting region Z spends 5.5 nights in the region
E. Expenditure	The amount of money spent per individual or by a defined community on leisure or particular leisure goods or services over a specified time period (C × spend per visit)	Consumer expenditure on leisure in Britain is over £50 billion a year	Tourists visiting region Z spend £25 million in the region per annum

* In tourism a further distinction is made between 'trips' (e.g. a complete holiday) and visits (i.e. places visited during the holiday)
** In tourism the measure 'bed-nights' is often used.

Figure 9.15 Measuring leisure and tourism demand

Figure 9.16
Opinion/attitude
question formats

a. *Open-ended/direct*: What attracted you to apply for this course?

_____

b. *Checklist*: Of the items on the card, which was the most important to you in applying for this course?

A.   Good reputation
B.   Easy access
C.   Curriculum
D.   Level of fees
E.   Easy parking

c. *Ranking*: Please rank the items on the card in terms of their importance to you in choosing a course. Please rank them 1 for the most important to 5 for the least important.

		Rank
A.	Good reputation	_____
B.	Easy access	_____
C.	Curriculum	_____
D.	Level of fees	_____
E.	Easy parking	_____

d. *Likert scales*: Looking at the items on the card, please say how important each was to you in choosing this course; was it: Very important, Quite important, Not very important or Not at all important?

	Very important	Quite important	Not very important	Not at all important
Good reputation	$\square_1$	$\square_2$	$\square_3$	$\square_4$
Easy access	$\square_1$	$\square_2$	$\square_3$	$\square_4$
Curriculum	$\square_1$	$\square_2$	$\square_3$	$\square_4$
Level of fees	$\square_1$	$\square_2$	$\square_3$	$\square_4$
Easy parking	$\square_1$	$\square_2$	$\square_3$	$\square_4$

d. *Attitude statements*: Please read the statements below and indicate your level of agreement or disagreement with them by ticking the appropriate box.

	Agree Strongly	Agree	No opinion	Disagree strongly	Disagree
The learning experience is more important than the qualification in education	$\square_1$	$\square_2$	$\square_3$	$\square_4$	$\square_5$
Graduate course fees are too high	$\square_1$	$\square_2$	$\square_3$	$\square_4$	$\square_5$

e. *Semantic differential*: Please look at the list below and tick the line to indicate where you think this course falls in relation to each factor listed.

Difficult	|_____|_____|_____|_____|	Easy
Irrelevant	|_____|_____|_____|_____|	Relevant
Professional	|_____|_____|_____|_____|	Unprofessional
Dull	|_____|_____|_____|_____|	Interesting

their agreement or disagreement with a proposition or the importance they attach to a factor, using a standard set of responses. One of the advantages of this approach is that the responses can be quantified, as discussed below under 'Attitude statements'.

Ranking

Asking respondents to rank items in order of importance is a relatively straightforward process, provided the list is not too long: more than five or six items could test respondents' patience. Again, the responses can be quantified – for example, in the form of average ranks.

Attitude statements

Attitude statements are a means of exploring respondents' attitudes towards a wide range of issues, including questions of a philosophical or political nature. Respondents are shown a series of statements and asked to indicate, using a scale, the extent to which they agree or disagree with them.

Responses to both Likert scale questions and attitude statements can be scored, as indicated by the numerals beside the boxes. For example, 'agree strongly' could be given a score of 5, 'agree' a score of 4, and so on to 'disagree strongly' with a score of 1. Scores can then be averaged across a number of respondents. So, for example, a group of people who mostly either 'agreed' or 'agreed strongly' with a statement would produce an average score between 4 and 5, whereas a group who 'disagreed' or 'disagreed strongly' would produce a low score, between 1 and 2. Such scores enable the strength of agreement with different statements to be compared, and the opinions of different groups of people to be compared.

Semantic differential

The semantic differential method involves offering respondents *pairs* of contrasting descriptors and asking them to indicate how the facility, place or service being studied relates to the descriptors. This technique is suitable for a respondent-completion questionnaire, since the respondent is required to place a tick on each line. It would be difficult to replicate this exactly in an interview situation with no visual prompts, such as in a telephone survey; the effect would be to reduce the possible answers to three: close to one end or the other and 'in the middle'. The choice of pairs of words used in a semantic differential list should arise from the research context and theory.

Repertory grid

A further development of this approach is the *repertory grid* technique, in which the pairs of words – called *personal constructs* – are developed by the respondent (Kelly, 1955). This technique is not explored further here, but references to examples of its use in leisure and tourism are given in the further reading section.

Ordering of questions and layout of questionnaires

Introductory remarks

Should a questionnaire include introductory remarks, for example, explaining the purpose of the survey and asking for the respondent's assistance? In the case of a mail survey such material is generally included in the covering letter. In the case of other forms of self-completion questionnaire such a note is advisable, unless the field-workers handing out the questionnaires have sufficient time to provide the necessary introduction and explanation. In the case of interviewer-administered questionnaires the remarks can be printed on the top of each questionnaire or can be included in the interviewers' written instructions.

In fact face-to-face interviewers are unlikely to approach potential interviewees and actually read from a script. When seeking cooperation of a potential interviewee it is usually necessary to maintain eye contact, so interviewers must know in advance what they want to say. In the case of household surveys, potential interviewees may require a considerable amount of information and proof of identity from the interviewer before agreeing to be interviewed. But in the case of site interviews, respondents are generally more interested in knowing how long the interview will take and 'what sort of questions' they will be asked – so only minimal opening remarks are necessary. For example, for a site survey the introduction could be as brief as: 'Excuse me, we are conducting a survey of visitors to the area; would you mind answering a few questions?'

It is usually necessary for an interviewer to indicate what organisation they represent, and this can be reinforced by an identity badge. Market research or consultancy companies often instruct interviewers to indicate only that they represent the company and not the client. This can ensure that unbiased opinions are obtained, although in some cases it can raise ethical considerations if it is felt that respondents have a right to know what organisation will be using the information gathered.

One function of opening remarks can be to ensure the respondent of confidentiality. In the case of site surveys, where names and addresses are not generally collected, confidentiality is easy to maintain. In the case of household and some postal surveys respondents can be identified. One way of ensuring that confidentiality is maintained is to arrange for names and addresses to be kept separate from the actual questionnaires and for questionnaires to include only an identifying number.

Ordering

It is important that an interview based on a questionnaire flows in a logical and comfortable manner. A number of principles should be borne in mind.

1. Start with easy questions.
2. Start with 'relevant' questions – for example if the respondent has been told that the survey is about holidays, begin with some questions about holidays.
3. Personal questions, dealing with such things as age or income, are generally best left to near the end: while they do not generally cause problems, and respondents

need not answer those personal questions if they object, they are less likely to cause offence if asked later in the interview when a rapport has been established between interviewer and respondent. Similar principles apply in relation to respondent-completion questionnaires.

Layout

A questionnaire must be laid out and printed in such a way that the person who must read it – whether interviewer or respondent – can follow all the instructions easily and answer all the questions that are meant to be answered. Layout becomes particularly important when a questionnaire contains filters – that is when answers to certain questions determine which subsequent questions must be answered. An example, with alternative ways of dealing with layout, is shown in Figure 9.17.

In the case of respondent-completion questionnaires extra care must be taken with layout because it can be very difficult to rectify faults 'in the field'. Clarity of layout, and the overall impression given by the questionnaire can be all-important in obtaining a good response.

Mail surveys, where the researcher does not have direct contact with the respondent, are the most demanding. A professionally laid out, type-set and printed questionnaire will pay dividends in terms of response rate and accuracy and completeness of responses. A type-set format can reduce the number of pages considerably, which may increase the response-rate if the perceived length of the questionnaire is a factor.

Even where interviewers are used there are advantages in keeping the questionnaire as compact as possible for ease of handling. A two-column format, as used in Case study 9.3 (p. 281), is worth exploring. Columns can be easily achieved with modern word-processing packages.

The questionnaire shown in Case study 9.1 is designed for respondent-completion and the layout therefore involves boxes for the respondent to tick. Boxes can, however, be laborious to type and lay out, so where an interviewer is being used, as in Case studies 9.2 and 9.3, the interviewer can circle codes.

The 'office use' column is not always necessary in such interviewer-administered questionnaires, but is included in Case studies 9.2 and 9.3 for exposition purposes. This type of layout can be used for respondent-completion in some situations – for example in certain 'captive group' situations or where respondents are known to be

---

Figure 9.17
Filtering:
examples

Layout 1

1. a. Have you studied at this university before?

           Yes $\square_1$

           No $\square_2$

    b. If YES: How long ago did you study here? ___ years

Layout 2

1. Have you studied at this university before?

           Yes $\square_1$ Go to question 3

           No $\square_2$ Go to question 2

2. How long ago did you study here? ___ years

highly literate and are unlikely to be deterred by the apparent technicalities of the layout.

Coding

Most questionnaire survey data are now analysed by computer. This means that the information in the questionnaire must be coded – that is converted into numerical codes and organised in a systematic, 'machine-readable', manner. Different procedures apply to pre-coded and open-ended questions and these are discussed in turn below.

Pre-coded questions

The principle for coding of pre-coded questions is illustrated in many of the examples in the example questionnaires. For example, for question 1 in Case study 9.1, the codes are as shown beside the boxes. Only one answer is possible, so only one *code* is recorded as the answer to this question.

Where the answer is already numerical, there is no need to code the answer because the numerical answer can be handled by the computer. For example, in question 4 of Case study 9.1 actual expenditure is asked for, which is a number and does not require coding.

Scaled answers, as in Likert scales and attitude statements, readily lend themselves to coding, as shown by the numerals in the examples given in Figure 9.16. In the case of the semantic differential each of the sections of the response line can be numbered, say, 1–4, so that answers can be given a numerical code, depending on where the respondent marks the line.

Open-ended questions

In the case of completely open-ended questions quite an elaborate procedure must be followed to devise a coding system. As already suggested, the answers to open-ended questions can be copied from the questionnaires and presented in a report 'raw', as in Figure 9.10. If this is all that is required from the open-ended questions then there is no point in spending the considerable labour necessary to code the information for computer analysis: the computer will merely reproduce what can be more easily achieved manually.

Computer analysis comes into its own if it is intended to analyse the results in more detail – for example comparing the opinions of two or more groups. If such comparisons are to be made it will usually be difficult to do so with, say, 50 or 60 different responses to compare, especially if many of the responses are only given by one or two respondents. The aim then is to devise a coding system which groups the responses into a manageable number of categories.

If a large sample is involved, it is advisable to select a representative sub-sample of the responses, say 50 or 100, and write out the responses, noting, as in Figure 9.18, the number of occurrences of each answer. Then give individual codes for the most

Figure 9.18
Coding open-
ended questions
– examples

Answers from 25 respondents to the question: 'What suggestions would you make for improving campus life?'

More live music ///
Upgrade facilities ///
More weekday events //
More lunch-time events /
More evening events //
Better PA system /
Cheaper drinks ///
Free transport from city /
More free events //
Less hard rock acts //

Better food ///
Keep out non-students //
Something with a theme, like a film festival //
Better acoustics in main hall //
Events for socialising, e.g. barbecues //
Events should start and finish on time ///
More unusual acts, films, etc . . . not just what can be seen in town ///
More participatory events – e.g. debates //
Free entry to all events //

Suggested coding system

Comments on programme content	1
Comments on timing	2
Comments on facilities	3
Comments on costs	4
Comments on organisation	5
Other	6

frequent responses and group the others into meaningful categories – this is a matter of judgement. The aim is not to leave too many responses in the 'other' category. An example of this process is given in Figure 9.18.

Recording coded information

Computer analysis is conducted using the coded information from a questionnaire. This is best illustrated by an example – a completed questionnaire from Case study 9.1 is set out in Figure 9.19.

The questionnaire is laid out for self-completion by the respondent, so it is made fairly simple by providing boxes to be ticked and the codes for the answers are discretely printed beside the boxes. An 'office use' column is provided into which the coded information is transferred ready for keying into the computer. This layout might be different for an interviewer-completed questionnaire, as discussed in the section on layout.

In the 'office use' column, *spaces* are provided into which the codes from the answers can be written. The 'variable names' in the office column – qno, crse, lib, etc. – are explained in Chapter 11.

■ Questionnaire number, in the 'office use' column, is an identifier so that a link can be made between data in the computer and actual questionnaires – the example questionnaire is number 001

Figure 9.19
Completed
questionnaire

Campus Life Survey 2003

Office Use

1. Which of the following best describes your current situation?

Full-time student with no regular paid work	☐1	
Full-time student with some regular paid work	☑2	
Part-time student with full-time job	☐3	
Part-time student – other	☐4	

_1_
    qno

_2_ status

2. Which of the following university services have you used in the last 4 weeks?

Used campus cafe/bar	☑1
Attended a live music performance on campus	☑1
Used campus sport facilities	☐1
Used campus travel service	☐1

_1_ cafebar
_1_ music
_0_ sport
_0_ travel

3. In thinking about the social and entertainment services provided on campus, what are the most important considerations for you?
Please rank the items below in terms of their importance to you.
Rank them from 1 for the most important to 5 for the least important.

	Rank	
Free or cheap access	_1_	
Day-time attractions	_4_	
Acts, films, etc. not available elsewhere	_2_	
Opportunities to socialise/meet people	_3_	
Quality of presentation	_5_	

_1_ cheap
_4_ daytime
_2_ unusual
_3_ meet
_5_ quality

4. Approximately how much do you spend in an average month on entertainment and social activities on and off campus?

£_100_

_100_ spend

5. Please indicate the importance of the following to you in relation to campus life.

	Very important	Important	Not at all Important	
Relaxation opportunities	☑3	☐2	☐1	_3_ relax
Social interaction	☑3	☐2	☐1	_3_ social
Mental stimulation	☐3	☐2	☑1	_1_ mental

6. What suggestions would you make for improving campus social life?

Provide more for minority tastes – less rock bands

_1_ sug1
___ sug2
___ sug3

7. You are: Male ☑1   Female ☐2

_1_ gender

8. Your age last birthday was: _18_ years

_18_ age

- Question 1 – only one answer/code can be given

- Question 2 – respondents can tick up to four boxes

- Question 3 – five ranks must be recorded

- Question 4 – asks for an actual number and this will be transferred into the computer without coding

- Question 5 – consists of three Likert-scale items

- Question 6 – an open-ended question. It is envisaged that some respondents might give more than one answer, so spaces have been reserved for three answers (although in the example, only one has been given). The answers have a coding system (devised as discussed above) as follows:

Comments on programme content	1
Comments on timing	2
Comments on facilities	3
Comments on costs	4
Comments on organisation	5
Other	6

The data from this particular completed questionnaire in Figure 9.19 therefore become a single row of numbers, as shown in the first row of Figure 9.20, which shows how data from 15 completed questionnaires would look. How such a set of data may be analysed by computer is discussed in Chapter 11.

The validity of questionnaire-based data

Questionnaires are designed to gather information from individuals about their characteristics, behaviour and attitudes. Whether or not they actually achieve this depends on a number of considerations. The interview situation is not always conducive to careful, thoughtful responses. Respondents may tend to exaggerate or understate in their answers to some questions. They may also have problems in recalling some information accurately. Respondents may tend to give answers which they believe will please the interviewer. Thus the *validity* of questionnaire-based data – the extent to which they accurately reflect what they are meant to reflect – is a constant source of concern. To some extent the researcher must simply live with these limitations of the survey method and hope that inaccuracies are not significant and that some of them cancel each other out. There are however some measures which can be taken to check on the presence of this type of problem.

One approach is to include 'dummy' categories in some questions. For example, in a survey of recreation managers in Britain in the early 1980s respondents were asked to indicate, from a list, what books and reports they had heard of and had read. Included in the list was one plausible, but non-existent title. A significant proportion of respondents indicated that they had heard of the report and a small proportion claimed to have read it! Such a response does not necessarily mean that respondents

qno	status	cafebar	music	sport	travel	cheap	daytime	unusual	meet	quality	spend	relax	social	mental	sug1	sug2	sug3	gender	age
1	2	1	1	0	0	1	4	2	3	5	100	3	3	1	1			1	18
2	2	1	1	1	0	1	4	2	3	5	50	2	3	1	2	1		1	19
3	3	1	0	0	0	2	5	1	3	4	250	2	2	2	3	4		2	19
4	4	0	0	0	0	2	3	1	4	5	25	3	2	2	1	2	4	1	22
5	3	1	0	0	1	1	4	3	2	5	55	3	3	1				2	24
6	3	1	1	1	0	2	4	1	3	5	40	2	3	1	2			2	20
7	2	1	0	0	0	3	2	1	4	5	150	2	3	2	3			2	20
8	2	1	0	1	0	3	4	2	1	5	250	1	2	2	4	5		1	21
9	4	0	1	0	0	1	5	2	3	4	300	2	3	2				1	21
10	3	1	1	0	0	2	3	1	5	4	100	1	2	1	1	1		2	21
11	3	1	1	0	1	2	3	1	4	5	75	2	2	1	2	3		2	19
12	2	1	0	1	0	1	4	3	2	5	50	2	3	1				1	22
13	1	1	0	1	0	1	5	2	3	4	55	2	3	2	1	2		2	21
14	3	1	1	0	0	2	4	1	3	5	75	3	3	2	4			2	20
15	1	1	1	0	0	3	2	1	5	4	150	3	3	1	1	2	5	1	20

Figure 9.20 Data from fifteen questionnaires

were lying – they may simply have been confused about the titles of particular publications. But it does provide cautionary information to the researcher on the degree of error in responses to such questions, since it suggests that responses to the genuine titles may also include a certain amount of inaccuracy. For example, if 2 per cent of respondents claim to have heard of the non-existent report, this could suggest that all answers are subject to an error of plus or minus two.

A similar approach is to include two or more questions in different parts of the questionnaire, which essentially ask the same thing. For example an early question could ask respondents to rank a list of activities or holiday areas in order of preference. Later in the questionnaire, in the context of asking some detailed questions, respondents could be asked to indicate their favourite activity or holiday area. In the analysis, the responses could be tested for consistency.

One possibility is that the interview experience itself may cause respondents to change their opinion, because it causes them to think through in detail something which they might previously have only considered superficially. Similar questions at the beginning and end of the interview may detect this. In an Australian survey of gambling behaviour and attitudes towards a proposed casino development Grichting and Caltabiano (1986) asked, at the beginning of the interview: 'What do you think about the casino coming to Townsville? Are you for it or against it?' At the end of the interview they asked: 'Taking everything you have said into consideration, what do you think now about the casino coming to Townsville? Are you for it or against it?' It was found that about 'one in six respondents changed their attitude toward the casino during the course of the interview'.

Fieldwork arrangements

The scale and complexity of the data collection, or fieldwork, part of a research project can obviously vary enormously. At one extreme the process is largely a matter of personal organisation; at the other extreme a staff of hundreds may need to be recruited, trained and supervised. Fieldwork must be organised in any empirical study involving primary data collection, but because of the popularity of the survey method and the likelihood that it will involve organisation of individuals other than the researcher, some attention is given to the task here in this chapter.

Some of the items which need consideration are listed in Figure 9.21. Brief notes on these tasks are given below.

a. Seek permissions
It is important to remember that permission is often needed to interview in public places, such as streets and beaches, because of local bye-laws. Many areas which are thought of as 'public' are in fact the responsibility of some public or private organisation – for example shopping centres and parks. Permission must be sought from these organisations to conduct fieldwork. It is also good practice to inform the local police if interviewing is being conducted in public places, in case of complaints from the public.

Figure 9.21
Fieldwork
planning tasks

a. Seek permissions – to visit sites, obtain records, etc.
b. Obtain lists for sampling – e.g. voters lists
c. Arrange printing – of questionnaires, etc.
d. Check insurance issues
e. Prepare written instructions for interviewers
f. Prepare identity badges/letters for interviewers
g. Recruit interviewers and supervisors
h. Train interviewers and supervisors
i. Obtain quotations for any fieldwork to be conducted by other organisations
j. Appoint and train data coders/processors

b. Obtain lists

Obtaining lists, such as voters or membership lists for sampling may seem routine, but often apparently straightforward tasks can involve delays, or the material may not be quite in the form anticipated and it takes time to 'sort out'. Often research projects are conducted on very tight schedules and delays of a few days can be crucial. Therefore the earlier these routine tasks are tackled the better.

c. Arrange printing

Printing sounds straightforward, but the in-house printshop has busy periods when it may not be possible to obtain a quick job turnround. Checking on printing procedures and turnround times at an early stage is therefore advisable.

d. Check insurance

When conducting fieldwork away from a normal place of work, insurance issues may arise, including public liability and workers' compensation for interviewers. In the case of educational institutions staff and students are normally covered as long as they are engaged in legitimate university/college activities, but these matters should be checked with a competent legal authority in the organisation.

e. Prepare written instructions for interviewers

Provision of written instructions for interviewers is advisable and may cover:

- detailed comments on questionnaires and/or other instruments
- instructions in relation to checking of completed questionnaires, etc. for legibility and completeness
- instructions on returning questionnaires, etc.
- dress and behaviour codes
- roster details
- 'wet weather' instructions, if relevant
- instructions on what to do in the case of 'difficult' interviewees, etc.
- details of time-sheets, payment, etc.
- contact telephone numbers.

A note on questionnaire-based interviewing is appropriate here. The general approach to interviewing when using a questionnaire is that the interviewer should be instructed to adhere precisely to the wording on the questionnaire. If the respondent does not understand the question, the question should simply be repeated exactly as before; if the respondent still does not understand then the interviewer should move on to the next question. If this procedure is to be adhered to then the importance of question wording and the testing of such wording in one or more pilot surveys is clear.

The above procedure is clearly important in relation to attitude questions. Any word of explanation or elaboration from the interviewer could influence, and therefore bias, the response. In relation to factual questions, however, it may be less important – a word of explanation from the interviewer may be acceptable if it results in obtaining accurate information.

f. Prepare identity badges/letters

If working in a public or semi-public place, fieldworkers should be clearly identified. A badge with the institutional logo and the fieldworker's name is advisable. A letter from the research supervisor indicating that the fieldworker is engaged in legitimate research activity for the organisation may also be helpful.

g. Recruit interviewers and supervisors

Where paid interviewers, supervisors or other fieldworkers are to be used it will be necessary to go through the normal procedures for employing part-time staff. Advice from the organisation's Human Resources Unit, or someone familiar with its procedures, will need to be sought.

h. Training

The length of training will vary with the complexity of the fieldwork and the experience of the fieldwork staff. Paid fieldworkers should be paid for the training session(s) (and this should be budgeted for). A two- or three-hour session is usually sufficient, but more may be necessary for a complex project. It is advisable for interviewers to practice interviews on each other and report back on difficulties encountered.

i. Obtain quotations

In some cases certain aspects of the project may be undertaken by other organisations – for example data processing. Obtaining detailed quotations on price as early as possible is clearly advisable.

j. Appoint and train data coders/processors

In some cases the coding, editing and processing of data for computer analysis is a significant task in its own right, requiring staff to be recruited. Recruitment and training procedures will need to be followed as for fieldworkers.

Conducting a pilot survey

Pilot surveys are small-scale 'trial runs' of a larger survey. Pilot surveys relate particularly to questionnaire surveys, but can, in fact, relate to trying out any type of research procedure. It is always advisable to carry out one or more pilot surveys before embarking on the main data collection exercise. The purposes of pilot surveys are summarised in Figure 9.22. Clearly the pilot can be used to test out all aspects of the survey, not just question wording. Item d., 'familiarity with respondents', refers to the role of the pilot in alerting the researcher to any characteristics, idiosyncrasies or sensitivities of the respondent group with which he or she may not have been previously familiar. Such matters can affect the design and conduct of the main survey. Items g and h, concerned with the response rate and length of interview, can be most important in providing information to 'fine tune' the survey process. For example, it may be necessary to shorten the questionnaire and/or vary the number of field staff so that the project keeps on schedule and within budget.

In principle at least some of the pilot interviews should be carried out by the researcher in charge, or at least by some experienced interviewers, since the interviewers will be required to report back on the pilot survey experience and contribute to discussions on any revisions to the questionnaire or fieldwork arrangements which might subsequently be made. The debriefing session following the pilot survey is very important and should take place as soon as possible after the completion of the exercise, so that the details are fresh in the interviewers' minds.

Figure 9.22
Pilot survey
purposes

a. Test questionnaire wording
b. Test question sequencing
c. Test questionnaire layout
d. Familiarity with respondents
e. Test fieldwork arrangements
f. Train and test fieldworkers
g. Estimate response rate
h. Estimate interview, etc. time
i. Test analysis procedures

Summary

This chapter provides an introduction to questionnaire surveys, arguably the most commonly used data collection vehicle in leisure and tourism research. The merits of questionnaire surveys are discussed, including the ability to quantify, transparency, succinctness in data presentation, the ability to study change over time, comprehensive coverage of complex phenomena and generalisability to the whole population. The second part of the chapter is devoted to discussing the features of seven different forms of the questionnaire survey: the household survey, the street survey, the telephone survey, the mail survey, the e-survey, the user/on-site/visitor survey and the captive group survey. The third part of the chapter considers questionnaire design and coding. Finally the chapter considers fieldwork arrangements for questionnaire surveys, including the conduct of pilot surveys.

Test questions

1. What are the merits of questionnaire surveys?

2. Seven types of questionnaire survey are discussed in the chapter, what are they?

3. List three of these questionnaire survey types and outline their characteristics in terms of: respondent- or interviewer-completion, cost, nature of the sample, possible length of questionnaire, and likely response rate.

4. What type of survey would you conduct for a sample of 500 of the following:
   a. Tourists visiting a seaside resort
   b. Members of 'Greenpeace'
   c. The users of a theatre
   d. The users of a large urban park
   e. Overseas visitors to Great Britain
   f. People who do not play sport
   g. People who play sport
   h. People who rent videos
   i. People aged 14 and over living in the local council area
   j. Young people aged 11–13 living in the local council area

5. What is quota sampling?

6. What measures might be used to increase response rates in mail surveys?

7. What principles should be followed in wording questions in questionnaires?

8. What is the difference between pre-coded and open-ended questions and what are the advantages and disadvantages of the two formats?

Exercises

1. Design a questionnaire in relation to one of the studies discussed in Case studies 3.1, 3.2 or 3.3, limiting the questionnaire to ten questions only.
2. Design a question on people's attitudes towards legalisation of drugs, using three alternative question formats.
3. If you are a member of a leisure/tourism class, invite members of the class to complete the questionnaire in Case study 9.1 (p. 279) and devise a coding system for the answers to open-ended questions based on the answers obtained.
4. Locate a published research report or thesis which includes a questionnaire survey and contains a copy of the questionnaire used (usually in an appendix) and provide a critique of the questionnaire design.

Further reading

Questionnaire design generally: Kidder (1981); Oppenheim (1992).

Life-cycle: Rapoport and Rapoport (1975).

Class: Giddens (1993), pp. 211–50. *Class and lifestyle*: O'Brien and Ford (1988).

Use of repertory grid technique: Stockdale (1984); Botterill (1989).

Time-budget diaries: Burton (1971); Szalai (1972); BBC (1978); Australian Bureau of Statistics (1994, 1998).

Large-scale, national household surveys: see further reading for Chapter 6.

Surveys generally: Williamson *et al*. (1982); Tourism and Recreation Research Unit (1983); Marriott (1987); Hudson (1988); Veal (1988); Ryan (1995).

Telephone surveys: Field (1972); Lavrakas (1993).

Mail surveys: Dillman (2000).

Visitor (user) surveys vs *conversion (coupon) surveys in tourism*: Perdue and Botkin (1988).

Case study 9.1 Example questionnaire: Site/street survey respondent-completed

Campus Life Survey 2003

		Office Use
Standard pre-coded	1. Which of the following best describes your current situation?	# ___ qno
	Full-time student with no regular paid work $\square_1$ Full-time student with some regular paid work $\square_2$ Part-time student with full-time job $\square_3$ Part-time student – other $\square_4$	___ status
Pre-coded Multiple response – dichotomous	2. Which of the following university services have you used in the last 4 weeks?	
	Used campus cafe/bar $\square_1$ Attended university club/association meeting $\square_1$ Attended a live music performance on campus $\square_1$ Watched a movie on campus $\square_1$	___ cafebar ___ club ___ music ___ movie
Ranking	3. In thinking about the social and entertainment services provided on campus, what are the most important considerations for you? Please rank the items below in terms of their importance to you. Rank them from 1 for the most important to 5 for the least important.	
	Rank Free or cheap access ___ Day-time attractions ___ Acts, films, etc. not available elsewhere ___ Opportunities to socialise/meet people ___ Cost ___	___ cheap ___ daytime ___ unusual ___ meet ___ cost
Numerical – uncoded	4. Approximately how much do you spend in an average week on entertainment and social activities on and off campus? £_____	
Likert scales	5. Please indicate the importance of the following to you in relation to campus life	_____ spend

	Very important	Important	Not at all Important	
Relaxation	$\square_3$	$\square_2$	$\square_1$	___ relax
Social interaction	$\square_3$	$\square_2$	$\square_1$	___ social
Mental stimulation	$\square_3$	$\square_2$	$\square_1$	___ mental

Open-ended Multiple response – categories	6. What suggestions would you make for improving campus social life? _____ _____	___ sug1 ___ sug2 ___ sug3
Standard pre-coded	7. You are: Male $\square_1$ Female $\square_2$	___ gend
Numerical – uncoded	8. Your age last birthday was: ___ years	___ age

_____

_____

_____

_____

Case study 9.2 Example questionnaire: household survey – interviewer-completed

Respondent No	**Short Stay Holiday Survey** _____#
Introductory remarks	Hallo. We are from St. Anthony's College and we are conducting a survey on people's short-stay holidays. Would you mind answering a few questions? It will take just a few minutes and the results will be kept confidential.

Respondent No   **Short Stay Holiday Survey**   _____#

Introductory remarks   Hallo. We are from St. Anthony's College and we are conducting a survey on people's short-stay holidays. Would you mind answering a few questions? It will take just a few minutes and the results will be kept confidential.

Pre-coded, factual

1. In the last six months, have you been on a short holiday trip of one, two or three nights away from home?

    Yes 1 – go to Q.2
    No 2 – go to Q.5   _____

Open-ended, factual, numerical

2. How many times did you go on such trips in the six months?

    Number of times: ___ go to Q.2   _____

Open-ended, factual

3. On your last trip, where did you go? _____   _____

Multiple responses

4. What were the main activities you engaged in on your visit?

a.	Sightseeing	$\square_1$	e. Arts activities/events	$\square_1$
b.	Eating and drinking	$\square_1$	f. Visit friends/relatives	$\square_1$
c.	Sporting activities	$\square_1$	g. Just doing nothing	$\square_1$
d.	Walking	$\square_1$	h. Other	$\square_1$

Simple pre-coded, factual

5. To what extent do you agree with the following statements?

	Agree strongly	Agree	Neither	Disagree	Disagree strongly	
A short break is as valuable as a long holiday	1	2	3	4	5	_____
Holidays make life worth living	1	2	3	4	5	_____

Pre-coded with showcard factual

6. Can you tell me which of the following age-groups you fall into?

Under 15	**A**
15–19	**B**
20–29	**C**
30–59	**D**
60+	**E**

    _____

Pre-coded with showcard factual

7. Which of the following best describes your current situation?

In full-time paid work	**A**
In part-time paid work	**B**
In full-time education	**C**
Full-time home/child care	**D**
Retired	**E**
Looking for work	**F**
Other	**G**

    _____

Pre-coded, factual, observed

THANK YOU FOR YOUR HELP

Observe gender:	Male	1	
	Female	2	_____

Case study 9.3   Example questionnaire: site survey – interviewer-completed

The survey is being carried out for the local council to find out what users of the park think of the park, and what changes they would like to see. A total of 100 users of the park are interviewed at the only entrance, in batches of 10, at different days of the week, at different times of the day, and in different weather conditions.

Ramsey Street Park Survey
Excuse me: we are carrying out a survey for the council to find out what people think about the park.
Could you spare a few minutes to answer a few questions?

Simple pre-coded	1.	How often do you visit this park?		
		Every day	1	
		Several times a week	2	
		Once a week	3	
		Every 2 or 3 weeks	4	
		Once a month	5	
		Less often	6	
		First visit	7	

Simple pre-coded, factual

2. Where have you travelled from today?

Home	1
Work	2
School/college/univ.	3
Other	4

Open-ended, factual

3. What suburb is that in?

_____

Simple pre-coded factual

4. How long did it take you to get here?

5 minutes or less	1
6–15 minutes	2
16–30 minutes	3
31 minutes or more	4

Simple pre-coded factual

5. How did you travel here?

Walk	1
Car	2
Motorbike	3
Bicycle	4
Bus/tram	5
Other	6

6. What do you like most about the park? Open-ended, opinion factual

_____

7. What do you like least about the park? Open-ended, opinion

_____

8. Looking at the card, where would you place this park, in relation to others you know? Attitude statement with show-card

A.	**Way below average**	1
B.	**Below average**	2
C.	**Average**	3
D.	**Above average**	4
E.	**Well above average**	5

9. Can you tell me which of these age-groups you fall into? Pre-coded factual with showcard

Under 15	A
15–19	B
20–29	C
30–59	D
60+	E

10. How many people are there in your group here today, including your self? Pre-coded

Alone	1
Two	2
3–4	3
5 or more	4

THANK YOU FOR YOUR HELP

_____

Observe:	Male	1	Observe,
	Female	2	factual

10 Sampling

Introduction – *SPSS*

This chapter is an introduction to the principles of sampling and considers: the idea of sampling; samples and populations; representativeness and random sampling; sample sizes and their consequences in terms of 'confidence intervals'; and weighting. It concludes with a note on sampling for qualitative research.

The idea of sampling

In most survey research and in some observational research it is necessary to *sample*. Mainly because of costs, it is not usually possible to gather data from *all* the people, organisations or other entities which are the focus of the research. For example, if the aim of a research project is to study the leisure patterns or holiday-making behaviour of the adult population of a country, no-one has the resources to conduct interviews with the millions of individuals who make up the adult population. The only time when the whole population is interviewed is every 5 or 10 years, when the government statistical agency conducts the official Census of Population – and the cost of collecting and analysing the data runs into tens of millions of pounds.

At a more modest level, it would be virtually impossible to conduct face-to-face interviews with all the users of an urban park or a busy tourist area since, in busy periods, many hundreds might enter the site and leave in a short space of time. It might be possible to hand respondent-completion questionnaires to all users but, as discussed in Chapter 9, this approach has disadvantages in terms of quality and level of response. The usual procedure is to interview a sample – a proportion – of the users.

In Chapter 7, on observation, the problems of continuous counting of numbers of users of leisure and tourism sites were discussed and it was noted that often available resources demand that sample counts be undertaken – that is the numbers entering the site or present at the site are counted on a sample of occasions. Sampling has implications for the way data are collected, analysed and interpreted.

Samples and populations

One item of terminology should be clarified initially. The total category of subjects which is the focus of attention in a particular research project is known as the *population*. A *sample* is selected from the population. The use of the term population makes obvious sense when dealing with communities of people – for instance when referring to the population of Britain or the population of London. But in social research the term also applies in other instances; for example the visitors to a resort over the course of a year constitute the *population of resort visitors*; and the users of a sports facility are the *population of users*.

The term *population* can also be applied to non-human phenomena – for example, if a study of the physical characteristics of Australia's beaches found that there were 10,000 beaches in all, from which 100 were to be selected for study, then the 10,000 beaches can be referred to as the *population of beaches* and the 100 selected for study would be the sample. In some texts the word *universe* is used instead of population.

If a sample is to be selected for study then two questions arise:

1. What procedures must be followed to ensure that the sample is representative of the population?
2. How large should the sample be?

These two questions are related, since, other things being equal, the larger the sample, the more chance it has of being representative.

Representativeness

A sample which is not representative of the population is described as *biased*. The whole process of sample selection must be aimed at *minimising* bias in the sample. The researcher seeks to achieve representativeness and to minimise bias by adopting the principles of *random sampling*. This is not the most helpful term since it implies that the process is not methodical. This is far from the case – random does not mean haphazard! The meaning of random sampling is as follows:

> In random sampling all members of the population have an equal chance of inclusion in the sample.

For example, if a sample of 1,000 people is to be selected from a population of 10,000 then every member of the population must have a 1 in 10 chance of being selected. In practice most sampling methods involving human beings can only approximate this rule. The problems of achieving random sampling vary with the type of survey and are discussed below in relation to: household surveys; site/user/visitor surveys; telephone surveys; street surveys and quota sampling; and mail surveys.

Sampling for household surveys

The problem of achieving randomness can be examined in the case of a household survey of the adult residents of a country. If the adult population of the country is, say, 40 million and we wish to interview a sample of 1,000, then every member of the adult population should have a 1 in 40,000 chance of being included in the sample. How would this be achieved? Ideally there should be a complete list of all 40 million of the country's adults – their names should be written on slips of paper and placed in a revolving drum, physically or electronically, as in a lottery draw, and 1,000 names should be drawn out. Each time a choice is made everyone has a one in 40 million chance of selection – since this happens 1,000 times, each person has a total of 1,000 in 40 million or one in 40,000 chance of selection.

This would be a very laborious process. Surely a close approximation would be to forget the slips of paper and the drum and choose every 40,000th name on the list. But where should the starting point be? It should be some random point between 1 and 40,000. There are published 'tables of random numbers', which can also be produced from computers, which can be used for this purpose. Strictly speaking the whole sample should be chosen using random numbers, since this would approximate most closely to the 'names in a drum' procedure.

In practice, however, such a list of the population being studied rarely exists. The nearest thing to it would be the electoral registers of all the constituencies in the country. Electoral registers are fairly comprehensive because adults are required by law to register, but they are not perfect. Highly mobile/homeless people are often not included; many who live in multi-occupied premises are omitted. The physical task of selecting the names from such a list would be immense, but there is another disadvantage with this approach. If every 40,000th voter on the registers were selected the sample would be scattered throughout the country. The cost of visiting every one of those selected for a face-to-face interview would be very high.

In practice therefore, organisations conducting national surveys compromise by employing 'multi-stage' sampling and 'clustered' sampling. Multi-stage means that sampling is not done directly but by stages. For example if the country had, say, four states or regions the proposed sample of 1,000 would be sub-divided in the same proportions as the populations of the regions. Within each region local government areas would then be divided into country and urban and, say four urban and two rural areas would be selected at random – with the intention of selecting appropriate sub-samples, of perhaps 25, 40 or 50 from each area. These sub-samples could be selected from electoral registers, or streets could be selected and individuals contacted by calling on, say, every fifth house in the street. In any one street interviewers may be instructed to interview, say, 10 or 15 people. By interviewing 'clusters' of people in this way costs are minimised. But care must be taken not to reduce the number of clusters too much since then the full range of population and area types would not be included.

Sampling for site/user/visitor surveys

Conditions at leisure/tourism sites or facilities vary enormously, depending on the type and size of facility, the season, day of the week, the time of day or the weather.

This discussion can only therefore be in general terms. To ensure randomness, and therefore representativeness, it is necessary for interviewers to adhere to strict rules. Site interviewers operate in two ways. First, the interviewer can be stationary and the users mobile – for instance when the interviewer is located near the entrance and visitors are interviewed as they enter or leave. Alternatively the users may be stationary and the interviewer mobile – for instance when interviewing beach users or users of a picnic site.

In the case of stationary interviewers, the instructions they should follow should be something like:

> When one interview is complete, check through the questionnaire for completeness and legibility. When you are ready with a new questionnaire stop the next person to enter the gate. Stick strictly to this rule and do not select interviewees on any other basis.

The important thing is that interviewers should not avoid certain types of user by picking and choosing whom to interview. Ideally there should be some rule such as interviewing every fifth person to come through the door/gate but, since users will enter at a varying rate and interviews vary in length, this is rarely possible.

In the case of stationary users and a mobile interviewer, the interviewer should be given a certain route to follow on the site and be instructed to interview, say, every fifth group they pass.

Where interviewers are employed, the success of the process will depend on the training given to the interviewers and this could involve observation of them at work to ensure that they are following the rules.

As indicated in Chapter 9, sampling in site/visitor surveys leads inevitably to variation in the proportion of users interviewed at different times of the day. Where users tend to stay for long periods – as in the case of beaches – this may not matter, but where people stay for shorter periods and where the type of user may vary during the course of the day or week, the sample will probably be unrepresentative – that is, biased. This should be corrected by weighting as discussed at the end of this chapter.

When surveys involve the handing out of questionnaires for respondent-completion – as for example, in a number of tourist en route/hotel surveys – unless field staff are available to encourage their completion and return, respondents will be self-selected. Busy hotel or leisure facility receptionists can rarely be relied upon to do a thorough job in handing out and collecting in questionnaires, unless the survey is a priority of the management and therefore closely supervised. Normally a significant proportion of the population will fail to return the questionnaire – but it is unlikely that this self-selection process will be random. For example, people with difficulties in reading or writing English, or people who are in a hurry, may fail to return their questionnaires. Those with 'something to say', whether positive or negative, are more likely to return their questionnaires than people who are apathetic or just content with the service, thus giving a misleading impression of the proportion of users who have strong opinions. Thus it can be seen that this type of 'uncontrolled' survey is at risk of introducing serious bias into the sample and should therefore be avoided if at all possible.

Sampling for street surveys and quota sampling

Although the technique of quota sampling can be used in other situations, it is most common in street surveys. The street survey is usually seen as a means of contacting a representative sample of the community or visitors to an area, but in fact it can also be seen as a sort of 'site survey', the site being the shopping or tourist area. As such a street survey which involved a random sample of the users of the street would be representative of the users of the area rather than the community or visitors as a whole – in a suburban shopping centre would for instance have a high proportion of retired people or full-time home/child carers.

If the aim is, in fact, to obtain a representative sample of the whole community, then to achieve this interviewers are given 'quotas' of people of different types to contact, the quotas being based on information about the community which is available from the census. For example, if the census indicates that 12 per cent of the population is retired then interviewers would be required to include 12 retired people in every 100 interviewed. In the case of tourist areas data may be available from official surveys/statistics. Once interviewers have filled their quota in certain age/gender groups, they are required to become more selective in whom they approach in order to fill the gaps in their quotas.

The quota method can only be used when background information on the target population is known – as with community surveys. In most user surveys this information is not known so the strict following of random sampling procedures must be relied upon.

Sampling for mail surveys

The initial list of people to whom the questionnaire is sent in a mail survey may be the whole population or a sample. If a sample is selected it can usually be done completely randomly because the mailing list for the whole population is usually available.

The respondents to a mail survey form a sample, although it is not randomly selected but self-selected. This introduces sources of bias similar to those in the uncontrolled self-completion site surveys discussed above. There is little that can be done about this except to make every effort to achieve a high response rate. In some cases information may be available on the population which can be used to weight the sample to correct for certain sources of bias – for example, in the case of a national survey the sample could be weighted to correct for any geographical bias in response because the geographical distribution of the population would be known. If, for example, the survey is of an occupational association and the proportion of members in various grades is known from records, then this can be used for weighting purposes. But ultimately, mail surveys suffer from an unknown and uncorrectable element of bias caused by non-response. It is inevitable that all surveys experience non-response, but the problem is greater with mail surveys because the level of non-response is usually greater.

Sample size

There is a popular misconception that the size of a sample should be decided on the basis of its relationship to the size of the population – for example that a sample should be, say, 5 per cent or 10 per cent of the population. *This is not so*. What is important is the absolute size of the sample, regardless of the size of the population. For example, a sample size of 1,000, is equally valid, provided proper sampling procedures have been followed, whether it is a sample of the British adult Britain (population 50 million), the residents of London (population 7 million), the residents of Brighton (population 100,000) or the students of a university (population, say, 10,000).

It is worth repeating that: it is the *absolute size of the sample* which is important, not its size relative to the population. This rule applies in all cases, except when the population itself is small – this exception and its implications are discussed later in the chapter.

On what criteria therefore should a sample size be determined? The criteria are basically threefold:

1.   the required level of precision in the results;
2.   the level of detail in the proposed analysis;
3.   the available budget.

Level of precision – confidence intervals

The idea of the level of precision can be explained as follows. The question to be posed is: to what extent do the findings from a sample precisely reflect the population from which it is drawn? For example, if a survey was designed to investigate holiday-making and it was found that 50 per cent of a sample of 500 people took a holiday in the previous year, how sure can we be that this finding – this *statistic* – is true of the population as a whole? How sure can we be, despite all efforts taken to choose a representative sample, that the sample is not in fact unrepresentative, and that the real percentage of holiday-taking in the population is in fact, say, 70 per cent or 30 per cent?

This question is answered in terms of probabilities. If the true value is around 50 per cent then, as long as random sampling procedures have been followed, the *probability* of drawing a sample which was so wrong that no-one in the sample had been on holiday would be very remote – almost impossible one might say. On the other hand the *probability* of coming up with say 48 or 49 per cent or 51 or 52 per cent would, one would think, be fairly high. The probability of coming up with 70 or 30 per cent would be somewhere in between.

Statisticians have examined the likely patterns of distribution of results from all possible samples of various sizes drawn from a population and established that, when a sample is randomly drawn, the sample value of a statistic has a certain probability of being within a certain range either side of the real value of the statistic. That range is plus or minus twice the 'standard error' of the statistic. The size of the standard error depends on the size of the sample and is unrelated to the size of the population. A properly drawn sample has a 95 per cent chance of producing a statistic with a value which is within two standard errors of the true population value so, conversely, there is a 95 per cent chance that the true population value lies within two standard errors of the sample statistic. This means that, if a hundred samples of the same size were drawn, in 95 cases we would expect the value of the statistic to be within two standard errors of the population value; in five cases we would expect it to be outside the range. Since we do not generally actually know the population value, we have to rely on this theoretical statement of probability about the likely accuracy of our finding: we have a 95 per cent chance of being approximately right and a five per cent chance of being wrong.

This 'two standard errors' range is referred to as the '95 per cent confidence interval' of a statistic. The relationships between standard errors and level of probability is a property of the 'normal curve' – a bell-shaped curve with certain mathematical properties, which we are not able to pursue here. The idea of a normal curve and 95 per cent confidence intervals is illustrated in Figure 10.1. The general idea of probabilities related to the properties of certain types of 'distribution' is pursued in more detail in Chapter 12.

Tables have been drawn up by statisticians which give the confidence intervals for various statistics for various sample sizes, as shown in Table 10.1. Down the side of the table are various sample sizes, ranging from 50 to 10,000. Across the top of the table are statistics which one might find from a survey – for example 20 per cent play tennis. The table shows 20 per cent together with 80 per cent because if it is found that 20 per cent of the sample play tennis, then clearly 80 per cent do not play tennis. Any conclusion about the accuracy of the statistic 20 per cent also applies to the corresponding statistic 80 per cent. In the body of the table are the *confidence intervals*.

An example of how the table is interpreted is as follows: suppose we have a sample size of 500 and we have a finding that 30 per cent of the sample have a certain characteristic – say, have been away on holiday in the previous summer (so 70 per cent have *not* been away on holiday). Reading off the table, for a sample size of 500, we find that a finding of 30 per cent (and 70 per cent) is subject to a confidence interval of plus or minus 4.0. So we can be fairly certain that the population value lies in the range 26.0 per cent to 34.0 per cent.

Figure 10.1
Normal curve
and confidence
intervals

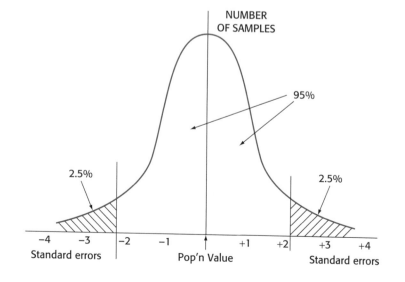

Table 10.1 Confidence intervals related to sample size

Sample size	Percentages found from sample ('results')							
	50%	40 or 60%	30 or 70%	20 or 80%	10 or 90%	5 or 95%	2 or 98%	1 or 99%
	Confidence intervals (± %)							
50	±13.9	±13.6	±12.7	±11.1	±8.3	*	*	*
80	±11.0	±10.7	±10.0	±8.8	±6.6	*	*	*
100	±9.8	±9.6	±9.0	±7.8	±5.9	±4.3	*	*
150	±8.0	±7.8	±7.3	±6.4	±4.8	±3.5	*	*
200	±6.9	±6.8	±6.3	±5.5	±4.2	±3.0	±1.9	*
250	±6.2	±6.1	±5.7	±5.0	±3.7	±2.7	±1.7	*
300	±5.7	±5.5	±5.2	±4.5	±3.4	±2.5	±1.6	*
400	±4.9	±4.8	±4.5	±3.9	±2.9	±2.1	±1.4	±1.0
500	±4.4	±4.3	±4.0	±3.5	±2.6	±1.9	±1.2	±0.9
750	±3.6	±3.5	±3.3	±2.9	±2.1	±1.6	±1.0	±0.7
1000	±3.1	±3.0	±2.8	±2.5	±1.9	±1.3	±0.9	±0.6
2000	±2.2	±2.1	±2.0	±1.7	±1.3	±1.0	±0.6	±0.4
4000	±1.5	±1.5	±1.4	±1.2	±0.9	±0.7	±0.4	±0.3
10,000	±1.0	±1.0	±0.9	±0.8	±0.6	±0.4	±0.3	±0.2

* confidence interval greater than the percentage

Interpretation of table: for example, for a sample size of 400 a finding of 30% is subject to a confidence interval of ±4.5 (that is to say, we can be 95% certain that the population value lies in the range 25.5% to 34.5%). For formula to calculate confidence intervals see Appendix 12.2.

An important point should be noted about these confidence intervals: to halve the confidence interval it is necessary to quadruple the sample size. In the example above, a sample of 2,000 people (four times the original sample) would give a confidence interval of plus or minus 2.0 per cent (half the original confidence interval). The cost of increasing the precision of surveys by increasing the sample is therefore very high.

Note that for smaller samples the confidence intervals become very large – for instance, the interval for a statistic of 50 per cent is plus or minus 13.9 per cent, meaning that a finding of 50 per cent can only be estimated to be within the range 36.1 to 63.9 per cent. For some statistics, for the smaller sample sizes, the confidence intervals are not calculable because the total margin of error is larger than the original statistic.

It should be noted that these confidence intervals apply only for samples which have been drawn using random sampling methods; other methods, such as multi-stage sampling, tend to produce larger confidence intervals, but the difference is often small, so the matter is not pursued here.

The implications of the precision criterion for deciding sample size now become clear. A sample size of, say, 1,000 would give a confidence interval for a finding of 50 per cent of plus or minus 3.1 per cent. If that margin of error was not considered acceptable then a larger sample size would be necessary. Whether or not it is considered acceptable depends on the uses to which the data will be put and is related to the type of analysis to be done, as discussed below. An alternative way of considering these relationships between sample size and confidence interval is presented in Table 10.2. This presents, in the body of the table, the necessary sample size to achieve a given confidence interval.

Table 10.2 Necessary sample sizes to achieve given confidence intervals

Conf. Interval	Percentages found from sample ('results')						
	50%	40 or 60%	30 or 70%	20 or 80%	10 or 90%	5 or 95%	1 or 99%
			Minimum necessary sample size				
±1%	9,600	9,216	8,064	6,144	3,456	1,824	380
±2%	2,400	2,304	2,016	1,536	864	456	*
±3%	1,067	1,024	896	683	384	203	*
±4%	600	576	504	384	216	114	*
±5%	384	369	323	246	138	73	*
±6%	267	256	224	171	96	*	*
±7%	196	188	165	125	71	*	*
±8%	150	144	126	96	54	*	*
±9%	119	114	100	76	43	*	*
±10%	96	92	81	61	35	*	*

* Confidence interval greater than the percentage

Detail of proposed analysis

The confidence intervals in Table 10.1 illustrate further the second criterion concerning the choice of sample size – the type of analysis to be undertaken. If many detailed comparisons are to be made, especially concerning small proportions of the population, then a small sample size may preclude very meaningful analysis. For instance, suppose a survey is conducted with a sample of 200 and it is found that 20 per cent of respondents went bowling and 30 per cent played tennis. The 20 per cent is subject to a margin of error of plus or minus 5.5 per cent and the 30 per cent is subject to a margin of plus or minus 6.3 per cent. Thus it is estimated that the proportions playing the two activities are as follows:

Bowling: between 14.5 and 25.5 per cent   Tennis: between 23.7 and 36.3 per cent

The confidence intervals overlap, so we cannot conclude that there is any 'significant' difference in the popularity of the two activities, despite a 10 per cent difference given by the survey. This is likely to be very limiting in any analysis. If the sample were 500 the confidence intervals would be 3.5 per cent and 4.0 per cent respectively, giving estimates as follows:

Bowling: between 16.5 and 23.5 per cent   Tennis: between 26.0 and 34.0 per cent

In this case the confidence intervals do *not* overlap and we can be fairly certain that tennis *is* more popular than bowling.

The detail of the analysis, the extent of sub-division of the sample into sub-samples, and the acceptable level of precision will therefore determine the necessary size of the sample. By and large this has nothing to do with the overall size of the original population, although there is a likelihood that the larger the population the greater its diversity and therefore the greater the need for sub-division into sub-samples.

Budget

A further point to be noted is that it could be positively wasteful to expend resources on a large sample when it can be shown to be unnecessary. For example, a sample of 10,000 gives estimates of statistics with a maximum confidence interval of ±1 per cent. Such a survey could cost, say, £200,000 to conduct. To halve that confidence interval to ±0.5 per cent would mean quadrupling the sample size to 40,000 at an additional cost of £600,000. There can be very few situations where such expenditure would be justified for such a small return.

Ultimately then, the limiting factor in determining sample size will be the third criterion, the resources available. Even if the budget available limits the sample size severely it may be decided to go ahead and risk the possibility of an unrepresentative sample. If the sample is small, however, the detail of the analysis will need to be limited. If resources are so limited that the validity of quantitative research is questionable, it may be sensible to consider qualitative research which may be more feasible. Alternatively the proposed research can be seen as a 'pilot' exercise, with the emphasis on methodology, preparatory to a more adequately resourced full-scale study in future.

How should the issue of sample size and confidence intervals be referred to in the report on the research? In some scientific research complex statistical tests are considered necessary in reporting statistical results from surveys. In much social science research, and leisure and tourism research in particular, requirements are less rigorous. This is true to some extent in academic research, but is markedly so in the reporting of applied research. While it is necessary to be aware of the limitations imposed by the sample size and not to make comparisons which the data cannot support, explicit reference to such matters in the text of a consultancy report is rare. A great deal of statistical jargon is not generally required: the lay reader expects the researcher to do a good job and expert readers should be given enough information to check the analysis in the report for themselves. It is recommended that an appendix be included in reports indicating the size of the sampling errors. Appendix 10.1 gives a possible format.

In academic journals the rules are somewhat different and there is an expectation that statistical tests be 'up front'. The variety of tests available is pursued in Chapter 12.

Sample size and small populations

The above discussion of sample size assumes that the population is large – in fact the statistical formulae used to calculate the confidence intervals are based on the assumption that the population is, in effect, infinite. The relationship between the size of confidence intervals and the size of the population becomes noticeable when the population size falls below about 50,000, as shown in Table 10.3. The table presents sample sizes necessary to produce 95 per cent confidence intervals of ±5 per cent and ±1 per cent for a sample finding of 50 per cent for different population sizes. Only the sample sizes for a 50 per cent finding are presented since, as shown in Figures 10.1 and 10.2, the 50 per cent finding is the most demanding in terms of sample size: for a given sample size, the confidence intervals for other findings – for example, 30/70 per cent – is always smaller. The table first indicates the sample size for an infinite population and it can be seen that the sample sizes are the same as indicated for a ±5 per cent or ±1 per cent confidence interval in the first column of Table 10.1. The details of the formula relating confidence intervals to population size can be found in Krejcie and Morgan (1970).

Table 10.3 Sample size and population size: small populations

Population size	Minimum sample sizes for confidence interval of ±5% and ±1% on a sample finding of 50%:	
	±5%	±1%
Infinite*	384	9,602
10,000,000	384	9,593
5,000,000	384	9,584
1,000,000	384	9,511
500,000	384	9,422
100,000	383	8,761
50,000	381	8,056
25,000	378	6,938
20,000	377	6,488
10,000	370	4,899
5000	357	3,288
2000	322	1,655
1000	278	906
500	217	475
200	132	196
100	80	99
50	44	50

* as in Tables 10.1 and 10.2 and formula in Appendix 12.2

Weighting

In this and previous sections, situations where weighting of survey or count data may be required have been indicated. In Chapter 11 the procedures for implementing weighting using the SPSS computer package are outlined. Here the principles involved are discussed. Take the example of the data shown in Table 10.4. In the sample of 45 interviews the number of interviews is spread fairly equally through the day, whereas more than half the actual users visit around the middle of the day (this information probably having been obtained by observation/counts). This can be a source of bias in the sample, since the mid-day users may differ from the others in their characteristics or opinions and they will be under-represented in the sample. The aim of weighting is to produce a weighted sample with a distribution similar to that of the actual users.

One approach is to 'gross up' the sample numbers to reflect the actual numbers – e.g. the 9–11am group is weighted by 25 ÷ 10 = 2.5, the 11–1pm group is weighted by 240 ÷ 12 = 20, and so on, as shown in Table 10.5.

Table 10.4 Interview/usage data from a site/visitor survey

Time	# of Interviews	%	Actual # of users (counts)	%
9–11 am	10	22.2	25	5.7
11.01–1 pm	12	26.7	240	55.2
1.01–3 pm	11	24.4	110	25.3
3.01–5 pm	12	26.7	60	2.7
Total	45	100.0	435	100.0

Table 10.5 Weighting

Time	A. # of Interviews	B. # of Users	C. Weighting Factors	D. Weighted Sample #
Source:	Survey	Counts	B/A	CxA
9–11 am	10	25	2.5	25
11.01–1 pm	12	240	20.0	240
1.01–3 pm	11	110	10.0	110
3.01–5 pm	12	60	5.0	60
Total	45	435		435

The weighting factors can be fed into the computer for the weighting to be done automatically, as discussed in Chapter 11. The initial weighting factors are equal to the user number divided by the sample number for that time-period. The weighted sample therefore is made to resemble the overall user numbers. It should be noted however, that the sample size is still 45, not 435! If statistical tests are to be carried out then it would be advisable to divide the weighting factors by 435 to bring the weighted sample total back to 45.

In this example the basis of the weighting relates to the pattern of visits over the course of the day, which happened to be information which was available in relation to this particular type of survey. Any other data available on the population could be used – for example, if age structure is available from the census, then age-groups rather than time-periods might be used.

Sampling for qualitative research

As discussed in Chapter 8, qualitative research generally makes no claim to quantitative representativeness and, by definition, does not involve statistical calculation demanding prescribed levels of precision. Generally, therefore, the quantitative considerations outlined above are not relevant to qualitative research. This is not to say that representativeness is ignored entirely. As Karla Henderson (1991: 132) puts it: '. . . the researcher using the qualitative approach is not concerned about adequate numbers or random selection, but in trying to present a working picture of the broader social structure from which the observations are drawn'. Thus if the population being studied includes young and old people, then both young and old people will be included in the sample, unless an explicit decision has been made to concentrate on one age-group only. But the sample will not necessarily reflect the proportions of young and old in the study population. Miles and Huberman (1994: 28) list 16 'strategies' for qualitative sampling. Some of these are presented in Table 10.6. In the research report, the qualitative sampling methods used should be adequately described. In all cases, just how individuals are selected and contacted should be described. For example, if the 'criterion' sampling method was used, what was the criterion used and how were the people who met the criterion contacted? If a 'snowball' method was used, how was it started? If 'convenience' sampling was used, what was the convenience factor – friendship, family, colleagues, students, neighbours?

Table 10.6 Selected qualitative sampling methods

Type of sampling	Characteristics
Convenience	Use of conveniently located persons or organisations – e.g. friends, colleagues, students, organisations in the neighbourhood, tourists visiting a local popular attraction.
Criterion	Individuals selected on the basis of a key criterion – e.g. age-group, membership of an organisation, purchasers of souvenirs.
Homogeneous	Deliberately selecting a relatively homogeneous sub-set of the population – e.g. university-educated male cyclists aged 20–30.
Opportunistic	Similar to 'convenience' but involves taking advantages of opportunities as they arise – e.g. studying a major sporting event taking place locally, or a holiday resort the researcher is holidaying at.
Maximum variation	Deliberately studying contrasting cases. Opposite of 'homogeneous'.
Purposeful	Similar to 'criterion' but may involve other considerations, e.g. 'maximum variation', 'typicality'.
Stratified purposeful	Selection of a range of cases based on set criteria, e.g. representatives of a range of age-groups or nationalities.

Summary

This chapter covers the topic of sampling, which is the process of selecting a proportion of the 'population' of subjects for study. It also examines the implications of sampling for data analysis. Two key issues are considered: *representativeness* of samples, and sample *size*. The researcher seeks representativeness by following the principles of *random sampling*, which means that, as nearly as possible, every member of the population has an equal chance of being selected. Different types of survey involve different practical procedures for achieving random sampling. If a sample has been randomly selected, the question still arises as to the extent to which the statistical findings from the sample truly reflect the population. Statistical procedures have been developed to assess the level of probability that a sample finding lies within a certain margin of the true population value. This margin is known as a *confidence interval* and its size is related to the size of the sample, regardless of the size of the population – the larger the sample the smaller the confidence interval or margin of statistical error. The necessary sample size for a study therefore depends on the precision required in the results, the detail of the analysis to be undertaken and the available budget. Finally, the chapter considers the practice of *weighting* to correct a sample for known bias and the issue of sampling for qualitative research.

Test questions

1. Define random sampling.
2. What is the opposite of a random/representative sample?
3. What is multi-stage sampling and why is it used?
4. What is a confidence interval?
5. What determines the size of the sample to be used in a study?
6. What is weighting?
7. What methods are available for qualitative sampling?

Exercises

1. Examine either a published research report or a journal article related to an empirical study and identify the procedures used to ensure a random sample.

2. Using the report used in exercise 1, produce confidence intervals for a range of percentage statistics occurring in the report.

3. In the example comparing bowling and tennis on page 291 above, what would the confidence intervals be if the sample size was 4,000?

4. Examine the results from a national recreation participation survey or a domestic or international tourism survey and produce confidence intervals for a number of the key findings.

Further reading

Sampling and the statistical implications of sampling are addressed in numerous statistics textbooks: including, Kidder (1981) Ch. 4; Spatz and Johnston (1989) Ch. 6. Sampling for qualitative research is discussed by Miles and Huberman (1994: 27–34).

Appendix 10.1   Suggested appendix on sample size and confidence intervals

This is a suggested wording for an appendix or note to be included in research reports based on sample data. Suppose the survey has a sample size of 500.

Statistical note

All sample surveys are subject to a margin of statistical error. The margins of error, or 'confidence intervals' for this survey, with a sample of 500, are as follows:

Finding from the survey	95% Confidence interval
50%	±4.4%
40% or 60%	±4.3%
30% or 70%	±4.0%
20% or 80%	± 3.5%
10% or 90%	±2.6%
5% or 95%	±1.9%
1% or 99%	±0.9%

This means, for example, that if 20 per cent of the sample are found to have a particular characteristic, there is an estimated 95 per cent chance that the true population percentage lies in the range 20 ± 3.5, ie. between 16.5 and 23.5 per cent.

These margins of error have been taken into account in the analyses in this report.

11 Survey analysis

Introduction – *SPSS*

In this chapter the use of a computer package for analysing data from questionnaire surveys is outlined. The chapter is organised as a step-by-step introductory manual for operating the *Statistical Package for the Social Sciences* (*SPSS*) software package for survey analysis and it is envisaged that the reader will have access to a computer with SPSS available on it, so that the procedures described here can be tried out in practice.

SPSS for Windows is the version of the package which is available for IBM-compatible personal computers using the Microsoft *Windows* system. Version 12 of the package is referred to here. Earlier editions of the book utilised earlier versions of *SPSS*. A *Studentware* version of *SPSS* exists, which is less expensive than the full version described here, but the size of the data set which it can handle is restricted and the range of analytical procedures included is limited (it can handle all the procedures covered in this chapter, except Multiple Response). Versions of *SPSS* also exist for Macintosh and mainframe computers – further details can be found on the *SPSS* website and in a number of published guides (see further reading section). *SPSS* is one of the most commonly used statistical packages; others include *Minitab*, *BMD* (Biomedical Data analysis), *SAS* (Statistical Analysis System) and *Turbostats*.

A full list of *SPSS* procedures can be found in the on-line *SPSS* manual which is included in the software package. In this chapter four main procedures only are described:

- *Frequencies* – which involves counts and percentages of individual variables;
- *Crosstabs* – the cross-tabulation of two or more variables;
- *Means* – obtaining means/averages of appropriate variables;
- *Graphs* – the production of graphics.

The areas covered in this chapter and the statistical procedures covered in Chapter 12 are summarised in Figure 11.1.

The chapter deals with the analysis of data from questionnaire surveys. But *SPSS* can also be used to analyse data from other sources. And although the package is ideally suited to dealing with numerical data it can also handle non-numerical data. Any data

Figure 11.1
SPSS Survey
analysis
overview

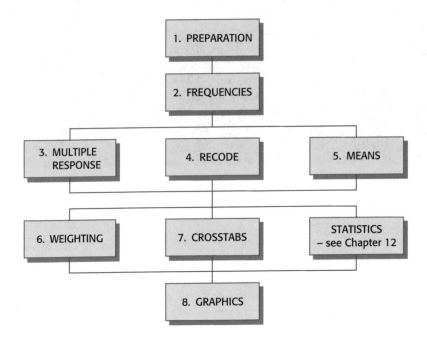

organised on the basis of *cases* and a common range of *variables* for each case can be analysed using the package (*cases* and *variables* are defined below).

The chapter does not deal with procedures for logging into a computer, file handling or the installation of the *SPSS* software onto the computer; it is assumed that *SPSS* for Windows is already installed on a computer available to the reader. The information in the chapter provides an introduction to the basics only. It is envisaged that most readers will have access to a teacher/tutor to assist as problems arise. The *SPSS* package itself includes a tutorial for beginners and there are numerous books available on the use of *SPSS*, as indicated in the further reading section. In higher education institutions *SPSS*, as with other computer packages, is generally made available in computer laboratories on licence. Further training is available in *SPSS*, and other survey packages, through universities, commercial computer training organisations and the *SPSS* company itself in major centres around the world.

Preparation

Cases and variables

SPSS – and any other statistical analysis package – deals with data which are organised in terms of *cases* and *variables*.

■ A *case* is a single example of the phenomenon being studied and for which data have been collected – for example, an individual member of a community who has been interviewed, a participant in a leisure activity, an employee of a company, a visitor to a country, a leisure or tourism organisation or a country for which data are available. So a *sample* is made up of a number of *cases*.

■ A *variable* is an item of information which is available for all or some of the cases, which can take on different values or categories – for example, the *gender* of an individual, which can take on the category 'male' or 'female'; the salary of an employee, which can be any monetary value; the *number of employees* of a company; the *population* of a country.

The use of *variables* in *SPSS* is further discussed here, while *cases* arise when entering data, as discussed later in the chapter.

Specifying variables

In order to communicate with the *SPSS* program it is necessary to identify each item of data in the questionnaire by a variable *name*. Figure 9.19, in Chapter 9, contains a copy of a simple questionnaire which is used to demonstrate the use of *SPSS* in this chapter. Chapter 9 dealt with the procedure for coding the data from this questionnaire in a form suitable for computer analysis. The questionnaire is *annotated with variable names* in the 'Office Use' column. The question numbers and corresponding variable names are listed in Figure 11.2, together with an additional nine items of information for each variable, which are required by the *SPSS* system. These items are discussed in turn below.

Name

■ In addition to variables related to the eight questions in the questionnaire, there is a variable *qno* to record a reference number for each case or questionnaire.

■ Every item of information on the questionnaire is given a *unique* name (no two variables with the same name).

■ The length of variable names is limited to 8 letters/numbers (no spaces), beginning with a letter. It is not permitted to use any of the following for variable names, because the *SPSS* program already uses these names for other purposes and would get confused!

ALL   AND   BY   EQ   GE   GT   LE   LT   NE   NOT   OR   TO   WITH

Three possible systems for naming variables are:

■ practice adopted here, which is to use variable names which are full or shortened versions of how the item might be described – for example *status* for student status, and *sug1* for improvement suggestion 1;

■ use a generalised name such as *var* for variable; so a questionnaire with 5 variables would have variable names: *var1*, *var2*, *var3*, *var4*, *var5* – in fact, *SPSS* has a system of 'default' variable names already set up in this form, which can be used instead of the customised names used here;

■ use of question numbers – for example, *Q1*, *Q2a*, *Q2b*, and so on.

Question No.	Name*	Type	Width**	Decimal places	Label	Values/Value labels	Missing values	Columns	Alignment	Measure/Data type
–	qno	Numeric	4	0	Questionnaire number	None	None	4	Right	Scale
1.	status	Numeric	1	0	Student status	1 F/T student – no work 2 F/T student – working 3 P/T student – F/T job 4 P/T student – other	None	4	Right	Nominal
2.	cafebar	Numeric	1	0	Campus cafe/bar in last 4 wks	1 Yes 0 No	None	4	Right	Nominal
	music	Numeric	1	0	Live campus music in last 4 wks	as for cafebar	None	4	Right	Nominal
	sport	Numeric	1	0	Sport facilities in last 4 wks	as for cafebar	None	4	Right	Nominal
	travel	Numeric	1	0	Travel service in last 4 wks	as for cafebar	None	4	Right	Nominal
3.	cheap	Numeric	1	0	Free/cheap (rank)	None	None	4	Right	Ordinal
	daytime	Numeric	1	0	Day-time events (rank)	None	None	4	Right	Ordinal
	unusual	Numeric	1	0	Not available elsewhere (rank)	None	None	4	Right	Ordinal
	meet	Numeric	1	0	Socialising (rank)	None	None	4	Right	Ordinal
	quality	Numeric	1	0	Quality of presentation (rank)	None	None	4	Right	Ordinal
4.	spend	Numeric	4	0	Expenditure on entertainment/month	None	None	4	Right	Scale
5.	relax	Numeric	1	0	Relaxation opportunities – importance	3 Very important 2 Important 1 Not at all important	None	4	Right	Scale
	social	Numeric	1	0	Social interaction – importance	as for relax	None	4	Right	Scale
	mental	Numeric	1	0	Mental stimulation – importance	as for relax	None	4	Right	Scale
6.	sug1	Numeric	2	0	Improvement suggestion – 1	1 Programme content*** 2 Timing 3 Facilities 4 Costs 5 Organisation	None	4	Right	Nominal
	sug2	Numeric	2	0	Improvement suggestion – 2	as for sug1	None	4	Right	Nominal
	sug3	Numeric	2	0	Improvement suggestion – 3	as for sug1	None	4	Right	Nominal
7.	gender	Numeric	1	0	Gender	1 Male 2 Female	None	4	Right	Nominal
8.	age	Numeric	2	0	Age	None	None	4	Right	Scale

* From Figure 9.19   ** max. no. of characters   *** See Fig. 9.18 for derivation of coding system

Figure 11.2   Variable names, labels and values

Type

SPSS requires the user to specify the variable *type* of variable. All the variables in the campus life survey questionnaire are *numeric* – that is, they can only be numbers. A number of other possibilities exist, including *date* and *string*, the latter meaning text comprising any combination of letters and numbers, but these options are not pursued here.

Width

Width specifies the maximum number of digits for the value of a variable. In the campus life survey questionnaire, all except two variables are single-digit. The width of variable *qno* will depend on the size of the sample – here a width of four digits is shown, indicating a maximum possible sample size of 9,999. The *cost* variable width has been put at four, suggesting maximum possible individual weekly expenditure on entertainment of £9,999 – which should accommodate all respondents!

Decimal places

None of the variables in the campus life questionnaire includes *decimal* places, so the number of decimal places is set to zero for all of them. Many variables could, however, include decimals or pounds/pence – for example, a person's height, or a tourist's expenditure per day.

Label

There is no restriction on the content of the variable *label*, which is a fuller, descriptive label for the variable which will be included in *SPSS* output tables, making them more readily understandable by the reader. This is often necessary with long questionnaires with many variables, and particularly when the short variable names are not immediately recognisable.

Values

The *values* and *value labels* for each variable, except those in question 6, are apparent from the questionnaire.

- The questionnaire number is just a reference number so it has no value labels.
- Variables based on questions 1, 2 and 5 have specific codes or values (1, 2, 3, etc.) with value labels as specified in the questionnaire.
- Variables based on question 3 are ranked from 1 to 5 – they have therefore been specified in Figure 11.2 as having no value labels. In fact, the values for these variables *could* be given value labels as follows: 1 = 'First', 2 = 'Second', 3 = 'Third', 4 = 'Fourth', 5 = 'Fifth'.
- The variable *cost* is a numerical sum of money – it therefore has no value labels.
- The values/labels for the open-ended question, 6, were derived as shown in Chapter 9 (Figure 9.18).

Missing

If a respondent does not answer a question in a questionnaire, the data entry may be left blank, or a 'No answer' or 'Not applicable' code may be provided. *SPSS* will automatically treat a blank in the data as a 'missing value', but 'No answer' and 'Not applicable' codes can be provided and specified as *missing values*. The implications are that *SPSS* excludes missing values when it is calculating means and percentages. In the campus life data set, the phenomenon of missing values becomes apparent in the case of variables *sug1*, *sug2* and *sug3*, since some respondents offer no suggestions at all, many offer only one and very few offer three – so there are usually numerous blanks in the data, particularly for *sug2* and *sug3*. It would be possible for non-use of services in question 2 to be left as a blank, giving rise to missing values, but in this case non-use has been coded as a zero. The *missing value* phenomenon is not pursued in detail in this chapter but is apparent in a number of the outputs from *SPSS*.

Columns

The number of columns or digits per variable is a presentational matter concerning the layout of the 'Data view' screen discussed below. A variable can be *displayed* with any number of columns regardless of the specified *width* of the underlying variable. In the campus life example, the specification is four columns for all variables enabling all the data to be seen on the 'Data view' screen at once, without scrolling, even on smaller computer screens.

Alignment

Alignment is also presentational. As in a spreadsheet, or table, numerical data are easier to read if aligned to the right, while text is often more suitably aligned to the left.

Measure

Data can be divided into *nominal*, *ordinal* and *scale* types.

- *Nominal data* are made up of non-numerical *categories*, such as the status categories in question 1 and 'Yes/No' in question 2 of the example questionnaire. In this situation, while numerical codes are used in computer analysis, they have no numerical meaning – for example, code 2 is not 'half' of code 4 – the 1/0 codes could equally well be 6 and 7, A and B, or X and Y. It does not make sense, therefore, to calculate, for example, an average or mean of *nominal data* codes.

- *Ordinal data* reflect a *ranking*, as in question 3 of the example questionnaire; the 1, 2, 3 in this question represent the *order of importance*, but rank 3 cannot be interpreted as being '3 times as high as' rank 1. It is, however, possible to take an average or mean rank – for example, to speak of an 'average ranking'.

- *Scale data*[1] are fully numerical – as in questions 4 and 8 of the example questionnaire. Numerical information, such as a person's age, travel expenditure or frequency of participation in an activity, are *scale data*. In this case an answer of 4 *is* twice as high as an answer of 2 and averages or means are clearly appropriate.

The data type, or type of measure, of a variable affects the range of statistical analysis which can be performed and the appropriate graphical presentation, and these are discussed later, particularly in Chapter 12.

In Figure 11.2 each variable is identified as nominal, ordinal and scale, as folows:

■ *qno* is identified as a *scale* variable, although it will not be used in analysis;

■ variables from questions 1, 2, 6 and 7 are *nominal*;

■ variables from question 3 are *ordinal*;

■ the question 4 variable, *spend* and question 8 variable, *age* are *scale* variables;

■ question 5 variables are 'Likert-style' variables, specified as *scale* variables for the reasons discussed below.

Attitude/Likert variables

Variables arising from *Attitude/Likert variables* have been used extensively in psychological and market research and have come to be seen almost as *scale* variables when, in reality, they are just ordinal. Means are therefore accepted as an appropriate form of analysis when using such variables. The scores of 1 to 3 in question 5 in the campus life questionnaire can be treated as numerical indicators of the level of importance respondents attach to the items listed. The means can be interpreted as average 'scores' on importance. It is possible to add scores in some circumstances.

Starting up

To start an *SPSS* session on a computer, activate the *SPSS* program using the *SPSS* icon (or selecting *SPSS* from *Start* and *Programs*). You are presented with a *dialog box* which asks: *What would you like to do?* Select *Type in data* and you will be presented with a spreadsheet-style window headed *Untitled – SPSS Data Editor*. This consists of two windows, a *Variable View* window, and a *Data View* window, as shown in Figure 11.3. You can toggle between the two windows using the tabs at the bottom of the screen. These two windows provide the basis for *SPSS* analysis. The *Variable View* window will receive the information on variables discussed above and the *Data View* screen will receive the data from completed questionnaires. Switch to the *Variable View* screen to start.

Entering information on variables – Variable View window

The information on the variables arising from a questionnaire – as shown in Figure 11.2 above – must be typed into the *Variable View* window. The result of this exercise for the campus life questionnaire is as shown in Figure 11.4.

Saving work

As with any computer work, the file should be saved to hard disk or floppy disk from time to time during the course of preparation and when completed, and a backup copy should also be made. The suffix for an *SPSS* datafile is .sav, so the example file could be

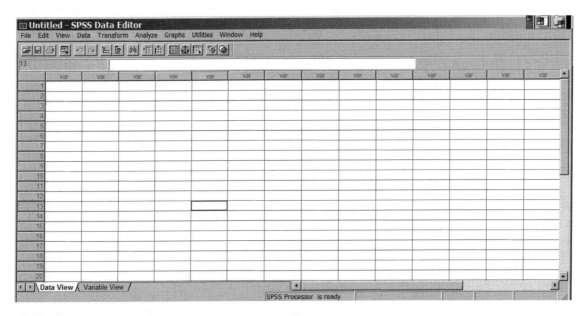

Figure 11.3   Blank *SPSS* Variable View and Data View windows

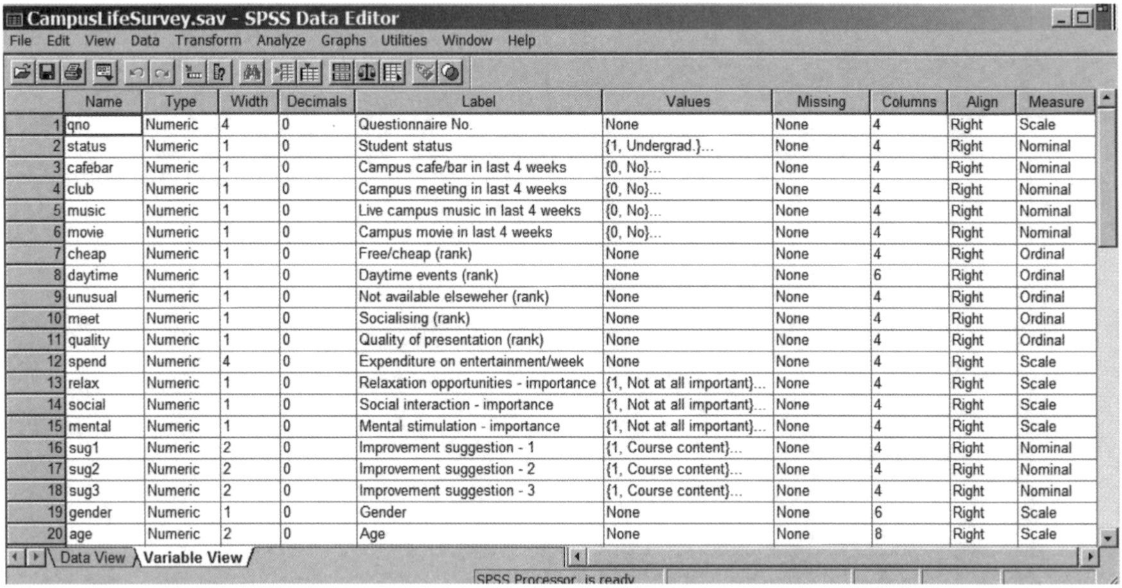

	Name	Type	Width	Decimals	Label	Values	Missing	Columns	Align	Measure
1	qno	Numeric	4	0	Questionnaire No.	None	None	4	Right	Scale
2	status	Numeric	1	0	Student status	{1, Undergrad.}...	None	4	Right	Nominal
3	cafebar	Numeric	1	0	Campus cafe/bar in last 4 weeks	{0, No}...	None	4	Right	Nominal
4	club	Numeric	1	0	Campus meeting in last 4 weeks	{0, No}...	None	4	Right	Nominal
5	music	Numeric	1	0	Live campus music in last 4 weeks	{0, No}...	None	4	Right	Nominal
6	movie	Numeric	1	0	Campus movie in last 4 weeks	{0, No}...	None	4	Right	Nominal
7	cheap	Numeric	1	0	Free/cheap (rank)	None	None	4	Right	Ordinal
8	daytime	Numeric	1	0	Daytime events (rank)	None	None	6	Right	Ordinal
9	unusual	Numeric	1	0	Not available elseweher (rank)	None	None	4	Right	Ordinal
10	meet	Numeric	1	0	Socialising (rank)	None	None	4	Right	Ordinal
11	quality	Numeric	1	0	Quality of presentation (rank)	None	None	4	Right	Ordinal
12	spend	Numeric	4	0	Expenditure on entertainment/week	None	None	4	Right	Scale
13	relax	Numeric	1	0	Relaxation opportunities - importance	{1, Not at all important}...	None	4	Right	Scale
14	social	Numeric	1	0	Social interaction - importance	{1, Not at all important}...	None	4	Right	Scale
15	mental	Numeric	1	0	Mental stimulation - importance	{1, Not at all important}...	None	4	Right	Scale
16	sug1	Numeric	2	0	Improvement suggestion - 1	{1, Course content}...	None	4	Right	Nominal
17	sug2	Numeric	2	0	Improvement suggestion - 2	{1, Course content}...	None	4	Right	Nominal
18	sug3	Numeric	2	0	Improvement suggestion - 3	{1, Course content}...	None	4	Right	Nominal
19	gender	Numeric	1	0	Gender	None	None	6	Right	Scale
20	age	Numeric	2	0	Age	None	None	8	Right	Scale

Figure 11.4 *SPSS* Variable View window with variable names and labels

called CampusLifeSurvey.sav. The title 'CampusLifeSurvey' appears at the top of the screen when the file is *saved*.

Entering data – Data View window

Switching to the *Data View* window reveals that the variable names entered via the *Variable View* window have automatically been put in place, and the system is ready to receive data. Data from the questionnaires can now be keyed in – one row on the screen per questionnaire, or *case*. Figure 11.5 shows the *Data View* window with data from the fifteen cases/questionnaires shown in Figure 9.20. While a sample of fifteen would generally be seen as too small for a typical leisure/ tourism survey, it is used here for demonstration purposes.

Survey data analysis and types of research

In Chapter 1 it was noted that research might be of three kinds: descriptive, explanatory and evaluative. Before considering the process of analysing questionnaire survey data, these types of research and their relationship to survey analysis by *SPSS* are discussed in turn below and summarised in Figure 11.6.

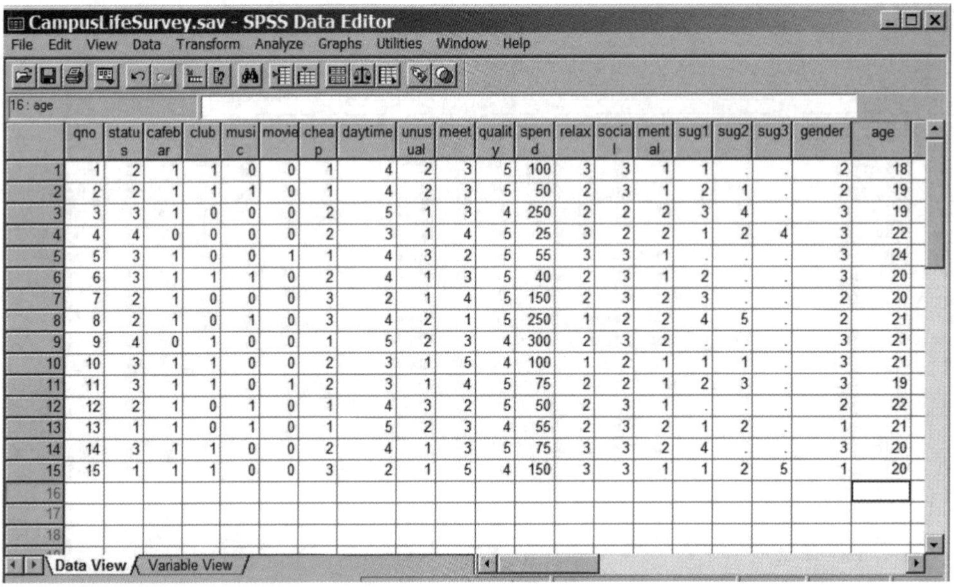

	qno	status	cafebar	club	music	movie	cheap	daytime	unusual	meet	quality	spend	relax	social	mental	sug1	sug2	sug3	gender	age
1	1	2	1	1	0	0	1	4	2	3	5	100	3	3	1	1	.	.	2	18
2	2	2	1	1	1	0	1	4	2	3	5	50	2	3	1	2	1	.	2	19
3	3	3	1	0	0	0	2	5	1	3	4	250	2	2	2	3	4	.	3	19
4	4	4	0	0	0	0	2	3	1	4	5	25	3	2	2	1	2	4	3	22
5	5	3	1	0	0	1	1	4	3	2	5	55	3	3	1	.	.	.	3	24
6	6	3	1	1	1	0	2	4	1	3	5	40	2	3	1	2	.	.	3	20
7	7	2	1	0	0	0	3	2	1	4	5	150	2	3	2	3	.	.	2	20
8	8	2	1	0	1	0	3	4	2	1	5	250	1	2	2	4	5	.	2	21
9	9	4	0	1	0	0	1	5	2	3	4	300	2	3	2	.	.	.	3	21
10	10	3	1	1	0	0	2	3	1	5	4	100	1	2	1	1	1	.	3	21
11	11	3	1	1	0	1	2	3	1	4	5	75	2	2	1	2	3	.	3	19
12	12	2	1	0	1	0	1	4	3	2	5	50	2	3	1	.	.	.	2	22
13	13	1	1	0	1	0	1	5	2	3	4	55	2	3	2	1	2	.	1	21
14	14	3	1	1	0	0	2	4	1	3	5	75	3	3	2	4	.	.	3	20
15	15	1	1	1	0	0	3	2	1	5	4	150	3	3	1	1	2	5	1	20
16																				
17																				
18																				

Figure 11.5 Data View window with data from fifteen questionnaires/cases

Figure 11.6 Research types and *SPSS* procedures

Research type	*SPSS* procedures
Descriptive	Frequencies, Means
Explanatory	Crosstabs, Compare Means
Evaluative	Frequencies – compared with targets or benchmarks Crosstabs – comparing user/customer-groups Means – compared with some benchmark or target

Descriptive research

Descriptive research usually involves the presentation of information in a fairly simple form. Of the *SPSS* procedures described in this chapter, the two most appropriate for descriptive research are *Frequencies* and *Means*. *Frequencies* presents counts and percentages for single variables. *Means* presents averages for numerical variables.

Explanatory research

Descriptive data do not, of themselves, *explain* anything. To explain the patterns in data it is necessary to consider the question of *causality* – how to determine whether A is caused by B. In Chapter 3 it was noted that to establish causality it is necessary to fulfil four criteria: association, time priority, non-spurious relation and rationale.

- *Associations* between variables can be explored using such *SPSS* procedures as *Crosstabs* and *Regression*.

- *Time priority* – involves establishing that, for A to be the *cause* of B, then A must take place *before* B – this is sometimes testable in social science research and is sometimes obvious, but is generally more appropriate for the conditions of the natural science laboratory.

- *Non-spurious* relationships are those which 'make sense' theoretically (that is, the relationship between A and B is not mediated by a third, extraneous variable C), and are not just a 'fluke' of the data. This can be approached using *SPSS*. For example, suppose it is found that leisure and tourism expenditure is inversely related to age for the whole sample. If leisure and tourism expenditure is also inversely related to age for, say, men and women separately, and for other sub-groups – even random sub-samples – this suggests a non-spurious relationship.

- *Rationale*, or *theory*, is of course not produced by *SPSS* but should be integral to the research design. As indicated in Chapter 3, the research may be *deductive* in nature, with pre-established hypotheses which are tested by the data analysis, or it may be *inductive*, in which development of theory and explanation building take place to a greater or lesser extent as part of the data analysis process. Either way, *explanation*, or the establishment of causality, is not complete without some sort of rational, conceptual explanation of the relationships found.

The example questionnaire offers only limited scope for *explanatory* research. For example, differences in attitudes between the various student groups – full-time and part-time or different age-groups for example – may indicate that varying expectations from campus life may be a function of student group characteristics.

The particular procedures which are appropriate for explanatory analysis and which are covered in this chapter are *Crosstabs*, which examines the relationship between two or more variables based on frequencies, and *Means*, which compares the means of two or more variables. These procedures can establish whether or not relationships exist between variables – whether or not they are spurious and/or supported by theory involves reference to the theoretical or conceptual framework.

Evaluative research

Evaluative research basically involves comparisons between survey findings and some benchmark derived from expectations, past figures, other similar facilities or programmes or target performance standards. The analysis called for is therefore relatively simple, is generally descriptive in nature, and is easily facilitated by *SPSS*.

The example questionnaire could be used for evaluative purposes – for example, a low level of use of one of the services listed in question 2 could imply that the existing programme is not performing well in meeting the needs of students and low levels of use by particular groups could indicate a failure to meet the needs of all groups.

Overlaps

Analysis does not always fall exclusively into one of the above three modes. For example, in presenting a descriptive account of the example campus life survey results, it would be natural to provide a breakdown of the participation patterns and preferences of the four student groups included. This would involve the use of *Crosstabs* and/or *Means*. While this could be descriptive in form, it would begin at least to hint at explanation, in that any differences in the groups' patterns of behaviour or opinions would seem to call for explanation; the analysis would be saying 'these groups are different' and would be implicitly posing the question 'why?'. In so far as the providers of campus services aimed to serve all sections of the student community, the data could be used in evaluating management.

Reliability

In Chapter 2 reference was made to questions of *validity* and *reliability*. It has been noted that some attempt at testing validity – whether the data are measuring what they are intended to measure – can be achieved in the design of questionnaires. Reliability – whether similar results would be obtained if the research were replicated – is a difficult issue in the social sciences, but an approach can be made at the analysis stage. While *SPSS* procedures are well suited to establishing the magnitude and strength of associations, the question of the reliability of such associations is more complex. Unlike the natural sciences, it is not always possible, for practical or resource reasons, to replicate research in the social sciences to establish reliability. While reference to previous research reported in the literature can be relevant and helpful in this respect, in fact, the changing nature of human nature over time and space means that consistency with previous research findings is by no means a guarantee of reliability.

If the sample is large enough, one approach to reliability is to split the sample into two or more sub-samples on a random basis, or on the basis of a selected variable, and see if the results for the sub-samples are the same as for the sample as a whole. This can be achieved using the *SPSS* procedure *split file*: the procedure is not covered here but is relatively straightforward to operate.

SPSS procedures

Starting an *SPSS* analysis session

The data-file with which you are dealing may already be on-screen (as in Figure 11.5) if you have just completed typing in data. If not, and in subsequent sessions, you will need to open the file, as shown in Figure 11.7.

Frequencies

The *Frequencies* procedure is the simplest form of descriptive analysis: it merely produces counts and percentages for individual variables – for example, the numbers and percentages of respondents registered in each student status group (*status*). The procedure can be run for one variable at a time or for a number of variables. It is advisable to begin the analysis of a data set by running *Frequencies* for one variable – so that the computer can read through the data and establish that the data file is in working order.

Figure 11.7
Starting an *SPSS*
analysis session

1. Start *SPSS* using the *SPSS* icon or *Start* and *Program*.
2. If the dialog box with the question *What do you want to do?* is presented, proceed with step 3, if not go to step 4.
3. Select *Open an existing data source* – if your file (e.g., CampusLifeSurvey.sav) is listed, select it, if not, select *More files* . . . and locate your file on the appropriate disk. Now skip to step 5.
4. If the dialog box with the question *What do you want to do?* is not presented, use the normal 'Windows' method for opening a file by selecting *File* at the top of the screen and *Open* and locating your file.
5. The *Variable View* and *Data View* windows should now be available, as shown in Figure 11.4 and 11.5.

Frequencies for one variable

The steps to obtain a table for the variable *status* are set out in Figure 11.8, together with the resultant output. The *Output* window presents two tables. The first, *Statistics*, indicates the number of 'valid cases' on which the analysis is based – in this case 15. The second table, headed *Student status*, shows:

- *Frequency* – count of the numbers of students in each status group;
- *Per cent* converts frequency numbers into percentages;
- *Valid per cent* is explained below under 'missing values'; and
- *Cumulative per cent* adds percentages cumulatively – which may be useful for a variable like *spend* or *age*, but is not particularly useful for the variable *status*.

Frequencies for a number of variables

If the single variable table has worked satisfactorily, frequency tables for all the variables can be obtained, by transferring all the variables (except *qno*) into the *Variable(s)* box in Step 2 in Figure 11.8. Running frequency tables for all variables is a common initial instruction in survey analysis: it is a good way of obtaining an overview of the results, and checking that all is well with the data. The results of this exercise for the example questionnaire are shown in Appendix 11.1.

> Note: The list of variables in the *Frequencies* dialog box can be in the form of *variable names* or the longer *variable labels* – the change from one format to the other can be made via *Edit, Options, Variable Lists*. Other changes to the format of output tables can also be made here.

Checking for errors

After obtaining the *Frequencies* printout for all variables it is necessary to check through the results to see if there are any errors. This could be, for example, in the form of an invalid code or an unexpected missing value. The error must be traced in the data file and corrected, perhaps by reference back to the original questionnaire. The data must then be corrected on the data file and the *Frequencies* table for that variable run again. *The corrected, 'clean' data file should then be saved to disk.*

Figure 11.8
Frequencies for
one variable –
SPSS procedures

Procedure

1. Select *Analyze* from the menu bar at the top of the screen, then *Descriptive Statistics*, then *Frequencies*. This opens the *Frequencies* dialog box.
2. In the *Frequencies* dialog box select the variable *status* by highlighting it. Then click on the right arrow box to transfer it to the *Variable(s)* box for analysis. Make sure that *Display frequency tables* in the dialog box is ticked.
3. Select *OK* and the results will appear in the *Output1 – SPSS Viewer*, as shown below.

Output

Frequencies

Statistics
Student status

N	Valid	15
	Missing	0

Student status

		Frequency	Per cent	Valid per cent	Cumulative per cent
Valid	F/T student/no paid work	2	13.3	13.3	13.3
	F/T student/paid work	5	33.3	33.3	46.7
	P/T student – F/T job	6	40.0	40.0	86.7
	P/T student/other	2	13.3	13.3	100.0
	Total	15	100.0	100.0	

F/T = full-time; P/T = part-time

Multiple response

Questions 2 and 6 in the example questionnaire are *multiple response* questions. They are single questions with a number of possible responses and must be analysed using a number of variables. Particular 'multiple response' analysis procedures are available in *SPSS* to handle their particular characteristics.

Question 2 on use of campus services is a *multiple response – dichotomous* variable, because each answer category is essentially a yes/no, dichotomous (two values) variable. Any one respondent could tick one, two, three or all four boxes, so each is a separate variable.

Question 6 on suggestions for improvements, is a *multiple response – categories* variable. It is open-ended and respondents might give any number of answers. In this case the designer of the questionnaire has assigned three variables to record the answers (*sug1*, *sug2* and *sug3*), on the assumption that a maximum of three answers would be given by any one respondent. Not all respondents will necessarily give three answers – this is no problem, because *sug2* and/or *sug3* can be left blank. Some may, however, give *more* than three answers, in which case it would not be possible to record the fourth and subsequent answers and that information would be lost. If more than a handful of respondents give more than three answers then a fourth variable (*sug4*) would need to be added. The decision on how many answers to allow for must depend on a preliminary scanning of the questionnaires. As an open-ended question, the coding system for question 6 applies to all three variables and was devised from the range of free-form answers as discussed in Chapter 10.

It can be seen from Appendix 11.1 that the normal *Frequencies* procedure produces output for these questions in a rather inconvenient format – four tables for question 2 and three tables for question 6. The *Multiple Response* procedure in *SPSS* combines multiple responses into single tables. The procedure is operated as shown in Figure 11.9, together with the results – one table each for questions 2 and 6. It should be noted that percentages are given related to the number of respondents and to the number of responses – which of these to use depends on the aims of the research.

Recode

As the name implies, *Recode* is a procedure which can be used to change the codes of variable values. The procedure can be applied to scale, ordinal or nominal variables. This might be done for a number of reasons:

- presentational purposes, when there are a large number of categories and several contain small numbers;
- theoretical purposes, when different parts of the analysis call for different groupings of response categories;
- for comparative reasons, when comparisons with previous research require different groupings;
- for statistical reasons, as will be discussed in Chapter 12.

Recode with scale and ordinal variables

Scale and ordinal variables are not 'pre-coded' – the actual value given by respondents is recorded rather than a code. In the case of scale variables in particular, this means that the *Frequencies* procedure outlined above produces a table with one line for every value in the data-set – as can be seen in Appendix 11.1 for variables *spend* and *age*. With large samples this can produce impractically large tables with possibly hundreds of lines, which would be unreadable and unmanageable for cross-tabulation (discussed below).

A *Recoded*, grouped, version of such variables can be produced using the method demonstrated in the first part of Figure 11.10.

Ordinal variables, such as those in question 3, can be recoded – for example ranks first and second could be grouped together, and third and fourth, and so on. Similarly Likert-type variables, as in question 5, can be recoded – for example, grouping 'very important' and 'important' together.

It might be asked: if the variable is to be grouped anyway, why not present groupings in the questionnaire, where respondents can tick a box? This is often done, but the advantage of not having the variable pre-coded is that it is possible to be flexible about what groupings are required and it is also possible to use such procedures as *Means* and *Regression*, which is not generally possible with pre-coded or nominal variables.

Figure 11.9
Multiple
response –
SPSS procedure

Procedures
1. select *Analyze*
2. then *Multiple Response*
3. then *Define Sets*

Multiple response – dichotomous	Multiple response – categories
4. Transfer *cafebar, music, sport* and *travel* into the *Variables in Set* box 5. under the *Variables are coded as . . .* box, select *Dichotomies* 6. enter *1* in the *Counted value* box (then press Tab) 7. give the 'set' a *Name* – e.g. *services* 8. add a *Label* – e.g. *Services used* 9. select *Add* 10. a new variable, *Services* is listed automatically 11. select *Close*	4. put *sug1, sug2, sug3* into the *Variables in Set* box 5. under *Variables are coded as . . .*, select *Categories* 6. enter *Range 1* through *6* 7. add *Name*, e.g. *sugs* 8. add *Label*, e.g. *Suggestions for improvement* 9. select *Add* 10. a new variable *$sugs* is listed automatically 11. select *Close*

To produce a table:
12. Select *Analyze*
13. Select *Multiple Response*
14. Select *Frequencies* and use the new variables

Output

Multiple response
Group: Service – Services used (Value tabulated = 1)

Dichotomy label	Name	Count	Responses (%)	Cases (%)
Campus cafe/bar in last 4 wks	Cafebar	13	46.4	92.9
Live campus music in last 4 wks	Music	8	28.6	57.1
Sport facilities in last 4 wks	Sport	5	17.9	35.7
Travel service in last 4 wks	Travel	2	7.1	14.3
Total responses		28	100.0	200.0

1 missing cases; 14 valid cases

Group: Sug – Suggestions for improvement

Category label	Code	Count	Responses (%)	Cases (%)
Programme content	1	7	31.8	58.3
Timing	2	6	27.3	50.0
Facilities	3	3	13.6	25.0
Costs	4	4	18.2	33.3
Organisation	5	2	9.1	16.7
Total responses		22	100.0	183.3

3 missing cases; 12 valid cases

Figure 11.10
Recode – *SPSS*
procedure

Part 1. For a scale or ordinal variable

Example: recode the variable *spend* as follows:

Proposed groupings	New code	Value labels
0–50	1	$0–50
51–100	2	$51–100
101–200	3	$101–200
201+	4	$201 and over

Procedures

1. From the top of the screen, select *Transform*, then *Recode*, then *Into Different Variable*.
2. Select the variable to be recoded, *spend*, and transfer to the *Numeric variable > Output variable* box.
3. Under *Output Variable*, add a *Name* (e.g., *spendr*) and *Label* (e.g., *Spend on books - recoded*).
4. Select *Old and New Values* and then the first *Range* option.
5. Enter *1* through *50*, then enter *1* against *Value*, then click on *Add* ('1 thru 50 → 1' should now appear in the *Old-New* box).
6. Repeat step 5. for: *51* through *100* – new value *2*; and *101* through 200 – new value *3*.
7. Select the third range option: *Range through Highest* : enter *201* and enter *4* against *Value*, then *Add*.
   The *'Old – New'* box should now contain: 1 thru 50 → 1, 51 thru 100 → 2, 101 thru 200 → 3, 201 thru Highest → 4.
8. Select *Continue*.
9. Select *Change*, then *OK*. The new variable now appears on the Data View and Variable View screens.
10. Add *Value Labels*, as above, via the *Variable View* window, as for any variable.
11. *Save* the data file with the new variable, if you will want to use it again.
12. Produce a *Frequencies* table for recoded variable *spendr* in the usual way, to produce the Output below.

Output: Spend Recoded

		Frequency	Per cent	Valid (%)	Cumulative (%)
Valid	$0–50	4	26.7	26.7	26.7
	$51–100	6	40.0	40.0	66.7
	$101–200	2	13.3	13.3	80.0
	$201+	3	20.0	20.0	100.0
	Total	15	100.0	100.0	

Figure 11.10
(*continued*)

Part 2. For a string (pre-coded) variable

Example: recode the variable *status* as follows:

Current coding	Recoded
1. F/T student – no work 2. F/T student – working	1. Full-time student
3. P/T student – F/T job 4. P/T student – other	2. Part-time student

F/T = full-time; P/T = part-time

Procedures

1. From the top of the screen, select *Transform*, then *Recode*, then *Into Different Variable*.
2. Select the variable to be recoded, *status* and transfer to the *Numeric variable > Output variable* box.
3. Under *Output Variable*, add a *Name* (e.g. *statusr*) and *Label* (e.g. *Status – recoded*).
4. Select *Old and New Values* and then the first *Value* option and type in *1*.
5. In the *New Value* box select *Copy old value*, then click on *Add* – now *1→ Copy* appears in the *Old → New* box.
6. In the *Value* box type *2*, and in the *New Value* box type *1*, then click on *Add*.
7. In *Range* type 3 through 4 and in the *New Value* box type *2*, then click on *Add*.
8. The *Old → New* box should now contain: *1→ Copy*, *2→ 1*, 3 thru 4 → 2.
9. Complete steps 8–12 in Part 1 to produce a *Frequencies* table for the recoded *status* variable, as follows:

Output: Course recoded

		Frequency	(%)	Valid (%)	Cumulative (%)
Valid	F/T student	72	46.7	46.7	46.7
	P/T student	8	53.3	53.3	100.0
	Total	15	100.0	100.0	

F/T = full-time; P/T = part-time

Recode with nominal/pre-coded variables

It is also possible to change the groupings of nominal or pre-coded variables using *Recode*. For instance, analysis could be conducted comparing all full-time students and all part-time students – that is, two groups rather than four. This is illustrated in the second part of Figure 11.10.

Means

A *mean* is the same as an *average*. It is often useful to be able to produce means – for instance mean ages, incomes or expenditure. Means can only be produced for scale or ordinal data. Means *cannot* be produced for nominal variables with codes which represent qualitative categories and not quantities.

Two procedures are available in *SPSS* for producing means, as shown in Figure 11.11:

Figure 11.11
Means – *SPSS*
procedures

Method 1. Using *Frequencies* procedure

a. Scale variable
1. Select *Analyze*, then *Descriptive Statistics* then *Frequencies*.
2. Select *spend* and transfer to the *Variable(s)* box.
3. Select *Statistics* and click on *Mean*.
4. Select *Continue*.
5. Select *OK* to run the *Frequencies* in the normal way. As shown below, the mean is given as 115.00.

Output–Statistics

Expenditure on entertainment/week

N	Valid	15
	Missing	0
Mean		115.00

b. Attitude statements/Likert scales
Using the procedure as in (a), above, to produce means for the three variables: *relax*, *social* and *mental*, resulting in output as follows. The mean scores on the 'importance scale' are: 2.20, 2.67 and 1.47.

Output–Statistics

	Relaxation opportunities – importance	Social interaction – importance	Mental stimulation – importance
N Valid	15	15	15
Missing	0	0	0
Mean	2.20	2.67	1.47

Method 2. Using *Means* procedure

1. Select *Analyze*, then *Compare Means*, then *Means*.
2. Select *status* and put it into the *Independent list** box.
3. Select *spend* and put it into the *Dependent list** box.
4. Select *OK*. Means for each course group are produced, as below, showing different mean expenditure levels for different groups.

* (The idea of dependent and independent variables and standard deviations are discussed in chapter 12.)

Output–Report

Expenditure on entertainment/week

Student status	Mean	N	Std. Deviation*
F/T student/no paid work	102.50	2	67.175
F/T student/paid work	120.00	5	83.666
P/T student – F/T job	99.17	6	76.643
P/T student/Other	162.50	2	194.454
Total	115.00	15	87.076

F/T = full-time; P/T = part-time

■ Method 1 uses a function of the *Frequencies* procedure – example 1a. shows that mean expenditure on entertainment among the sample is £115. Example 1b demonstrates the use of the procedure for producing mean scores on Likert-type scales. Note that this is purely *descriptive*.

■ Method 2 uses the *SPSS* procedure *Means*, which produces means for sub-groups as well as for the whole sample. For example, in Figure 11.11, mean expenditures on entertainment are shown for students of different statuses. Note that this moves into the area of *explanation*, since it reveals that a student's full-time/part-time and employment status leads to different levels of expenditure.

Presenting the results: statistical summary

The layout of the frequency tables produced by *SPSS* contains more detail than is necessary for most reports. It is recommended that a *Statistical Summary* be prepared for inclusion in any report, rather than including a copy of the *SPSS* printout. The summary must be prepared with a word-processor, either typing it out afresh or editing the saved *SPSS Output* file. For example, the output from the *Frequencies* analysis covered so far, including the initial *Frequencies* run reproduced in Appendix 11.1 and the *Recodes, Multiple responses* and *Means* discussed above could be summarised as in Figure 11.12.

The following should be noted about the summary.

■ The results from *Multiple Response* variables are presented in single tables.
■ Recoded versions of *spend* and *age* are included.
■ The mean *spend* and *age* and the mean scores for the attitude/Likert-type variables come from the *Means* procedure discussed above.
■ It is generally not necessary to include actual frequency counts as well as percentages in reports, since the sample size is indicated. Readers can work out the raw numbers for themselves if required.

Cross-tabulation

Introduction

After *Frequencies*, the most commonly used *SPSS* command is probably *Crosstabs*. This procedure relates two or more variables to produce tables of the sort commonly encountered in social research. In analysing the relationships between variables, cross-tabulation marks the move from purely descriptive to explanatory analysis. The procedure and output are demonstrated in part 1 of Figure 11.13.

Rows and columns

Having been specified as the *row* variable, *status* appears down the side of the table, while the *column* variable, *music*, appears across the top. Specifying the two variables the other way round would produce a table with *status* across the top and *music* down the side.

Figure 11.12
Campus Life
Survey 2003:
statistical
summary

Student status	%
F/T student/no paid work	13.3
F/T student/paid work	33.3
P/T student – F/T job	40.0
P/T student/Other	13.3
Total	100.0

F/T = full-time; P/T = part-time

Campus services used in the last four weeks

	%
Cafe/bar	86.7
Live campus music	53.3
Sport facilities	33.3
Travel service	13.3

Importance of factors in campus services

	Average rank
Free/cheap access	1.8
Day-time events	3.7
Not available elsewhere	1.6
Opportunities for socialising	3.2
Quality of presentation	4.7

Expenditure on entertainment/month

	%
£0–50	26.7
£51–100	40.0
£101–200	13.3
Over £200	20.0
Average expenditure	£115.00

Importance of factors in campus services

	Very important %	Important %	Not Important %	Mean score*
Relaxation opportunities	33.3	53.3	13.3	2.2
Social interaction	66.7	33.3	0.0	2.7
Mental stimulation	0.0	46.7	53.3	1.5

* 3 = very important, 2 = important, 1 = not important

Figure 11.12
(*continued*)

Suggestions for improving the course (sample size, 15)

	% of cases
Comments on programme content	58.3
Comments on timing	50.0
Comments on facilities	25.0
Comments on costs	33.3
Comments on organisation	16.7

Gender
Male	53.3
Female	46.3

Age
18–19	26.7
20–21	53.4
22 and over	20.0

Figure 11.13
Crosstabs –
SPSS procedure

1. Crosstabs – Counts only

Procedure

1. Select *Analyze*, then *Descriptive Statistics*, then *Crosstabs*.
2. Transfer *music* to the *Columns* box.
3. Transfer *status* to the *Rows* box.
4. Select *OK*. Output is as below.

Output

Student status * Live campus music in last 4 wks Crosstabulation

		Live campus music in last 4 wks		Total
		No	Yes	
Student status	F/T student/no paid work	1	1	2
	F/T student/paid work	3	2	5
	P/T student – F/T job	2	4	6
	P/T student/Other	1	1	2
Total		7	8	15

F/T = full-time; P/T = part-time

Figure 11.13
(*continued*)

2. Crosstabs with percentages

Procedure

1. Repeat steps 1–3 above.
2. In the *Crosstabs* dialog box select *Cells* . . . to produce the *Crosstabs: Cell Display* dialog box.
3. Under *Percentages*, select *Row*.
4. Select *Continue* then *OK*. Output appears as follows.

Output

Student status * Live campus music in last 4 wks Crosstabulation

| | | | Live campus music in last 4 wks | | |
			No	Yes	Total
Student status	F/T student/no paid work	Count	1	1	2
		% within student status	50.0	50.0	100.0
	F/T student/paid work	Count	3	2	5
		% within student status	60.0	40.0	100.0
	P/T student – F/T job	Count	2	4	6
		% within student status	33.3	66.7	100.0
	P/T student/Other	Count	1	1	2
		% within student status	50.0	50.0	100.0
Total		Count	7	8	15
		% within student status	46.7	53.3	100.0

F/T = full-time; P/T = part-time

3. Three-way crosstabulation

Procedure

1. Repeat steps 1–3 in part 1 above.
2. In the *Crosstabs* dialog box: transfer *gender* into the *Layer* box.
3. Select *OK* to produce output as follows.

Output

Student status * Live campus music in last 4 wks * Gender Crosstabulation

| | | | Live campus music in last 4 wks | | |
Gender			No	Yes	Total
Male	Student status	F/T student/no paid work	1	1	2
		P/T student – F/T job	2	3	5
		P/T student/other	0	1	1
	Total		3	5	8
Female	Student status	F/T student/paid work	3	2	5
		P/T student – F/T job	0	1	1
		P/T student/other	1	0	1
	Total		4	3	7

F/T = full-time; P/T = part-time

Percentages

In most cases percentages are required in tables rather than just the raw figures. The crosstab table contains only counts of the raw data, not percentages. To produce percentages it is necessary to specify the 'cell contents'. There are four relevant options for individual cell contents:

■ counts
■ row percentages – where percentages add up to 100 going across a row
■ column percentages – where percentages add up to 100 going down the column
■ total percentages – where all cell percentages add up to 100.

The choice of which percentages to use depends on the context and the purpose of the analysis – it generally becomes apparent in the course of discussing the contents of a table; often 'trial and error' is involved in testing out the use of particular percentages in particular situations. The procedures for producing percentages in *Crosstabs* are as shown in part 2 of Figure 11.13.

Three-way cross-tabulations

Often three-way cross-tabulations are required. For example, the table in part 2 of Figure 11.13 could be further subdivided by gender. This is demonstrated in part 3 of Figure 11.13. Further subdivision is possible, although often sample size places limits on how far this can go.

Weighting

The weighting of data to correct for biassed samples is discussed in Chapter 10, where the procedure for calculating a weighting factor is discussed. The simplest way of introducing a weighting factor to the *SPSS* process is to add the weights as an additional variable. For example, the 'weighting' variable might be called *wt* and the weights typed into the data-file like any other item of data.

To weight data, use the *Weight* feature in *Transform*, specifying the appropriate variable (e.g. *wt*) as weighting variable. To save having to type in the weights for every respondent, *SPSS* provides a logical procedure. For example, if all Masters course students are to be given a weight of 1.3, it is possible to indicate this in the *Weight* procedure. It is not intended to explain the detail of this procedure here – the reader is referred to the *SPSS* Help index.

Graphics

Graphical presentation of data is an aid to communication in most situations: for example, trends and patterns can be seen more easily in graphic form by most people. Computer packages generally offer the following graphic formats for data presentation:

■ Bar graph

■ Stacked bar graph

■ Pie chart

■ Line graph.

Computers can produce all four formats from any one set of data. But all formats are not equally appropriate for all data types: the appropriate type of graphic depends on the type of data or level of measurement involved. The three data types therefore lend themselves to different graphical treatment. The relationships between these types of data and permitted graphical types is summarised in Figure 11.14.

■ The *bar graph* or *histogram* is perhaps the most commonly used graphic in leisure and tourism research. Because it deals with *categories* for each bar, any scale variable must first be divided into groups – using the *Recode* procedure. The 'stacked' bar graph includes information on two variables – the graphical equivalent of the cross-tabulation.

■ The *pie chart* is just that: it divides something into sections like a pie. The segments making up the pie chart must therefore add up to some sort of meaningful total – often the total sample.

■ The *line graph* is the most constrained and is used more generally in research in more quantified fields such as economics and the natural sciences. Strictly speaking they should only be used with *scale* variables.

  – A line graph with a single *scale* variable indicates the distribution of a variable although, for the type of data in the example survey, this is probably best done by means of a bar chart.

  – A line graph can be used to show the relationship between two *scale* variables – with one variable on each axis. However, a fitted *regression* line, as will be discussed in Chapter 12, is generally more meaningful than a line traced through all observation points.

■ A *scatterplot* is based on two *scale* variables, but involves just plots of the observation points, rather than drawing a line through them. The use of such a diagram in relation to *correlation* and *regression* is explored further in Chapter 12.

Data type	Characteristics	Example questions in Figure 9.19	Mean/ average possible	Types of graphic			
				Bar graph	Pie chart	Line graph	Scatter gram
Nominal	Qualitative categories	1, 2, 6	No	Yes	Yes	No	No
Ordinal	Ranks	3, 5	Yes	Yes	Yes	No	No
Scale	Numerical	4	Yes	Yes (grouped)	Yes (grouped)	Yes	Yes

Figure 11.14 Data types and graphics

Graphics are easily produced in *SPSS* using the *Graphs* option and specifying the variable required. Examples of graphics output from *SPSS* are shown in Figure 11.15. It is not proposed to consider graphics procedures in detail here; details can be found in the *SPSS* Help index.

Figure 11.15
Graphics from
SPSS

Procedures

Note: In all cases, double clicking on the *SPSS* graphic offers a number of options to edit the appearance of the chart, for example, the colouring.

a. Bar chart
1. Select *Graphs* at the top of the screen.
2. Select *Bar* and then *Simple* then *Define* to produce the dialog box: *Define Simple Bar: Summaries for Groups of Cases*.
3. Transfer *status* to the *Category axis* box.
4. Select *N of cases* or *% of cases*. In example here, *% of cases* has been selected.
5. Select *OK* to produce the bar chart.

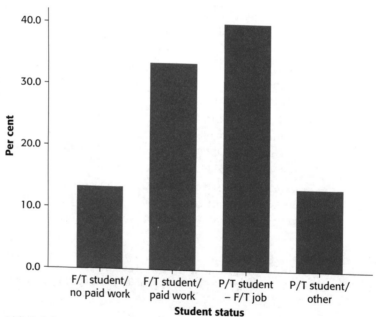

F/T = full-time; P/T = part-time

Figure 11.15
(*continued*)

b. Stacked bar chart
1. Select *Graphs* at the top of the screen.
2. Select *Bar* and then *Stacked* then *Define* to produce the dialog box: *Define Stack Bar: Summaries for Groups of Cases*.
3. Transfer *status* to the *Category axis* box and *gender* to the *Define Stacks by* box.
4. Select *N of cases* or *% of cases*. In the example here, *N of cases* has been selected.
5. Select *OK* to produce the graphic.

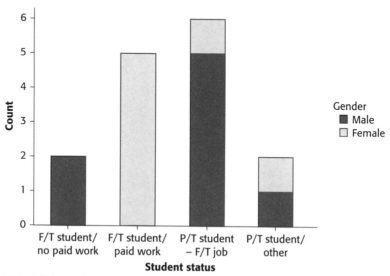

F/T = full-time; P/T = part-time

c. Pie chart
1. Select *Graphs* at the top of the screen.
2. Select *Pie* and then *Summary for Groups of Cases* then *Define* to produce the dialog box: *Define Pie: Summaries for Groups of Cases*.
3. Transfer *status* to the *Define slices by* box.
4. Select *N of cases* or *% of cases*. In the example here, *N of cases* has been selected.
5. Select *OK* to produce the pie chart.

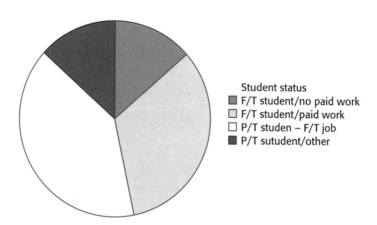

Figure 11.15
(*continued*)

d. Line graph
1. Select *Graphs* at the top of the screen.
2. Select *Line* and then *Simple* then *Define* to produce the dialog box: *Define Simple Line: Summaries for Groups of Cases*.
3. Transfer *age* to the *Category axis* box.
4. Select *N of cases* or *% of cases*. In the example here, *N of cases* has been selected.
5. Select *OK* to produce the graphic.

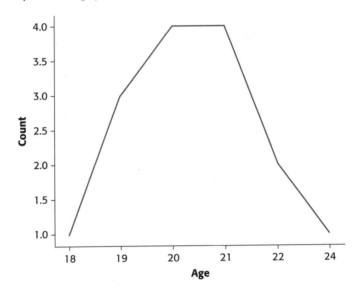

e. Scattergram
1. Select *Graphs* at the top of the screen.
2. Select *Scatter* and then *Simple* then *Define* to produce the dialog box: *Simple Scatterplot*.
3. Transfer *spend* to the *Y-axis* box and *age* to the *X-axis* box.
4. Select *OK* to produce the graphic.

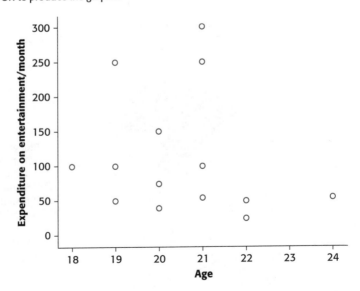

The analysis process

The above is only a brief introduction to the mechanics of survey data analysis. While *SPSS* is capable of much more sophisticated analyses, mastery of the procedures presented here can provide a good basis for a sound programme of analysis, especially in the context of management, as discussed in Chapter 1.

Summary

This chapter provides an introduction to the use of the *SPSS* software package for analysis of data from a questionnaire survey. Based on the introduction to coding in Chapter 9, the process of introducing survey data and information on variables into the *SPSS* package is demonstrated. This includes a discussion of levels of measurement and three corresponding variable types: nominal, ordinal and scale. Following a discussion of the relationship between types of research and types of data analysis, the chapter covers six *SPSS* analysis procedures, as follows.

- *Frequencies* provides counts and percentages for individual and multiple variables.
- *Multiple response* creates single tables for the two or more variables arising from questions with multiple responses.
- *Recode* is used to create groups for scale variables and regroup pre-coded variables.
- *Means* calculates the means, or averages of variables and compares means for sub-samples.
- *Crosstabs* creates cross-tabulations or frequency tables showing the relationships between two or more variables.
- *Weight* is used to weight data according to some criterion variable, as discussed in Chapter 10.
- *Graphs* produces graphical representations of data in various forms, including bar charts, pie charts, line graphs and scattergrams.

Test questions

1. Explain the difference between nominal, ordinal and scale variables and give examples.
2. What is the advantage of using an uncoded format for a scale variable in a questionnaire, rather than coding it into groups?
3. Outline the characteristics of the two types of multiple response question.
4. Why might an analyst wish to recode variables?
5. What are the two methods for obtaining means in *SPSS*?

Exercises

1. The major exercise for this chapter is to replicate the *SPSS* analyses presented in the chapter. This can be done by typing the data and variable definition data in Figures 11.4 and 11.5, and carrying out the instructions for the various procedures in the chapter.

2. Repeat each of the procedures in exercise 1 using at least one different variable in each procedure.

3. Conduct a survey of students using the questionnaire in Figure 9.19; and analyse the data using SPSS, following the analyses procedures outlined in this chapter.

Further reading

Regarding *SPSS*:

■ The *SPSS* website is at: www.spss.com
■ A number of guides to the use of *SPSS* exist, including the following: Coakes and Steed (1999); Pallant (2004); Carver and Nash (2005); George and Mallery (2005); Bryman and Cramer (2005).

Regarding questionnaire survey analysis generally:

■ It is difficult to locate published research reports which give full details of questionnaire surveys and their analysis. While many journal articles are based on survey research, they typically do not provide a copy of the questionnaire and provide only a brief summary of the analysis process – often only part of the analysis arising from the data. Few commercially published books are based primarily on questionnaire survey data, and even when they are they invariably fail to include a copy of the questionnaire used; one exception is Bennett *et al.* (1999), which not only provides a listing of the questions in the questionnaire, but also provides a detailed discussion of the relationship between existing theory (by Bourdieu) and the empirical research described in the book. Government-sponsored survey reports, by the government statistical agency or other agencies, often contain these details – although inevitably they are generally either purely descriptive or related in a fairly straightforward manner to policy issues. Such reports are inconsistently available in libraries, but are sometimes available on the Internet. Examples include:
  – *Australian sport/recreation participation surveys*: Dale and Ford (2002), Standing Committee on Recreation and Sport (2003, 2004);
  – British sport/recreation survey: office for National Statistics (1996)
  – USA outdoor recreation survey: Cordell *et al.* (1999)
■ International reviews of survey evidence: *leisure, time-use and tourism surveys in fifteen countries*: Cushman *et al.* (2005b); *the arts in eight countries*: Hantrais and Kamphorst, (1987); *sport in fifteen countries*: Kamphorst and Roberts (1989); *leisure/lifestyles in nine countries*: Olszewska and Roberts (1989).

Note

1. In earlier versions of the book the term 'ratio' was used rather than 'scale'. Later versions of *SPSS* use the term 'scale', which makes more intuitive sense, so this term has been adopted in this edition.

Appendix 11.1: *SPSS* frequencies output file

Statistics (only scale and ordinal variables included here)

	Free/ cheap	Day-time events	Not available elsewhere	Socialising	Quality of presentation	Expenditure on entertainment/ month	Relaxation – importance	Social interaction: importance	Mental stimulation: importance
N Valid	15	15	15	15	15	15	15	15	15
Missing	0	0	0	0	0	0	0	0	0
Mean	1.80	3.73	1.60	3.20	4.67	115.0	2.20	1.67	1.47

Student status

		Frequency	Per cent	Valid per cent	Cumulative per cent
Valid	F/T student/no paid work	2	13.3	13.3	13.3
	F/T student/paid work	5	33.3	33.3	46.7
	P/T student – F/T job	6	40.0	40.0	86.7
	P/T student/Other	2	13.3	13.3	100.0
	Total	15	100.0	100.0	

Campus cafe/bar in last 4 wks

		Frequency	Per cent	Valid per cent	Cumulative per cent
Valid	No	2	13.3	13.3	13.3
	Yes	13	86.7	86.7	100.0
	Total	15	100.0	100.0	

Live campus music in last 4 wks

		Frequency	Per cent	Valid per cent	Cumulative per cent
Valid	No	7	46.7	46.7	46.7
	Yes	8	53.3	53.3	100.0
	Total	15	100.0	100.0	

Sports facilities in last 4 wks

		Frequency	Per cent	Valid per cent	Cumulative per cent
Valid	No	10	66.7	66.7	66.7
	Yes	5	33.3	33.3	100
	Total	15	100.0	100.0	

Travel service in last 4 wks

		Frequency	Per cent	Valid per cent	Cumulative per cent
Valid	No	13	86.7	86.7	86.7
	Yes	2	13.3	13.3	100
	Total	15	100.0	100.0	

Free/cheap (rank)

		Frequency	Per cent	Valid per cent	Cumulative per cent
Valid	1	6	40.0	40.0	40.0
	2	6	40.0	40.0	80
	3	3	20.0	20.0	100.0
	Total	15	100.0	100.0	

Daytime events (rank)

		Frequency	Per cent	Valid per cent	Cumulative per cent
Valid	2	2	13.3	13.3	13.3
	3	3	20.0	20.0	33.3
	4	7	46.7	46.7	80.0
	5	3	20.0	20.0	100.0
	Total	15	100.0	100.0	

Not available elsewhere (rank)

		Frequency	Per cent	Valid per cent	Cumulative per cent
Valid	1	8	53.3	53.3	53.3
	2	5	33.3	33.3	86.7
	3	2	13.3	13.3	100.0
	Total	15	100.0	100.0	

Socialising (rank)

		Frequency	Per cent	Valid per cent	Cumulative per cent
Valid	1	1	6.7	6.7	6.7
	2	2	13.3	13.3	20.0
	3	7	46.7	46.7	66.7
	4	3	20.0	20.0	86.7
	5	2	13.3	13.3	100.0
	Total	15	100.0	100.0	

Quality of presentation (rank)

		Frequency	Per cent	Valid per cent	Cumulative per cent
Valid	4	5	33.3	33.3	33.3
	5	10	66.7	66.7	100.0
	Total	15	100.0	100.0	

Expenditure on entertainment/month

		Frequency	Per cent	Valid per cent	Cumulative per cent
Valid	25	1	6.7	6.7	6.7
	40	1	6.7	6.7	13.3
	50	2	13.3	13.3	26.7
	55	2	13.3	13.3	40.0
	75	2	13.3	13.3	53.3
	100	2	13.3	13.3	66.7
	150	2	13.3	13.3	80.0
	250	2	13.3	13.3	93.3
	300	1	6.7	6.7	100.0
	Total	15	100.0	100.0	

Relaxation opportunities – importance

		Frequency	Per cent	Valid per cent	Cumulative per cent
Valid	Very important	2	13.3	13.3	13.3
	Important	8	53.3	53.3	66.7
	Not at all important	5	33.3	33.3	100
	Total	15	100	100	

Social interaction – importance

		Frequency	Per cent	Valid per cent	Cumulative per cent
Valid	Important	5	33.3	33.3	33.3
	Not at all important	10	66.7	66.7	100
	Total	15	100	100	

Mental stimulation – importance

		Frequency	Per cent	Valid per cent	Cumulative per cent
Valid	Very important	8	53.3	53.3	53.3
	Important	7	46.7	46.7	100
	Total	15	100	100	

Improvement suggestion – 1

		Frequency	Per cent	Valid per cent	Cumulative per cent
Valid	Programme content	5	33.3	41.7	41.7
	Timing	3	20.0	25.0	66.7
	Facilities	2	13.3	16.7	83.3
	Costs	2	13.3	16.7	100
	Total	12	80.0		
Missing	System	3	20.0		
Total		15	100.0		

Improvement suggestion – 2

		Frequency	Per cent	Valid per cent	Cumulative per cent
Valid	Programme content	2	13.3	25.0	25
	Timing	3	20.0	37.5	62.5
	Facilities	1	6.7	12.5	75
	Costs	1	6.7	12.5	87.5
	Organisation	1	6.7	12.5	100
	Total	8	53.3	100.0	
Missing	System	7	46.7		
Total		15	100.0		

Improvement suggestion – 3

		Frequency	Per cent	Valid per cent	Cumulative per cent
Valid	Costs	1	6.7	50.0	50
	Organisation	1	6.7	50.0	100
	Total	2	13.3	100.0	
Missing	System	13	86.7		
Total		15	100.0		

Gender

		Frequency	Per cent	Valid per cent	Cumulative per cent
Valid	Male	8	53.3	53.3	53.3
	Female	7	46.7	46.7	100.0
	Total	15	100.0	100.0	

Age

		Frequency	Per cent	Valid per cent	Cumulative per cent
Valid	18	1	6.7	6.7	6.7
	19	3	20.0	20.0	26.7
	20	4	26.7	26.7	53.3
	21	4	26.7	26.7	80
	22	2	13.3	13.3	93.3
	24	1	6.7	6.7	100.0
	Total	15	100.0	100.0	

12 Statistical analysis

Introduction

This chapter provides an introduction to statistics, building on the outline of sampling theory presented in Chapter 10 and the introduction to the *SPSS* package outlined in Chapter 11. It *is* only an introduction: it is not intended to be a complete course in statistics. There are many textbooks covering approximately the same ground as is covered here, but in more detail and more depth, and reference to some of these texts is given in the further reading section. The outline of survey analysis in Chapter 11 deals with quantification and the generation and analysis of statistical information, but this chapter is concerned with more than just quantification. Given that, as discussed in Chapter 10, data based on samples are subject to a margin of error when generalising to the population from which they were drawn, this chapter examines how the accuracy of sample-based statistical data can be assessed and in particular how relationships between variables might be analysed.

After dealing with some general concepts related to the statistical method, the chapter covers a number of statistical tests which are appropriate for different types of data. These tests are: the chi-square test, the t-test, analysis of variance, correlation, linear and multiple regression and multi-variate analysis. In each case the *SPSS* procedures for carrying out the tests are described.

The statistics approach

Before examining particular statistical tests, some preliminary statistical concepts and ideas should be discussed, namely: the idea of probabilistic statements; the normal distribution; probabilistic statement formats; significance; the null hypothesis; and dependent and independent variables.

Probabilistic statements

In general, the science of 'inferential statistics' seeks to make *probabilistic* statements about a *population* on the basis of information available from a *sample* drawn from that population. The statements are *probabilistic* because, as discussed in Chapter 10, it is not possible to be absolutely sure that any sample is truly representative of the population from which it has been drawn, so we can only estimate the *probability* that results obtained from a sample are true of the population. The 'statements' which might be made on the basis of sample survey findings can be descriptive, comparative or relational:

- descriptive: for example: 10 per cent of adults play tennis
- comparative: for example: 10 per cent play tennis, but 12 per cent play golf
- relational: for example: people with high incomes play tennis more than people with low incomes.

If they are based on data from samples, such statements cannot be made without qualification. The *sample* may indicate these findings, but it is not certain that they apply precisely to the population from which the sample is drawn, because there is always an element of doubt about any sample. Inferential statistics modifies the above example statements to be of the form:

- we can be 95 per cent confident that the proportion of adults that plays tennis is between 9 per cent and 11 per cent;
- the proportion of golf players is *significantly* higher than the proportion of tennis players (at the 95 per cent level of probability);
- there is a positive relationship between level of income and level of tennis playing (at the 95 per cent level).

The normal distribution

Descriptive statements and 'confidence intervals' are discussed in general terms in Chapter 10 in relation to the issue of sample size. The probability or confidence interval statement is based on the *theoretical* idea of drawing repeated samples of the same size from the same population. The sample drawn in any one piece of research is only one of a large number of *possible* samples which *might* have been drawn. If a large number of samples *could* be drawn, such an exercise would produce a variety of results, some very unrepresentative of the population but most, assuming random sampling procedures are used, tending to produce results close to the true population values. Statistical theory – which we are unable to explore in detail here – is able to quantify this tendency, so that we can say that, in 95 or 99 out of a hundred of such samples, the values found from the sample will fall within a certain range either side of the true population value – hence the idea of 'confidence intervals' as discussed in Chapter 10.

The theory relates to the bell-shaped 'normal distribution' which would result if repeated samples were drawn and the values of a statistic (for example the proportion who play tennis) plotted, as shown in Figure 12.1. The 'normal curve' which would result if a very large number of samples was drawn was shown in Figure 10.1. The value of a statistic (such as a percentage or an average) for the population lies at the centre of the distribution but the value of the statistic found from a sample in a particular

Figure 12.1
Drawing
repeated
samples and
the normal
distribution

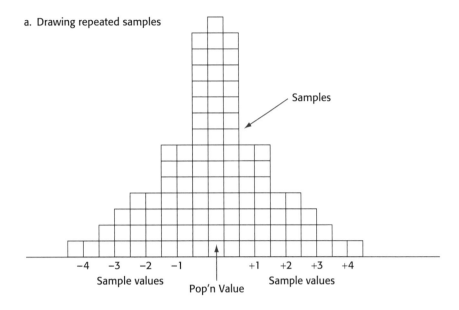

a. Drawing repeated samples

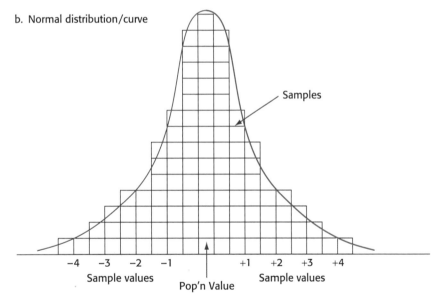

b. Normal distribution/curve

research project is just one among the many values which might arise from various samples which might be drawn from the population. The probabilistic statement is made on the basis of this distribution of possible sample values, which has theoretically known properties for different samples and statistics.

This idea of levels of probability about the accuracy of sample findings based on the theoretical possibility of drawing many samples, is common to most of the statistical procedures examined in this chapter.

Statement formats

It is customary in social research to use probability levels of 95 per cent or 99 per cent – and occasionally 90 per cent or 99.9 per cent. As probability estimates these can be interpreted exactly as in everyday language – for example when we say '90 per cent certain', '50:50' or '9 times out of ten' we are making probabilistic statements. So, if a survey finding is *significant* (a concept discussed further below) at the '99 per cent level', we are saying that we believe that there is a 99 per cent chance that what we have found is true of the population – there is therefore, conversely, a 1 per cent chance that what we have found is *not* true. If we can only say that something is significant at the lower 95 per cent level, we are less confident – there is a 5 per cent chance that what we have found is not true. Thus the terminology *highly significant* is sometimes used in relation to findings at the 99 per cent level and *significant* for the 95 per cent level.

In some cases, instead of the computer-generated results of statistical tests using these conventional cut-off points, they present the exact probability – for example, it might be found that a result is significant at the 96.5 per cent level or the 82.5 per cent level. It is then left up to the researcher to judge whether such levels are acceptable.

Note also, that sometimes the result is expressed as 1 per cent and sometimes as 99 per cent, or 5 per cent rather than 95 per cent. A further variation is to express the probability as a proportion rather than a percentage – for example 0.05 rather than 5 per cent or 0.01 rather than 1 per cent. Similarly the exact calculations may be expressed as proportions, for example 0.035 rather than 3.5 per cent or 96.5 per cent.

In the following, therefore, the three forms in each row are equivalent:

5%	95%	0.05
1%	99%	0.01
0.1%	99.9%	0.001
3.5%	96.5%	0.035
7.5%	92.5%	0.075

In computer printouts from SPSS, if the probability is below .0005 it sometimes comes out as .000 because it is printed only to three decimal places. In some research reports and computer printouts results which are significant at the 5 per cent level are indicated by a single asterisk (*) and those significant at the 1 per cent level are indicated by two asterisks (**).

Significance

The second common feature of statistical tests and procedures is that they deal with the idea of *significance*. A *significant* difference or relationship is one which is *unlikely to have happened by chance*. So, for example, the greater the difference between two sample percentages the more likely it is that the difference is *real* and not just a statistical chance happening.

For example, if it was found from a sample that 10.1 per cent of women played tennis and 10.2 per cent of men played tennis we would be inclined, even from a common-sense point of view, to say that the difference is not significant. This is because, if another sample were selected, it is quite likely that the figures would be different, and even the opposite way around: it is 'too close to call'. However, whether or not such a small difference is *statistically* significant depends on the sample size. If the findings were based on a small sample, say around 100 people, the difference would not be significant – the chances of getting a different result from a different sample of 100 people from the same population would be high (and the statistical procedures outlined below would establish this). But if the sample were large – say several thousand people – then it might be found to be statistically significant: that is, if the result is based on such a large sample we can be much more confident that it is 'real' and would be reproduced if another sample of similar size were drawn.

Statistical theory enables us to quantify and assess 'significance' – that is, to say what sizes of differences are significant for what sizes of sample.

Statistical significance should not, however, be confused with *social, theoretical*, or *managerial* significance. For example, if the above finding about men's and women's tennis playing was based on a sample of, say, 10,000 people, it would be *statistically* significant, but this does not make the difference significant in any social sense. For all practical purposes, on the basis of such findings, we would say that men's and women's tennis playing rates are the same. This is a very important point to bear in mind when reading research results based on statistics; large samples can produce many 'statistically significant' findings; but that does not necessarily make them 'significant' in any other way.

The null hypothesis

A common feature of the statistical method is the concept of the *null hypothesis*, referred to by the symbol H_0. It is based on the idea of setting up two mutually incompatible hypotheses, so that only one can be true. For example *either* more people play tennis than golf *or* the number of people who play tennis is less than or equal to the number who play golf – if one proposition is true then the other is untrue. The null hypothesis usually proposes that there is *no difference* between two observed values or that there is *no relationship* between variables. There are therefore two possibilities:

H_0 – Null hypothesis: there is *no* significant difference or relationship
H_1 – Alternative hypothesis: there *is* a significant difference or relationship.

Usually it is the *alternative* hypothesis, H_1, that the researcher is interested in, but statistical theory explores the implications of the *null* hypothesis.

In terms of the types of research discussed in Chapter 2, this is very much a *deductive* approach: the hypothesis is set up in advance of the analysis, possibly within a theoretical framework.

The use of the null hypothesis idea can be illustrated by example. Suppose, in a study of leisure participation patterns, using a sample of 1,000 adults, part of the study focuses on the relative popularity of golf and tennis. The null hypothesis would be that the participation levels are the same.

H_0 – tennis and golf participation levels are the same;
H_1 – tennis and golf participation levels are significantly different.

Suppose it is found that 120 (12 per cent) play tennis and 120 (12 per cent) play golf. Clearly there is no difference between the two figures; they are consistent with the null hypothesis. The null hypothesis is accepted and the alternative hypothesis is rejected.

But suppose the numbers playing tennis were found to be 121 (12.1 per cent) and the number playing golf was 120 (12.0 per cent). Would we reject the null hypothesis and accept the alternative, that tennis and golf participation levels are different? From what we know of samples, clearly not: this would be too close to call. Such a small difference between the two figures would still be consistent with the null hypothesis. So how big would the difference have to be before we reject the null hypothesis? A difference of 5, 10, 15? This is where statistical theory comes in, to provide a test of what is and is not a significant difference. And this is basically what the rest of this chapter is all about: providing tests of the relationship between sample findings and the null hypothesis for different situations. The null hypothesis is used in each of the tests examined.

Dependent and independent variables

The terminology *dependent variable* and *independent variable* is frequently used in statistical analysis. If there is a significant relationship between a dependent and an independent variable, the *implication* is that changes in the former are caused by changes in the latter: the independent variable *influences* the dependent variable.

For example, if it is suggested that the level of holiday taking is influenced by a person's income level then the level of holiday-taking is the *dependent* variable and income is the *independent* variable. Even though a certain level of income does not *cause* people to go on holiday, it makes more sense to suggest that level of income facilitates or constrains the level of holiday-taking, than to suggest the opposite. So it makes some sense to talk of holiday taking being *dependent* on income. One variable can be dependent on a number of independent variables, as illustrated in Figure 12.2 – for example it may be hypothesised that holiday taking is dependent on income *and* occupation *and* age.

Figure 12.2
Dependent and independent variables

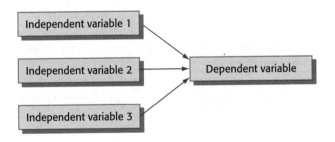

Statistical tests

What tests?

The idea of levels of measurement, or types of data, was introduced in Chapter 11, when nominal, ordinal and scale data were discussed. The higher the level of measurement the greater the range of analysis that can be carried out on the data. For example, it is possible to calculate means/averages of ordinal and scale measures, but not of nominal data. Consequently, different statistical tests are associated with different levels of measurement. The rest of the chapter sets out different statistical tests to be used in different situations; as summarised in Figure 12.3. The tests all relate to comparisons between variables and relationships between variables. The appropriate type of test to be used depends on the format of the data, the level of measurement and the number of variables involved.

In what follows fictitious data are used to illustrate the various tests. The data arise from a questionnaire survey similar to that used in Chapter 11, but with a larger sample and additional leisure and tourism participation variables added. Listings of the

Task	Format of data	No. of variables	Types of variable	Test
Relationship between two variables	Cross-tabulation of frequencies	2	Nominal	Chi-square
Difference between two means – paired	Means – for a whole sample	2	Two scale/ordinal	t-test – paired
Difference between two means – independent samples	Means – for two sub-groups	2	1. scale/ordinal (means) 2. nominal (2 grps only)	t-test – independent samples
Relationship between two variables	Means – for 2 sub-groups	2	1. scale/ordinal (means) 2. nominal (2 groups)	One-way analysis of variance
Relationship between three or more variables	Means – cross-tabulated	3+	1. scale/ordinal (means) 2. three or more nominal	Factorial analysis of variance
Relationship between two variables	Individual measures	2	Two scale/ordinal	Correlation
Linear relationship between two variables	Individual measures	2	Two scale/ordinal	Linear regression
Linear relationship between three or more variables	Individual measures	3+	Three or more scale/ordinal	Multiple regression
Relationships between large numbers of variables	Individual measures	Many	Large numbers of scale/ordinal	Factor analysis Cluster analysis

Figure 12.3 Types of data and types of statistical test

variables and data used are included as Appendix 12.1. As in Chapter 11, the examples have been created using *SPSS* for Windows, Version 12.

Chi-square

Introduction

The 'Chi-square test' (symbol: χ^2, pronounced ky, to rhyme with sky) can be used in a number of situations, but its use is demonstrated here in relation to cross-tabulations of two *nominal* variables – the familiar tables produced from such packages as *SPSS*. When examining cross-tabulations it is possible to use 'common-sense' and an underlying knowledge of the size of confidence intervals, as discussed in Chapter 10, to make an approximate judgement as to whether there is any sort of relationship between the two variables involved in the table. However, unless the pattern is very clear, it can be difficult to judge whether the overall differences are *significant*. The chi-square test is designed to achieve this.

Figure 12.4 shows the *SPSS* procedures to obtain a cross-tabulation with a chi-square test, and the resultant output. The example chosen relates student full-time/part-time status (*statusr*) to gender (*gender*). The interpretation of this output is discussed below.

Null hypothesis

The null hypothesis is that *there is no difference in student full-time/part-time status between male and female respondents*: that is:

H$_0$ – there is *no* relationship between student status and gender in the population of students

H$_1$ – there *is* a relationship between status and gender in the population of students.

Note that the proposition being tested can therefore be expressed in three ways, as shown in Figure 12.5.

Expected frequencies

The cells of the table include counts and column percentages, as discussed in relation to cross-tabulations in Chapter 11. But they also include *expected counts*. These are the counts which *would be expected* if the null hypothesis were true – that is, if there was no difference between males and females in their full-time/part-time status. In this case we have an equal number of men and women in the sample, so the expected values show a 50:50 split for each status.

The value of chi-square

Chi-square is a statistic based on the sum of the differences between the counts and the expected counts: the greater this sum the greater the value of chi-square. However, if the differences between the observed and expected counts in the table are simply

Figure 12.4
SPSS procedure
for chi-square
test

Procedures

1. Select *Analyze*, then *Descriptive Statistics*, then *Crosstabs*.
2. Select variables to be crosstabulated – *Row(s): status Column(s): gender*
3. Select *Statistics* ... then, in the *Crosstabs: Statistics* dialog box, select *Chi-square* then *Continue*
4. Select *Cells* ... then, in the *Crosstabs; cells display* dialog box:
   - in *Counts*: select *Observed* and *Expected*
   - in *Percentages*: select *Column* then *Continue*
5. Select *OK* to produce the output below (*Case Processing Summary* table omitted).

Output

Student status recoded * Gender Cross-tabulation

			Gender		
			Male	**Female**	**Total**
Student status recoded	Full-time	Count	18	9	27
		Expected Count	13.5	13.5	27.0
		% within gender	72.0%	36.0%	100.0%
	Part-time	Count	7	16	23
		Expected Count	11.5	11.5	23.0
		% within gender	28.0%	64.0%	100.0%
Total		Count	25	25	50
		Expected Count	25.0	25.0	50.0
		% within student status recoded	50.0%	50.0%	100.0%

Chi-square tests **(key items highlighted)**

	Value	**df**	**Asymp. Sig. (2-sided)**	**Exact Sig. (2-sided)**	**Exact Sig. (1-sided)**
Pearson chi-square	**6.522(b)**	**1**	**.011**		
Continuity Correction(a)	5.153	1	.023		
Likelihood Ratio	6.676	1	.010		
Fisher's Exact Test				.022	.011
Linear-by-Linear Association	6.391	1	.011		
N of Valid Cases	50				

a Computed only for a 2×2 table
b **0 cells (.0%) have expected count less than 5. The minimum expected count is 11.50**

added, it will be found that the positives cancel out the negatives, giving zero. chi-square is therefore based on the sum of the *squared* values of the differences. For readers who are mathematically inclined, the formula for chi-square is shown in Appendix 12.2. Fortunately the *SPSS* package calculates the value of chi-square, so it is not necessary to know the details of the formula. It is sufficient to understand that chi-square is a statistical measure of the difference between the observed and expected counts in the table.

In the example in Figure 12.4, the value of chi-square is 6.522. We are using the 'Pearson' value, devised by the statistician Pearson – the other values (Likelihood Ratio, Fisher's Exact Test and Linear-by-Linear Association) do not concern us here.

Option 1	Option 2	Option3
Null hypothesis (H₀): there is *no* relationship between full-time/ part-time status and gender in the population of students.	Male and female full-time/ part-time status in the population of students is the same	Observed and expected values are not significantly different
Alternative hypothesis (H₁) there *is* a relationship between full-time/ part-time status and gender in the population of students.	Male and female full-time/ part-time status in the population of students is different	Observed and expected values are significantly different

Figure 12.5   Alternative expressions of hypotheses

How should this value of chi-square be interpreted? We have noted that the greater the difference between the observed and expected values the greater the value of chi-square. Our null hypothesis is that there is *no* difference between the two sets of values. But clearly, we would accept some *minor* differences between two sets of values and still accept the null hypothesis. But just how big would the differences have to be before we would reject the null hypothesis and conclude that there *is* a difference between male and female full-time/part-time status?

For a given size of table (in this case two cells by two) statisticians have been able to calculate the likelihood of obtaining various values of chi-square when the null hypothesis is true. As with the normal distribution discussed above and in Chapter 11, this is based on the theoretical possibility of drawing lots of samples of the same size. This is shown in Figure 12.6. It shows that, for a particular table size, if the null hypothesis is true (population counts and expected counts are the same), some differences in observed and expected counts can be expected from most samples drawn from a

Figure 12.6
Distribution of chi-square assuming null hypothesis is true

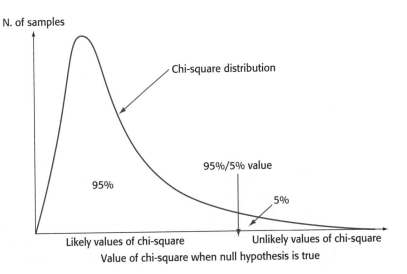

given population, so a *range of values* of chi-square can be expected. Most values of chi-square would be expected to be fairly small; some larger values would occur, but only rarely – they are unlikely.

As with the normal curve, it is customary to adopt either a 5 per cent or a 1 per cent cut-off to decide what is considered to be 'unlikely'. In the ensuing discussions 5 per cent is used. Therefore, if any value of chi-square is in the range to the right of the 5 per cent point in the diagram it is considered unlikely and *inconsistent* with the null hypothesis: we *reject* the null hypothesis. If it is in the range to the left of the 5 per cent point we *accept* the null hypothesis.

In Figure 12.4, the *SPSS* output tells us the value of chi-square for the table: 6.522. It also indicates the likelihood of this value: 0.011, or 1.1 per cent. Our value of chi-square is therefore an unlikely one (it has a likelihood less than 5 per cent), so we reject the null hypothesis and conclude that there *is* a significant difference between the male and female full-time/part-time status.

Degrees of freedom

The values of chi-square depend on the table size, which is indirectly measured by the *degrees of freedom*. Degrees of freedom are calculated by: *the number of rows minus one* multiplied by *the number of columns minus one*. So, for the table in Figure 12.4, the degrees of freedom are: $(2 - 1) \times (2 - 1) = 1 \times 1 = 1$. This is shown in the *SPSS* output under *df*.

Expected counts rule

One rule for the application of chi-square is that there should not be more than one-fifth of the cells of the table with expected counts of less than five, and none with an expected count of less than one. The *SPSS* output indicates whether such cells exist. The note at the bottom of the table indicates that no cells have an expected count of less than five and the minimum expected count is 11.5, so there is no problem. Grouping of some of the values by recoding can be used to reduce the number of cells and thus increase the expected frequencies. In fact this was done in the example with the recoded variable – if the analysis is run with unrecoded *status* variable the test infringes the expected counts rule and is invalid.

Reporting

How should the results of statistical tests such as chi-square be reported? Four solutions can be considered, as follows.

1. Include the results of the test in the table in the research report, as in Figure 12.7. The commentary might then merely say: 'The relationship between full-time/part-time status and gender was significant at the 5 per cent level.'

2. Include the test results in the text, for example: 'The relationship between full-time/part-time status and gender was significant at the 5 per cent level ($\chi^2 = 6.5$, 1 DF).'

Figure 12.7
Presentation of
chi-square test
results

Table x: Full-time/part-time status by gender

Status	Male	Female	Total
		%	
Full-time student	72.0	36.0	54.0
Part-time student	28.0	64.0	46.0
Total	100.0	100.0	100.0
Sample size:	25	25	50

$\chi^2 = 6.52$, DF 1, significant at the 5% level

3. Make the statistics less intrusive by including a note in the report or paper indicating that all tests were conducted at the 5 per cent level and that test values are included in the tables, or are listed in an appendix, or even excluded altogether for non-technical audiences.

4. Use the * and ** approach to indicate significant and highly significant results in tables, as discussed above.

Comparing two means: the t-test

Introduction

So far we have dealt only with proportions or percentages, either singly or in cross-tabulations; but many research results are in the form of averages – for example the average age of a group of participants in an activity, the average holiday expenditure of visitors from different countries, or the average score of a group on a Likert scale. In statistical parlance an average is referred to as a *mean*. Means can only be calculated for *ordinal* and *scale* variables, not nominal variables.

The simplest form of analysis is to compare two means to see whether they are significantly different. For example, we might want to test whether the average age of golf players in a sample is significantly different from that of the tennis players, or whether the average amount spent on holidays by a group of people is greater or less than the amount spent on the arts and entertainment. In this situation the null hypothesis is expressed as follows:

H_0 – Null hypothesis: there is *no* difference between the means
H_1 – Alternative hypothesis: there *is* a difference between the means.

For this situation, rather than chi-square, a statistic referred to as 't' is calculated – but the interpretation is similar. This is based on a formula involving the sample size and the two means to be compared (see Appendix 12.2). If there is *no difference* between two means in the population (H_0) then, for a given sample size, t has a known 'distribution' of likely values (see Figure 12.8): high values are rare, so if the value from a sample is high – in the top 5 per cent of values for that sample size – then we reject H_0 and accept H_1; that is, we conclude that there *is* a significant difference at the 5 per cent level of

Figure 12.8
Chi-square and
t distributions

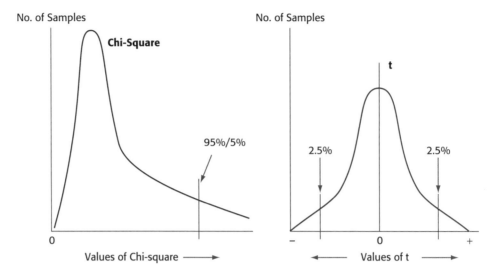

probability respectively. Note that, because 't' can take on negative or positive values there are two 'tails' to its distribution – hence the reference to 'two-tailed test' in some of the *SPSS* output discussed below.

There are two situations where we might want to compare means:

A. To compare the means of two variables which apply to the whole sample – for example comparing the average amount spent on holidays with the average amount spent on the arts and entertainment (for everybody in the sample). This is known as a *paired samples test.*

B. To compare the means of one variable for two sub-groups – for example comparing the average age of men in the sample with that of women. The sample is divided into two sub-groups, men and women; this is known as a *group* or *independent samples* test.

A. Paired samples test

Figure 12.9 presents two examples of the paired samples test. The *SPSS* output provides a range of statistics with which we are not concerned here – including a correlation, which is discussed later in this chapter. The items we are interested in are depicted in bold in Figure 12.9.

Example 1 compares the frequency of playing sport/fitness with the frequency of visiting national parks. The people in the sample play sport/fitness on average 12.2 times in three months and visit national parks on average 9.8 times, a difference of 2.4 – the question is: is this difference significant? The value of t is 1.245 and its (2-tail) significance is 0.219 or 21.9 per cent. The result is consistent with the null hypothesis (0.219 is much higher than 0.05), so we accept the null hypothesis, that the

SPSS Procedures

1. Select *Analyze*, then *Compare Means*
2. Select *Paired Samples T-Test*
3. Highlight the two variables to be compared in the *Current Selections* box, then transfer to the *Paired variables* box.
4. Select *OK* to obtain t-test output.

Output

Example 1: Playing sport vs Visiting national parks

Paired Samples Statistics

		Mean	N	Std. Deviation	Std. Error Mean
Pair 1	**Play sport/fitness**	**12.20**	50	13.095	1.852
	Visit national park	**9.80**	50	8.804	1.245

Paired Samples Correlations (IGNORE)

		N	Correlation	Sig.
Pair 1	Play sport/fitness & Visit national park	50	.274	.054

Paired Samples Test

		Paired Differences					t	df	Sig. (2-tailed)
		Mean	Std. Deviation	Std. Error Mean	95% Confidence Interval of the Difference				
					Lower	Upper			
Pair 1	**Play sport/fitness – Visit national park**	**2.400**	13.632	1.928	−1.474	6.274	**1.245**	49	**.219**

Example 2: Visit national parks vs Going out for a meal

Paired Samples Statistics

		Mean	N	Std. Deviation	Std. Error Mean
Pair 1	**Visit national park**	**9.80**	50	8.804	1.245
	Go out for meal	**6.54**	50	3.157	.446

Paired Samples Correlations – IGNORE

		N	Correlation	Sig.
Pair 1	Visit national park & Go out for meal	50	−.044	.759

Paired Samples Test

		Paired Differences					t	df	Sig. (2-tailed)
		Mean	Std. Deviation	Std. Error Mean	95% Confidence Interval of the Difference				
					Lower	Upper			
Pair 1	**Visit national park Go out for meal**	**3.260**	9.484	1.341	.565	5.955	**2.431**	49	**.019**

Figure 12.9   Comparing means: t-test: paired samples – *SPSS* procedures

Procedures

1. Select *Analyze* and then *Compare Means*
2. Select *Independent Samples T-Test*
3. Select the variable for which the mean is required (*spend*) and transfer to *Test variables* box
4. Select variable to be used to divide the sample into two groups (*gender*) and transfer to *Grouping variable* box
5. Select *Define groups* and enter the values used to divide the sample into two groups (in the example: 1 for Male and 2 for Female). Select *OK* and the two values appear in brackets following the name of the grouping variable (*gender* [1,2]).
6. Select *OK* to obtain t-test.

Output

Group statistics

	Gender	N	Mean	Std. Deviation	Std. Error Mean
Course costs, £ p.a.	**Male**	25	**110.00**	77.607	15.521
	Female	25	**138.60**	84.613	16.923

Independent samples test

	Levene's Test for Equality of Variances		t-test for Equality of Means						
	F	Sig.	t	df	Sig. (2-tailed)	Mean Difference	Std. Error Difference	95% Confidence Interval of the Difference	
								Lower	Upper
Equal variances assumed	.431	.514	−1.245	48	.219	−28.600	22.963	−74.770	17.570
Equal variances not assumed			−1.245	47.646	.219	−28.600	22.963	−74.779	17.579

Figure 12.10   Comparing means: t-test: independent samples – *SPSS* procedures

difference between the level of sport playing and the level of visits to national parks is *not* significant.

   Example 2 compares the frequency of visiting national parks and going out for a meal. In this case the difference is 3.26, the value of t is 2.431 and its significance level is 0.019, which is below 0.05, so we reject the null hypothesis and conclude that there *is* a significant difference between the frequency of visiting national parks and going out for meals.

B. Independent samples test

Figure 12.10 compares levels of expenditure on entertainment by male and female students. For males expenditure is £110 and for females it is £138.60, a difference of £28.60. In this case t has a value of −1.25 and a significance level of 0.219. Since 0.219 is above 0.05, this is consistent with the null hypothesis, so we accept that there is no significant difference between the two expenditure figures.

Procedures

To obtain a table showing the means to be compared:
1. Select *Analyze* and then *Compare Means*
2. Select *Means*
3. Select the variables for which the mean is required (*sportfit, theatre, npark, meal, hols*) and transfer to the *Dependent list* box.
4. Select variable for grouping (*status*) and transfer to the *Independent list* box
5. In *Options* ensure that *Mean* and *Number of cases* are in the *Cell statistics* box.
6. Select *OK* to produce the output.

Output

Student status		Play sport/ fitness	Visit theatre	Visit national park	Go out for meal	Holiday expenditure
F/T student/no paid work	Mean	9.69	2.62	9.77	6.46	328.46
	N	13	13	13	13	13
F/T student/paid work	Mean	9.64	2.93	8.64	4.00	342.50
	N	14	14	14	14	14
P/T student – F/T job	Mean	19.06	2.25	8.63	8.19	425.63
	N	16	16	16	16	16
P/T student/Other	Mean	6.29	3.29	14.86	8.00	752.86
	N	7	7	7	7	7
Total	Mean	12.20	2.68	9.80	6.54	422.90
	N	50	50	50	50	50

Figure 12.11 Comparing ranges of means – *SPSS* procedures

A number of means: one-way analysis of variance (ANOVA)

Introduction

The t-test was used to examine differences between means two at a time. *Analysis of variance* (ANOVA) is used to examine *more than two* means at a time. This begins to resemble the cross-tabulation process, but with *means* appearing in the cells of the table instead of counts, as shown in the examples in Figure 12.11, which compares mean leisure participation levels and holiday expenditure for the various student status groups. Here the question which we seek to answer with ANOVA is whether, for each activity/expenditure item, the means for the different groups of students are different from the overall mean – that is, whether participation/expenditure is related to student status.

Null hypothesis

The null hypothesis is therefore: that all the means are equal to the overall mean. How different must the group means be from the overall mean before we reject this hypothesis?

Figure 12.12
Comparing
means and
variances

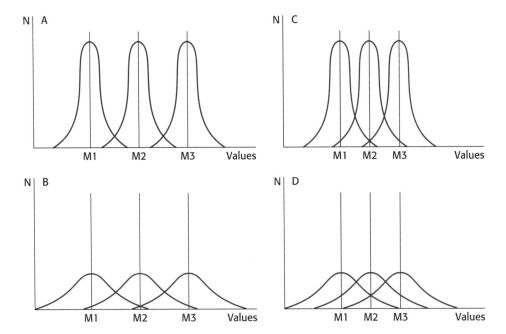

Variance

Whether or not the means are in effect from *one* population (with *one* mean) or from *different* sub-populations (with *different* means) depends not only on the differences between the means but also on their 'spread', or *variance*. Figure 12.12 shows four examples of three means, with the associated 'spread' of cases around them. In example A, the means are well spaced and there is very little overlap in the cases, but in example C the means are closer together and there is considerable overlap suggesting that they may be from the same population. In example B the means are spaced as in A, but the spread around the means is greater and so overlap is considerable. Example D presents the worst case of overlap. So we might expect to find that for example A there *is* a significant difference between the means, while for example D there is not. Examples B and C raise doubts because of the overlaps. (Note that a visual presentation of this type of information, although in a different format, can be obtained using the *Boxplot* feature within the *Graphics* procedure of SPSS).

The 'spread' of sample values is referred to as the *variance* and can be measured by adding up the differences between the scores of individual observations/cases and the mean score. The formula for calculating variance is shown in Appendix 12.2.

Analysis of variance

Whether or not the means are significantly different from the overall means depends on:

1. the spread of the separate sub-group means around the overall mean – the *between groups* variance; and

2. the spread of sub-group observations around the means of the sub-groups – the *within groups* variance.

The greater the *between groups* variance the *greater* the likelihood of significant difference. The greater the *within groups* variance the *less* the likelihood of significant difference. Analysis of variance is based on the ratio of these two measures, which produces a statistic referred to as 'F'. As with the other statistics examined, values of F for a given number of degrees of freedom (based on sample sizes and number of groups) have a known probability distribution in the null hypothesis situation. High values are unlikely and result in the rejection of the null hypothesis.

SPSS procedures for analysis of variance

SPSS procedures and examples of output are shown in Figure 12.13. For 'between groups' and 'within groups' the output shows: the degrees of freedom (DF); the 'mean squares' (variance); the value of F; and the F probability/significance.

In Figure 12.13, it can be seen that the significance for the first three activities is above 0.05, so the null hypothesis is accepted and it is included that participation in

Figure 12.13 One-way analysis of variance – *SPSS* procedures

Procedures

1. Select *Analyze* and then *Compare Means*
2. Select *One-way ANOVA*
3. Select variables for which means are required (*sportfit, theatre, npark, meal, hols*) and put in the *Dependent list* box
4. Select variable for grouping (*status*) and put in the *Independent list* box
5. Select *OK* to produce the output.

Output

ANOVA

		Sum of Squares	df	Mean Square	F	Sig.
Play sport/fitness	Between Groups	1,171.650	3	390.550	2.485	.072
	Within Groups	7,230.350	46	157.182		
	Total	8,402.000	49			
Visit theatre	Between Groups	6.446	3	2.149	.411	.746
	Within Groups	240.434	46	5.227		
	Total	246.880	49			
Visit national park	Between Groups	219.871	3	73.290	.942	.428
	Within Groups	3,578.129	46	77.785		
	Total	3,798.000	49			
Go out for meal	Between Groups	148.752	3	49.584	6.715	.001
	Within Groups	339.668	46	7.384		
	Total	488.420	49			
Holiday expenditure	Between Groups	968,661.162	3	322,887.054	6.644	.001
	Within Groups	2,235,593.338	46	48,599.855		
	Total	3,204,254.500	49			

these activities is not related to student status. For the last two, going out for a meal and holiday expenditure, the significance is below 0.05 for the null hypothesis is rejected and we conclude that there is a relationship between these activities and student status.

A table of means: factorial analysis of variance (ANOVA)

Introduction

As with one-way analysis of variance, factorial analysis of variance deals with *means*. But while one-way analysis of variance deals with means of groups determined on the basis of *one* variable, factorial analysis of variance is designed for sets of means grouped by more than one classifying variable, or 'factor'. An example is shown in Figure 12.14, examining frequency of theatre going by status and gender. It can be seen that, while there is little difference in frequency of attendance by status, with the lowest mean frequency 2.62 and the highest 3.29, or between male and female students (2.24 and 3.12 respectively), when the two variables are put together, considerable differences emerge, with the lowest mean frequency at 1.40 and the highest at 5.40. Analysis of variance examines this 'cross-tabulation of means' and determines whether the differences revealed are significant. As with the one-way analysis of variance, the procedure examines the differences between group means and the spread of values within groups.

Null hypothesis

The null hypothesis is that there is no interaction between the variables – that the level of theatre going of the students in the various courses is not affected by gender. A table of 'expected counts' consistent with the null hypothesis could be produced as for the chi-square example, but the values would be means rather than numbers of cases.

SPSS factorial analysis of variance

Figure 12.15 shows the results of a factorial analysis of variance on the above data. The underlined F probabilities indicate:

- relationship between theatre-going and status alone: not significant: Sig. = 0.250;
- relationship between theatre-going and gender: not significant: Sig. = 0.242;
- relationship between theatre-going and course and gender together: significant at the 5 per cent level: Sig. = 0.019.

The F probability for the analysis involving the two independent variables is less than 0.05; the null hypothesis is therefore rejected and it is concluded that the interaction between gender and status with regard to theatre going is significant at the 5 per cent level.

Figure 12.14
A table of
means – SPSS
procedures

Procedures

1. Select *Analyze* then *Compare Means*
2. Select the *Dependent* variable (*theatre*)
3. Select *Independent* variable (*status*)
4. Click on *Next* to get *Layer 2 of 2*, then enter the second independent variable (*gender*)
5. Select *OK* to obtain the output.

Output

Visit theatre

Student status	Gender	Mean	N	Std. Deviation
F/T student/no paid work	Male	3.11	9	1.833
	Female	1.50	4	2.380
	Total	2.62	13	2.063
F/T student/paid work	Male	1.56	9	1.130
	Female	5.40	5	2.191
	Total	2.93	14	2.433
P/T student – F/T job	Male	1.40	5	2.074
	Female	2.64	11	2.730
	Total	2.25	16	2.543
P/T student/Other	Male	3.50	2	2.121
	Female	3.20	5	1.643
	Total	3.29	7	1.604
Total	Male	2.24	25	1.786
	Female	3.12	25	2.587
	Total	2.68	50	2.245

How the above might be presented in a report

Table: Frequency of visiting theatre, by status and gender

	Mean number of visits in three months		
Course	Male	Female	Total
F/T student/no paid work	3.1	1.5	2.6
F/T student/paid work	1.6	5.4	2.9
P/T student – F/T job	1.4	2.6	2.3
P/T student/Other	3.5	3.2	3.3
Total	2.2	3.1	2.7

Correlation

Introduction

Correlation can be used to examine the relationships between two or more *ordinal or scale* variables. If two phenomena are related in a systematic way they are said to be *correlated*. They can be:

Figure 12.15
Factorial analysis
of variance –
SPSS procedures

Relating to data in Figure 12.14.

Procedures

1. Select *Analysis* then *General Linear Model*
2. Select *Univariate*
3. Select the *Dependent* variable – the one for which the means are to be calculated (*theatre*)
4. Select the *Fixed Factors* – the two variables affecting the dependent variable (*status* and *gender*)
5. Select *OK* to obtain the output.

Output

Tests of Between-Subjects Effects
Dependent Variable: Visit theatre (**key items in bold**)

Source	Type III Sum of Squares	df	Mean Square	F	Sig.
Corrected Model	66.523(a)	7	9.503	2.213	.052
Intercept	299.090	1	299.090	69.650	.000
status	18.308	3	6.103	**1.421**	**.250**
gender	6.041	1	6.041	**1.407**	**.242**
status * gender	47.424	3	15.808	**3.681**	**.019**
Error	180.357	42	4.294		
Total	606.000	50			
Corrected Total	246.880	49			

a R Squared = .269 (Adjusted R Squared = .148)

- *positively* correlated (as one variable increases so does the other),
- *negatively* correlated (as one variable increases the other decreases); or
- *un-correlated* (there is no relationship between the variables).

It is often helpful to think of correlation in visual terms. Relationships between income and the four variables are shown in Figure 12.16, illustrating a variety of types of correlation. The graphics were produced using the *SPSS* graphics *Scatterplot* procedure discussed in Chapter 11. Each dot represents one person (or 'case' or 'observation'). The correlation coefficients, r, are explained below.

Correlation coefficient (r)

Correlation can be measured by means of the *correlation coefficient*, usually represented by the letter r. The coefficient is:

- zero if there is no relationship between two variables;
- +1.0 if there is perfect positive correlation between two variables;
- −1.0 if there is perfect negative correlation between two variables;
- between 0 and +1.0 if there is *some* positive correlation;
- between 0 and −1.0 if there is *some* negative correlation.

Figure 12.16
Relationships
between
variables

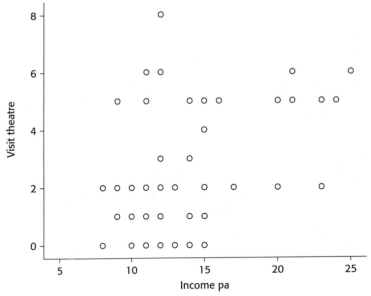

a. Theatre-going increases with income – a weak positive correlation (r = 0.46)

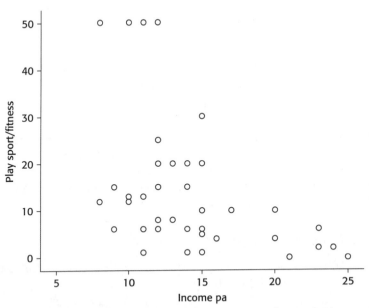

b. Sport/fitness participation declines with income – a moderate negative correlation (r = −0.44)

Figure 12.16
(*continued*)

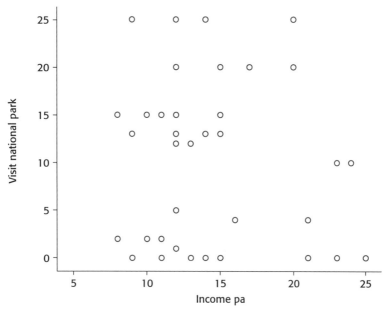

c. No apparent relationship between national park visiting and income – almost zero correlation (r = 0.024)

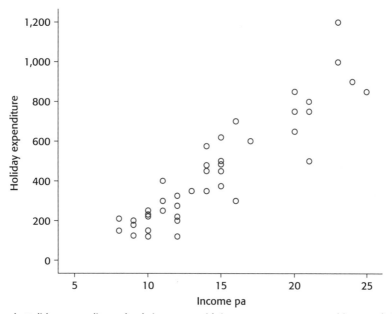

d. Holiday expenditure clearly increases with income – very strong positive correlation r = 0.91)

Figure 12.17
Correlation

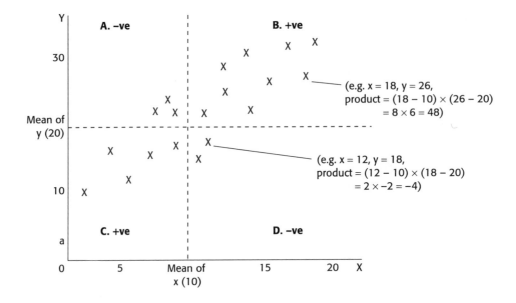

The closer the coefficient is to 1.0, the greater the correlation – for example, 0.9 is a *high positive* correlation, 0.2 is a *low positive* correlation and –0.8 is a *high negative* correlation.

The correlation coefficient is calculated by measuring how far each data point is from the mean of each variable and multiplying the two differences. In Figure 12.17 it can be seen that the result will be a positive number for data points in the top right hand and bottom left hand quadrants (B and C) and negative for data points in the other two quadrants (A and D). The calculations are shown for two of the data points by way of illustration. If most of the data points are in quadrants B and C a positive correlation will result, while if most of the data points are in A and D a negative correlation will result. If the data points are widely scattered in all four quadrants, then the negatives cancel out the positives, resulting in a low value for the correlation. This explains in very broad terms the basis of the positive and negative correlations, and high and low correlations. It is beyond the scope of this book to explain how the 'perfect' correlation is made to equal one, but, for those with the requisite mathematics, this can be deduced from the formula for r, which is given in Appendix 12.2.

Significance of r

The *significance* of a correlation coefficient depends on its size, as discussed above, and also the sample size, and is assessed by means of a t-test (see formula in Appendix 12.2).

Null hypothesis

The null hypothesis is that the correlation is zero. The t-test therefore indicates only whether the correlation coefficient is *significantly different from zero*. Quite low coefficients can therefore emerge as 'significant' if the sample is large enough.

Procedures

1. Select *Analyze*
2. Select *Correlate*
3. Select *Bivariate*
4. Select variables to be included (*inc, sportfit, theatre, npark, meal, hols*)
5. Select *OK* to produce output.

Output

Correlations

		Income pa	Play sport	Visit theatre	Visit national park	Go out for meal	Holiday expenditure
Income pa	Pearson Correlation	1.000	−.439**	.460**	.024	.076	.915**
	Sig. (2-tailed)	.	.001	.001	.866	.598	.000
	N	50	50	50	50	50	50
Play sport	Pearson Correlation	−.439**	1.000	−.679**	.274	.454**	−.368**
	Sig. (2-tailed)	.001	.	.000	.054	.001	.008
	N	50	50	50	50	50	50
Visit theatre	Pearson Correlation	.460**	−.679**	1.000	−.292*	−.286*	.379**
	Sig. (2-tailed)	.001	.000	.	.039	.044	.007
	N	50	50	50	50	50	50
Visit national park	Pearson Correlation	.024	.274	−.292*	1.000	−.044	.058
	Sig. (2-tailed)	.866	.054	.039	.	.759	.688
	N	50	50	50	50	50	50
Go out for meal	Pearson Correlation	.076	.454**	−.286*	−.044	1.000	.119
	Sig. (2-tailed)	.598	.001	.044	.759	.	.410
	N	50	50	50	50	50	50
Holiday expenditure	Pearson Correlation	.915**	−.368**	.379	.058	.119	1.000
	Sig. (2-tailed)	.000	.008	.007	.688	.410	.
	N	50	50	50	50	50	50

** Correlation is significant at the 0.01 level (2-tailed)
* Correlation is significant at the 0.05 level (2-tailed)

Figure 12.18 Correlation matrix – *SPSS* procedures

SPSS and correlation

SPSS can be used to produce correlation coefficients between pairs of variables, as shown in Figure 12.18. The output is in the form of a symmetrical matrix, so that, for example, the correlation between sport and income is the same as between income and sport. For each pair of variables, the output includes the correlation coefficient, the sample size (the number in brackets) and P, the probability related to the t-test. The starring system discussed above is used to indicate significance at the 5 per cent and 1 per cent levels. As with other tests, if the probability is below the 0.05 or 0.01 levels we reject the null hypothesis and conclude that the correlation is significantly different from zero, at 5 per cent or 1 per cent respectively.

Linear regression

Introduction

Linear regression takes us one step further in this type of quantitative analysis – in the direction of 'prediction'. If the correlation between two variables is consistent enough, one variable can be used to 'predict' the other. In particular, easily measured variables (such as age or income) can be used to predict variables which are more difficult or costly to measure (such as participation in leisure or tourism activities). Examples of how knowledge of the relationship between variables might be used for prediction purposes are as follows; they suggest more sophisticated approaches to the analysis of Case-studies 6.1 and 6.2.

- Knowledge of the relationship between age and leisure participation can be used in planning leisure facilities for a community: the future age-structure of the community can be relatively easily estimated and with this information demand for leisure activities can be estimated.
- Relationships between income per head and amount of overseas air travel per head in different countries or over various time-periods can be used to predict growth of air travel as incomes rise.

The procedures described here are just another format in which the relationships between variables of interest can be examined. If the variables can be quantified, then the techniques also enable the strength and nature of the relationship to be quantified.

Regression model

To predict one variable on the basis of another a *model* or equation is needed of the type:

Example 1: Leisure participation = *some number* times AGE
Example 2: Demand for overseas travel = *some number* times INCOME

Suppose leisure participation is measured in terms of the number of visits or days participation for some activity over the course of a year, and demand for travel is measured by the number of overseas trips in a year. Regression analysis produces an equation of the form:

Example 1: Days participation = a + b times AGE
Example 2: Trips = a + b times INCOME

The *coefficients* or *parameters*, a and b, are determined from examination of existing data, using regression analysis. The process of finding out the values of the parameters or coefficients is referred to as *calibration* of the model.

In general terms this is represented by the equation: $y = a + bx$, where y stands for participation or travel demand and x stands for age or income. Note that here

Figure 12.19
Regression line

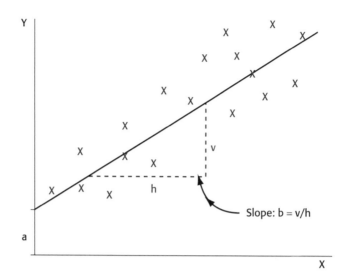

Participation and *Travel demand* are the *dependent* variables and AGE and INCOME are the *independent* variables.

In visual terms this describes a 'regression line' fitted through the data, with 'intercept' or 'constant' of *a* and 'slope' of *b*, as shown in Figure 12.19. The regression procedure finds the 'line of best fit' by finding the line which minimises the sum of the (squared) differences between it and the data points, and specifies this line by giving values for a and b.

SPSS and regression

Examples of regression output from *SPSS* are shown in Figure 12.20. The *SPSS* program produces a large amount of output with which we are not concerned here – only the items in bold are discussed. However, the output illustrates the point that regression is an involved process and only the broad outlines are dealt with in this book. The output relates to *multiple* regression, which involves more than one independent variable, as discussed in the next section – but here we have only one independent variable, income.

The items we are interested in are the value of the regression coefficient, R (similar to the correlation coefficient, r), the value of R^2, which is an indicator of how well the data fit the regression line, its test of significance, and the coefficients listed under B. For Example 1 in Figure 12.20, the relationship between income and holiday expenditure, the value of R is 0.915, R^2 is 0.836, and the probability (as measured by an F test) is 0.000 which makes it highly significant. The *constant* (a) is –323.493 and the *coefficient* of *slope* (b) for income is 52.563. The regression equation is therefore:

Holiday expenditure (£ pa) = –323.493 + 52.563 × income (in £'000s pa)

This regression line can be plotted onto a graph, as shown in Figure 12.21, using the *SPSS Curve estimation* procedure. With this equation, if we knew a student's income we

Figure 12.20
Regression
analysis – *SPSS*
procedures

Procedures

1. Select *Analyze* then *Regression*
2. Select *Linear*
3. Select *dependent* and *independent* variables
4. Select *OK* to produce the output.

Output (key items in bold)

Example 1: Income (independent) by holiday expenditure (dependent)

Model summary

Model	R	R Square	Adjusted R Square	Std. Error of the Estimate
1	.915	.836	.833	104.51

a Predictors: (Constant), Income pa

ANOVA

Model		Sum of Squares	df	Mean Square	F	Sig.
1	Regression	2,679,971.336	1	2,679,971.336	245.361	.000
	Residual	524,283.164	48	10922.566		
	Total	3,204,254.500	49			

a Predictors: (Constant), Income pa   b Dependent Variable: Holiday expenditure

Coefficients

		Unstandardised Coefficients		Standardised Coeffs	t	Sig.
Model		B	Std. Error	Beta		
1	(Constant)	−323.493	49.890		−6.484	.000
	Income pa	52.563	3.356	.915	15.664	.000

a Dependent Variable: Holiday expenditure

Example 2: Income (independent) by theatre-going (dependent)

Model Summary

Model	R	R Square	Adjusted R Square	Std. Error of the Estimate
1	.460	.212	.195	2.01

a Predictors: (Constant), Income pa

ANOVA

Model		Sum of Squares	df	Mean Square	F	Sig.
1	Regression	52.284	1	52.284	12.896	.001
	Residual	194.596	48	4.054		
	Total	246.880	49			

a Predictors: (Constant), Income pa   b Dependent Variable: Visit theatre

Coefficients

		Unstandardised Coefficients		Standardised Coefficients	t	Sig.
Model		B	Std. Error	Beta		
1	(Constant)	−.617	.961		−.642	.524
	Income pa	.232	.065	.460	3.591	.001

a Dependent Variable: Visit theatre

Figure 12.21
Regression
line – curve fit –
SPSS procedure

Procedure

1. Select *Analyze* then *Regression* then *Curve Estimation*
2. Select *dependent* and *independent* variables (*hols* and *inc*)
3. Select *OK* to produce output.

Output

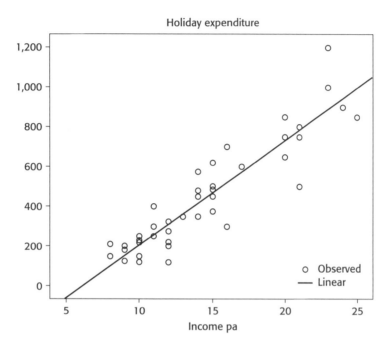

Holiday expenditure

could estimate their level of holiday expenditure, either by reading it off the graph or calculating it. For example, for a student with an income of £10,000 a year:

Holiday expenditure $= -323.49 + 52.56 \times 10 = -323.49 + 525.60 = £202.11$

So we would estimate that such a student would spend £202 on holidays in a year. Of course we are not saying that *every* student with that income will spend this sum: the regression line/equation is a sort of average; it is not precise.

Example 2 in Figure 12.20 produces similar output for the relationship between theatre-going and income. In this case the resultant regression equation would be:

Theatre-going (times in 3 months) $= -0.62 + 0.23 \times$ income

Non-linear regression

In Figure 12.22 the relationship between the two variables, is *non-linear* – that is, the relationship indicated is curved, rather than being a straight line. The *SPSS Curve fit* procedure offers a number of *models* which may produce lines/curves which fit the data better than a simple straight line. Theory or trial and error may lead to a suitable

Figure 12.22

Regression – curve fit – non-linear – *SPSS* procedures

Procedure

1. Select *Analyze* then *Regression* then *Curve Fit*
2. Select *dependent* and *independent* variables (*hols* and *inc*)
3. Under *Models* select *Cubic*
4. Select *OK* to produce output.

Output

Independent: inc

Dependent	Mth	Rsq	d.f.	F	Sigf	b0	b1	b2	b3
hols	CUB	.843	46	82.43	.000	494.351	−113.10	10.5471	−.2118

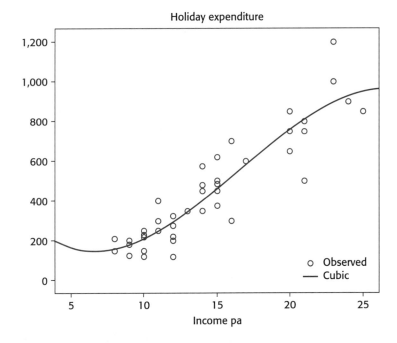

model. In Figure 12.22 a 'cubic' model is presented, in which the independent variable is raised to the power of three – this results in the curved line indicated and a small increase in the value of R^2 to 0.843.

The standard regression procedure seeks to fit a straight line to these data, which is not necessarily an accurate reflection of the relationship. This emphasises the importance of examining the data *visually*, as done here, and not relying just on correlation coefficients. Where theory or observation of the data suggests that the relationship would be better represented by a *curved* line, *non-linear* methods may be used. Non-linear regression analyses are available in *SPSS* and involve applying logarithms or other formulae to the data, but exploration of these techniques in detail is beyond the scope of this book.

Multiple regression

Multiple regression is linear regression involving more than one independent variable. For example, we might hypothesise that sports participation is dependent not just on income but also on age, or that overseas travel is dependent not just on income but also on the price of airfares. Thus our models, or regression equations, would be:

Example 1: Sports participation = a + b × income + c × age
Example 2: Travel = a + b × income + c × fares

In *linear* regression, as discussed above, the procedure fits a straight line to the data – the line of *best fit*. In *multiple* regression the procedure fits a *surface* to the data – the surface of best fit. It is possible to visualise this in three dimensions (one dependent and two independent variables), with the axes forming a three-dimensional box, the observations suspended in space and the regression surface being a flat plane somewhere within the box (*SPSS* offers a 3-D graphical option to represent this in the *scatterplot* procedure). When additional variables are included then four, five or 'n' dimensions are involved and it is not possible to visualise the process, but the mathematical principles used to establish the regression equation are the same.

An example, in which theatre-going is related to income and age, is shown in Figure 12.23. It will be noticed that the value of R has risen from 0.46 in the single variable case (Figure 12.20, Example 2) to 0.5799, indicating an improvement in the 'fit' of the data to the model. The model equation is now:

Theatre-going (per 3 months) = −0.3.49 + 0.056 × income + 0.0227 × age

It is possible, in theory, to continue to add variables to the equation. This should, however, be done with caution, since it frequently involves *multi-collinearity*, where the independent variables are themselves inter-correlated. The 'independent' variables should be, as far as possible, just that: independent. Various tests exist to test for this phenomenon. Often, in leisure and tourism, a large number of variables is involved, many inter-correlated, but each contributing something to the leisure or tourist phenomenon under investigation. Multi-variate analysis procedures, such as cluster and factor analysis, discussed below, are designed partly to overcome the problems associated with handling large numbers of variables.

Cluster and factor analysis

Introduction

Cluster and factor analysis are techniques which are available in *SPSS* and are used when the number of independent variables is large and there is a desire to group them in some way. The theoretical counterpart to this is that there are some complex phenomena which cannot be measured by one or two variables, but require a 'battery' of variables, each contributing some aspect to the make-up of the phenomenon. Examples are:

■ a person's 'lifestyle' or 'psychographic' group (made up of variables such as leisure and work patterns, income and expenditure patterns, values, age and family situation);

Figure 12.23
Multiple
regression –
SPSS procedures

Procedures

1. Select *Analyze* then *Regression* then *Linear*
2. Select *dependent* variable (*theatre*) and (more than 1) *independent* variables (*age, income*)
3. Select *Enter* for all the selected variables to be included immediately, or *Stepwise* for the program to select and include variables in order of influence
4. Select *OK* to produce the output.

Output (key items in bold)

Variables Entered/Removed[b]

Model	Variables Entered	Variables Removed	Method
1	**Age, Income pa**[a]	.	Enter

a All requested variables entered   b Dependent Variable: Visit theatre

Model Summary

Model	R	R Square	Adjusted R Square	Std. Error of the Estimate
1	**.580**[a]	**.336**	.308	1.87

a Predictors: (Constant), Age, Income pa

ANOVA[b]

Model		Sum of Squares	df	Mean Square	F	Sig.
1	Regression	83.023	2	41.512	**11.907**	**.000**[a]
	Residual	163.857	47	3.486		
	Total	246.880	49			

a Predictors: (Constant), Age, Income pa   b Dependent Variable: Visit theatre

Coefficients[a]

Model		Unstandardised Coefficients		Standardised Coefficients	t	Sig.
		B	Std. Error	Beta		
1	(Constant)	**−3.493**	1.316		−2.654	.011
	Income pa	**.056**	.084	.111	.662	.511
	Age	**.227**	.076	.497	2.969	.005

a Dependent Variable: Visit theatre

■ a person's characteristics as a tourist – a 'tourist type' (made up of variables such as travel experience, expenditure patterns, products desired and satisfactions sought).

Each of these is often researched using a large number of data items – for example, lifestyles/psychographics have been measured by asking people as many as 300 questions about their attitudes to work, politics, morals, leisure, religion and so on.

Figure 12.24
Simple manual
factor analysis

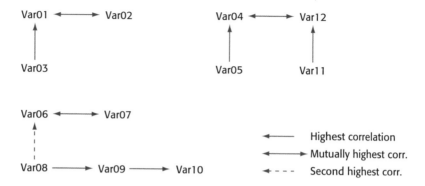

Factor analysis

Factor analysis is based on the idea that certain variables 'go together', in that people with a high score on one variable also tend to have a high score on certain others, which might then form a group – for example, people who go to the theatre might also visit galleries; people with strong pro-environment views might be found to favour certain types of holiday. Analysis of this type of phenomenon can be approached using a simple, manual technique involving a correlation matrix of the variables, as illustrated in Figure 12.24. Groupings of variables can be produced by indicating which variables have their highest correlations with each other. In Figure 12.24 three groupings of variables is shown, where the arrows indicate highest correlations.

This procedure only takes account of the highest correlation, with some use being made of the second highest, as indicated. But variables will have a range of lower order relationships with each other which this method cannot take account of. A number of lower order correlations may, cumulatively, be more significant than a single 'highest' correlation. Factor analysis is a mathematical procedure which groups the variables taking account of *all* the correlations. The details of the method are, however, beyond the scope of this book.

Cluster analysis

Cluster analysis is another 'grouping' procedure, but it focuses on the individuals directly rather than the variables. Imagine a situation with two variables, age and some behavioural variable, and data points plotted in the usual way, as shown in Figure 12.25. It can be seen that there are three broad 'clusters' of respondents – two young clusters and one older cluster. Each of these clusters might form, for example, particular market segments. With just two variables and a few observations it is relatively simple to identify clusters visually. But with more variables and more cases this would not be possible.

Cluster analysis involves giving the computer a set of rules for building clusters. It first calculates the 'distances' between data points, in terms of a range of specified variables. Those points which are closest together are put into a first round 'cluster' and a new 'point' halfway between the two is put in their place. The process is repeated to

Figure 12.25
Plots of 'clusters'

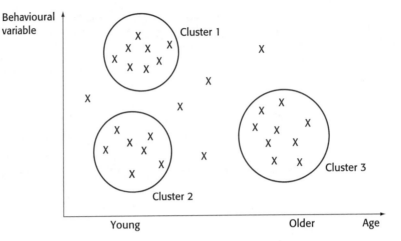

Figure 12.26
Dendrogram

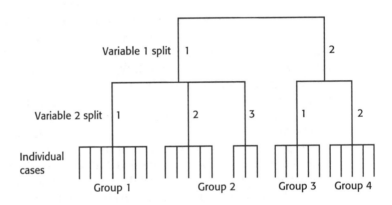

form a second round of clustering, and a third and fourth and so on, until there are only two 'points' left. The result is usually illustrated by a 'dendrogram', of the sort shown in Figure 12.26.

In conclusion

Much leisure and tourism research, even of a quantitative nature, is conducted without the use of the techniques covered in this chapter. This is a reflection of the descriptive nature of much of the research in the field, as discussed in Chapter 1, the nature of the data involved and the needs of the audience or client for the research. Often in leisure and tourism the need is for 'broad brush' research findings: accuracy is required but a high level of precision is not. Contrast this with medical research, where precision can be a matter of life or death. To some extent the level of use of statistical techniques is related to disciplinary traditions. Thus, for example, the use of statistical techniques in the American *Journal of Leisure Research* is quite common, as a result of the heavy involvement of psychologists in American leisure research, whereas in the British journal *Leisure Studies* statistical techniques are less often deployed, reflecting the British tradition of qualitative sociology. In the case of tourism journals statistical techniques such as regression and correlation tend to arise quite often because of the strong economic dimension of some tourism research.

Many leisure or tourism researchers could therefore find that they rarely make use of the techniques presented in this chapter, but they should be able to interpret research reports which do make use of them, and they should be able to utilise them if called upon.

As has been stressed throughout this book, data collection and analysis should be determined by a theoretical, conceptual or evaluative framework. At the analysis stage the researcher should, ideally, not be wondering what to relate to what, and choosing variables and analyses in an *ad hoc* manner. While a certain amount of inductive exploration and even serendipity is inevitable, ideally there should be a basic analysis plan from the beginning. Key variables and the question of relationships between them should have been thought about in advance, for example as a result of an early 'concept mapping' exercise. Thus, while the examples given in this chapter may appear *ad hoc* and 'data driven', in a real research project the procedures used should be driven by theory, research problems or hypotheses.

Summary

This chapter builds on Chapter 10, which introduces the idea of sampling and its effects, and on Chapter 11, which deals with the analysis of questionnaire survey data using the package *SPSS*. Here, the principles and processes involved in statistical analysis are introduced. The phenomenon of statistics, in this context, does not refer just to quantification, but to the processes required to generalise from findings from samples to the wider population. Statistical concepts are initially introduced, including: the idea of probabilistic statements; the normal distribution; significance; the null hypothesis; and dependent and independent variables. The chapter then outlines *SPSS* procedures and presents outputs for a number of statistical tests, as follows.

- Chi-square – for examining the relationship between variables in a frequency table;
- the t-test – for comparing the significance of the difference between two means;
- one-way analysis of variance (ANOVA) – for examining the relationship between two variables as expressed by a set of means;
- factorial analysis of variance (ANOVA) – for examining the relationship between one dependent variable and two independent variables based on means;
- correlation – the relationship between two scale variables;
- linear regression – which establishes the 'line of best fit' between two variables;
- multiple regression – which examines the relationship between one dependent variable and two or more independent variables;
- cluster and factor analysis – which deal with summarising the relationships among large numbers of variables.

Exercises

It is suggested that the reader replicate the various analyses set out in this chapter, first using the data in Appendix 12.1 and then using your own data set. This can be based on data which may have been collected for Chapter 11, but will involve adding a range of scale variables to the questionnaire, similar to those listed in Appendix 12.1.

Further reading

There are many excellent statistics textbooks available which cover the range of techniques included in this chapter and, of course, much more. Texts vary in terms of the degree of familiarity with algebra that they assume on the part of the reader, so readers with limited mathematical knowledge should 'shop around' to find a text which deals with the topic in conceptual terms rather than in detailed mathematical terms. However, a certain amount of mathematical aptitude is, of course, essential. Examples of general research methods texts which include statistics are Ryan (1995) and Burns (1994); and a specialist text: Spatz and Johnston (1989).

For examples of the use of the techniques covered here, the reader should browse through the *Journal of Leisure Research* and, to a lesser extent, *Leisure Sciences*.

Appendix 12.1 Details of example data file used – variable details and data

Name	Type	Width	Decimals	Lab	Values	Missing	Columns	Align	Measure
qno	Numeric	5	0	Questionnaire number	None	None	8	Right	Scale
status	Numeric	5	0	Student status	1 F/T student – no work 2 F/T student – working 3 P/T student – F/T job 4 P/T student – other	None	8	Right	Nominal
cafebar	Numeric	5	0	Campus cafe/bar in last 4 wks	0 No 1 Yes	None	8	Right	Nominal
music	Numeric	5	0	Live campus music in last 4 wks	0 No 1 Yes	None	8	Right	Nominal
sport	Numeric	5	0	Sport facilities in last 4 wks	0 No 1 Yes	None	8	Right	Nominal
travel	Numeric	5	0	Travel service in last 4 wks	0 No 1 Yes	None	8	Right	Nominal
cheap	Numeric	5	0	Free/cheap (rank)	None	None	8	Right	Ordinal
daytime	Numeric	5	0	Day-time events (rank)	None	None	8	Right	Ordinal
unusual	Numeric	5	0	Not available elsewhere (rank)	None	None	8	Right	Ordinal
meet	Numeric	5	0	Socialising (rank)	None	None	8	Right	Ordinal
quality	Numeric	5	0	Quality of presentation (rank)	None	None	8	Right	Ordinal
spend	Numeric	5	0	Expenditure on entertainment/month	None	None	8	Right	Scale
relax	Numeric	5	0	Relaxation opportunities – importance	1 Not Important 2 Important 3 Very Important	None	8	Right	Scale
social	Numeric	5	0	Social interaction – importance	As above	None	8	Right	Scale
mental	Numeric	5	0	Mental stimulation – importance	As above	None	8	Right	Scale
sug1	Numeric	5	0	First suggestion	1 Programme content 2 Timing 3 Facilities 4 Costs 5 Organisation	None	8	Right	Nominal
sug2	Numeric	5	0	Second suggestion	As above	None	8	Right	Nominal
sug3	Numeric	5	0	Third suggestion	As above	None	8	Right	Nominal
age	Numeric	5	0	Age	None	None	8	Right	Scale
gender	Numeric	5	0	Gender	1 male 2 Female	None	8	Right	Nominal
inc	Numeric	5	0	Income pa, $000s	None	None	8	Right	Scale
sport	Numeric	5	0	Played sport – times in last 3 months	None	None	8	Right	Scale
theatre	Numeric	5	0	Visit theatre – times in last 3 months	None	None	8	Right	Scale
npark	Numeric	5	0	Visit national park – times in last 3 months	None	None	8	Right	Scale
hols	Numeric	5	0	Holiday expenditure	None	None	8	Right	Scale

Data

qno	status	cafebar	music	sport	travel	cheap	daytime	unusual	meet	quality	spend	relax	social	mental	sug1	sug2	sug3	age	gender	inc	sportft	theatre	npark	meal	hols
1	2	1	1	0	0	1	4	2	3	5	100	3	3	1	1	–	–	18	1	12	25	1	5	8	220
2	2	1	1	1	0	1	4	2	3	5	50	2	3	1	2	1	–	23	1	15	30	0	15	10	485
3	3	1	0	0	0	2	5	1	3	4	250	2	2	2	3	4	–	28	2	15	5	4	20	2	450
4	4	0	0	0	0	2	3	1	4	5	25	3	2	2	1	2	4	35	2	21	0	5	4	12	750
5	3	1	0	0	1	1	4	3	2	5	55	3	3	1	–	–	–	29	2	20	4	5	25	4	650
6	3	1	1	0	0	2	4	1	3	5	40	2	3	1	2	–	–	29	1	14	20	0	0	8	480
7	2	1	0	1	0	3	2	1	4	5	150	2	3	2	3	–	–	23	2	11	6	6	0	3	250
8	2	1	0	0	0	3	4	2	1	5	250	1	2	2	4	5	–	22	1	12	8	0	12	1	120
9	4	0	1	1	0	1	5	2	3	4	300	2	3	2	–	–	–	22	2	15	10	2	20	6	450
10	3	1	0	0	0	2	3	1	5	4	100	1	2	1	1	1	–	19	2	12	50	0	15	10	220
11	3	1	0	0	0	2	3	1	4	5	75	2	2	2	2	3	–	20	1	11	13	1	2	9	300
12	2	1	1	0	1	1	4	3	2	5	50	2	3	1	1	–	–	19	1	14	6	3	13	5	575
13	1	1	0	1	0	1	5	2	3	4	55	2	3	2	4	2	–	21	2	11	1	5	0	7	300
14	3	1	0	0	0	2	4	1	5	5	75	3	3	2	1	–	–	35	2	25	0	6	0	9	850
15	1	1	1	0	0	3	2	1	2	4	150	3	3	2	4	2	5	22	1	9	15	1	25	6	200
16	2	0	1	0	0	3	4	2	3	5	200	1	2	1	–	5	–	28	2	12	6	8	1	2	220
17	1	1	0	0	0	1	5	1	5	4	175	2	3	1	1	–	–	20	2	12	20	0	20	11	275
18	1	1	0	1	0	2	3	1	4	4	100	1	2	2	1	2	–	21	1	8	12	2	2	8	150
19	4	1	1	0	1	2	3	3	2	5	105	2	3	2	2	3	4	32	2	23	2	5	10	10	1,200
20	1	1	1	1	0	1	4	1	4	5	50	2	2	2	3	–	–	23	1	16	4	5	4	0	300
21	1	1	0	0	0	3	2	2	1	5	150	2	3	2	4	–	–	18	1	11	6	2	0	3	250
22	2	1	0	1	0	3	4	2	3	5	250	1	2	2	–	5	–	25	1	12	8	2	12	1	325
23	4	0	1	0	0	1	5	2	3	4	300	2	3	2	–	–	–	22	2	17	10	2	20	6	600

Case																									
24	400	12	15	0	50	11	2	29	–	1	1	1	2	1	100	4	5	1	3	2	0	0	1	1	3
25	230	9	2	1	13	10	1	23	–	3	2	1	2	2	75	5	4	1	3	2	0	0	1	1	3
26	125	5	13	5	6	9	2	19	–	–	–	1	3	2	50	5	2	3	4	1	1	1	0	1	2
27	350	7	0	5	1	14	1	21	–	2	4	2	3	2	55	4	3	2	5	1	0	1	0	1	1
28	500	9	0	6	0	21	2	35	5	–	–	2	3	3	75	5	3	1	4	2	0	0	1	1	3
29	200	6	25	1	15	12	1	22	–	2	–	1	3	3	150	4	5	1	2	3	0	0	1	1	1
30	850	4	25	5	4	20	1	29	–	–	2	–	3	3	55	5	2	3	4	1	1	0	0	1	3
31	350	8	0	0	20	13	1	20	–	–	3	1	3	2	40	5	3	1	4	2	0	0	1	1	3
32	1,000	3	0	2	6	23	2	23	–	–	4	2	3	2	150	5	4	1	2	3	0	0	0	1	2
33	275	4	12	6	8	12	2	25	–	5	–	2	2	1	250	5	1	2	4	3	0	0	1	0	2
34	750	6	20	2	10	20	1	22	–	–	1	2	3	2	300	4	3	2	5	1	0	1	0	1	4
35	150	10	15	0	50	10	1	19	–	1	2	1	2	1	100	4	5	1	3	2	0	0	1	0	3
36	250	9	2	1	13	10	–	20	–	3	–	1	2	2	75	5	4	1	3	2	1	0	1	1	3
37	450	5	13	5	6	15	2	19	–	–	2	1	3	2	50	5	2	3	5	1	0	0	0	0	2
38	500	7	0	6	1	15	2	21	–	2	–	2	3	3	55	4	3	2	4	1	0	1	1	1	1
39	800	9	0	1	0	21	2	35	5	–	4	2	3	3	75	5	3	1	2	2	0	0	0	0	3
40	450	6	25	0	15	14	1	22	–	2	1	1	3	3	150	4	5	2	5	3	0	0	1	1	–
41	375	11	20	2	20	15	1	20	–	3	–	2	2	2	175	4	3	1	3	1	0	0	0	0	1
42	220	8	2	5	12	10	2	21	4	–	2	2	2	1	100	4	5	2	4	2	0	1	1	1	–
43	900	10	10	5	2	24	1	32	–	5	3	2	3	2	105	5	4	1	2	3	1	0	1	1	4
44	700	4	4	2	4	16	1	28	–	–	4	1	2	1	50	5	2	3	4	1	0	1	1	1	1
45	180	3	0	2	6	9	2	23	–	1	–	2	3	3	150	5	4	1	2	3	0	0	0	1	2
46	350	1	12	2	8	13	1	25	–	–	1	2	2	1	250	5	1	3	5	1	0	1	0	0	2
47	620	6	20	0	10	15	2	22	–	3	2	2	3	2	300	4	3	1	3	2	0	0	0	1	4
48	210	10	15	1	50	8	2	19	–	–	2	1	2	1	100	5	5	2	3	2	1	0	1	1	3
49	120	9	2	3	13	10	1	20	–	–	1	1	2	2	75	4	4	2	3	2	0	0	1	1	3
50	220	5	13	3	6	12	1	19	–	5	–	1	3	2	50	5	2	3	4	1	0	1	0	0	2

Appendix 12.2   Statistical formulae

- **95% Confidence Interval for Normal Distribution for percentage p**

  C.I. $= 1.96\sqrt{(p(100-p)/(n-1))}$

  Where n = sample size

- **Chi-square**

  $\Pi^2 = \sqrt{3((O-E)/E)^2}$

- **t for difference between means**

  $t = \sqrt{((0_1 - 0_2)/(s_1^2/n_1 + s_2^2/n_1))}$

- **Standard Deviation**

  $SD = \sqrt{(3(x-0)^2/n)}$

- **Correlation Coefficient**

  $r = 3((x-0)(y-\hat{y}))^2/(s_1^2/n_1 + s_2^2/n_2)$

- **Value of t for Correlation Coefficient, r**

  $t = r\sqrt{((N-2)/(1-r)^2)}$

13 Preparing a research report

Introduction

This chapter outlines key aspects of the preparation and presentation of written research reports, including discussion of content, structure and layout. It considers the varying requirements and conventions of different reporting formats, including academic articles, consultancy reports, books and theses. It concludes with brief consideration of non-written formats, particularly the oral presentation.

Written reports of research are a key element of the world of management and planning. Applied studies of the sort discussed in Chapter 1, namely feasibility studies, marketing plans, recreation needs studies, tourism development plans, market research studies and performance appraisals, all tend to be presented in the form of written reports. The results of academic studies are produced in article, report, book, or thesis format. In this chapter we deal with three report formats: management/ planning/project reports, academic articles and theses. The first of these may arise in a management/planning context or may arise from a funded academic project when the researcher reports to the funding body; this style of report is referred to as a *project report* in the discussion below. The main distinguishing characteristics of these three styles of report are summarised in Figure 13.1.

The medium is the message and in this case the medium is the written report. The ability to prepare a report, and the ability to recognise good quality and poor quality reports, should be seen as a key element in the skills of the manager. While form is no substitute for good content, a report which is poorly presented can undermine or even negate good content. While most of the researcher's attention should of course be focussed on achieving high quality substantive content, the general aspects raised in this chapter also merit serious attention.

Getting started

In discussing research proposals in Chapter 3 it was noted that researchers invariably leave too little time for report writing. Even when adequate time has been allocated in the timetable this is often whittled away and the writing of the report is delayed,

Characteristic	Management/planning/project report	Academic article	Thesis
Authors	'In-house' staff, external consultants or funded academics	Academics	Honours, masters or doctoral students
Content	Report of commissioned or grant-funded project	Report of academic research	Report of academic research
Brief	Provided by commissioning organisation or outlined in grant application	Generally self-generated (although may arise from commissioned work)	Generally self-generated (although may arise in part from grant-funded project)
Quality assurance	In-house: internal Consultants/academics: reputation of consultants/researchers	Anonymous refereeing process (see Chapter 1)	Supervision + examination by external examiners
Readership	Professional managers/planners and possibly elected or appointed board/council/committee members	Primarily academics	Primarily academic
Published status	May or may not be publicly available	Publicly available (often on-line) in published academic journals	Publicly available in libraries and, recently, on-line; findings generally published in summary form in one or more academic articles
Length	Varies	In the social/management sciences, including leisure/tourism studies, generally 5,000–7,000 words	In the social/management sciences, including leisure/ tourism studies: Honours: c. 20,000 words Masters: c. 40,000 words PhD: c. 70,000 words +
Emphasis	Emphasis on findings rather than links with the literature/ theory and methodology (although the latter must be described)	Methodology, theory, literature as important as the findings	Methodology, theory, literature as important as the findings

Figure 13.1   Types of research report

leaving too little time. There is a tendency to put off report writing because it is difficult, and it is often felt that, with just a little more data analysis or a little more reading of the literature, the process of writing the report will become easier. This is rarely the case – it is always difficult!

A regrettably common practice is for writers of reports to spend a great deal of their depleted time, with the deadline looming, writing and preparing material which could have been attended to much earlier in the process. There are often large parts of any report which can be written before data analysis is complete, or even started. Such parts include the introduction, statement of objectives, outline of theoretical or evaluative framework, literature review and description of the methodology. In addition, time-consuming activities such as arranging for maps, illustrations and cover designs to be produced need not be left until the last minute!

Report components

Reports generally include some standard components, although some are unique to certain report styles, as shown in Figure 13.2. The components listed are discussed in turn below.

Cover

For a project report the cover should include minimal information, such as title, author(s) and publisher or sponsor. The lavishness and design content will vary with the context and the resources available. If the report is available for sale it should include an International Standard Book Number (ISBN) on the back cover. All publications in the Western world have a ten-digit ISBN, the first five identifying the publisher (as can be seen on the back of this book, for example). ISBNs are allocated by National Libraries, which receive free deposit copies of all publications in their country. The ISBN makes it easy to order publications through bookshops and ensures that the publication is catalogued in library systems around the world.

Title page

The title page is the first page inside the cover of a project report. It may include much the same information as the cover or considerably more detail, as indicated in Figure 13.2. In some cases, as in commercially published books, some of the detail is provided on the reverse of the title page.

List of contents

Lists of contents are required in project reports and theses and may include just chapter titles, but usually also include full details of sub-sections. An example of a contents list is shown in Figure 13.3. Word-processing packages include procedures for compiling tables of contents and lists, such as tables and diagrams.

Component	Content	Management/Planning/ Research report	Academic article	Thesis
Cover	– Title of report – Author(s) – Institution/publisher – ISBN (if published) back cover	As indicated	Not applicable	Prescribed by university regulations
Title page	– Title of report – Author(s) – Institution/publisher, including address, phone, fax numbers, email, web-site* – Sponsoring body (e.g. 'Report to the Tourism Commission') – Date of publication* – If the report is for sale: ISBN* (*sometimes on reverse of title page)	As indicated	Submitted article includes: – Title of articles – Author(s) – Institutional affiliation – Contact details (This page omitted by editors when article is sent for anonymous refereeing)	Prescribed by university regulations
Contents page(s)	See Figure 13.3 for example	As in Figure 13.3	Not applicable	As in Figure 13.3 but may not include section numbering
Summary	Summary of *whole* report, including background, aims, methods, main findings, conclusions and (where applicable) recommendations	Executive Summary: Length: 20 pp report: ½–1 page 21–50 pp report: 3–4 pp 50–100 pp report: 5–6 pp	Abstract: Length: typically c. 300 words	Synopsis: Length: typically 3–4 pages
Preface/Foreword	Optional. Contains background information, sometimes an explanation of reasons for authors' involvement with the project. Or may be by a significant individual not directly involved in the project. Not applicable in academic article, where such information may be included in an endnote.			
Acknowledgements	– Funding organisations – Liaison officers of funding organisations – Members of steering committees – Organisations/individuals providing access to information etc. – Staff employed (e.g. including interviewers, coders, computer programmers, secretaries, wordprocessors) – Individuals (including academic supervisors) who have given advice, commented on report drafts, etc. – (Collectively) Individuals who responded to questionnaires, etc.			
Main body of report	Discussed separately			
Appendices	Text and statistical material included for the record but which, because of its size, would interrupt the flow if included in the main body of the report.			

Figure 13.2 Report style and components

Figure 13.3
Example of
contents page

CONTENTS

Page

Summary

A summary is required for all three styles of report except for very short project reports. The summary is called, *executive summary*, *abstract* or *synopsis*, depending on the context. An executive summary is sometimes thought of as the summary for the 'busy executive' who does not have time to read the whole report, but really refers to the idea that it should contain information necessary to take *executive action* on the basis of the report. A summary should contain a summary of *the whole report, article or thesis*, as indicated in Figure 13.2; it is *not* the introduction. The summary should, of course, be written *last*.

Preface/foreword

Prefaces or Forewords are used for a variety of purposes. Usually they explain the origins of the study and outline any qualifications or limitations, and acknowledgements of assistance if there is no separate 'acknowledgements' section. Sometimes a significant individual is asked to write a Foreword, such as the director of an institution, a minister or an eminent academic.

Acknowledgements

It is clearly a matter of courtesy to acknowledge any assistance received during the course of a research project. People and institutions who might be acknowledged are listed in Figure 13.2.

Main body of the report – technical aspects

Clearly the main body of the report is its most important component. The substantive content is discussed in the next section; here we consider a number of technical aspects of organisation and presentation, as listed in Figure 13.4.

Figure 13.4
Main body of report: technical aspects

- Section numbering
- Paragraph numbering
- 'Dot point' lists
- Page numbering
- Headers/footers
- Heading hierarchy
- Typing layout/spacing
- Tables and graphics
- Referencing
- Which person?

Section numbering

It is usual to number not only the major sections/chapters, but also sub-sections within chapters, as shown in the example in Figure 13.3. Once a numbering section is established it should be carried through consistently throughout the report. Word-processing packages often provide 'style' templates to facilitate this process.

In project reports, section numbers may extend to several levels, for example, within section 4.2, there could be sub-sections: 4.2.1, 4.2.2, etc. Further levels can become cumbersome and are generally not required throughout the report, so if there is an occasional need for further sub-sections it is often advisable to use a simple a., b., c. or (i), (ii), (iii), etc.

Journal articles rarely include section numbering; when it is included it is typically one level only. In theses chapters are, of course, numbered, and possibly one level of sections within chapters, but sub-section numbering is not generally used.

Paragraph numbering

In some reports paragraphs are individually numbered, although this is rare. This can be useful for reference purposes when a report is being discussed in committees, etc. Paragraphs can be numbered in a single series for the whole report or chapter by chapter: in chapter 1: paragraphs 1.1, 1.2, 1.3, etc.; in chapter 2: paragraphs 2.1, 2.2, 2.3 etc., and so on.

'Dot point' lists

'Dot point' lists are very common in management reports, and quite common in the other reporting formats. Management reports are often discussed in committee or written comments are offered in various consultation exercises. To ease this process, numbered lists may be more helpful than 'dot points': it is easier for a commentator to refer to 'item 4' than to 'the third dot point on page 3'.

Where possible, grammatical rules should be followed in dot-point lists. For example, in Figure 13.5, the list is, in effect, all one sentence. There are therefore, semi-colons at the end of each list item, a full-stop at the end and no capital letters at the beginning of each item. This principle is difficult to follow when the individual dot points are lengthy, perhaps themselves involving more than one sentence: if this is the case, then all the dot-points in a sequence should be treated as one or more complete sentences with capital letters and full-stops.

Figure 13.5
Dot-point list
example

In preparing a research report, the author should take account of:
- the likely readership;
- the requirements of the funding agency, as indicated in the study brief;
- printing or other distribution format;
- likely costs; and
- delivery of a clear message.

Page numbering

One problem in putting together long reports, especially when different authors are responsible for different sections, is to organise page numbering so that it follows on from chapter to chapter. This can be avoided by numbering each chapter separately, for example: Chapter 1: pages 1.1, 1.2, 1.3, etc.; Chapter 2: pages 2.1, 2.2, 2.3, etc. and so on. Such a numbering system can also aid readers in finding their way around a report. Word-processors can be made to produce page numbers in this form by using the header and/or page-numbering facilities.

It is general practice for the title page, contents page(s), acknowledgements, and the executive summary pages to be numbered using roman numerals (as in this book) and for the report proper to start at page 1 with normal (arabic) numbers. Most word-processors will facilitate this.

Headers/footers

Word-processing packages provide the facility to include a running header or footer across the top or bottom of each page. This can be used to indicate sections or chapters, as in this book, or, in the case of a consultancy report, can be used to indicate title and authorship of the report, perhaps even displaying the consultancy logo on each page.

Heading hierarchy

In the main body of the report a hierarchy of heading styles should be used, with the major chapter/section headings being in the most prominent style and with decreasing emphasis for sub-section headings. For example:

1. Chapter Titles
1.1 Section Headings
1.1.1 Sub-section Headings

Such a convention helps readers to know where they are in a document. When a team is involved in writing a report it is clearly sensible to agree these heading styles in advance. Modern word-processing systems provide a hierarchy of headings and report 'styles' which standardise heading formats and section numbering systems, linked to assembly of tables of contents.

Typing layout/spacing

Essays and books tend to use the convention of starting new paragraphs by indenting the first line. Report style is to separate paragraphs by a blank line and not to indent the first line. Report style also tends to have more headings. For a document in report style it is usual to leave wide margins, which raises the question as to whether it is necessary to print documents in 1.5 or double space format or whether single spacing is adequate (and more environmentally friendly!). Different journals have different format specifications for submission of articles, usually indicated in the journal itself and/or on the journal website. Universities provide guidelines for the layout of theses.

Tables and graphics

Balance

When presenting the results of quantitative research, an appropriate balance must be struck between the use of tables, graphics and text. In most cases, very large or complex tables are consigned to appendices and simplified versions included in the body of the report. It may be appropriate to place *all* tables in appendices and provide only reader-friendly graphics in the body of the report. The decision on which approach to use depends partly on the complexity of the data to be presented, but mainly on the prospective readership.

Tables/graphics vs text

Tables, graphics and text each have a distinctive role to play in the presentation of the study findings. Tables provide information; graphics illustrate that information so that patterns can be seen in a visual way. The text should be telling a story or developing an argument and 'orchestrating' tables and graphics to support that task.

There seems to be little point in the text of a report simply repeating what is in a table or graphic. At the least the text should highlight the main features of the data; ideally it should develop an argument or draw conclusions based on the data. In Figure 13.6 Commentary A does little more than repeat what is in the table: it says nothing to the reader about the difference between men's and women's participation patterns, which is presumably the purpose of the exercise. Commentary B, on the other hand, is more informative, pointing out particular features of the data in the table.

In the more quantitative disciplines there is a convention that, in academic reports such as journal articles and theses, the results of statistical tests should be mentioned in the text, even if the information is also available in a table. Thus, for example, a sentence in the text might read: 'Mean weekly frequency of participation by men (2.1) is significantly higher than for women (1.7, $t = 5.6$, $p < 0001$, see Table 2). Clearly the information in brackets 'clutters' the text and makes it less 'reader-friendly' if there are a number of such insertions; it seems unnecessary to include it in the text if it can be seen in the table; and the information on the t-test may be meaningless to readers without statistical knowledge. In less quantitative fields it is not necessary to include the information in brackets, particularly the t-test result, in the text if it is available in a table and it is generally not appropriate for management reports.

Presentation

Diagrams and tables should, as far as possible, be complete in themselves. That is, the title should be informative and the columns, rows or axes should be fully labelled so that the reader can understand them without necessarily referring to the text (for example, see table in Figure 13.6). Thus tables or graphics presenting data from leisure and tourism surveys or other data sources should include information on: the geographical area, the year, gender and age-range of the sample or population to which the data relate, sample size, where relevant, and units of measurement.

Figure 13.6
Table and
commentaries

Table X: Participation in top five sports/physical activities, persons aged 16+, Great Britain, 1986

Activity	% Participating in four weeks prior to interview (most popular quarter)	
	Males	**Females**
Walking	21	18
Snooker/billiards	17	3
Swimming – indoor	9	10
Darts	9	3
Football	6	*
Keep fit/yoga	1	5

Source: General Household Survey, OPCS

* less than 0.05%

Commentary A
The table indicates that the top five sports and physical recreation activities for men are walking (21%), snooker/billiards (17%), indoor swimming (9%), darts (9%) and football (6%), whereas for women the five most popular activities are walking (18%), indoor swimming (10%), keep fit/yoga (5%), snooker/billiards (3%) and darts (3%).

Commentary B
Men and women may have more in common in their patterns of leisure activity than is popularly imagined. The table indicates that four activities – walking, swimming, snooker/ billiards and darts – are included in the top five most popular sport and physical recreation activities for both men and women. While in general men's participation levels are higher than those of women, the table shows that women's participation rate exceeds that of men for two of the activities, namely keep fit/yoga and swimming.

Reproductions of secondary data should indicate the source of data, but tables or graphics presenting results from the primary data collection of the study, such as a survey, do not need to indicate this on every table and diagram – however, some consultants tend to do this for intellectual property reasons so that if a user copies just one table or diagram then its source is still indicated.

Referencing

References to the literature and other sources in academic reports should follow the referencing conventions as set out in Chapter 5. This may, however, be inappropriate for the non-academic readerships of management reports. While sources should be acknowledged in such reports, it is generally appropriate to do so in an unobtrusive manner – for example by use of the endnote rather than author/date reference style. In some management reports the 'review of the literature' is relegated to an appendix with just the conclusions being presented in the body of the report.

Which person?

In academic reports, it is conventional to report the conduct and findings of research in an 'impersonal style' – for example to say: 'A survey was conducted' rather than 'I/we conducted a survey'; and 'It was found that . . .' rather than 'I/we found that . . .'. Some believe that this attempt to appear 'scientific' is inappropriate in the social sciences, particularly in qualitative research where the researcher personally engages with the research milieu. First person accounts are therefore sometimes, but not commonly, used in some leisure and tourism reports. The first person plural is also quite commonly used by consultants in management reports, especially when the consultants wish to convey the impression that they are bringing particular personal skills and experience to bear on a project.

The impersonal style can appear odd or pretentious when authors refer to their own work. Thus for me to say: 'Veal (2002) has argued that leisure is pluralistic' seems odd. For me to say: 'The author has argued that leisure is pluralistic (Veal, 2002)' seems pretentious. The solution in such a situation is to use the first person: 'I have argued that leisure is pluralistic (Veal, 2002)', or to 'de-centre' the author: 'It has been argued that leisure is pluralistic (Veal, 2002)'.

Main body of the report – structure and content

Structure

It could be said that the three most important aspects of a research report are: 1.structure, 2. structure, and 3. structure! The *structure* of a report is of fundamental importance and needs to be thoroughly considered and discussed, particularly when a team is involved. While all reports have certain structural features in common, the important aspects of any one report concern the underlying argument and how that relates to the objectives of the study and any data collection and analysis involved. This is linked fundamentally to the *research questions*, the *theoretical or evaluative framework* and the *overall research strategy*, as discussed in Chapter 3.

Before writing starts it can be useful to agree not only the report structure and format, but also target word-lengths for each chapter or section. While an agreed structure is a necessary starting point, it is also necessary to be flexible. As drafting gets going it may be found that what was originally conceived as one chapter needs to be divided into two or three chapters, or what was thought of as a separate chapter can be incorporated into another chapter or into an appendix. Throughout, consideration needs to be given to the overall length of the report, in terms of words or pages.

When a questionnaire survey is involved, there is a tendency to structure the presentation according to the sequence of questions in the questionnaire and, correspondingly, the sequence of tables as they are produced by the computer. This is not an appropriate way to proceed! Questionnaires are structured for ease of interview, for the convenience of interviewer and/or respondent: they do *not* provide a suitable sequence and structure for a report.

The table of contents, as shown in Figure 13.3, indicates the structure of the report to the reader. The example relates to management reports and theses, which tend to be lengthy and to be divided into chapters and to have tables of contents. Journal articles are shorter and do not have tables of contents, but structure is, of course, still important. There is a conventional overall structure for journal articles involving about six sections, as shown in Figure 13.7.

Being clear in your own mind about structure is one thing; conveying it to the reader can be quite another. While the contents page and general organisation of a report should make the reader aware of the structure, this is rarely enough: it must be *explained* – often more than once. Thus it is good practice, particularly in the case of a lengthy report, to provide an outline of the structure of the whole report in the introductory chapter, and outlines of each chapter in the introduction to each chapter. Summaries are useful at the end of each chapter and these can be revisited and summarised at the end of the report when drawing conclusions together. It is advisable to provide numerous references backwards and forwards, as reminders to the reader as to where they are in the overall 'story' of the report. When a list of 'factors', 'issues' or 'topics' is about to be discussed, one by one, it is useful to list the factors or issues to be discussed, and then summarise at the end of the section to indicate what the review of factors or issues has achieved.

Between methods and results

All empirical research reports, regardless of format, should include a clear summary of the methods used to gather data. In journal articles the description is often quite short, because of the limitation of word-length. In management reports the description may be short in the body of the report because of the type of readership, but there is scope to provide more detail in appendices. In a thesis an extensive and 'up front' description of methods used is essential.

In all formats, but particularly in a thesis, the *choice* of methods should also be discussed. Why was a particular method selected? What alternatives were considered and why were they rejected? Such a discussion should be related to the nature of the research questions/hypotheses. It is not sufficient merely to lists the characteristics and merits of the methods chosen, but to indicate why those *particular* characteristics were appropriate in *this particular project*. Factors to consider in selecting a research method are discussed at the end of Chapter 4 and these should be referred to in justifying the choice of method.

Figure 13.7
Conventional academic article structure

- Background/introduction/justification for the research/nature of the problem
- Review of the literature
- Methods
- Results
- Conclusion
- References

Part of the reporting of results of empirical research involves provision of some very basic information on the success of the chosen method in achieving a suitable sample. Since this is technical in nature and not concerned directly with the substantive findings, it can be reported in the 'methods' section, although it is often reported as the first part of the 'results' sections. This component of the report should provide information on:

- the size of the sample achieved;
- response rates and an indication as to whether they are deemed to be acceptable or likely to have caused bias;
- characteristics of the sample, particularly in so far as they can indicate the representativeness of the sample – thus a sample from a household or community survey might be compared with the known age/gender structure of the local population from the population census data for the area, while the age-structure of a site-survey sample might be compared with junior/adult ticket sales ratios or information from other similar surveys;
- any measures taken to correct sample bias by means of weighting, and a description of that process.

Audiences and style

The style, format and length of a report is largely influenced by the type of audience at which it is aimed. The amount of technical jargon used and the detail with which data are presented will be affected by this question of audience. Audiences may be: popular; decision-makers; experts.

- A *popular audience* consists of members of the general public who might read a report of research in a newspaper or magazine – full research reports are therefore not generally written for a popular readership.
- *Decision-makers* are groups, such as elected members of councils, government ministers, members of boards of companies, or senior executives, who may not have a detailed knowledge of a particular field, or may have a particular knowledge, which might be technical, managerial or political.
- *Experts* are professionals or academics who are familiar with the subject matter of the report.

Report functions: record and narrative

A research report can be thought of in two ways: first the report as narrative and, second, the report as record. *Narrative* means that a report has to tell a *story* to the reader. The writer of the report therefore needs to think of the flow of the argument – the 'story' – in the same way that the writer of a novel has to consider the plot. The report as *record* means that a report is often also a reference source where future readers may wish to look for information. Being a good record may involve including extensive detailed information which may interfere with the process of 'story telling'.

The report as narrative may call for presentation of only simplified factual information or key features of the data, possibly in graphical form, to demonstrate and illustrate the argument. The report as record is likely to call for the presentation of detailed information – even data which were collected but did not prove particularly relevant for the overall study conclusions. Thus balancing these demands as the report is being put together can be a major challenge.

Report as narrative

The narrative of a research report usually develops as indicated in Figure 13.8. The items listed may emerge in a variety of chapter/section configurations. For example, sections A and B could be one chapter/section or three or four, depending on the complexity of the project.

The introductory section(s), A, should reflect the considerations which emerged in the initial steps in the planning stages of a project (1, 2 and 6 – see Figure 3.1, p.46). The term 'context' is used to include the environment in which the research is situated, including any initial literature review which may be involved. Section(s) B should reflect steps 3–5 and 7–8 in the research planning process and may include further reference to the literature.

In sections B and C it is important that the relation between data requirements and the research questions and theoretical or evaluative framework be explained, as discussed in Chapter 3. It should be clear from the discussion why the data are being collected – and how this relates to the planning/management/theoretical issues raised;

Figure 13.8
Report as narrative – structure

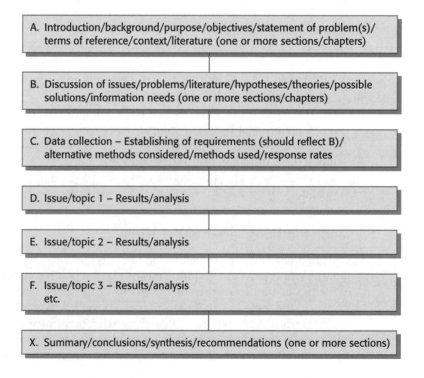

A. Introduction/background/purpose/objectives/statement of problem(s)/ terms of reference/context/literature (one or more sections/chapters)

B. Discussion of issues/problems/literature/hypotheses/theories/possible solutions/information needs (one or more sections/chapters)

C. Data collection – Establishing of requirements (should reflect B)/ alternative methods considered/methods used/response rates

D. Issue/topic 1 – Results/analysis

E. Issue/topic 2 – Results/analysis

F. Issue/topic 3 – Results/analysis etc.

X. Summary/conclusions/synthesis/recommendations (one or more sections) how it was anticipated that the information collected would solve or shed light on the problems/issues raised, or aid decision-making.

In section C methodology should be described in detail; it should be clear why particular techniques were chosen, how samples or subjects were selected, and what data collection instruments were used. Where sample surveys are involved full information should be given on response rates and sample sizes obtained and some indication given of the consequences in terms of confidence intervals, as discussed in Chapter 10. These technical aspects of the results of any survey work can be included in the methodology section of the report or in the first of the results sections.

The results/analysis sections (D, E, F, etc.) should ideally be structured by the earlier conceptual or theoretical discussion (B) around issues and elements of the research problem.

Sometimes conclusions are fully set out in the results/analysis section(s) and all that is required in the final conclusions section is to reiterate and draw them together. In other cases the final section includes the final stage of analysis and the drawing of conclusions from that analysis. In writing the final section it is vital to refer back to the terms of reference/objectives of the study to ensure that all objectives have been met. Not all research reports include 'recommendations'. Recommendations are most likely to arise from evaluative research and in management research where the brief has explicitly asked for them. It should, of course, be clear to whom such recommendations are addressed.

The report as 'record'

It is wise to think beyond the immediate readership and use of a research report, and think of it also as the definitive record of the research conducted. It should therefore contain a summary of all the relevant data collected in a form which would be useful for any future user of the report. This means that, while data may be presented in the main body of the report in a highly condensed and summarised form in order to produce a readable narrative, it should also be presented in as much detail as possible, 'for the record'. Data included 'for the record' can be placed in appendices or, when large amounts of data are involved, in a separate statistical volume.

In the case of questionnaire survey data it can be a good idea to provide a statistical appendix which includes tables from all the questions in the order they appear in the questionnaire, as discussed in Chapter 11. Any reader interested in a specific aspect of the data is then able to locate and use it. The main body of the report can then be structured around issues and not be constrained by the structure of the questionnaire.

In conclusion

Ultimately the writing of a good research report is an art and a skill which develops with practice. Reports can be improved enormously as a result of comments from others – often because the writer has been 'too close' to the report for too long to be able to see glaring faults or omissions. The researcher/writer can also usually spot opportunities for improvement if he or she takes a short break and returns to the draft report with 'fresh eyes'. Finally, *checking and double checking the report for typing, spelling and typographical errors is well worth the laborious effort.*

Other media

While the written report is still the most common medium for the communication of research results, this is likely to change in future. In particular, the researcher is often required to present final or interim results of research in person and some sort of audio-visual aids are usually advisable, including: handouts; posters; overhead transparencies; slides; video clips; computer-based devices. The most common medium is the oral presentation aided by computer-based visuals using such packages as Microsoft 'PowerPoint'.

An important point to bear in mind is the obvious fact that the audio-visual presentation is *not* the same as a written report. The presentation must be designed as a medium/message in its own right. The information to be presented must fit into the time allotted and must be suitable for the medium. Constant references to what is *not* being covered in the presentation because of lack of time, or to slides which it 'may not be possible to read from the back of the room', are an indication of an unprofessional approach.

It goes without saying that the presenter should *practice* presenting the material to ensure that it fits into the time allotted. Such practice sessions can be seen as the equivalent of various drafts of the written report. Typically it is necessary to be selective in making such a presentation. Judgement must be used in deciding what to include and what to leave out. As with the writing of abstracts and synopses, this can be a considerable challenge. Practice runs help in this process since programs such as PowerPoint include a 'rehearse timings' procedure which help in deciding how long to spend on particular parts of the presentation and what to leave out on grounds of time. For example, if there are six 'key findings' from a study, rather than rushing to cover all six, it is in most cases better to say to an audience: 'There are six findings from the study and in this presentation I am going to concentrate on the three most important.'

The standard slide templates available in programs such as PowerPoint provide a default font size and a default number of 'dot points' on a slide. This is for a good reason. Viewing an image on a personal computer screen from less than a metre is different from viewing the same image projected on a screen in a lecture hall or meeting room. Thus, while a table or graphic with 30 lines of data may be readable in a printed report and on a personal computer screen, it may not be readable to someone 20 metres from a projection screen. In such a situation the most important, say, ten lines of the table or items in the graphic must be selected, or the table or graphic must be divided into two and presented on two sequential slides. Again, a practice run-through with a full-size screen is advisable.

Summary

This chapter considers the preparation of what is generally the final outcome of a research project, namely a written report. It considers the varying demands of three types of report: the management/planning/research project report, the academic journal article and the thesis, each with different audiences, different constraints and different conventions. The chapter reviews the various ancillary components of a report, including the cover, cover page, title page, list of contents, synopsis/abstract/executive summary, preface/foreword and acknowledgements. It then considers the main body of the report in terms of technical aspects, largely to do with format, and structure and content. Structure is emphasised as the key feature of research reports, particularly in their longer formats.

A final comment

Research is a creative process which, in the words of Norbert Elias with which we began this text, aims to 'make known something previously unknown to human beings . . . to advance human knowledge, to make it more certain or better fitting . . . the aim is . . . discovery'. It is hoped that this book will provide some assistance in that process of discovery and that the reader will enjoy some of the satisfactions and rewards which can come from worthwhile research.

Test questions/exercises

No specific exercises are offered here. By now the reader should be capable of venturing into the world of research by carrying out a research project from beginning to end.

Further reading

The best reading relevant to this chapter is the critical reading of research reports. As regards non-print media, most readers of this book have ample opportunity in the course of their academic and/or professional lives to see good and bad examples of audio-visual presentations from which they can discern good and bad practice!

References

ABS *see* Australian Bureau of Statistics.

Adler, P.A. and Adler, P. (1994) Observational techniques. In N.K. Denzin and Y.S. Lincoln (eds) *Handbook of Qualitative Research*. Thousand Oaks, CA: Sage, 377–92.

Age, The (1982) *The Age Lifestyle Study for the Eighties*. Melbourne: D. Syme & Co.

Aitchison, C. (2000) Poststructural feminist theories of representing Others: a response to the 'crisis' in leisure studies' discourse. *Leisure Studies*, 19(3), 127–45.

Aitchison, C. (2003) *Gender and Leisure: Social and Cultural Perspectives*. London: Routledge.

Aitchison, C., MacLeod, N.E. and Shaw, S.J. (2000) *Leisure and Tourism Landscapes: Social and Cultural Geographies*. London: Routledge.

American Psychological Association (2001) *Publication Manual of the American Psychological Association*, 5th edn. Washington, DC: APA.

Anderson, H.-C. and Robinson, M. (eds) (2002) *Literature and Tourism: Reading and Writing Tourism Texts*. London: Continuum.

Anderson, R. (1975) *Leisure: An Inappropriate Concept for Women?* Canberra: AGPS.

Archer, B.H. (1994) Demand forecasting and estimation. In J.R.B. Ritchie and C.R. Goeldner (eds) *Travel, Tourism and Hospitality Research*, 2nd edn. New York: John Wiley, 105–14.

Atkinson, R. (1998) *The Life Story Interview*. London: Sage.

Australian Bureau of Statistics (ABS) (1994) *How Australians Use their Time, 1992*. (Cat. No. 4153.0), Canberra: ABS.

Australian Bureau of Statistics (ABS) (1998) *How Australians Use their Time, 1997*. (Cat. No. 4153.0), Canberra: ABS.

Australian Bureau of Statistics (ABS) (2000a) *Children's Participation in Cultural and Leisure Activities*. (Cat. No. 4901.0), Canberra: ABS.

Australian Bureau of Statistics (2005) *2003–04 Household Expenditure Survey, Detailed Expenditure Items*. (Cat. No. 6535.0), Canberra: ABS.

Australian Bureau of Statistics (ABS) (2003a) *Participation in Sport and Physical Activities, Australia, 2002*. (Cat. No. 4177.0), Canberra: ABS.

Australian Bureau of Statistics (ABS) (2003b) *Sports Attendance, Australia, 2002*. (Cat. No. 4174.0), Canberra: ABS.

Australian Bureau of Statistics (ABS) (2003c) *Attendance at Selected Cultural Venues, Australia, 2002*. (Cat. No. 4114.0), Canberra: ABS.

Australian Bureau of Statistics (ABS) (2004) *Work in Selected Culture and Leisure Activities*. (Cat. No. 6281.0), Canberra: ABS.

Bachman, J.G. and O'Malley, P.M. (1981) When four months equal a year: inconsistencies in student reports of drug use. *Public Opinion Quarterly*, 45(4), 536–48.

Bailey, P. (1978) *Leisure and Class in Victorian England*. London: Routledge.

Bailey, P. (1989) Leisure, culture and the historian: reviewing the first generation of leisure historiography in Britain. *Leisure Studies*, 8(2), 107–28.

Baretje, R. (1964) *Bibliographie Touristique*, Aix-en-Provence: Centre d'Etudes du Tourisme.

Barnett, L.A. (ed.) (1988) *Research about Leisure: Past, Present and Future*. Champaign, IL: Sagamore Publishing.

Barry, P. (1990) *The Rise and Fall of Alan Bond*. Sydney: Bantam/ABC Books.

Barry, P. (1994) *The Rise and Rise of Kerry Packer*. Sydney: Bantam/ABC.

Bazeley, P. and Richards, L. (2000) *The NVivo Qualitative Project Book*. London: Sage.

Bennett, T. and Frow, J. (1991) *Art Galleries: Who Goes?* Redfern, NSW: Australia Council.

Bennett, T., Emmison, M. and Frow, J. (1999) *Accounting for Tastes: Australian Everyday Cultures*. Cambridge: Cambridge University Press.

Bertaux, D. (ed.) (1981) *Biography and Society*. London: Sage.

Bickmore, D., Shaw, M. and Tulloch, T. (1980) Lifestyles on maps. *Geographical Magazine*, 52(11), 763–9.

Billings, A.C. and Tyler Eastman, S. (2002) Selective representation of gender, ethnicity and nationality in American television coverage of the 2000 Summer Olympics. *International Review for the Sociology of Sport*, 37(3/4), 351–70.

Birenbaum, A. and Sagarin, E. (eds) (1973) *People in Places: The Sociology of the Familiar*. London: Nelson.

Bitgood, S., Patterson, D. and Benefield, A. (1988) Exhibit design and visitor behaviour. *Environment and Behaviour*, 20(4), 474–91.

Bittman, M. (1998) The land of the lost weekend? Trends in free time among working age Australians, 1974–1992. *Society and Leisure*, 21(2), 353–78.

BMRA *see* British Market Research Association.

Boothby, J. (1987) Self-reported participation rates: further comment. *Leisure Studies*, 6(1), 99–104.

Borman, K.M., LeCompt, M.D. and Goetz, J.P. (1986) Ethnographic and qualitative research design and why it doesn't work. *American Behavioral Scientist*, 30(1), 42–57.

Botterill, T.D. (1989) Humanistic tourism? Personal constructions of a tourist: Sam visits Japan. *Leisure Studies*, 8(3), 281–94.

Bramham, P. and Henry, I. (1985) Political ideology and leisure policy in the United Kingdom. *Leisure Studies*, 4(1), 1–19.

Bramham, R., Henry, I., Mommaas, H. and Van Der Poel, H. (eds) (1993) *Leisure Policies in Europe*. Wallingford, UK: CAB International.

Brandenburg, J., Greiner, W., Hamilton-Smith, E., Scholten, H., Senior, R. and Webb, J. (1982) A conceptual model of how people adopt recreation activities. *Leisure Studies*, 1(3), 263–76.

British Broadcasting Corporation (BBC) (1978) *The People's Use of Time*. London: BBC.

British Market Research Association (BMRA) (n.d.) *Code of Business Practice*. London: BMRA. (Available at: www.bmra.org.uk, accessed October 2005 – search under 'Code of Practice'.)

Bromley, D.B. (1986) *The Case Study Method in Psychology and Related Disciplines*. New York: John Wiley & Sons.

Brown, P. (1995) Women, sport and the media: an historical perspective on sports coverage in the *Sydney Morning Herald*, 1890–1990. In C. Simpson and B. Gidlow (eds) *Australian and New Zealand Association for Leisure Studies, Second Conference – Leisure Connexions*, Canterbury, New Zealand: Lincoln University, 44–50.

Brown, P.R., Brown, W.J. and Powers, J.R. (2001) Time pressure, satisfaction with leisure and health among Australian women. *Annals of Leisure Research*, 4, 1–16.

Brukner, P., Khan, K. and John Kron, J. (eds) (2003) *Encyclopedia of Exercise, Sport and Health*. Crows Nest, NSW: Allen & Unwin.

Bruner, G.C. and Hensel, P.J. 1992, *Marketing Scales Handbook: A Compilation of Multi-Item Measures*. Chicago, IL: American Marketing Assoc.

Bryman, A. and Bell, E. (2003) Breaking down the quantitative/qualitative divide, and Combining quantitative and qualitative research. *Business Research Methods*. Oxford: Oxford University Press, 465–94.

Bryman, A. and Cramer, D. (2005) *Quantitative Data Analysis with SPSS 12 and 13: A Guide for Social Scientists*. London: Routledge.

BTA/Keele University (1967) *Pilot National Recreation Survey*. Keele: University of Keele/British Travel Association.

Bryman, A. (1995) *Disney and his Worlds*. London: Routledge.

Bryman, A. and Bell, E. (2003) *Business Research Methods*. Oxford: Oxford University Press.

Bulmer, M. (ed.) (1982) *Social Research Ethics*. London: Macmillan.

Burch, W.R., Jr. (1964) *A New Look at an Old Friend – Observation as a Technique for Recreation Research*. Portland, OR: Pacific Northwest Forest and Range Experiment Station.

Burch, W.R. (1981) The ecology of metaphor: spacing regularities for humans and other primates in urban and wild habitats. *Leisure Sciences*, 4(3), 213–30.

Burdge, R. (1989) The evolution of leisure and recreation research from multidisciplinary to interdisciplinary. In E.L. Jackson and T.L. Burton (eds) *Understanding Leisure and Recreation: Mapping the Past and Charting the Future*, State College, PA: Venture, 29–48.

Bureau of Tourism Research (2002) *National Visitor Survey, 2001*. Canberra: BTR. Summary tables available at: Tourism Research Australia: www.tra.australia.com/ (accessed Feb. 2005).

Burgess, R.G. (ed.) (1982) *Field Research: A Sourcebook and Field Manual*. London: Allen & Unwin.

Burkart, A.J. and Medlik, S. (1981) *Tourism: Past, Present and Future*, 2nd edn. London: Heinemann.

Burns, R.B. (1994) *Introduction to Research Methods*, 2nd edn. Melbourne: Longman Cheshire.

Buzan, T. (1995) *The Mind Map Book*. London: BBC Books.

Cairns, J., Jennet, N. and Sloane, P.J. (1986) The economics of professional team sports: a survey of theory and evidence. *Journal of Economic Studies*, 13(1), 3–80.

Calantone, R.J., Di Benedetto, C.A. and Bojanic, D. (1987) A comprehensive review of the tourism forecasting literature. *Journal of Travel Research*, 26(2), 28–39.

Calder, A. and Sheridan, D. (1984) *Speak for Yourself: A Mass Observation Anthology, 1937–49*, London: Jonathan Cape.

Calder, B. (1977) Focus groups and the nature of qualitative marketing research. *Journal of Marketing Research*, 14, 353–64.

Campbell, F.L. (1970) Participant observation in outdoor recreation. *Journal of Leisure Research*, 2(4), 226–36.

Carty, V. (1997) Ideologies and forms of domination in the organization of the global production and consumption of goods in the emerging postmodern era: a case study of Nike Corporation and the implications for gender. *Gender, Work and Organization*, 4(4), 189–201.

Carver, R.H. and Nash, J.G. (2005) *Doing Data Analysis with SPSS Version 12.0*. Belmont, CA: Thomson/Brooks/Cole.

Casey, B., Dunlop, R. and Selwood, S. (1996) *Culture as Commodity? The Economics of the Arts and Built Heritage in the UK*. London: Policy Studies Institute.

Chadwick, R.A. (1994) Concepts, definitions, and measures used in travel and tourism research. In J.R.B. Ritchie and C.R. Goeldner (eds) *Travel, Tourism and Hospitality Research*, 2nd edn. New York: John Wiley, 65–80.

Chase, D.R. and Godbey, G.C. (1983) The accuracy of self-reported participation rates. *Leisure Studies*, 2(2), 231–6.

Chase, D. and Harada, M. (1984) Response error in self-reported recreation participation. *Journal of Leisure Research*, 16(4), 322–9.

Child, E. (1983) Play and culture: a study of English and Asian children. *Leisure Studies*, 2(2), 169–86.

Chisnall, P.M. (1991) Market segmentation analysis. *The Essence of Marketing Research*, New York: Prentice-Hall, 76–91.

Christensen, J.E. (1980) A second look at the informal interview. *Journal of Leisure Research*, 12(2), 183–6.

Christensen, J.E. (1988) Statistical and methodological issues in leisure research. In Barnett, L.A. (ed.) *Research about Leisure: Past, Present and Future*. Champaign, IL: Sagamore Publishing, 175–92.

Clarke, J. and Critcher, C. (1985) *The Devil Makes Work: Leisure in Capitalist Britain*, London: Macmillan.

Claxton, J.D. (1994) Conjoint analysis in travel research: a manager's guide. In J.R.B. Ritchie and C.R. Goeldner (eds) *Travel, Tourism and Hospitality Research*, 2nd edn. New York: John Wiley, 513–22.

Coakes, S.J. and Steed, L.G. (1999) *SPSS Analysis Without Anguish: (Version 11.0 for Windows)*. Brisbane: John Wiley & Sons.

Coalter, F. (with Long, J. and Duffield, B.) (1988) *Recreational Welfare*. Aldershot: Avebury/Gower.

Coalter, F. (1990) Analysing leisure policy. In I. Henry (ed.) *Management and Planning in the Leisure Industries*. London: Macmillan, 149–78.

Coalter, F. (1993) Sports participation: price or priorities? *Leisure Studies*, 12(3), 171–82.

Cohen, E. (1972) Towards a sociology of international tourism. *Social Research*, 39(1), 164–82.

Cohen, E. (1984) The sociology of tourism: approaches, issues, and findings. *Annual Review of Sociology*, 10, 373–92.

Cohen, E. (1988) Traditions in the qualitative sociology of tourism. *Annals of Tourism Research*, 15(1), 29–46.

Cohen, E. (1993) The study of touristic images of native people: mitigating the stereotype of a stereotype. In D.G. Pearce and R.W. Butler (eds) *Tourism Research: Critiques and Challenges*. London: Routledge, 36–69.

Connell, J. and Lowe, A. (1997) Generating grounded theory from qualitative data: the application of inductive methods in tourism and hospitality management research. *Progress in Tourism and Hospitality Research*, 3, 165–73.

Coopers & Lybrand Associates (1981) *Service Provision and Pricing in Local Government*. London: HMSO.

Coppock, J.T. (1982) Geographical contributions to the study of leisure. *Leisure Studies*, 1(1), 1–28.

Coppock, J.T. and Duffield, B.S. (1975) *Recreation in the Countryside: A Spatial Analysis*. London: Macmillan.

Cordell, H.K., McDonald, B.L., Teasley, R.J., Bergstrom, J.C., Martin, J., Bason, J. and Leeworthy, V.R. (1999) Outdoor recreation participation trends. In H.K. Cordell (ed.) *Outdoor Recreation in American Life: A National Assessment of Demand and Supply Trends*. Champaign, IL: Sagamore Publishing, 219–32.

Cordell, H.K., Green, G.T., Leeworthy, V.R., Stephens, R., Fly, M.J. and Betz, C.J. (2005) United States of America: outdoor recreation. In G. Cushman, A.J. Veal and J. Zuzanek (eds) *Free Time and Leisure Participation: International Perspectives*. Wallingford, UK: CAB International, 245–64.

Corley, J. (1982) Employment in the leisure industries in Britain 1960–80. *Leisure Studies*, 1(1), 109–11.

Cowling, D. *et al.* (1983) *Identifying the Market: Catchment Areas of Sports Centres and Swimming Pools*. Study 24, London: Sports Council.

Craig Smith, N. (1991) The case study: a vital yet misunderstood research method. In N. Smith and P. Dainty (eds) *The Management Research Handbook*. London: Routledge, 145–58.

Critcher, C. (1992) Is there anything on the box? Leisure studies and media studies. *Leisure Studies*, 11(2), 97–122.

Crouch, D. (ed.) (1999) *Leisure/Tourism Geographies: Practices and Geographical Knowledge*. London: Routledge.

Crouch, G.I. and Shaw, R.N. (1991) *International Tourism Demand: A Meta-Analytical Integration of Research Findings*. Management Paper No. 36, Melbourne: Graduate School of Management, Monash University.

Crouch, G.I., Perdue, R.R., Timmermans, H.J.P. and Uysal, M. (eds) (2004) *Consumer Psychology of Tourism, Hospitality and Leisure*, Vol. 3. Wallingford: CABI Publishing.

Csikszentmihalyi, M. (1990) *Flow: The Psychology of Optimal Experience*. New York: Harper & Row.

Csikszentmihalyi, M. and Larson, R. (1987) Validity and reliability of the experience-sampling method. *Journal of Nervous and Mental Disease*, 175, 526–36.

Cumming, E. and Henry, W. (1961) *Growing Old: The Process of Disengagement*. New York: Praeger.

Cuneen, C. and Lynch, R. (1988) The social meaning of conflict in riots at the Australian Grand Prix motorcycle races. *Leisure Studies*, 7(1), 1–20.

Cuneen, C., Findlay, M., Lynch, R. and Tupper, V. (1989) *Dynamics of Collective Conflict: Riots at the Bathurst 'Bike Races*. North Ryde, NSW: Law Book Co.

Cunningham, H. (1980) *Leisure in the Industrial Revolution*, London: Croom Helm.

Cushman, G., Veal, A.J. and Zuzanek, J. (eds) (2005a) *Free Time and Leisure Participation: International Perspectives*, Wallingford, UK: CAB International.

Cushman, G., Veal, A.J. and Zuzanek, J. (2005b) National leisure participation and time-use surveys: a future. In G. Cushman, A.J. Veal and J. Zuzanek, J. *Free Time and Leisure Participation: International Perspectives*, Wallingford, UK: CAB International, 283–92.

Dale, T. and Ford, I. (2002) *Participation in Exercise, Recreation and Sport, 2001*. Canberra: Australian Sports Commission, available at: www.ausport.gov.au/scorsresearch/ research.asp (accessed March 2005).

Dann, G.M.S. (ed.) (2002) *The Tourist as a Metaphor of the Social World*. Wallingford, UK: CAB International.

Dann, G. and Cohen, E. (1991) Sociology and tourism. *Annals of Tourism Research*, 18(1), 155–69.

Dann, G., Nash, D. and Pearce, P. (1988) Special issue: methodological issues in tourism research. *Annals of Tourism Research*, 15(1).

Darcy, S. (1994) Australian leisure participation: the monthly data. *Australian Journal of Leisure and Recreation*, 4(1), 26–32.

Darcy, S. (1998) *People with a Disability and Tourism: A Bibliography*. School of Leisure and Tourism Studies, University of Technology, Sydney, On-line Bibliography 7, available at: www.business.uts.edu.au/lst/research/ bibs.html (accessed March 2005).

Davies, B. (2003) The role of quantitative and qualitative research in industrial studies of tourism. *Journal of Travel Research*, 30(1), 59–63.

Dawson, J. and Hillier, J. (1995) Competitor mystery shopping: methodological considerations and implications for the MRS Code of Conduct. *Journal of the Market Research Society*, 37(4), 417–43.

Deem, R. (1986) *All Work and No Play? The Sociology of Women and Leisure*. Milton Keynes: Open University Press.

Denzin, N.K. and Lincoln, Y.S. (eds) (1994) *Handbook of Qualitative Research*, Thousand Oaks, CA: Sage.

Department of the Arts, Sport, the Environment, Tourism and Territories (DASETT) (1988a) *The Economic Impact of Sport and Recreation – Household Expenditure*. Technical Paper No. 1, Canberra: AGPS.

Department of the Arts, Sport, the Environment, Tourism and Territories (DASETT) (1988b) *The Economic Impact of Sport and Recreation – Regular Physical Activity*. Technical Paper No. 2, Canberra: AGPS.

Dillman, D.A. (2000) *Mail and Telephone Surveys: The Total Design Method*, 2nd edn. New York: Wiley.

Douglas, J.D., Rasmussen, P.K. and Flanagan, C.A. (1977) *The Nude Beach*. Beverley Hills, CA, Sage.

Driver, B.L. and Bruns, D.H. (1999) Concepts and uses of the benefits approach to leisure. In E.L. Jackson and T.L. Burton (eds) *Leisure Studies: Prospects for the Twenty-First Century*. State College, PA: Venture, 349–70.

Driver, B.L., Brown, P.J. and Peterson, G.L. (eds) (1991) *Benefits of Leisure*. State College, PA: Venture.

Driver, B.L., Tinsley, H.E.A. and Manfredo, M.J. (1991) The 'Paragraphs About Leisure' and 'Recreation Experience Preference' scales: results from two inventories designed to assess the breadth of perceived psychological benefits of leisure. In B.L. Driver, P.J. Brown and G.L. Peterson (eds) *Benefits of Leisure*. State College, PA: Venture, 263–301.

Duffy, M.E. (1987) Methodological triangulation: a vehicle for merging qualitative and qualitative research methods. *IMAGE: Journal of Nursing Scholarship*, 19, 130–3.

Dunne, S. (1995) *Interviewing Techniques for Writers and Researchers*. London: A & C. Black.

During, S. (ed.) (1993) *The Cultural Studies Reader*. London: Routledge.

Dyer, R. (1993) Entertainment and utopia. In S. During (ed.) *The Cultural Studies Reader*, London: Routledge, 271–83.

Eadington, W.R. and Redman, M. (1991) Economics and tourism. *Annals of Tourism Research*, 18(1), 41–56.

Echtner, C.M. and Ritchie, J.R.B. (1993) The measurement of destination image: an empirical assessment. *Journal of Travel Research*, 21(1), 3–13.

Edwards, A. (1991) The reliability of tourism statistics. *Economist Intelligence Unit: Travel and Tourism Analyst*, 1, 62–75.

Elias, N. (1986) Introduction. In Elias, N., and Dunning, E. *Quest for Excitement: Sport and Leisure in the Civilizing Process*. Oxford: Basil Blackwell, 19–62.

Elias, N. and Dunning, E. (1986) *Quest for Excitement: Sport and Leisure in the Civilizing Process*. Oxford: Basil Blackwell.

Ely, M. (1981) Systematic observation as a recreation research tool. In D. Mercer (ed.) *Outdoor Recreation: Australian Perspectives*. Malvern, Vic.: Sorrett, 57–67.

Faulkner, B., Pearce, P., Shaw, R. and Weiler, B. (2003) Tourism research in Australia: confronting the challenges of the 1990s and beyond. In L. Fredline, L. Jago and C. Cooper (eds) *Progressing Tourism Research – Bill Faulkner*. Channel View Publications, Clevedon, UK, 303–40.

Field, D.N. (1972) The telephone interview in leisure research. *Journal of Leisure Research*, 5(1), 51–9.

Finn, M., Elliott-White, M. and Walton, M. (2000) *Tourism and Leisure Research Methods*. Harlow, UK: Longman.

Fiske, J. (1983) Surfalism and sandiotics: the beach in Oz popular culture. *Australian Journal of Cultural Studies*, 1(2), 120–49.

Fogleson, R.E. (2001) *Married to the Mouse: Walt Disney World and Orlando*. New Haven, CN: Yale University Press.

Foucault, M. (1979) *Discipline and Punish*. Harmondsworth: Penguin.

Franklin, A. (2003) *Tourism; An Introduction*. London: Sage.

Geary, C., Taylor, T., Toohey, K. and Lynch, R. (1996) *Leisure, Sport and Ethnicity: A Bibliography*. School of Leisure and Tourism Studies, University of Technology, Sydney, On-line Bibliography 6, available at: www.business.uts.edu.au/lst/research/ bibs.html (accessed March, 2005).

George, D. and Mallery, P. (2005) *SPSS for Windows Step by Step: A Simple Guide and Reference, 12.0 Update*. Boston, MA: Pearson Education.

Gibbs, G. (2002) *Qualitative Data Analysis: Explorations with NVivo*. London: Open University Press.

Giddens, A. (ed.) (1974) *Positivism and Sociology*. London: Heinemann.

Giddens, A. (1993) *Sociology*. Cambridge: Polity Press.

Glancy, M. (1986) Participant observation in the recreation setting. *Journal of Leisure Research*, 18(2), 59–80.

Glancy, M. (1993) Achieving intersubjectivity: the process of becoming the subject in leisure research. *Leisure Studies*, 12 (1), 45–60.

Glaser, B. and Strauss, A.L. (1967) *The Discovery of Grounded Theory: Strategies for Qualitative Research*, Chicago, IL: Aldine.

Glass, G.V., McGaw, B. and Smith, M.L. (1981) *Meta-Analysis in Social Research*. Beverley Hills, CA: Sage.

Glyptis, S.A. (1981a) People at play in the countryside. *Geography*, 66, 277–85.

Glyptis, S.A. (1981b) Room to relax in the countryside. *The Planner*, 67(5), 120–22.

Godbey, G. and Scott, D. (1990) Reorienting leisure research – the case for qualitative methods. *Society and Leisure*, 13(1), 189–206.

Goeldner, C.R. (1994) Travel and tourism information sources. In J.R.B. Ritchie and C.R. Goeldner (eds) *Travel, Tourism and Hospitality Research*, 2nd edn. New York: John Wiley, 81–90.

Goeldner, C.R. and Dicke, K. (1980) *Bibliography of Tourism and Travel Research*. (9 vols), Boulder, CO: University of Colorado.

Goffman, I. (1959) *The Presentation of Self in Everyday Life*. Garden City, NY: Doubleday/ Anchor.

Gold, S.M. (1972) The non-use of neighbourhood parks. *Journal of the American Institute of Planners*, November, 369–78.

Graburn, N.H.H. and Jafari, J. (1991) Introduction: tourism social sciences. *Annals of Tourism Research*, 18(1) (Special Issue: Tourism Social Sciences), 1–11.

Graburn, N.H.H. and Moore, R.S. (1994) Anthropological research on tourism. In J.R.B. Ritchie and C.R. Goeldner (eds) *Travel, Tourism and Hospitality Research*, 2nd edn. New York: John Wiley, 233–42.

Grant, D. (1984) Another look at the beach. *Australian Journal of Cultural Studies*, 2(2), 131–8.

Gratton, C. and Taylor, P. (1995) From economic theory to leisure practice via empirics: the case of demand and price. *Leisure Studies*, 14(4), 245–62.

Gratton, C. and Taylor, P. (2000) *Economics of Sport and Recreation*. London: E & F N Spon.

Gratton, C. and Tice, A. (1994) Trends in sports participation in Britain 1977–1987. *Leisure Studies*, 13(1), 49–66.

Gratton, C. and Veal, A.J. (2005) Great Britain. In G. Cushman, A.J. Veal and J. Zuzanek (eds) *Free Time and Leisure Participation: International Perspectives*. Wallingford, UK: CAB International, 109–26.

Green, E., Hebron, S. and Woodward, B. (1990) *Women's Leisure, What Leisure?* London: Macmillan.

Green, H., Hunter, C. and Moore, B. (1990) Application of the Delphi technique in tourism. *Annals of Tourism Research*, 17(2), 270–9.

Greenbaum, T.L. (1998) *The Handbook for Focus Group Research*, 2nd edn. Thousand Oaks, CA: Sage.

Greenbaum, T.L. (2000) *Moderating Focus Groups: A Practical Guide for Group Facilitation*. Thousand Oaks, CA: Sage.

Grichting, W.L. and Caltabiano, M.L. (1986) Amount and direction of bias in survey interviewing. *Australian Psychologist*, 21(1), 69–78.

Griffin, C., Hobson, D., MacIntosh, S. and McCabe, T. (1982) Women and leisure. In J. Hargreaves (ed.) *Sport, Culture and Ideology*. London: Routledge, 99–116.

Hall, S. and Jefferson, T. (eds) (1976) *Resistance through Rituals: Youth Culture in Post-war Britain*. London: Hutchinson.

Hamilton-Smith, E. (ed.) (1994) Play: a reflection of society. Theme issue of *Society and Leisure*, 17(1).

Hantrais, L. and Kamphorst, T.J. (1987) *Trends in the Arts: A Multinational Perspective*. Amersfoot, Holland: Giordano Bruno.

Harper, J.A. and Balmer, K.R. (1989) The perceived benefits of public leisure services: an exploratory investigation. *Society and Leisure*, 12(1), 171–88.

Harper, W. and Hultsman, J. (1992) Interpreting leisure as text: the whole. *Leisure Studies*, 11(3), 233–42.

Harris, R. and Leiper, N. (eds) (1995) *Sustainable Tourism: An Australian Perspective*. Melbourne: Butterworth-Heinemann.

Harvard Business School (n.d.), Harvard Business School Case Studies. Cambridge, MA: Harvard University, available at: www.hbsp.harvard.edu (accessed Oct. 2004).

Hatry, H.P. and Dunn, D.R. (1971) *Measuring the Effectiveness of Local Government Services: Recreation*, Washington, DC: The Urban Institute.

Havitz, M.E. and Sell, J.A. (1991) The experimental method and leisure/recreation research: promoting a more active role. *Society and Leisure*, 14(1), 47–68.

Hedges, B. (1986) *Personal Leisure Histories*. London: Sports Council/Economic and Social Research Council.

Hemingway, J. (1995) Leisure studies and interpretive social inquiry. *Leisure Studies*, 14(1), 32–47.

Henderson, K.A. (1990) Reality comes through a prism: method choices in leisure research. *Society and Leisure*, 13(1), 169–88.

Henderson, K.A. (1991) *Dimensions of Choice: A Qualitative Approach to Recreation, Parks, and Leisure Research*, State College, PA: Venture.

Henderson, K.A. and Bialeschki, D. (1995) *Evaluating Leisure Services: Making Enlightened Decisions*. State College, PA: Venture.

Henderson, K.M., Bialeschki, D., Shaw, S.M. and Freysinger, V.J. (1989) *A Time of One's Own: A Feminist Perspective on Women's Leisure*. State College, PA: Venture.

Henley Centre for Forecasting (1986) *The Economic Impact and Importance of Sport in the United Kingdom*. London: Sports Council.

Henley Centre for Forecasting (quarterly) *Leisure Futures*, London: HCF.

Henry, I.P. (1993) *The Politics of Leisure Policy*. Basingstoke: Macmillan.

Henry, I.P. (2001) *The Politics of Leisure Policy*, 2nd edn. Basingstoke: Palgrave.

Henry, I. and Paramio Salcines, J.L. (1998) Sport, culture and urban regimes: the case of Bilbao. In M.F. Collins and I.S. Cooper (eds) *Leisure Management: Issues and Applications*. Wallingford, UK: CAB International, 97–112.

Henry, I. and Spink, J. (1990) Planning for leisure: the commercial and public sectors. In I.P. Henry (ed.) *Management and Planning in the Leisure Industries*. London: Macmillan, 33–69.

Hodder, I. (1994) The interpretation of documents and material culture. In N.K. Denzin and Y.S. Lincoln (eds) *Handbook of Qualitative Research*. Thousand Oaks, CA: Sage, 393–402.

Hollands, R.G. (1985) Working class youth, leisure and the search for work. In S.R. Parker and A.J. Veal (eds) *Work, Non-work and Leisure*. London: Leisure Studies Association, 3–29.

Howard, K. and Sharp, J.A. (1983) *The Management of a Student Research Project*. Aldershot, UK: Gower.

Howat, G., Crilley, G., Absher, J. and Milne, I. (1996) Measuring customer service quality in sports and leisure centres. *Managing Leisure*, 1(2), 77–90.

Howat, G., Crilley, G., Mikilewicz, S., Edgecombe, S., March, H., Murray, D. and Bell, B. (2003) Service quality, customer satisfaction and behavioural intentions of Australian aquatic centre customers, 1999–2001. *Annals of Leisure Research*, 5, 52–65.

Howe, C.Z. (1991) Considerations when using phenomenology in leisure inquiry: beliefs, methods and analysis in naturalistic research. *Leisure Studies*, 10(1), 49–62.

Howell, S. and Badmin, P. (1996) *Performance, Monitoring and Evaluation in Leisure Management*. London: Pitman.

Huberman, A.M. and Miles, M.B. (1994) Data management and analysis methods. In N.K. Denzin and Y.S. Lincoln (eds) *Handbook of Qualitative Research*. Thousand Oaks, CA: Sage, 428–44.

Hudson, S. (1988) *How to Conduct Community Needs Assessment Surveys in Public Parks and Recreation*. Columbus, OH: Publishing Horizons.

Hudson, S., Snaith, T., Miller, G. and Hudson, P. (2001) Distribution channels in the travel industry: using mystery shoppers to understand the influence of travel agency recommendations. *Journal of Travel Research*, 40(2), 148–54.

Huizinga, J. (1955) *Homo Ludens: A Study of the Play Element in Culture*. Boston, MA: Beacon Press.

Hultsman, J. and Harper, W. (1992) Interpreting leisure as text: the part. *Leisure Studies*, 11(2), 135–46.

Hurst, F. (1994) En route surveys. In J.R.B. Ritchie and C.R. Goeldner (eds) *Travel, Tourism and Hospitality Research*, 2nd edn. New York: John Wiley, 453–72.

Iacocca, L.A. (1984) *Iacocca: An Autobiography*. Toronto: Bantam Books.

Ingham, R. (1986) Psychological contributions to the study of leisure – Part One. *Leisure Studies*, 5(3), 255–80.

Ingham, R. (1987) Psychological contributions to the study of leisure – Part Two. *Leisure Studies*, 6(1), 1–14.

Iso-Ahola, S.E. (1980) *The Social Psychology of Leisure and Recreation*. Dubuque, IA: Wm. C. Brown.

Jackson, E.L. and Burton, T.L. (eds) (1989) *Understanding Leisure and Recreation: Mapping the Past and Charting the Future*. State College, PA: Venture.

Jackson, E.L. and Burton, T.L. (eds) (1999) *Leisure Studies: Prospects for the Twenty-First Century*. State College, PA: Venture.

Jackson, E.L. and Scott, D. (1999) Constraints to leisure. In E.L. Jackson and T.L. Burton (eds) *Leisure Studies: Prospects for the Twenty-First Century*. State College, PA: Venture, 299–322.

Jafari, J. (ed.) (2000) *Encyclopedia of Tourism*. London: Routledge.

Jafari, J. and Aaser, D. (1988) Tourism as the subject of doctoral dissertations. *Annals of Tourism Research*, 15(3), 407–29.

James, K. and Embrey, L. (2002) Adolescent girls' leisure: a conceptual framework highlighting factors that can affect girls' recreational choices. *Annals of Leisure Research*, 5, 14–26.

Jarvie, G. and Maguire, J. (1994) *Sport and Leisure in Social Thought*. London: Routledge.

Jenkins, J. and Pigram, J. (eds) (2003) *Encyclopedia of Leisure and Outdoor Recreation*. London: Routledge.

Jenkins, J. and Stolk, P. (2003) Statutory authorities dancing with enterprise: WA Inc., the Western Australian Tourism Commission and the 'Global Dance Affair'. *Annals of Leisure Research*, 6(3), 222–44.

Jordan, F. and Gibson, H. (2004) Let your data do the talking: researching the solo travel experiences of British and American women. In J. Phillimore and L. Godson (eds) *Qualitative Research in Tourism: Ontologies, Epistemologies and Methodologies*. London: Routledge, 215–35.

Kamphorst, T.J. and Roberts, K. (eds) (1989) *Trends in Sports: A Multinational Perspective*. Culemborg, Holland: Giordano Bruno.

Kamphorst, T.J., Tibori, T.T. and Giliam, M.J. (1984) Quantitative and qualitative research: shall the twain ever meet? *World Leisure & Recreation*, 26, 25–7.

Kasprzyk, D., Duncan, G., Kalton, G. and Singh, M.P. (1989) *Panel Surveys*. New York: John Wiley & Sons.

Keirle, I. and Walsh, S. (1999) Objective assessment of countryside recreation by observation. *Journal of Environmental Planning and Management*, 42(6), 875–87.

Kellehear, A. (1993) *The Unobtrusive Researcher: A Guide to Methods*. Sydney: Allen & Unwin.

Kelly, G.A. (1955) *The Psychology of Personal Constructs*. New York: Norton.

Kelly, J.R. (1980) Leisure and quality: beyond the quantitative barrier in research. In T.L. Goodale and P.A. Witt (eds) *Recreation and Leisure: Issues in an Era of Change*. State College, PA: Venture, 300–14.

Kelly, J.R. (1983) *Leisure Identities and Interactions*. London: Allen & Unwin.

Kelly, J.R. (1987a) *Freedom to Be: A New Sociology of Leisure*. New York: Macmillan.

Kelly, J.R. (1987b) *Recreation Trends – Toward the Year 2000*. Champaign, IL: Management Learning Laboratories.

Kelly, J.R. (1994) The symbolic interaction metaphor and leisure: critical challenges. *Leisure Studies*, 13(2), 81–96.

Kelly, J.R. (1997) Leisure as life: outline of a poststructuralist reconstruction. *Loisir et Société/Society and Leisure*, 20(2), 401–18.

Kelly, J.R. and Godbey, G. (1992) *The Sociology of Leisure*. State College, PA: Venture.

Kelsey, C. and Gray, H. (1986a) *The Citizen Survey Process in Parks and Recreation*. Reston, VA: American Alliance for Health, P.E., Recreation and Dance.

Kelsey, C. and Gray, H. (1986b) *The Feasibility Study Process for Parks and Recreation*. Reston, VA: American Alliance for Health, P.E., Recreation and Dance.

Kidder, L.H. (1981) *Selltiz, Wrightsman and Cook's Research Methods in Social Relations*. New York: Holt, Rinehart & Winston.

Kimmel, A.J. (1988) *Ethics and Values in Applied Social Research*. Newbury Park, CA: Sage.

Kleiber, D. (1999) *Leisure Experience and Human Development*. New York: Basic Books.

Klein, N. (1999) *No Logo: Taking Aim at the Brand Bullies*. New York: Picador.

Klugman, K., Kuenz, J., Waldrop, S. and Willis, S. (1995) *Inside the Mouse: The Project on Disney*. Durham, NC: Duke University Press.

Kraus, R. and Allen, L. (1987) *Research and Evaluation in Recreation, Parks, and Leisure Studies*. Columbus, OH: Publishing Horizons.

Kraus, R. and Allen, L. (1998) *Research and Evaluation in Recreation, Parks, and Leisure Studies,* 2nd edn. Boston, MA: Allyn & Bacon.

Krejcie, R.V. and Morgan, D.W. (1970) Determining sample size for research activities. *Educational and Psychological Measurement,* 30, 607–10.

Krenz, C. and Sax, G. (1986) What quantitative research is and why it doesn't work. *American Behavioral Scientist,* 30(1), 58–69.

Krippendorf, J. (1987) *The Holiday Makers: Understanding the Impact of Leisure and Travel.* Oxford: Heinemann.

Krueger, R.A. (1988) *Focus Groups: A Practical Guide for Applied Research.* Newbury Park, CA: Sage.

Labovitz, S. and Hagedorn, R. (1971) *Introduction to Social Research.* New York: McGraw-Hill.

Ladkin, A. (2004) The life and work history methodology: a discussion of its potential use for tourism and hospitality research. In J. Phillimore and L. Godson (eds) *Qualitative Research in Tourism: Ontologies, Epistemologies and Methodologies.* London: Routledge, 236–54.

Langer, M. (1997) *Service Quality in Tourism.* Frankfurt: Peter Lang.

Lainsbury, A. (2000) *Once upon an American Dream: The Story of Euro Disneyland.* Lawrence, KS: University of Kansas Press.

LaPage, W.F. (1981) A further look at the informal interview. *Journal of Leisure Research,* 13(2), 174–6.

LaPage, W.F. (1994) Using panels for tourism and travel research. In J.R.B. Ritchie and C.R. Goeldner (eds) *Travel, Tourism and Hospitality Research,* 2nd edn. New York: John Wiley, 481–6.

Lavrakas, P.K. (1993) *Telephone Survey Methods: Sampling, Selection and Supervision,* 2nd edn. Newbury Park, CA: Sage.

Leiper, N. (1995) *Tourism Management.* Collingwood, Vic.: RMIT Press/TAFE Publications.

Levinson, D. and Christensen, K. (eds) (1996) *Encyclopedia of World Sport: From Ancient Times to the Present.* Santa Barbara, CA: ABC-CLIO.

Lofland, J. and Lofland, L.H. (1984) *Analyzing Social Settings: A Guide to Qualitative Observation and Analysis,* 2nd edn. Belmont, CA: Wadsworth.

Long, P. (2000) Tourism development regimes in the inner city fringe: the case of Discover Islington, London. In B. Bramwell and B. Lane (eds) *Tourism Collaboration and Partnerships: Politics, Practice and Sustainability.* Clevedon, UK: Channel View Publications, 183–99.

Loomis, R.J. (1987) *Museum Visitor Evaluation: New Tool for Management.* Nashville, TN: American Association for State and Local History.

Lucas, R.C. (1970) *User Evaluation of Campgrounds.* St. Paul, MN: US Forest Service.

Lundberg, G.A., Komarovsky, M. and McInerny, M.A. (1934) *Leisure: A Suburban Study.* New York: Columbia University Press.

Lynch, R. and Brown, P. (1995) *An Australian Leisure Research Agenda.* Canberra: AGPS.

Lynch, R. and Brown, P. (1999) Utility of large-scale leisure research agendas. *Managing Leisure,* 4(2), 63–77.

Lynch, R. and Veal, A.J. (1996) *Australian Leisure.* Melbourne: Longman Australia.

MacCannell, D. (1976) *The Tourist: A New Theory of the Leisure Class.* London: Macmillan.

MacCannell, D. (1993) *The Empty Meeting Grounds.* London: Routledge.

McCall, G.J. and Simmons, J.L. (eds) (1969) *Issues in Participant Observation.* Reading, MA: Addison-Wesley.

McFee, M. (1992) *LSA Publications Index Book.* Eastbourne: Leisure Studies Association.

McGuiggan, R.L. (2000) The Myers-Briggs Type Indicator and leisure attribute preference. In Woodside, A.G., Crouch, G.I., Mazanec, J.A., Oppermann, M. and Sakai, M.Y. (eds)

Consumer Psychology of Tourism, Hospitality and Leisure. Wallingford, UK: CAB International, 245–67.

McNiff, J. and Whitehead, J. (2002) *Action Research: Principles and Practice*. London: Routledge/Falmer.

McRobbie, A. (1994) *Postmodernism and Popular Culture*. London: Routledge.

Maguire, J. (1988) Doing figurational sociology: some preliminary observations on methodological issues and sensitizing concepts. *Leisure Studies*, 7(2), 187–94.

Mallon, B. (1984) *The Olympics: A Bibliography*. New York: Garland.

Marans, R.W. and Mohai, P. (1991) Leisure resources, recreation activity, and the quality of life. In B.L. Driver, P.J. Brown and G.L. Peterson (eds) *Benefits of Leisure*. State College, PA: Venture, 351–64.

Marriott, K. (1987) *Recreation Planning: A Manual for Local Government*, Adelaide: Dept. of Recreation and Sport, South Australia.

Marsh, P., Rosser, E. and Harré, R. (1978) *The Rules of Disorder*. London: Routledge.

Martilla, J.A. and James, J.C. (1977) Importance-performance analysis. *Journal of Marketing*, 41(1), 77–9.

Matthews, H.G. and Richter, L. (1991) Political science and tourism. *Annals of Tourism Research*, 18(1), 120–35.

Mazanec, J.A., Crouch, G.I., Brent Ritchie, J.R. and Woodside, A.G. (eds) (2001) *Consumer Psychology of Tourism, Hospitality and Leisure*, Vol. 2. Wallingford, UK: CAB International.

Meyersohn, R. (1958) A comprehensive bibliography on leisure. In E. Larrabee and R. Meyersohn (eds) *Mass Leisure*. Glencoe, IL: Free Press, 389–420.

Miles, M.B. and Huberman, A.M. (1994) *Qualitative Data Analysis*, 2nd edn. Thousand Oaks, CA: Sage.

Miles, M. and Weitzman, E. (1994) *Computer Programs for Qualitative Data Analysis*. Thousand Oaks, CA: Sage.

Mitchell, A. (1985) *The Nine American Lifestyles*. New York: Collier Macmillan.

Mitchell, L.S. (1994) Research on the geography of tourism. In J.R.B. Ritchie and C.R. Goeldner (eds) *Travel, Tourism and Hospitality Research, 2nd edn*. New York: John Wiley, 197–208.

Mitchell, L.S. and Murphy, P.E. (1991) Geography and tourism. *Annals of Tourism Research*, 18(1), 57–70.

Moeller, G.H., Meschner, M.A., More, T.A. and Shafer, E.L. (1980a) The informal interview as a technique for recreation research. *Journal of Leisure Research*, 12(2), 174–82.

Moeller, G.H., Meschner, M.A., More, T.A. and Shafer, E.L. (1980b) A response to 'A second look at the informal interview'. *Journal of Leisure Research*, 12(2), 187–8.

Moeller, G.H. and Shafer, E.L. (1994) The Delphi technique: a tool for long-range tourism and travel planning. In J.R.B. Ritchie and C.R. Goeldner (eds) *Travel, Tourism and Hospitality Research*, 2nd edn. New York: John Wiley, 473–80.

Moorhouse, H.F. (1989) Models of work, models of leisure. In C. Rojek (ed.) *Leisure for Leisure*. London: Macmillan, 15–35.

Morgan, D.L. (ed.) (1993) *Successful Focus Groups: Advancing the State of the Art*. Newbury Park, CA: Sage.

Morgan, D. (1994) It began with the piton: the challenge to British rock climbing in a post-modernist framework. In I. Henry (ed.) *Leisure: Modernity, Postmodernity and Lifestyles*. Eastbourne, Sussex: Leisure Studies Association, 341–54.

Morse, J. and Richards, L. (2002) *Readme First for a User's Guide to Qualitative Methods*. Thousand Oaks, CA: Sage.

Murphy, P. (1991) Data gathering for community-oriented tourism planning: a case study of Vancouver Island, British Columbia. *Leisure Studies*, 10(1), 65–80.

Myerscough, J. (1988) *The Economic Importance of the Arts in Britain*. London: Policy Studies Institute.

Nash, D. and Smith, V.L. (1991) Anthropology and tourism. *Annals of Tourism Research*, 18(1), 170–7.

Noonan, D.S. (2003) Contingent valuation and cultural resources: a meta-analytic review of the literature. *Journal of Cultural Economics*, 27(3/4), 159–70.

O'Brien, S. and Ford, R. (1988) Can we at last say goodbye to social class? An examination of the usefulness and stability of some alternative methods of measurement. *Journal of the Market Research Society*, 30(3), 289–332.

O'Connor, B. and Boyle, R. (1993) Dallas with balls: televised sport, soap opera and male and female pleasures. *Leisure Studies*, 12(2), 107–20.

OECD – Organisation for Economic Cooperation and Development (annual) *International Tourism and Tourism Policies in OECD Member Countries*. Paris: OECD.

Office for National Statistics (ONS) (Annual (a)) *Family Spending: A Report on the Family Expenditure Survey*. London: ONS.

Office for National Statistics (ONS) (Annual (b)) *General Household Survey*. London: ONS.

Office for National Statistics (ONS) (1996) *Living in Britain, 1996*. London: HMSO.

Office for National Statistics (ONS) (1997) *General Household Survey*. London: ONS.

Office for National Statistics (ONS) (2004a) *Travel Trends 2003: A Report on the International Passenger Survey*. London: Office for National Statistics.

Office for National Statistics (ONS) (2004b) *Family Spending: A Report on the 2002–2003 Expenditure and Food Survey*. London: HMSO.

Office of Population Censuses and Surveys (OPCS) (annual) *General Household Survey*. London: HMSO.

Olszewska, A. and Roberts, K. (eds) (1989) *Leisure and Lifestyle: A Comparative Analysis of Free Time*. Sage: London.

Oppenheim, A.N. (1992) *Questionnaire Design, Interviewing and Attitude Measurement*. London: Pinter.

Oppermann, M. (1998) *Sex Tourism and Prostitution: Aspects of Leisure, Recreation and Work*. Elmsford, NY: Cognizant.

Pallant, J.F. (2004) *SPSS Survival Manual: A Step by Step Guide to Data Analysis Using SPSS*. Sydney: Allen & Unwin.

Palmer, I. and Dunford, R. (2002) Managing discursive tension: the co-existence of individualist and collaborative discourses in Flight Centre. *Journal of Management Studies*. 39(8), 1045–70.

Parker, S. (1971) *The Future of Work and Leisure*. London: Palladin.

Parker, S.R. (1976) *The Sociology of Leisure*. London: George Allen & Unwin.

Parker, T. (1988) *Red Hill: A Mining Community*. London: Coronet.

Parry, N.C.A. (1983) Sociological contributions to the study of leisure. *Leisure Studies*, 2(1), 57–82.

Parsons, W. (1995) *Public Policy*. Cheltenham: Edward Elgar.

Patmore, A. (1983) *Recreation and Resources*. Oxford: Basil Blackwell.

Pearce, D. (1987) *Tourism Today: A Geographical Analysis*. Harlow: Longman.

Pearce, D.G. and Butler, R.W. (eds) (1993) *Tourism Research: Critiques and Challenges*. London: Routledge.

Pearce, P.L. (1982) *The Social Psychology of Tourist Behaviour*. Oxford: Pergamon.

Pearce, P.L. (1988) *The Ulysses Factor: Evaluating Visitors in Tourist Settings*. New York: Springer-Verlag.

Pearce, P.L. and Stringer, P.F. (1991) Psychology and tourism. *Annals of Tourism Research*, 18(1), 136–54.

Pendergast, T. and Pendergast, S. (eds) (1999) *St James Encyclopedia of Popular Culture*. Detroit, MI: St James Press.

Pentland, W.E., Harvey, A.S., Powell Lawton, M. and McColl, M.A. (eds) (1999) *Time Use Research in the Social Sciences*. New York: Kluwer/Plenum.

Perdue, R.R. and Botkin, M.R. (1988) Visitor survey versus conversion study. *Annals of Tourism Research*, 15(1), 76–87.

Perkins, H.C. and Cushman, G. (eds) (1993) *Leisure, Recreation and Tourism*, Auckland: Longman Paul.

Perkins, H.C. and Cushman, G. (eds) (1998) *Time Out? Leisure, Recreation and Tourism in New Zealand and Australia*. Auckland: Longman.

Peterson, K.I. (1994) Qualitative research methods for the travel and tourism industry. In J.R.B. Ritchie and C.R. Goeldner (eds) *Travel, Tourism and Hospitality Research*, 2nd edn. New York: John Wiley, 487–92.

Philips, D. (2004) Stately pleasure domes – nationhood, monarchy and industry: the celebration exhibition in Britain. *Leisure Studies*, 23(2), 95–108.

Phillimore, J. and Godson, L. (eds) (2004a) *Qualitative Research in Tourism: Ontologies, Epistemologies and Methodologies*. London: Routledge.

Phillimore, J. and Godson, L. (eds) (2004b) Progress in qualitative research in tourism. In *Qualitative Research in Tourism: Ontologies, Epistemologies and Methodologies*. London: Routledge, 3–29.

Pieper, J. (1963) *Leisure: The Basis of Culture*. New York: Random House.

Pigram, J. (1983) *Outdoor Recreation and Resource Management*. London: Croom Helm.

Pizam, A. (1994) Planning a tourism research investigation. In J.R.B. Ritchie and C.R. Goeldner (eds) *Travel, Tourism and Hospitality Research*, 2nd edn. New York: John Wiley, 91–104.

Pollard, W.E. (1987) Decision making and the use of evaluation research. *American Behavioral Scientist*, 30(6), 661–76.

Prior, L. (2003) *Using Documents in Social Research*. London: Sage.

Project on Disney (1995) *Inside the Mouse: Work and Play at Disney World*. Durham, NC: Duke University Press.

Punch, M. (1994) Politics and ethics in qualitative research. In N.K. Denzin and Y.S. Lincoln (eds) *Handbook of Qualitative Research*. Thousand Oaks, CA: Sage, 83–98.

Rapoport, R. and Rapoport, R.N. (1975) *Leisure and the Family Life Cycle*. London: Routledge.

Reason, P. and Bradbury, H. (eds) (2001) *Handbook of Action Research: Participative Inquiry and Practice*. London: Sage.

Reynolds, F. and Johnson, D. (1978) Validity of focus group findings. *Journal of Advertising Research*, 19(1), 3–24.

Richards, T.J. and Richards, L. (1994) Using computers in qualitative research. In N.K. Denzin and Y.S. Lincoln (eds) *Handbook of Qualitative Research*. Thousand Oaks, CA: Sage, 445–62.

Richter, L.K. (1989) *The Politics of Tourism in Asia*. Honolulu, HA: University of Hawaii Press.

Richter, L.K. (1994) The political dimensions of tourism. In J.R.B. Ritchie and C.R. Goeldner (eds) *Travel, Tourism and Hospitality Research*, 2nd edn. New York: John Wiley, 219–32.

Riley, R.W. and Love, L.L. (2000) The state of qualitative tourism research. *Annals of Tourism Research*, 27(1), 164–87.

Ritchie, J.R.B. (1994) Tourism research: policy and managerial priorities for the 1990s and beyond. In Pearce, D.G. and Butler, R.W. (eds) *Tourism Research: Critiques and Challenges*. London: Routledge, 201–16.

Ritchie, J.R.B. and Goeldner, C.R. (eds) (1994) *Travel, Tourism and Hospitality Research*, 2nd edn. New York: John Wiley.

Roberts, B. (2002) *Biographical Research*. Buckingham, UK: Open University Press.

Roberts, K. (1978) *Contemporary Society and the Growth of Leisure*. London: Longman.

Roberts, K. (1983) *Youth and Leisure*. London: Allen & Unwin.

Roberts, K. (1999) *Leisure in Contemporary Society*. Wallingford, UK: CAB International.

Robertson, R.W. and Veal, A.J. (1987) *Port Hacking Visitor Use Study*, Sydney: Centre for Leisure and Tourism Studies, University of Technology, Sydney.

Rojek, C. (1985) *Capitalism and Leisure Theory*. London: Tavistock.

Rojek, C. (1989) Leisure and recreation theory. In E.L. Jackson and T.L. Burton (eds) *Understanding Leisure and Recreation: Mapping the Past and Charting the Future*. State College, PA: Venture, 69–88.

Rojek, C. (1993) Disney culture. *Leisure Studies*, 12(2), 121–36.

Rojek, C. (1995) *Decentring Leisure: Rethinking Leisure Theory*. London: Sage.

Rojek, C. (2000) *Leisure and Culture*. Basingstoke: Macmillan.

Rose, D. (ed.) (2000) *Researching Social and Economic Change: the Uses of Household Panel Studies*. London: Routledge.

Rose, H. (1991) Case studies. In G. Allen and C. Skinner (eds) *Handbook for Research Students in the Social Sciences*. Brighton: Falmer, 190–202.

Rowe, D. (1995) *Popular Cultures: Rock Music, Sport and the Politics of Pleasure*. London: Sage.

Rowe, D. (ed.) (2004) *Critical Readings: Sport, Culture and the Media*. Maidenhead: Open University Press.

Rowe, D. and Brown, P. (1994) Promoting women's sport: theory, policy and practice. *Leisure Studies*, 13(2), 97–110.

Ruddell, E.J. and Hammit, W.E. (1987) Prospect refuge theory: a psychological orientation for edge effect in recreation environments. *Journal of Leisure Research*, 19(4), 249–60.

Ryan, C. (1991) *Recreational Tourism: A Social Science Perspective*. London: Routledge.

Ryan, C. (1995) *Researching Tourist Satisfaction: Issues, Concepts, Problems*. London: Routledge.

Ryan, C. and Hall, C.M. (eds) (2001) *Sex Tourism: Marginal People and Liminalities*. London: Routledge.

Sahlins, M. (1972) *Stone Age Economics*. New York: Aldine.

Saunders, D.M. and Turner, D.E. (1987) Gambling and leisure: the case of racing. *Leisure Studies*, 6(3), 281–300.

Schneider, B., Ainbinder, A.M. and Csikszentmihalyi, M. (2004) Stress and working parents. In J.T. Haworth and A.J. Veal (eds) *Work and Leisure*. London: Routledge, 145–67.

Scraton, S. (1994) The changing world of women and leisure: feminism, 'postfeminism' and leisure. *Leisure Studies*, 13(4), 249–61.

Seaton, A.V. (1994) Intimations of modernity: the cocktail cult between the wars. In I. Henry (ed.) *Leisure: Modernity, Postmodernity and Lifestyles*. Eastbourne, Sussex: Leisure Studies Association, 323–40.

Semeneoff, B. (1976) *Projective Techniques*. London: John Wiley & Sons.

Settle, J.G. (1977) *Leisure in the North West: A Tool for Forecasting*. London: Sports Council.

Shadish, W.R.Jr., Cook, T.D. and Leviton, L.C. (1991) *Foundations of Program Evaluation: Theories of Practice*. Newbury Park, CA: Sage.

Shaw, M. (1984) *Sport and Leisure Participation and Life-styles in Different Residential Neighbourhoods*. London: Sports Council/SSRC.

Sherrow, V. (ed.) (1996) *Encyclopedia of Women and Sports*. Santa Barbara, CA: ABC-CLIO.

Shih, D. (1986) VALS as a tool of tourism marketing research. *Journal of Travel Research*, 25(1), 2–11.

Shrestha, R.K. and Loomis, J.B. (2003) Meta-analytic benefit transfer of outdoor recreation economic values: testing out-of-sample convergent validity. *Environmental and Resource Economics*, 25(1), 79–100.

Sieber, J.E. (1992) *Planning Ethically Responsible Research*. Newbury Park, CA: Sage.

Sillitoe, K.K. (1969) *Planning for Leisure*. London: HMSO.

Silverman, D. (1993) *Interpreting Qualitative Data: Methods for Analysing Talk, Text and Interaction*. London: Sage.

Skelton, A., Bridgwood, A., Duckworth, K., Hutton, L., Fenn, C., Creaser, C. and Babbidge, A. (2002) *Arts in England: Attendance, Participation and Attitudes in 2001: Findings of A Study Carried Out by Social Survey Division of the Office for National Statistics*. London: Arts Council of England, available at: www.artscouncil.org.uk/information/publications.html (accessed Oct. 2004).

Small, J. (2004) Memory work. In J. Phillimore and L. Godson (eds) *Qualitative Research in Tourism: Ontologies, Epistemologies and Methodologies*. London: Routledge, 255–72.

Smith, M. (1985) A participant observer study of a 'rough' working class pub. *Leisure Studies*, 4(3), 293–306.

Smith, S.L.J. (1983) *Recreation Geography*. Harlow: Longman.

Smith, S.L.J. (1989) *Tourism Analysis: A Handbook*. Harlow: Longman.

Snape, R. (2004) The Co-operative Holidays Association and the cultural formation of countryside leisure practice. *Leisure Studies*, 23(2), 143–58.

Snooks and Co. (2002) *Style Manual for Authors, Editors and Printers*, 6th edn. Milton, Qld: John Wiley & Sons.

Sönmez, S., Shinew, K., Marchese, L., Veldkamp, C. and Burnett, G.W. (1993) Leisure corrupted: an artist's portrait of leisure in a changing society. *Leisure Studies*, 12(4), 266–76.

Spatz, C. and Johnston, J.O. (1989) *Basic Statistics: Tales of Distribution*, 4th edn. Pacific Grove, CA: Brooks/Cole Publishing.

Sport Industries Research Centre (annual) *Leisure Forecasts and Sport Market Forecasts*. Sheffield: SIRC, Sheffield Hallam University.

Stake, R.E. (1994) Case studies. In N.K. Denzin and Y.S. Lincoln (eds) *Handbook of Qualitative Research*. Thousand Oaks, CA: Sage, 236–47.

Stake, R.E. (1995) *The Art of Case Study Research*. Thousand Oaks, CA: Sage.

Standing Committee on Recreation and Sport (SCORS) (2003) *Participation in Exercise, Recreation and Sport 2002*. Canberra: Australian Sports Commission/SCORS, available at: www.ausport.gov.au info/scorsresearch/scors.asp (accessed March 2005).

Standing Committee on Recreation and Sport (SCORS) (2004) *Participation in Exercise, Recreation and Sport 2003*. Canberra: Standing Committee on Recreation and Sport, available at: www.ausport.gov.au info/scorsresearch/scors.asp (accessed March 2005).

StarUK (2003) *UK Tourism Facts*. London: Statistics on Tourism and Research (Star) UK, available at: www.staruk.org.uk (accessed Jan. 2005).

Stebbins, R. (1992) *Amateurs, Professionals and Serious Leisure*. Montreal: McGill-Queen's University Press.

Stewart, D.W. and Shamdasani, P.N. (1990) *Focus Groups: Theory and Practice*. Newbury Park, CA: Sage.

Stockdale, J. (1984) People's conceptions of leisure. In A. Tomlinson (ed.) *Leisure: Politics, Planning and People*. London: Leisure Studies Association, 86–115.

Storey, W.K. (2004) *Writing History: A Guide for Students*. New York: Oxford University Press.

Strauss, A.L. (1987) *Qualitative Analysis for Social Scientists*. Cambridge: Cambridge University Press.

Strauss, A. and Corbin, J. (1994) Grounded theory methodology. In N.K. Denzin and Y.S. Lincoln (eds) *Handbook of Qualitative Research*. Thousand Oaks, CA: Sage, 273–85.

Straw, W. (1993) Characterising rock music culture: the case of heavy metal. In S. During (ed.) *The Cultural Studies Reader*. London: Routledge, 368–81.

Sydney Morning Herald (1996) Our green future. 7 June, p. 12.

Szalai, A. (ed.) (1972) *The Use of Time: Daily Activities of Urban and Suburban Populations in Twelve Countries*. The Hague: Mouton.

Tomlinson, A. (ed.) (1990) *Consumption, Identity, and Style: Marketing, Meanings, and the Packaging of Pleasure*. London: Comedia/Routledge.

Toohey, K. (1990) A content analysis of the Australian television coverage of the 1988 Seoul Olympics. Paper to the *Commonwealth and International Conference of Physical Education, Sport, Health, Dance, Recreation and Leisure*, January, Auckland.

Torkildsen, G. (2005) *Leisure and Recreation Management*, 5th edn. London: Routledge.

Tourism and Recreation Research Unit (TRRU) (1983) *Recreation Site Survey Manual: Methods and Techniques for Conducting Visitor Surveys*. London: E & FN Spon.

Tourism Australia (2004) *Inbound Tourism Trends, Year Ended 30 June 2004*. Sydney: Tourism Australia, accessed from: www.tourism.australia.com (accessed Jan. 2005).

Towner, J. and Wall, G. (1991) History and tourism. *Annals of Tourism Research*, 18(1), 71–84.

Treuren, G. and Lane, D. (2003) The tourism planning process in the context of organised interests, industry structure, state capacity, accumulation and sustainability. *Current Issues in Tourism*, 6(1), 1–22.

Tyre, G.L. and Siderelis, C.D. (1978) Instant-count sampling – a technique for estimating recreation use in municipal settings. *Journal of Leisure Research*, 10(2), 173–80.

United Nations Statistics Division (n.d.) *Time Use Classifications*. New York: United Nations. (Available at: http://unstats.un.org/unsd/methods/timeuse/tuaclass.htm; accessed October 2005.)

Urry, J. (1990) *The Tourist Gaze: Leisure and Travel in Contemporary Societies*. London: Sage.

Urry, J. (1994) Cultural change and contemporary tourism. *Leisure Studies*, 13(4), 233–8.

Van der Zande, A.N. (1985) Distribution patterns of visitors in large areas: a problem of measurement and analysis. *Leisure Studies*, 4(1), 85–100.

Van Doren, C.S. and Solan, D.S. (1979) Listing of dissertations and theses in leisure and recreation: August 1975 to August 1977. *Journal of Leisure Research*, 10(3), 219–44.

Van Doren, C.S. and Stubbles, R. (1976) Listing of dissertations and theses in leisure and recreation. *Journal of Leisure Research*, 7(1), 69–80.

Veal, A.J. (1984) Leisure in England and Wales. *Leisure Studies*, 3(2), 221–30.

Veal, A.J. (1987) The leisure forecasting tradition. *Leisure and the Future*. London: Allen & Unwin, 125–56.

Veal, A.J. (1988) Are user surveys useful? In J. and N. Parry (eds) *Leisure, The Arts and the Community*. Conference papers No. 30, Eastbourne, UK: Leisure Studies Association, 20–7.

Veal, A.J. (1989a) Leisure, lifestyle and status: a pluralistic framework for analysis. *Leisure Studies*, 8(2) 141–54.

Veal, A.J. (1989b) The doubtful contribution of economics to leisure management. *Society and Leisure*, 12(2), 147–56.

Veal, A.J. (1993a) The concept of lifestyle: a review. *Leisure Studies*, 12(4), 233–52.

Veal, A.J. (1993b) Leisure participation in Australia, 1985–1991: a note on the data. *Australian Journal of Leisure and Recreation*, 3(1), 37–43.

Veal, A.J. (1993c) Leisure surveys in Australia. *ANZALS Leisure Research Series*, 1, 197–210.

Veal, A.J. (1994) Intersubjectivity and the transatlantic divide: a comment on Glancy (and Ragheb and Tate). *Leisure Studies*, 13(3), 211–16.

Veal, A.J. (1995) Leisure studies: frameworks for analysis. In H. Ruskin and A. Sivan (eds) *Leisure Education: Towards the 21st Century*. Provo, UT: Brigham Young University Press, 124–36.

Veal, A.J. (1997) *Recreational Use of Beaches: Bibliography*. School of Leisure and Tourism Studies, University of Technology, Sydney, On-line Bibliography 1, available at: www.business.uts.edu.au/lst/research/bibs.html (accessed March 2005).

Veal, A.J. (2000) *Lifestyle and Leisure: A Bibliography and Review*. School of Leisure and Tourism Studies, University of Technology, Sydney, On-line Bibliography 8, available at: www.business.uts.edu.au/lst/research/bibs.html (accessed March 2005).

Veal, A.J. (2002) *Leisure and Tourism Policy and Planning*. Wallingford, UK: CAB International.

Veal, A.J. (2003a) *Education, Training and Professional Development in Leisure: A Bibliography*. School of Leisure and Tourism Studies, University of Technology, Sydney, On-line Bibliography 10, available at: www.business.uts.edu.au/lst/ research/bibs.html (accessed March 2005).

Veal, A.J. (2003b) Tracking change: leisure participation and policy in Australia, 1985–2002. *Annals of Leisure Research*, 6(3), 246–78.

Veal, A.J. (2004) *Urban Parks and Open Space Planning and Management: A Bibliography*. School of Leisure and Tourism Studies, University of Technology, Sydney, On-line Bibliography 9, available at: www.business.uts.edu.au/lst/research/bibs.html (accessed March 2005).

Veal, A.J. (2005) Australia. In G. Cushman, A.J. Veal and J. Zuzanek (eds) *Free Time and Leisure Participation: International Perspectives*. Wallingford, UK: CAB International, 17–40.

Veal, A.J. and Lynch, R. (2001) *Australian Leisure, 2nd edn*. Sydney: Longman.

Veal, A.J. and Toohey, K. (2003) *The Olympic Games: A Bibliography*. School of Leisure and Tourism Studies, University of Technology, Sydney, On-line Bibliography 5, available at: www.business.uts.edu.au/lst/research/bibs.html (accessed March 2005).

Vickerman, R.W. (1983) The contribution of economics to the study of leisure. *Leisure Studies*, 2(3), 345–64.

Walker, J.C. (1988) *Louts and Legends*. Sydney: Allen & Unwin.

Walker, J.R. and Taylor, T. (1998) *The Columbia Guide to Online Style*. New York: Columbia University Press.

Walle, A. (1997) Quantitative versus qualitative tourism research. *Annals of Tourism Research*, 24(3), 524–36.

Ware, J.E., Kosinski, M. and Keller, S.D. (1994) *SF 36 Physical and Mental Health Summary Scales: A User's Manual*. Boston, MA: The Health Institute, New England Medical Centre.

Wearing, B. (1998) *Leisure and Feminist Theory*. London: Sage.

Weaver, D. (ed.) (2000) *Encyclopedia of Ecotourism*. Wallingford, UK: CAB International.

Weiler, B. and Hall, C.M. (eds) (1992) *Special Interest Tourism*. London: Belhaven.

Wells, W.D. (ed.) (1974) *Life Style and Psychographics*. Chicago, IL: American Marketing Assn.

West, P. (1989) Urban regional parks and black minorities: subculture, marginality, and interracial relations in park use in the Detroit metropolitan area. *Leisure Sciences*, 11(1), 11–28.

White, J. (2004) Gender, work and leisure. In J.T. Haworth and A.J. Veal (eds) *Work and Leisure*. London: Routledge, 67–84.

Whyte, W.F. (1955) *Street Corner Society*. Chicago, IL: University of Chicago Press.

Whyte, W.F. (1982) Interviewing in field research. In R.G. Burgess (ed.) *Field Research: A Sourcebook and Field Manual*. London: Allen & Unwin, 111–22.

Williams, A.M. and Shaw, G. (1988) *Tourism and Economic Development: Western European Experience*. London: Belhaven.

Williams, C. (1998) Is the SERVQUAL model an appropriate management tool for measuring service delivery quality in the UK leisure industry? *Managing Leisure*, 3(2), 98–110.

Williams, E.A., Jenkins, C. and Neville, A.M. (1988) Social area influences on leisure activity – an exploration of the ACORN classification with reference to sport. *Leisure Studies*, 7(1), 81–95.

Williams, R.C. (2003) *The Historian's Toolbox: A Student's Guide to the Theory and Craft of History*. Armonk, NY: M. E. Sharpe.

Williams, S. (1995) *Outdoor Recreation and the Urban Environment*. London: Routledge.

Williamson, J.B., Barry, S.T. and Dorr, R.S. (1982) *The Research Craft*. Boston, MA: Little, Brown.

Wilson, J. (1988) *Politics and Leisure*. London: Allen & Unwin.

Wilson, K. (1995) Olympians or lemmings? The postmodernist fun run. *Leisure Studies*, 14(3), 174–85.

Wimbush, E. and Talbot, M. (eds) (1988) *Relative Freedoms: Women and Leisure*. Milton Keynes: Open University Press.

Witt, C.A. and Wright, P.L. (1992) Tourist motivation: life after Maslow. In P. Johnston and B. Thomas (eds) *Choice and Demand in Tourism*. London: Mansell, 33–55.

Woodside, A.G. and Ronkainen, I.A. (1994) Improving advertising conversion studies. In J.R.B. Ritchie and C.R. Goeldner (eds) *Travel, Tourism and Hospitality Research, 2nd edn.* New York: John Wiley, 545–58.

Woodside, A.G., Crouch, G.I., Mazanec, J.A., Oppermann, M. and Sakai, M. (eds) (1999) *Consumer Psychology of Tourism, Hospitality and Leisure*, Vol. 1. Wallingford: CAB International.

World Tourism Organisation (annual) *Yearbook of Tourism Statistics*. Madrid: WTO.

Wynne, D. (1986) Living on 'The Heath'. *Leisure Studies*, 5(1), 109–16.

Wynne, D. (1998) *Leisure, Lifestyle and the New Middle Class: A Case Study*. London: Routledge.

Yin, R.K. (2003) *Case Study Research: Design and Methods*, 3rd edn. Thousand Oaks, CA: Sage.

Young, M. and Willmott, P. (1973) *The Symmetrical Family*. London: Routledge.

Young, C.H., Savola, K.L. and Phelps, E. (1991) *Inventory of Longitudinal Studies in the Social Sciences*. Newbury Park, CA: Sage.

Zikmund, W.G. (1997) *Business Research Methods*, 5th edn. Orlando, FL: Dryden Press.

Zuzanek, J. and Mannell, R. (1998) Life-cycle squeeze, time pressure, daily stress, and leisure participation: a Canadian perspective. *Loisir et Société/Society and Leisure*, 21(2), 513–44.

Zuzanek, J. and Veal, A.J. (eds) (1998) Time pressure, stress, leisure participation and well-being. Special issue of *Loisir et Société/Society and Leisure*, 21(2).

Zukin, S. (1990) Socio-spatial prototypes of a new organization of consumption: the role of real cultural capital. *Sociology*, 24(1), 37–55.

INDEX